Credit Derivatives

Credit Derivatives
Application, Pricing, and Risk Management

An Interactive Book with Pricing Models and Examples on the Internet

Gunter Meissner

BLACKWELL PUBLISHING
350 Main Street, Malden, MA 02148-5020, USA
108 Cowley Road, Oxford OX4 1JF, UK
550 Swanston Street, Carlton, Victoria 3053, Australia

First published 2005 by Blackwell Publishing Ltd

Library of Congress Cataloging-in-Publication Data

Meissner, Gunter, 1957–
Credit derivatives: application, pricing, and risk management/Gunter Meissner.
p. cm.
Includes bibliographical references and index.
ISBN 1-4051-2676-0 (hardback : alk. paper)
1. Credit derivatives. I. Title.

HG6024.A3M436 2005
332.63′2–dc22

2004017623

A catalogue record for this title is available from the British Library.

Set in 11 on 13 Perpetua
by SNP Best-set Typesetter Ltd., Hong Kong
Printed and bound in the United Kingdom
by MPG Books, Bodmin, Cornwall

The publisher's policy is to use permanent paper from mills that operate a sustainable forestry policy, and which has been manufactured from pulp processed using acid-free and elementary chlorine-free practices. Furthermore, the publisher ensures that the text paper and cover board used have met acceptable environmental accreditation standards.

For further information on
Blackwell Publishing, visit our website:
www.blackwellpublishing.com

Contents Overview

Contents

Preface

Target audience

This book is written for practitioners in the credit derivatives area such as executives, traders, risk managers, product developers, structurers, marketers, settlement employees and brokers. The main target group though are advanced undergraduate and graduate students of finance. In chapters 1 to 4, the products and applications of credit derivatives are explained at a basic level, so that also beginners should benefit from this book. Chapters 5 and 6, pricing and risk management, require some mathematical knowledge. Hence it is recommended that the reader has taken basic algebra, calculus and statistics courses.

Interactive models and examples

One feature that differentiates this book from other credit derivatives books is that most pricing models in this book are programmed and can be operated on the Internet. The models are written in VBA (visual basic application) with an easy to use Excel interface. In addition, most of the examples are displayed as Excel sheets on the Internet. Hence the user can verify the examples and can vary the input parameters for educational purposes.

Answers to questions and problems

At the end of each chapter, questions and problems are displayed. The answers, available for instructors, are on the Internet. The Internet site can be accessed by sending an email to gmeissne@aol.com.

Feedback

The author welcomes feedback on the book. Please send comments and suggestions to gmeissne@aol.com.

Acknowledgements

I would like to thank all the people that helped. But I can't, I did it all myself. (Herman Munster)

Numerous students, academics and practitioners have contributed in the production of this book. I am grateful to many of the professors and students at Hawaii Pacific University (HPU), especially Marianne Noergaard and Lars Foss, for detailed discussions on many issues in the book. I would like to thank the Trustees' Scholarly Endeavors Program of Hawaii Pacific University for two research grants to support this book. I am also thankful to students of Thammasat University in the summer of 2002 and 2003 for reviewing the book. I am also grateful for a research scholarship at the University of Technology Sydney in the summer 2003. UTS Professors Carl Ciarella, Tony Hall, Vladimir Kasakov, Eckhard Platen, Erik Schlogl, and Chris Terry contributed with constructive comments and suggestions.

I am grateful for discussions on mathematical issues with Ranjan Bhaduri, Janne Kettunen, Dima Ksendzosky, and Christos Kyritsis. Daniel Fitzpatrick, Janne Kettunen, Dima Ksendzovsky, Sidharth Sood, Iovo Stefanov, and Shigeharu Takemura have co-programmed several interactive models found in this book. Helpful comments and suggestions were provided by Daniel Ahlgren, Roar Berg, Wojtek Bratek, Tsai Chia-Che, Steve Haywood, Tsui-Hsuan Huang, Andres Huerta, Chan-Ho Kim, Paul Klinteby, Tobias Kohls, Mei-hui Lu, Rudolf Meissner, Marilyn Moreaux, Pukpring Phuphaichitkul, Anak Sankanae, Sascha Schanz, Sebastian Schmidt, Fredrik Setterwall, Sven Steude, Supradit Tanpraset, Young-Soon Yoon, and Bogdan Zdziech.

I would like to thank Ranjan Bhaduri, Erik Schlogl, and Jonathan Simms for a detailed review of the final manuscript.

I further appreciate the enthusiasm, encouragement, and support of the managing editor Seth Ditchik of Blackwell Publishing.

Introduction: The Basics of Credit Derivatives

Make everything as simple as possible, but not simpler. (Albert Einstein)

What is Credit Risk?

Credit risk is the risk of a financial loss due to a reduction in the credit quality of a debtor. There are principally two types of credit risk: default risk and credit deterioration risk. *Default risk* is the risk that an obligor does not repay part or his entire financial obligation. If default occurs, the creditor will only receive the amount recovered from the debtor, called recovery rate. *Credit deterioration risk* is the risk that the credit quality of the debtor decreases. In this case, the value of the assets of the debtor will decrease, resulting in a financial loss for the creditor. If the debtor is rated by a public rating agency such as Standard & Poors, Moody's, or Fitch, credit deterioration risk is expressed as a downgrade to a lower rating category, for example from AA to A, called *migration risk* or *downgrade risk*.

Default risk can actually be seen as a subcategory of credit deterioration risk, since default occurs for a large credit deterioration. However, there are quite different dynamics involved if a debtor only deteriorates in credit quality or defaults. For example, a bond investor will receive his full notional amount at bond maturity, if the credit quality of the bond issuer has only deteriorated. However, the investor will only receive the recovery rate, if the bond issuer has defaulted. Hence, it is reasonable to differentiate default risk and credit deterioration risk.

What are Credit Derivatives?

Credit derivatives are financial instruments designed to transfer credit risk from one counterpart to another. Legal ownership of the reference obligation is usually not transferred. Credit derivatives can have the form of forwards, swaps, and options, which may be imbedded in financial assets such as bonds or loans. Credit derivatives allow an investor to reduce or eliminate credit risk or to assume credit risk, expecting to profit from it.

From a more technical point of view, credit derivatives are financial instruments, whose value is derived from the credit quality of an underlying obligation, which is usually a bond or a loan. For example, a put option on the credit-spread between a risky bond and a risk-free bond will increase in value, if the yield of the risky bond increases due to credit deterioration.

Why Credit Derivatives?

The number of credit derivatives transactions has increased dramatically worldwide in recent years (see chapter 1: "The Market for Credit Derivatives"). The main reasons for the rise of credit derivatives are:

- The general desire to reduce credit risk in the financial markets, expressed by increased regulatory requirements as the Basel II Accord (see chapter 4);
- An increase in personal bankruptcies and recent corporate and sovereign bankruptcies, such as the Asian financial crisis in 1997, Russia 1998, Argentina 2001, or Enron 2001 and WorldCom 2002 (see chapter 1);
- An increase in the ability to value and risk-manage credit risk (see chapters 5 and 6).

There are many ways in which financial managers can utilize credit derivatives. The main applications, which are discussed in chapter 4, are:

- Hedging various types of risk such as default risk and credit deterioration risk, as well as other types of risk such as market risk and types of operational risk;
- Yield enhancement, mainly achieved by assuming credit risk;
- Convenience and cost reduction (e.g. the fact that a client will not notice when his credit risk is transferred to a third party);
- Arbitrage, due to the fact that many credit derivatives can be replicated by other financial instruments;
- Credit Line Management, which can reduce regulatory capital.

Chapter One
The Market for Credit Derivatives

The Phoenicians invented the money – But why so little of it? (Nestroy)

Credit Events That Have Led to the Birth of Credit Derivatives

The dramatic rise of credit derivatives (for the definition see Introduction) has its origin in several severe credit crises in the recent past. Some of them will be discussed in the following.

The Latin American debt crisis in the early 1980s. In August 1982, the debt situation in Latin America turned into a severe crisis when Mexico suspended coupon payments to its creditors. The crisis worsened over the next 7 years and spread to other Latin American countries as inflation grew and investors pulled capital out of the plagued debtor nations. Private lenders were unwilling to provide new money, but at the same time lending by official, taxpayer-supported institutions increased steadily.

In March 1989, the United States Treasury Department under then Treasury Secretary Nicholas F. Brady put together a new strategy for dealing with developing country debt. The strategy, better known as the "Brady Plan," acknowledged that reversing the flight of capital from debtor nations was critical, and that global capital markets would direct resources to any country that had the will to implement genuine reforms based upon sound economic fundamentals.

As a result, the Brady Plan focused on debt service reduction for those debtors who agreed to implement substantial economic reform programs. The plan offered banks credit enhancements in exchange for their agreement to reduce claims. These credit enhancements were created by first converting commercial bank loans into bonds, and then collateralizing the notional amount with US Treasury zero-coupon bonds, purchased with the proceeds of IMF and World Bank loans. Thus, the Brady bonds represented a form of default insurance, similar to a default swap, the most popular credit derivative in today's trading practice.

The junk bond crisis in the 1980s. In the early 1980s, the investment bank Drexel Burnham Lambert with its West-Coast chief, the self-made millionaire, Michael Milken, engaged in high volume trading of junk bonds. Junk bonds, or the more benign term, high yield bonds are bonds with a rating lower than BBB. The high yield of the junk bonds naturally reflects the high default probability of the junk bond issuer.

At first Milken's trading activities in junk bonds resulted in enormous profits. However, his trading success deteriorated and he was later charged with securities fraud and Drexel Burnham had to shut down its operation. In addition, many Savings & Loan (S&L) institutions had invested in high-yield bonds, which sparked the S&L crisis of the late 1980s, while simultaneously tainting the junk bond name.

The Savings and Loan (S&L) crisis in the late 1980s. Exploding interest rates during the early 1980s were one of the primary causes of the crisis. The S&L associations typically provided long-term mortgage loans, usually at a fixed interest rate, for a period up to thirty years. These long-term loans were usually financed with short-term depository funds. The huge difference between the long-term mortgage rates and short-term depository funds, coupled with highly speculative investments, partly in junk bonds, by some Savings and Loan institutions caused most of the industry to become insolvent. Losses kept compounding since the insolvent institutions were allowed to remain open, leading to accumulating losses. The US government finally had to step in and take over and bail out many S&L institutions. In 1990, the General Accounting Office estimated that the insurance losses would ultimately exceed $325 billion, over $1,000 for each resident of the United States.

The Asian financial crisis in 1997–1998. Falling interest rates in industrialized countries throughout the 1990s resulted in lower cost of capital for investing companies and nations. Coupled with overconfidence in the growth perspectives of South-East Asian nations, huge amounts of capital had poured into South-East Asia. Moreover, the financial flows were mostly "hot money" i.e. short-term with less than 1-year maturity. When growth rates declined in the mid 1990s, creditors did not renew their credits. Since most of the funds were invested long term (or unprofitable), these maturity mismatches led to the Asian financial crisis.

On July 2, 1997 the crisis broke out when the Thai government released the Thai baht from the US dollar peg. Aggravated by currency speculators, many South-East Asian currencies devalued sharply and the countries could not meet their financial obligations since most of them were in US dollars. The IMF and the World Bank stepped in and prevented bankruptcy by lending the hardest hit countries South Korea $58.4 billion, Indonesia $42.3 billion and Thailand $17.2 billion.

The Russian debt crisis 1998. The origins of the Russian crisis in 1998 are to be found in the country's gradual transition process from totalitarianism towards democracy and economic liberalization.

Due to the monetary policy implemented in 1995, banks had limited funds to lend to enterprises. To compensate for the low availability of loans, enterprises were forced to use barter relationships with customers, suppliers and workforces. A barter relationship is one in which goods or services, rather than cash, are exchanged for debt. These kinds of relationships allow companies to balance their accounting books, thus overstating many companies' financial status. Additionally, Russia's administrative tax collection was little developed leading to low government revenues from taxes, resulting in high government debt.

To attempt to increase government revenue, the state decided to issue short-term ruble-denominated bonds (called GKOs) at attractive interest rates. However, the state was unable to pay back these bonds and was thus forced to issue more GKOs at even higher rates.

Struggling to repay its debt, the central bank was forced to devalue the ruble. It did so by increasing the ruble's fluctuation band against the dollar by 50%. In addition, the central bank decided to print more rubles, which naturally led to higher inflation. Consequently, confidence dwindled and many investors converted their money into US dollars, aggravating the downfall of the ruble. Furthermore, oil prices fell sharply in 1998, reducing Russia's income further. In August 1998 the Russian government forced restructuring of the ruble-denominated internal debt and imposed a 90-day moratorium on repayments of foreign loans. Thus, Russia was officially in a state of bankruptcy.

Argentinean crisis 2001. One of the main factors for the demise of the Argentine economy in the late 1990s was the peg of the Argentine peso to the US dollar. With the dollar appreciating in the 1990s against nearly all currencies, Argentina's exports and foreign investment in Argentina had become increasingly less attractive. It was estimated that productivity had to increase by around 20% to make Argentine exports competitive. Together with poor political and economic leadership, Argentina experienced a severe recession in 2001.

In order to reduce capital outflow, the interest rate on 3-month treasury bills was raised from 9% to 14% in July 2001 despite an ongoing deflation, which increased the real burden of high interest payments.

In order to manage the crisis, a new currency, the "Argentino," was created, not tied to the dollar. Prices, rents, and interest payments were supposed to stay in dollars or pesos, whereas pensions and wages were to be paid in Argentinos, whose value was suspected to decrease relative to the dollar or the peso. The wide majority of the population anticipated the rise in cost and decrease in income, and President Rodriguez Saa had to resign.

In early December 2001, Argentina required investors to swap $50 billion of 11% and 12% bonds into 7% yielding bonds. On December 23, 2001 Argentina's capital reserves were depleted and Argentina declared a moratorium, officially defaulting on their debt. For investors, who had bought credit protection maturing in mid December in the form of default swaps, it was crucial whether the forced yield swap constituted the event of default. The issue depends on the definition used in the specific contract and will be solved in court.

The Enron bankruptcy filing. On December 2, 2001, corporate America was shocked to hear the Chapter 11 filing of utility giant Enron. Enron's principal activity was the provision of products and services related to natural gas, electricity and communications to wholesale and retail customers. Reasons for Enron's bankruptcy filing, the biggest petition in US history, were over-expansion, mismanagement, and personal enrichment. Before the filing, Enron accountants had tried to hide financial problems with numerous special purpose entities (SPE), located in the Cayman Islands and other tax havens. Thousands of former Enron employees and shareholders are seeking financial retribution for the billions of dollars lost in the company collapse.

Arthur Andersen, working for Enron as a consultant *and* auditor, was found guilty of obstruction of justice in June 2002 for destroying thousands of its Enron audit records after learning federal regulators were investigating. With its reputation badly damaged, Arthur Andersen did not see any prospects to survive, selling its tax and audit practices in ten cities to Ernst & Young LLP and its offices in fives cities to KPMG LLP.

Market Size and Products

In 2003, credit derivatives comprised about 0.8% of the overall derivatives market, as seen in figure 1.1. However, credit derivatives have increased sharply in recent years and have grown from $54 billion to $840 billion from 1998 to 2003, as seen in figure 1.2.

Broadly, the credit derivatives market can be divided into four categories: default swaps (DS) also called credit default swaps (CDS), total rate of return swaps (TRORs), credit-spread products, and synthetic structures (for details see chapter 3). Over two-thirds of all traded credit derivatives in 2002 were default swaps and about 25% were synthetic structures. Total rate of return swaps, which had about the same trading volume as default swaps in 1998, only comprised about 1.3% of the credit derivatives market in 2002. One reason for the rise in default swaps is the provision of a standardized legal documentation by ISDA (International Swaps and Derivatives Association) in 1999, with an update in 2003.[1] Once standard legal documentation for TRORs is available, TRORs might regain their previous

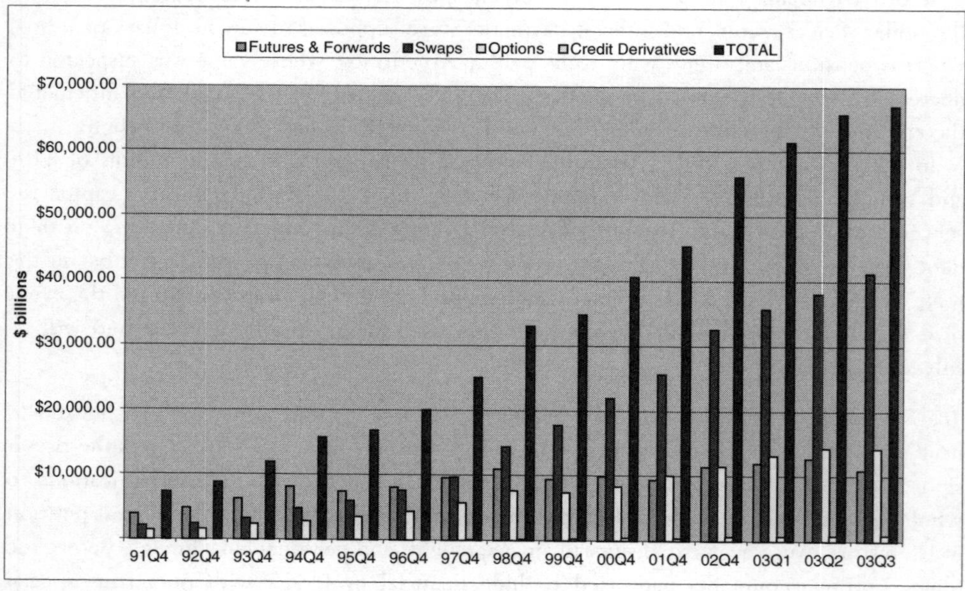

Figure 1.1: Total quarterly US derivative activity from 1998 to 2003 (notional amount)
Source: Comptroller of the Currency Administrator of National Banks, OCC Bank Derivatives Report.

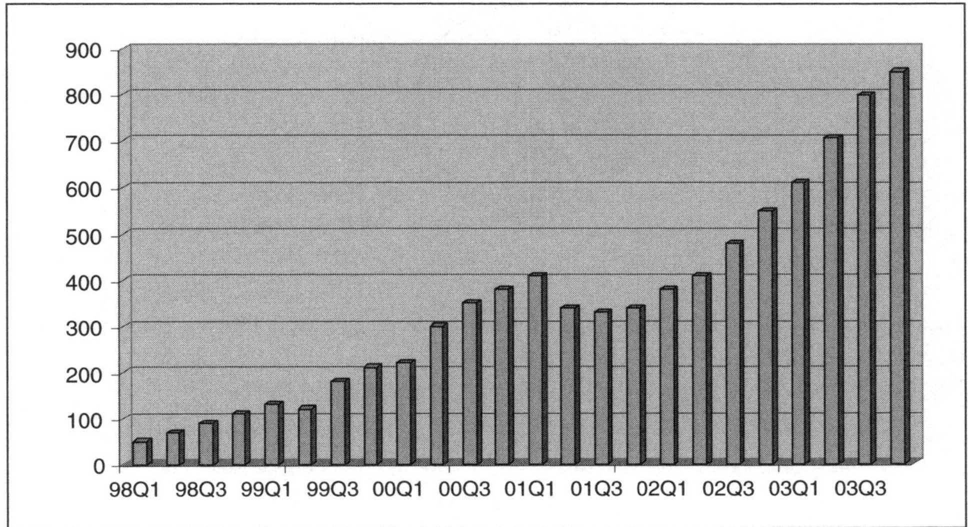

Figure 1.2: Credit derivatives quarterly growth in the US from 1998 to 2003 (notional amount in millions)
Source: Comptroller of the Currency Administrator of National Banks, OCC Bank Derivatives Report Fourth Quarter 2000 to 2003.

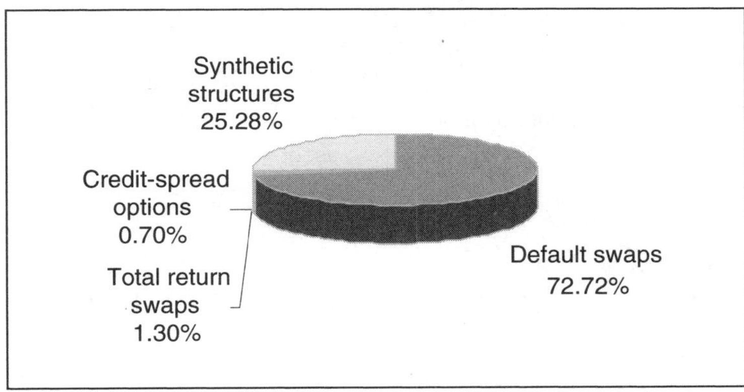

Figure 1.3: Credit derivatives in percent of trading volume in the US in 2002
Source: Risk Magazine, February 2003, pp. 20–3.

trading volume. Figure 1.3 shows the distribution of credit derivatives products in the US in 2002.

In terms of regional trading activity, the American market has a slightly higher trading volume than Europe, as seen in figure 1.4.

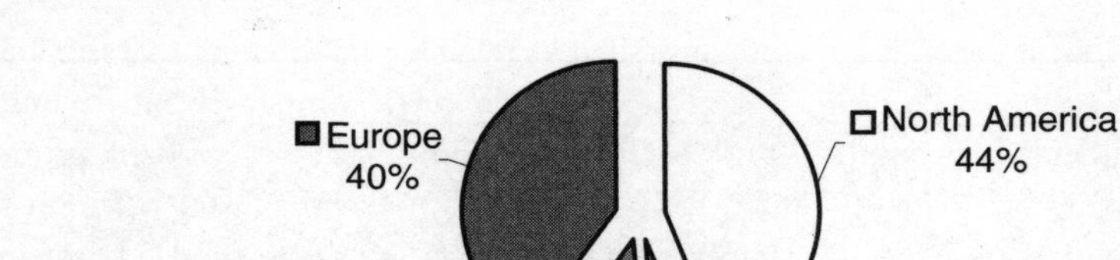

Figure 1.4: Trading volume with respect to geographical regions in 2002 by origin of underlying credit
Source: Risk Magazine, February 2003, third survey of credit derivatives, pp. 20–3.

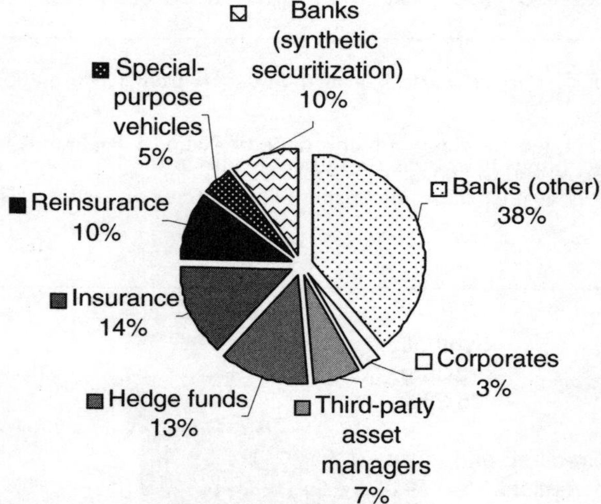

Figure 1.5: End-user breakdown
Source: Risk Magazine, February 2003, third survey of credit derivatives, pp. 20–3.

With respect to end users, we can see from figure 1.5 that banks, insurance companies, and hedge funds are the main buyers and sellers of credit derivatives.

Credit Derivatives Have Been Around in Different Forms

Credit derivatives started trading actively in the mid 1990s. However, they are not a recent invention. Other forms of credit protection such as letters of credit and bond guarantees such as the Brady bonds have been around for many years.

Letter of credit. A letter of credit is a document issued by a bank guaranteeing that the loan of a foreign investor will be repaid. Let's look at an example: a US company wants to build a power plant in Thailand. It needs 10,000,000 Thai baht from Thai Farmers Bank immediately. The US company asks its house bank, Bank of America, to send a letter of credit to Thai Farmers Bank, which guarantees the repayment of the loan. This way, the US company can receive the money immediately without lengthy and costly credit checks by Thai Farmers Bank. Thus a letter of credit is effectively an insurance against default of a third party (the US company), therefore quite similar to a standard default swap.

Brady bonds. Brady bonds, as already briefly discussed above, are US dollar denominated bonds issued mainly by Latin American countries, that were exchanged for Latin American commercial bank loans in default. US Treasury zero-coupon bonds guaranteed the notional amount of these bonds. Therefore, the US government acted de facto as a default swap seller. The fee in this "default swap" was however zero, since the US government guaranteed the notional amount for free, trying to re-establish investor confidence in the plagued Latin American countries.

The QBI Contract

Personal bankruptcy filings have increased dramatically in the US in recent years as seen in figure 1.6. To protect against these increasing bankruptcies or assume risk on it, the CME

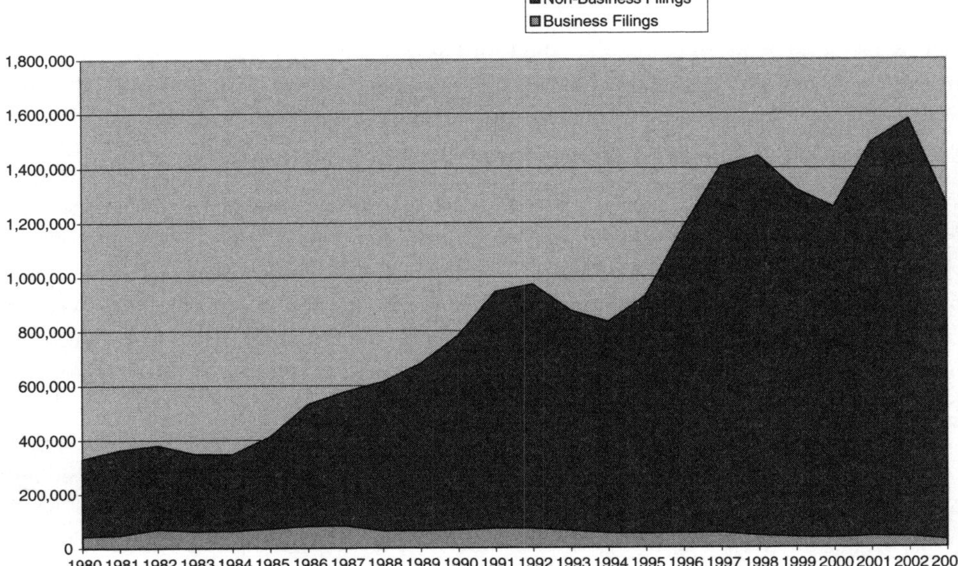

Figure 1.6: Business and non-business bankruptcy filings in the US from 1980 to 2003
Source: American Bankruptcy Institute, http://www.abiworld.org/stats/1980annual.html.

(Chicago Mercantile Exchange) launched derivatives contracts on the QBI (Quarterly Bankruptcy Index) in September 2000, the first ever exchange-traded credit derivative product. Investors who want to take a position in future bankruptcy filings can buy or sell the QBI Futures[2] (Ticker symbol QB) or the QBI Options[3] on Futures contract (Ticker Symbol 8Q).

The QBI Futures contract. Due to the unusual underlying, which is personal bankruptcy filings during a specific quarter, the QBI Futures contract has some unique features. It principally trades on the March, June, September, December cycle (i.e. there are four Futures contracts per year). However, to accommodate for possible late bankruptcy reporting during a quarter, the QBI Futures contract is settled two business days before the fifteenth of April, July, October, and January. Conveniently, one bankruptcy filing increases the QBI index by $1. The index is rounded to the nearest $25 and expressed in units of 1,000.

Buying a QBI Futures contract means that the buyer believes the market underestimates future bankruptcy filings; selling a QBI Futures contract means that the seller believes the market overestimates future bankruptcy filings.

Example 1.1: An investor believes that the QBI Futures contract underestimates the personal bankruptcy filings during the quarter from January to March. In February, he buys one QBI Futures contract at the current QBI future price of 355. At future maturity on April 13, the QBI has a settlement price of 360,127, which is rounded to the nearest 25, so 360,125. Thus, the profit for the investor is 360,125 – 355,000 = $5,125. Naturally, if the settlement price had been below 355,000, the investor would have lost money.

It is also interesting to notice how the QBI Futures contract is traded. Traders are able to enter bids and offers at anytime during a "pre-opening" period each day from 7:30 a.m. until 1:30 p.m. Chicago Time. Orders become "firm" (i.e. they cannot be canceled or modified) between 1:20 p.m. and 1:30 p.m., when the orders are matched and executed.

The QBI Options on Futures contract. Investors can also hedge or assume risk on personal bankruptcy filings using the QBI Options on Futures contract. A QBI call option gives the call buyer the right, but not the obligation, to buy one QBI Futures contract at the strike price, which is determined at the purchase date. A QBI put option gives the put buyer the right, but not the obligation, to sell one QBI Futures contract at the strike price. The QBI option contract is American style, thus an option buyer can exercise his option anytime before or at option maturity.

Trading of the QBI Options contract takes place in the same form as the QBI Futures contract. That is, traders are able to enter bids and offers at anytime during a "pre-opening" period each day from 7:30 a.m. until 1:30 p.m. Chicago Time, and orders become "firm" (i.e. cannot be canceled or modified) between 1:20 p.m. and 1:30 p.m., when the orders are matched and executed.

An investor should buy the QBI Futures contract rather than the QBI call option, if he is very certain that the market underestimates future bankruptcy filings, because a future contract does not require paying a premium, and thus has higher leverage. If an investor believes the market consensus about future bankruptcies is too low but he is not very certain, he should buy the call option rather than the Futures contract, because the downside of the call option is just the call premium. However, the downside of the future contract can be significant (the maximum loss of selling a future is unlimited; the maximum loss when buying a future is the future price, in case the future price goes to zero).

Example 1.2: A credit card company wants to protect against rising bankruptcy filings but at the same time wants to maintain the advantage of decreasing bankruptcy filings. The company buys 10 call options on the March QBI Futures contract with a strike of 350, with a call premium of $0.50 for one option. Since the option contract is quoted in thousands, he pays 10 × $0.50 × 1,000 = $5,000. At option maturity the QBI Futures contract is at 365,146, thus rounded to the next 25, it is 365,150. Thus the overall payoff for the company is 10 × (365,150 − 350,000) − 5,000 = $146,500 (ignoring the interest rate effects of having paid the $5,000 at an earlier point in time).

Creditex and CreditTrade

Creditex and CreditTrade, both founded in 1999, are Internet-based electronic platforms for trading and obtaining information on credit derivatives.

Creditex, headquartered in New York, is a broker/dealer approved by the NASD (National Association of Securities Dealers) and is officially supported by the major derivatives players such as JP Morgan Chase, Deutsche Bank, UBS, CSFB, etc. On average, 40 institutions place about 4,000 bids and offers per month on the platform mainly in default swaps. However, in 2002, a wide range of other credit derivatives such as total rate of return swaps and synthetic structures were also executed. Creditex also offers two data management services. The first is *Data Download,* where subscribers receive a comprehensive download of all transactions posted (or traded) to date on the Creditex trading platform. In addition, Creditex provides daily, weekly or monthly updates to the data. Data Download is delivered as an attachment to an automated email. The second service is *PriceTracker,* a desktop application, allows subscribers to view all current prices posted on the Creditex trading platform. Subscribers can search on a single name, as well as search for an entire portfolio at once.

CreditTrade, the London-based European competitor, is different to Creditex in that it offers a combined traditional voice and electronic brokerage service. In February 2000, CreditTrade acquired the credit derivative team of the broker Prebon Yamane and has today an exclusive correspondent relationship with Prebon. JP Morgan Chase and ICG are major shareholders of CreditTrade. Besides its brokerage service, CreditTrade offers, like Creditex, a historical data subscription service (CreditTrade Benchmarks) and an intra-day price tracing service (CreditTrade Market Prices). In January 2000, CreditTrade set up a structured products desk to diversify their product range away from standard single name default swaps.

Trac-x and Iboxx

Trac-x (pronounced "tracks") is a family of credit derivatives indexes launched by JP Morgan and Morgan Stanley in April 2003. Just as other indexes, for example the Dow Jones Industrial Index, the Trac-x consists of a basket of underlying financial instruments, whose price is expressed as a single number. The underlying for the Trac-x are prices of 50 or 100 default swaps (discussed in chapter 2). At the beginning of 2004, several Trac-x indexes existed: TRAC-X Europe, TRAC-X NA (North America), TRAC-X NA High Yield, TRAC-X Japan, TRAC-X Australia, and TRAC-X EM (Emerging Markets).

In November 2003, JP Morgan and Morgan Stanley handed over the management and marketing of the Trac-x to Dow Jones and Company (see www.dowjones.com). The indexes were renamed as "Dow Jones TRAC-X Indexes." However, ownership of the Trac-x will remain with JP Morgan and Morgan Stanley.

Main users of the Trac-x are financial institutions, which can buy one of the Trac-x indexes to perform a broad hedge against credit risk (see chapter 2 and 4 on hedging). Investors can also sell one of the Trac-x indexes to assume credit risk. Hedging and assuming credit risk can be done conveniently, since the Trac-x, as any index, is expressed as a single number. The trading volume of the Trac-x has been very satisfactory, with over $100 billion of Trac-x traded in the first nine months after the launch.

In October 2003, 11 credit dealers launched a rival index to the Trac-x, termed Iboxx. The dealers cited discontent with the licensing and reconstitution of the Trac-x. It is to be expected that the Trac-x and Iboxx will merge in the future to ensure high liquidity in a single index.

Summary of Chapter 1

The credit derivatives market has increased dramatically since its inception in the mid 1990s. The reasons for the increase are the general desire of the financial system to decrease credit risk, and thus increase stability. Furthermore, several severe debt crises of sovereigns and corporates have led to an increased awareness of credit risk. Among them are the Asian financial crisis in 1997–8, the Russian debt crisis 1998, the Argentinean crisis 2001, and corporate bankruptcy filings such as Enron or WorldCom in 2001 and 2002.

Credit protection is, however, not a new phenomenon, but has been around in forms such as letters of credit or Brady bonds. Brady bonds are effectively a default insurance, similar to a default swap.

The QBI Futures and the QBI Options on Future contract are the first two credit-related contracts to be traded on exchanges. The underlying of the QBI is the number of personal bankruptcy filings in a certain quarter, whereby one bankruptcy filing increases the QBI value by $1. A credit card issuer, who wants to protect against personal bankruptcy filings, can either buy a QBI Futures contract or a call option of the futures contract. The QBI Futures contract should be bought if the hedger is very sure that bankruptcy filings will increase. If the investor is not so sure, a call option should be bought, which protects against rising bankruptcy filings but at the same time maintains the advantage of decreasing bankruptcy filings.

Currently, two Internet-based credit derivatives trading platforms exist, the New York based Creditex and the London based CreditTrade. Both platforms provide an electronic brokerage system; CreditTrade also provides a traditional voice brokering. Both electronic trading systems also offer a historical and intra-day data subscription service.

The Trac-x index, launched in April 2003, is an index based on default swap prices. In October 2003, 11 credit dealers launched a rival index to the Trac-x, termed Iboxx. The Trac-x and the Iboxx allow investors to conveniently hedge or assume credit risk, since both indexes are expressed as a single number.

References and Suggestions for Further Readings

Davidson, C., "The demand of innovation," *Risk Magazine,* August 2003, pp. S8–S10.

DeLong, B., "The Mexican Peso Crisis," www.j-bradford-delong.net.

Ferry, J., "Argentine sovereign debt sparks bitter credit default row," *Risk Magazine,* January 2002, p. 10.

Fitchratings, "Global Credit Derivatives: Risk Management or Risk?" www.fitchratings.com, September 2003.

Hull, J., *Options, Futures and Other Derivatives*, Fifth edn, Prentice Hall, 2003.

Humphries, N., "Software Survey 2002," *Risk Magazine,* January 2002, pp. 100–9.

ISDA, "ISDA Credit Derivatives Definitions," www.ISDA.org.

Leander, J., "The Credit Implosion," *Risk Magazine,* October 2002, p. S2.

Meissner, G., Trading *Financial Derivatives*, Prentice Hall, 1998.

Patel, N., "Flow Business Booms," *Risk Magazine,* February 2003, pp. 20–3.

Ticktin, H., "The Russian Crisis; Capitalism is in Question," www.igc.org.

Questions and Problems

Answers, available for instructors, are on the Internet. Please email gmeissne@aol.com for the site.

1.1 *Define credit derivatives! What are the reasons for the strong growth of credit derivatives since the mid 1990s?*

1.2 *What are the main applications of credit derivatives?*

1.3 *Define credit risk! Do you believe is it reasonable to differentiate default risk and credit deterioration risk?*

1.4 *Name several credit crises in the past years that have highlighted the need to reduce credit risk!*

1.5 *Why have default swaps dominated the credit derivatives market in the recent past? Why has the trading volume of TRORs diminished?*

1.6 *Discuss the underlying of the QBI Futures and the QBI Options on Futures contract. Describe the unusual trade execution of the QBI contract.*

1.7 *How do the dominant electronic trading platforms for credit derivatives Creditex and CreditTrade differ?*

1.8 *What is the main objective of the Trac-x and Iboxx indexes?*

Notes

1 ISDA, www.ISDA.org, "ISDA Credit Derivatives Definitions"; ISDA, www.ISDA.org, "2003 Definitions."
2 A futures contract is the agreement to trade an underlying asset in the future at a price, which is determined at the start of the futures contract. The buyer of a futures contract has the obligation to buy the underlying asset at the maturity date of the future contract; the seller of a futures contract has the obligation to sell the underlying asset at the maturity date of the future contract. For more on futures see Hull (2003) or Meissner (1998).
3 In an option, the buyer has the right to buy (in case of a call) or sell (in case of a put) the underlying asset at a price, which is agreed at the start of the option contract. The seller of an option has to sell (in case of a call) or buy (in case of a put) the underlying asset, if the option buyer exercises her option. For more on futures see Hull (2003) or Meissner (1998).

Chapter Two
Credit Derivatives Products

Why haven't we thought of this before? (John O'Brien on credit derivatives)

As stated in the Introduction, credit derivatives are financial instruments designed to transfer credit risk from one counterpart to another. Broadly, credit derivatives can be divided into four main categories, as seen in figure 2.1.

It should be mentioned that synthetic structures are not really a product by themselves. They are bonds and loans with embedded credit derivatives. As mentioned in chapter 1, default swaps comprised about 73% of all derivatives in the US in 2002; reason enough to have a closer look at them.

Default Swaps

What is a default swap?

In a default swap (DS), also called credit default swap (CDS), the buyer makes a periodic or an upfront payment to the seller of the default swap. The default swap seller promises to make a payment in the event of default of a reference obligation, which is usually a bond or a loan. This basic structure of a default swap is seen in figure 2.2.

More technically, a default swap can be viewed as a put option[1] on the reference obligation. The default buyer owns this put, allowing him to sell the reference obligation to the default swap seller in case of default. This put option is usually far out-of-the-money, since the probability of default is usually low. More precisely, a default swap is similar to a knock-in put option[2]. The knock-in event is the default of the reference obligation. If default occurs, the put is knocked in, triggering the payment of the default swap seller.

It is important to note that the default swap buyer has a short position in the credit quality of the reference obligation: If the credit quality and the price of the bond decrease, the present value (the premium, if paid upfront) of the default swap will increase. Thus the premium that the default swap buyer paid in the original contract is lower than the market premium after the bond price decrease. If desired, the default swap buyer can sell the default swap at the higher market premium with a profit.

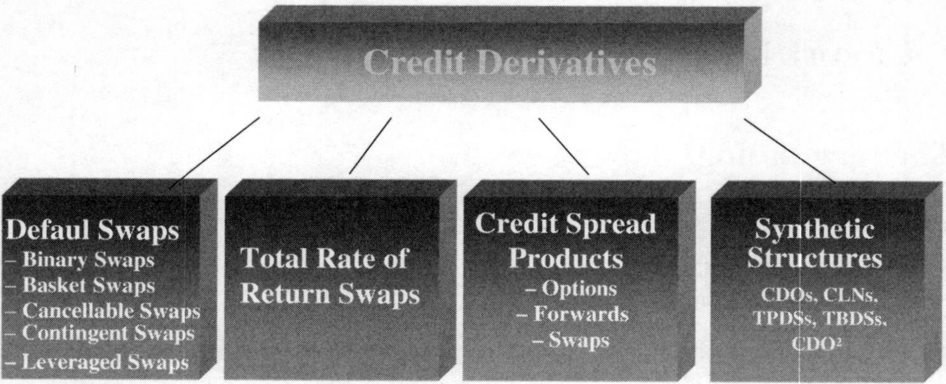

Figure 2.1: Main categories of credit derivatives

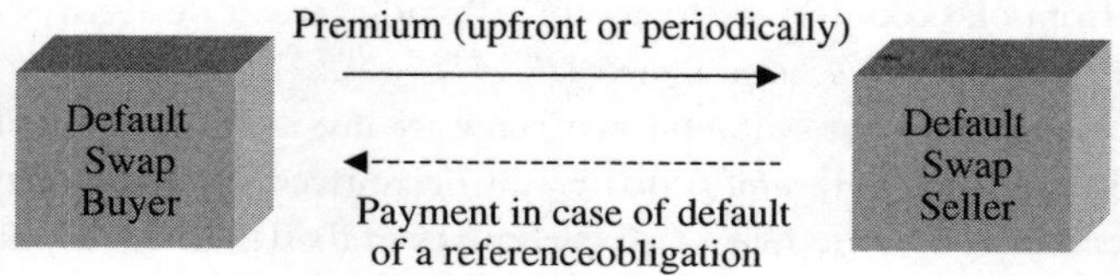

Figure 2.2: The structure of a default swap

Using the same logic, the default swap seller has a long position in the credit quality of the reference obligation. If the credit quality and the price of the reference obligation increase, the present value of the default swap decreases. Thus, after a bond price increases, the premium that the default swap seller receives in the original default swap contract will be an above market premium. The default swap seller can buy back the default swap at the lower current market premium with a profit.

Why default swaps?

The reasons for the rise of default swaps are many. They can be categorized as follows.

- *Hedging:* Reducing various types of risk such as default risk, credit deterioration risk, and also other types of risk such as market risk and operational risk.
- *Yield enhancement:* Usually by assuming credit risk on a reference obligation.
- *Convenience and Cost Reduction:* A default swap allows a lender to eliminate the credit exposure to a debtor without knowledge of the debtor, thus maintaining a good bank-debtor relationship.
- *Arbitrage:* Since default swaps (and other credit derivatives) can be replicated with other financial instruments, arbitrage opportunities may exist.

- *Regulatory Capital Relief:* Default swaps can help reduce the amount of regulatory capital.

These applications of defaults swaps will be discussed in detail in chapter 4.

The terminology

Buying a default swap or paying a fixed rate in a default swap is also called *buying protection* (Default Swap Buyer in figure 2.2). Selling a default swap or paying a floating rate in a default swap is also called *selling protection* or *assuming risk* (Default Swap Seller in figure 2.2). The default swap premium, also called fee, price or fixed rate, is often referred to as the *default swap spread*. This should not be confused with the bid-offer spread of default swaps, which reflects the buying and selling price of a trader or broker. Being *long the default swap basis* means buying the reference obligation and buying protection; being *short the default swap basis* means selling the reference obligation and selling protection.

Features of default swaps

There is a lot to discuss when it comes to default swaps, so we better get started. In a default swap contract, the following terms have to be agreed between a buyer and seller: The premium, which will be discussed in detail in chapter 5 on pricing; the reference obligation, its notional amount and the maturity of the swap; the definition of the default event; and the type of settlement (physical or cash).

The default swap premium

The default swap premium, also called price, fee, spread, or fixed rate is the periodic or upfront payment that the default swap buyer makes to the default swap seller. It is important to note that in most default swap contracts the periodic premium terminates in the event of default. However, in the event of default, the default swap buyer will typically have to pay accrued interest on the swap premium from the last premium payment date to the default date. The way the value of the default swap premium is derived will be discussed in greater detail in chapter 5 on pricing.

The reference obligation

The reference obligation is the obligation that, if in default, triggers the default swap payment. The reference obligation can be a single bond or a loan issued by a corporate or sovereign. In most default swap contracts, the default event applies to several bonds or loans with similar characteristics. This protects the default insurance buyer from the event that many obligations but coincidently or deliberately not his obligation have defaulted.

The most common type of reference obligation is a bond. This is because it is easier to price and hedge a default swap based on a bond, since bonds usually trade in a secondary market. Thus the bond can be bought as a hedge for a long default swap position or shorted as a hedge against a short default swap position. Furthermore, a bond price that is observed in the market serves as a basis for the derivation of the default swap premium (see pricing chapter 5 for details).

If the reference obligation is a loan, things are trickier. Loans often do not trade in a secondary market, thus their price is not directly observable. The value of a loan must be derived from the company's characteristics such as debt to equity ratio, return on capital, quality of management, etc. Since loans often do not publicly trade they cannot be bought or sold in the market as a hedge. Furthermore, since the price of a loan is not directly obtainable, the pricing of the default swap is difficult, since one crucial input parameter, the price of the underlying asset, is uncertain.

What constitutes default?

One of the most critical issues in a default swap is the event that constitutes default, thus the event which triggers the payment by the default swap seller. Conveniently, the 1999 ISDA documentation, with an update in February 2003, offers a guideline of possible credit events[3]. ISDA specifies six possible events:

1 Bankruptcy;
2 Failure to pay;
3 Obligation acceleration;
4 Obligation default;
5 Repudiation/moratorium (a standstill or deferral of the reference entity with respect to the underlying reference obligation);
6 Restructuring.

Default swap counterparties can agree on all or selected credit events from the above list. It is a bit surprising that the event of a downgrade (a public agency such as Moody's, Standard & Poors, or Fitch lowering the publicized rating of a debtor) is not included in the list of credit events. ISDA claims that in past default swap contracts the event of a downgrade was a rare case[4]. Another reason for not including a downgrade in the list of possible credit events is the fact that the rating agencies would have a direct influence on triggering a default swap payment. Lawsuits questioning the neutrality of the agencies or the correctness of the ratings should be the unpleasant consequence.

A further important issue when dealing with default events is *materiality*. It has to be ensured that the credit event is significant and not the mistake of a settlement employee, who forgot to make a small payment. Thus, most default swaps include a *materiality clause*. ISDA suggests that the "default requirement" is $10,000,000 (i.e. the notional amount of the reference obligation is at least $10,000,000)[5]. Furthermore, ISDA suggests that the "payment requirement" is at least $1,000,000. If this is applied, a payment failure of less than $1,000,000 does not constitute the event of default.

The importance of accurately defining the credit event was brought to light in December 2001 in the Argentine debt crisis. On December 23, 2001 Argentina's then prime minister Rodriguez Saa declared a moratorium, which clearly constituted a default event.

However, prior to December 23, Argentina forced creditors to accept a restructuring of their debt, swapping $50 billion of 11% and 12% bonds into 7% yielding bonds. JP Morgan Chase and other investment banks that were the default swap sellers argued that the restructuring was not a credit event defined in the default swap contract. The issue depends to a certain extent on which type of ISDA master agreement was used and will most likely be resolved in court.

Cash versus physical settlement

As in a standard option, the settlement of a default swap is either in cash or is physical. Cash settlement is easier from an administrative point of view since no bonds are transferred from the default swap buyer to the default swap seller, as occurs with physical settlement.

Cash Settlement: In the case of cash settlement, the cash paid from the default swap seller to the default swap buyer in case of default is usually determined as

$$N \times [\text{Reference price} - (\text{Final price} + \text{Accrued interest on reference obligation})]$$

where N is the notional amount, also called calculation amount or principal amount of the default swap. The reference price is determined at the inception of the default swap and is typically the par value of 100. The final price, also called recovery rate, is determined at the time of default. The reference price as well as the final price are quoted in percent.

The above settlement amount, which includes accrued interest, assumes that the default swap buyer will eventually receive the coupon. Hence, part of the coupon, the accrued interest at the time of default, is subtracted from the settlement amount. However, since the issuer is in a state of default, the coupon might not be paid at the next coupon date. Therefore, in some default swap contracts, the accrued interest is excluded from the settlement amount.

Let's just look at a simple example including accrued interest.

Example 2.1: The notional amount of a default swap is $50,000,000. The reference price is 100%, and a dealer poll determines the final price of the reference bond as 35.00%. The last coupon payment was 45 days ago and the bond has an annual coupon of 9%. What is the cash settlement amount in case of default of the reference bond? It is:

$$\$50{,}000{,}000[100\% - (35\% + 9\% \times 45/360)] = \$31{,}937{,}500.$$

As in the above example, in a cash settled swap a dealer poll of at least five dealers determines the final price of the reference obligation. This can be problematic since the defaulted obligation is usually quite volatile after the default event and often does not actively trade. In most default swap contracts the bid price of the dealer poll is used to determine the final price. This is reasonable since the default swap buyer, who typically owns the asset, should mark-to-market his bonds at the bid price, since he has to sell it at the market bid.

Physical Settlement: In the case of physical settlement, the default swap buyer delivers the defaulted bond to the default swap seller and receives the reference price of the bond, which is typically 100. In most default swap contracts, the buyer has the right to deliver a bond from a pre-specified basket of bonds. This protects the default swap buyer from getting squeezed[6] in case he does not own the reference bond.

The physical settlement amount paid by the default swap seller to the default swap buyer is simply calculated as

$$N \times \text{Reference price}$$

where N is the notional amount of the default swap. The reference price is quoted in percent.

Let's look at a very simple example.

Example 2.2: The notional amount of a default swap is $10,000,000 and the reference price is 100%. What is the physical settlement amount paid by the default swap seller in case of default?

$$\$10{,}000{,}000 \times 100\% = \$10{,}000{,}000$$

Note that the physical settlement amount, unless otherwise specified, does not include accrued interest. This is because the default swap seller receives the accrued interest via receiving the bond. Naturally, this accrued interest might not be paid at all or only in part, since the issuer is in a state of bankruptcy.

Hedging with default swaps

Clearly the main application of default swaps is hedging against default of a reference obligation. Various aspects of hedging will be discussed in more detail in chapter 4. However, some crucial properties will be discussed in this basic chapter.

Default swaps are usually purchased if the default swap buyer owns the reference obligation and wants to protect against default of this obligation. Hence, when owning the underlying reference obligation, the default swap functions as an *insurance against default*. This is seen in figure 2.3.

In figure 2.3, the investor is hedged against default of the reference obligation: In the case of physical settlement, the investor takes the obligation and hands it to the default insurance seller, who will pay $1 million. In the case of cash settlement, the investor can sell the reference obligation at the final price in the market and receive the 100 – final price from the default swap seller. For details on settlement, see the discussion above.

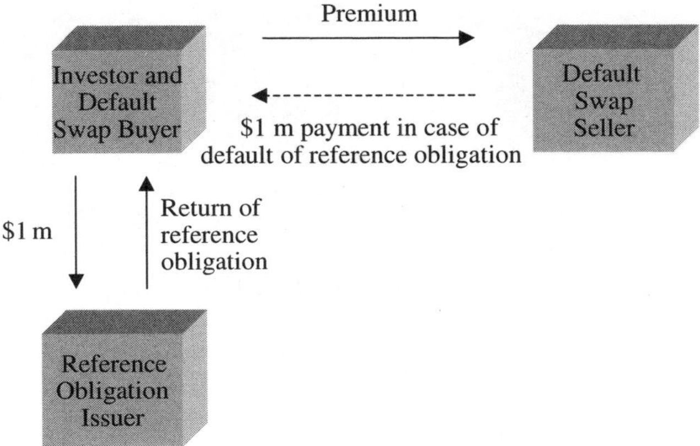

Figure 2.3: An investor hedges his $1 million investment with a default swap

Does a default swap hedge credit deterioration risk?

As just discussed, a default swap protects against default risk; if the reference obligation of the reference entity defaults, the default swap buyer receives a payment from the default swap seller. A crucial question remains: Does a default swap hedge credit deterioration risk (i.e. the risk that the credit quality of the reference entity decreases and thus the obligation of the reference entity decreases in price)? The answer to the question is a clear "That depends!" It depends whether the default swap is marked-to-market[7] or not.

If the default swap is not marked-to-market, an obligation will decrease in price if the credit quality of the reference entity decreases with no compensating effect of the default swap. In this case, the default swap does not protect against credit deterioration risk.

However, if the default swap is marked-to-market, a default swap does protect against credit deterioration risk. This will be demonstrated by the following arbitrage argument: In an arbitrage-free environment, the returns of two portfolios must be identical if the risk is identical. Assuming the notional and maturity of the risk-free bond, the risky bond and the default swap are identical, we get equation (2.1):

$$\text{Long a risk-free bond} = \text{Long a risky bond} + \text{Long a default swap} \tag{2.1a}$$

or stated in form of returns

$$\text{Return on risk-free bond} = \text{Return on risky bond} - \text{Default swap premium (p.a.).} \tag{2.1b}$$

The minus term in equation (2.1b) stems from the fact that the default swap is purchased, thus the default swap premium is an expense. Diagrammatically, equation (2.1) can be represented in figure 2.4.

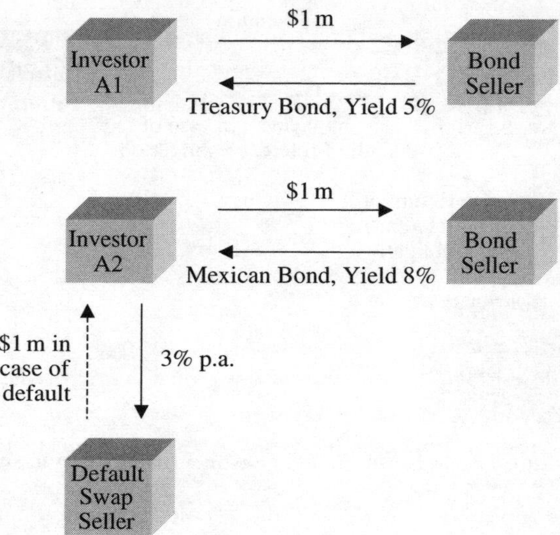

Figure 2.4: Identical returns of investor A1, who invests in a risk-free asset, and investor A2, who invests in a risky asset and buys a default swap with a 3% annual premium

In figure 2.4, the risk profiles and returns of investors A1 and A2 are identical. To begin with, the reader should recall that the reference obligation can only have two states: default and no default. If the reference obligation is in the state of no default, A1 and A2 both make a 5% return. If the reference obligation is in default, A1 is not affected. A2 can use its default insurance, give the Mexican bond to the default swap seller and receive $1 million. Assuming that the risk-free bond trades at par, it is also worth $1 million. Thus we can conclude that at any point in time, bankruptcy or no bankruptcy, equation (2.1) holds.

Consequently for any deterioration of credit quality, equation (2.1) must also hold: If the credit quality of Mexico decreases and the Mexican bond yield increases, the default swap premium for Mexico must increase by the same percentage for equation (2.1) to hold. For example, in figure 2.4, if the Mexican bond yield increases to 10%, the Mexican default swap premium must increase to 5% for equation (2.1) to hold.

As a result, if the change of the default swap premium is marked-to-market, the decrease in the risky bond price will be offset by the increase of the value of the default swap. Thus, on a marked-to-market basis, a default swap protects against credit deterioration risk.

However, in equation (2.1), we have so far ignored several important points.

- We have not considered *counterparty risk*, i.e. the risk that the default swap seller may default. Including counterparty default risk would lower the default swap premium, since the default swap buyer wants to be compensated for the risk. Also, the correlation of the default risk of the reference asset and the counterparty has to be considered when pricing a default swap. These issues will be discussed in chapter 5 on pricing.
- Equation (2.1) is only correct if the no-default value of the risky bond and the current price of the risk-free bond are both par. This is because the par value of the risky bond

is received in case of default (minus the recovery rate), which is compared to the par value of the risk-free bond. Equation (2.1) still holds if we assume that both bonds trade away from par, but interest rate changes affect the yield of the risk-free bond and the risky bond to the same extent. However, considering the different duration and convexity of the bonds, this will mostly not be true in practice. Also, a bond close to default or in default will not be very sensitive to interest rate changes, but rather to recovery rate assessments.

- In equation (2.1) we have also not included the accrued interest of the risky bond. Besides the recovery rate, the accrued interest is typically deducted from the payoff. Hence, in case of default, the default swap buyer does not receive the notional amount N, which is based on the par value of the reference bond (N = $1,000,000 in figure 2.4), but an amount N(1-RR-a), where N: notional amount, RR: recovery rate of the reference entity, and a: accrued interest from the last coupon date until default.
- In equation (2.1) we have also ignored *liquidity risk*. This means that due to the rather illiquid nature of many risky bonds, the bid-offer spread might be so high, that a trade leads to an uneconomical price. Due to the illiquid nature of the bond, it might also be the case that investors are hesitant to buy the bond, resulting in a lower price of the bond than economically justified, termed a *liquidity premium*.

Hence, we have to conclude that equation (2.1) can only serve as an approximation.

Does a default swap hedge against market risk?

For bonds and loans, market risk is primarily the risk that interest rates in the economy change unfavorably. (Other types of market risk are liquidity and volatility risk, see chapter 4.) In the case of holding a bond or loan, naturally interest rate increases will decrease the bond or loan price. Does a default swap protect against market risk? The answer is, principally, no. Regardless of whether the default swap is marked-to-market or not, the value of the swap will not change if the reference asset decreases in price due to interest rate increases. Thus, if interest rates increase, the bond or loan price will decrease without any compensation effect of the default swap (in figure 2.4 the Mexican bond price will decrease but the market default swap premium of 3% will not increase).

However, there is a small effect of interest rate changes on a default swap due to the fact that all expected future cash flows of the default swap are discounted with the interest rate curve. However, for a hedged position, this interest rate effect largely cancels out, if the same discount rates are used to discount the risky bond's future cash flows and the default swap's future cash flows.

Types of default swaps

There are numerous variations of default swaps. The most actively traded are these.

Binary or Digital Default Swaps: In a binary or digital default swap, the payoff in the event of default is a fixed dollar amount, which is specified at the commencement of the swap.

The payoff is often related to historical recovery rates. Binary swaps have become increasingly popular in the recent past. One reason for the increasing popularity is administrative simplicity. No dealer poll has to determine the final price as in a standard default swap, but the pre-specified amount is simply paid from the default swap seller to the default swap buyer. A binary default swap also avoids the problem of volatility of the reference asset after default, which can lead to a distortion of the final price and thus a distortion of the payoff.

Basket Credit Default Swaps: In a basket credit default swap, the reference obligation consists of a basket of obligations. There are several types of basket credit default swaps. In an *N-to-default basket swap* a payoff is triggered when the Nth reference entity defaults. If N = 1, this swap is a *first-to-default basket credit swap*. N is also referred to as the attachment point. After the Nth credit event has occurred, the swap ceases to exist and there is no further exposure to following credit events. In an *add-up credit default swap* (or *linear credit default swap*), the investor is exposed to all reference entities in the basket.

Naturally, basket default swaps hold higher default risk, especially when the default probabilities of the obligations in the basket have a low correlation. Thus, the lower the correlation of the obligations in the basket, the higher is the basket default swap premium, and vice versa. Basket default swaps can be integrated into synthetic structures, which are customized for specific user needs. These tranched basket default swaps are discussed in chapter 3 on synthetic structures.

Cancelable Default Swap: A cancelable default swap is a combination of a default swap and a default swap option. Either the buyer (callable default swap) or the seller (putable default swap), or both, have the right to terminate the default swap. In trading practice, callable default swaps are much more common. The motivation for the callable default swap buyer can be an investment in an asset that can be terminated by the issuer. In the case of termination of the asset, the default swap buyer does not need the protection anymore and can terminate the swap. In a callable default swap, the default swap buyer effectively owns a receiver's option, i.e. an option to receive the periodic default swap premium (which in the case of exercise cancels out). This option increases in value if the default swap premium decreases, i.e. if the credit quality of the reference entity increases.

Contingent Default Swap: In a contingent default swap, the payoff is triggered if both the standard credit event and an additional event occur. The additional credit event might be the default of another obligation. Naturally, contingent default swaps are cheaper than standard default swaps (unless the correlation between the default events is equal to 1). The motivation for the buyer can be – besides the lower premium – that he only seeks quite weak protection, i.e. protection if both reference obligations default.

Leveraged Default Swap: In a leveraged or geared default swap the payoff is a multiple of the loss amount. The payoff is usually determined as the payoff of a standard default swap plus a certain percentage of the notional amount. Naturally leveraged default swaps are more expensive than standard swaps. The motivation for the leveraged default swap buyer is speculation but often also administrative simplicity. Rather than hedging default risk on different assets individually, a single leveraged default swap can hedge a large notional amount. However, if the underlying asset in the leveraged default swap does not match the true exposure of the portfolio, the default swap buyer is exposed to basis risk: Certain assets in the portfolio might default, which are not protected in the leveraged single asset default swap.

Tranched Portfolio Default Swaps and Tranched Basket Default Swaps: Portfolio default swaps are a variation of collateralized debt obligations (CDOs). An original loan or asset is bought by a special-purpose vehicle (SPV) and transformed into notes with different tranches, each tranche having a different degree of risk. Investors can choose the tranche with a degree of risk reflecting their own risk preference. Tranched portfolio default swaps and tranched basket default swaps will be discussed in more detail in chapter 3 on synthetic structures.

Key benefits of default swaps

On an aggregate level, the key advantage of default swaps is that default risk in an economy is reduced. Naturally, in a default swap the default risk is only transferred from the default swap buyer to the default swap seller. However, default swap sellers are usually financial institutions, which aggregate the risk, which can have offsetting effects in itself. Furthermore, the aggregated default risk is managed and reduced with the expertise of financial institutions. Thus, the usage of default swaps and other credit derivatives stabilizes the financial system in an economy.

Protecting an obligation with a default swap can also reduce the price deterioration of the reference obligation; instead of selling the obligation, the holder buys protection, thus the price decrease is reduced.

On an individual level, default swaps have several key benefits. One is obviously the reduction or elimination of default risk for the individual default swap buyer.

Another benefit of default swaps is maintaining a good bank–client relationship. If a bank questions the credit quality of a debtor, it can reduce the default risk of the debtor by entering into a default swap. This requires no consent or knowledge by the debtor, since the bond or loan officially remains in the balance sheet of the bank. Thus a good bank–client relationship is maintained and the credit line of the debtor can stay open, even though the bank questions the debtor's credit quality.

A further benefit for the individual is the reduction of regulatory capital. Regulatory capital can be reduced significantly with default swaps, since the risk of default is reduced with default swaps and consequently so is the required regulatory capital. This will be discussed in more detail in chapter 4.

A further application of default swaps is speculation, which adds liquidity to the default swap market. Also, since a default swap can be replicated by other financial instruments, arbitrage opportunities can exist. Last but not least, default swaps can reduce costs, since they can be cheaper than alternative financial instruments. These applications will be discussed in detail in chapter 4.

Total Rate of Return Swaps (TRORs)

In 1997, total rate of return swaps comprised about 17% of the credit derivatives market. However, in 2002, this number has decreased to about 1%. The reason for this sharp decline

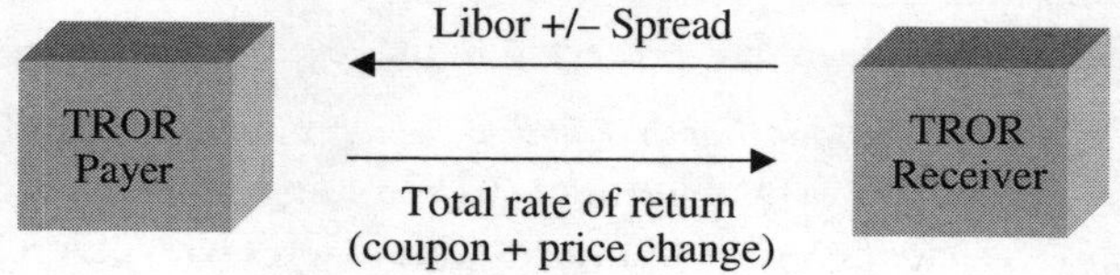

Figure 2.5: The structure of a TROR (both payments are made periodically)

is at least partially to be found in the standardized documentation that ISDA provides for default swaps but not TRORs. Once ISDA supplies standardized documentation, TRORs should regain at least part of their market share. Reason enough to discuss them.

What is a TROR?

A TROR can be viewed as a non-funded position in an obligation, which is usually a bond or a loan. The TROR receiver is synthetically long the obligation, which means he will benefit if the price of the obligation increases. The TROR payer is synthetically short the obligation, which means he will benefit if the price of the obligation decreases. Since the TROR receiver receives the coupon, he pays an interest rate to the TROR payer, usually Libor plus or minus a spread, as seen in figure 2.5.

It is important to note that the TROR receiver takes the default risk and credit deterioration risk: If the reference asset defaults, the TROR receiver has to pay the price decline to the TROR payer. Even in the event of credit deterioration and consequently price deterioration, the TROR receiver bears the risk: He has to pay the price decline to the TROR payer. If the price decline is bigger than the coupon, the TROR receiver will have to make *two* payments, Libor plus or minus a spread *and* the price decrease minus the coupon.

Why TRORs?

Since the TROR receiver has a long position in the reference obligation, which is usually a bond or a loan, the question arises: Why does the TROR receiver not simply buy the asset[8] in the market? The reason arises due to several issues. First, the TROR receiver has no need for funding, i.e. he does not have to borrow cash to buy the bond. This is especially advantageous if the credit rating of the TROR receiver is poor and his potential funding costs are high. However, the credit rating of the TROR receiver will partly determine the spread over Libor. The lower the rating of the TROR receiver, the higher the spread over Libor will be. Second, due to the lack of funding, the leverage[9] for the TROR receiver is extremely high. Third, TRORs are currently off-balance-sheet investments. Thus, the TROR receiver does not have to set aside regulatory capital for the investment. It can be expected, though, that the regulators will require TRORs to be listed on the balance sheet in the future. Fourth, the TROR market might be more liquid than the market for the underlying asset.

For the TROR payer, who has a short position in the asset, the motives are similar. He can conveniently short the asset, which is often difficult in the rather illiquid secondary

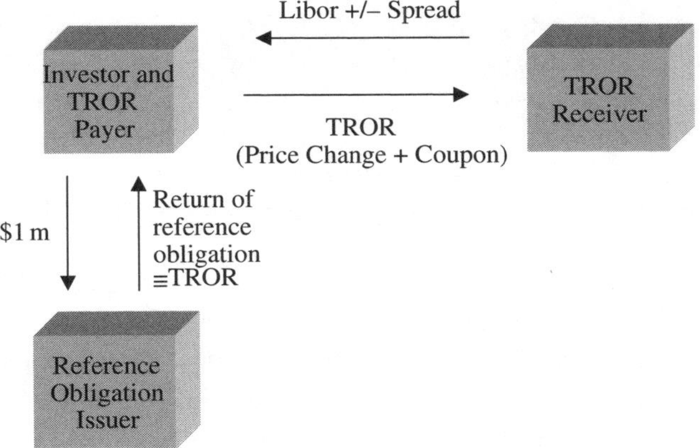

Figure 2.6: An investor hedges a $1 million investment with a TROR (instead of a long position in the reference obligation, the TROR payer now receives Libor +/− a spread)

bond market. (For loans the situation is even worse; hardly any secondary market exists.) As is the case for the TROR receiver, the TROR payer has an off-balance-sheet position. Most importantly, the TROR payer hedges the default risk and price deterioration risk, as well as the market risk of the asset, which will be discussed now.

Hedging with TRORs

A TROR payer is protected against default risk and price deterioration risk, since the TROR receiver pays the price decrease. Is the TROR payer also hedged against market risk? As already mentioned, for bonds and loans, market risk is primarily the risk that interest rates in the economy change unfavorably. In the case of holding a bond or loan, naturally interest rate increases will reduce the bond or loan price. Does a TROR protect against market risk? The answer is yes: The TROR receiver will pay the price decrease to the TROR payer, whether the price decrease is due to credit deterioration or interest rate increase, as seen in figure 2.6.

The difference between a TROR and a default swap

Since a TROR assumes a position in the market risk and credit risk of an asset, but a default swap just assumes credit risk, a TROR is equivalent to a default swap plus market risk:

$$\text{TROR} = \text{Default swap} + \text{Market risk} \tag{2.2}$$

More precisely, equation (2.2) is:

$$\text{Receiving in a TROR} = \text{Short a default swap} + \text{Long a risk-free asset} \tag{2.2a}$$

(Long credit quality + Long market price = Long credit quality + Long market price)

"Long credit quality" means that the position generates a profit if the credit quality of the reference asset improves, and vice versa. "Long market price" means that the position generates a profit if the market price of the reference asset increases, and vice versa. Also, it is true that:

Paying in a TROR = Long a default swap + Short a risk-free asset (2.2b)
(Short credit quality + Short market price = Short credit quality + Short market price)

Equations (2.2), (2.2a), and (2.2b) assume that the TROR and the default swap are marked-to-market. Furthermore, the default swap premium has to be equal to the Libor (+/− a spread) payment in the TROR, and the calculation amount, maturity, underlying obligation, and settlement procedure are identical. Equation (2.2) will come in handy when pricing TRORs. We can simply price a default swap and then add the market risk by going long or short a risk-free asset, which represents the market risk without incurring default risk, (see chapter 5). Example 4.20 in chapter 4 shows an arbitrage opportunity if equation (2.2) is not satisfied.

The difference between a TROR and an asset swap

In an asset swap, one party pays a fixed rate, which originates from an asset, thus the coupon in the case of a bond. The other party pays a floating rate, usually Libor plus a spread. This spread is referred to as the *asset swap spread*.

It is typically assumed that the Libor curve and swap curve are risk-free curves. It follows that the asset swap spread is equal to or greater than zero, since the probability of default of a corporate is equal to or greater than zero. For example, if the risk-free 10-year swap rate is 4%, then in a zero-cost 10-year swap, a 4% fixed rate is exchanged against Libor flat. If a BB-rated corporate issues a 10-year bond with a coupon of 6%, in an asset swap based on this bond, the 6% coupon would be exchanged against Libor + 200 basis points (assuming identical payment frequencies for the 6% fixed rate and the Libor). Including the original investment, an asset swap is seen in figure 2.7.

An asset swap together with owning the reference asset, as in figure 2.7, does not protect the asset swap fixed rate payer against credit risk but against market rate risk.

With respect to credit risk, the asset swap fixed rate payer is not protected against credit deterioration risk as well as default risk: If the reference asset deteriorates in credit quality or defaults, there is no compensation in the asset swap value. Following the above discussed default swap, if the coupon of the reference asset increases to 7%, the new asset swap will have a Libor spread of 300 basis points.

With respect to market risk (i.e. interest rate risk), in an asset swap a fixed rate (the coupon) is swapped into Libor (+ a spread). Hence, when owning the reference asset, the coupons cancel out (see figure 2.7), and the investor receives a Libor rate (+ a spread), which is readjusted periodically.

So what is the difference between a TROR and an asset swap? In a TROR the total return of an asset is exchanged against Libor. In an asset swap, a fixed rate based on the coupon of an asset is exchanged against Libor. As a consequence, a TROR hedges credit risk as well as market risk, however, an asset swap only hedges market risk.

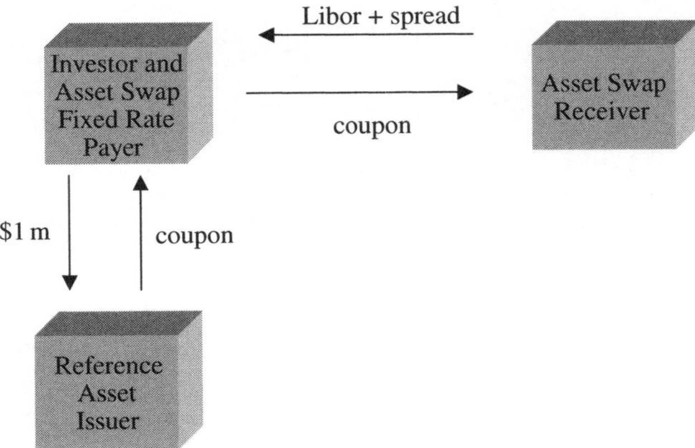

Figure 2.7: An investor hedging his asset with an asset swap

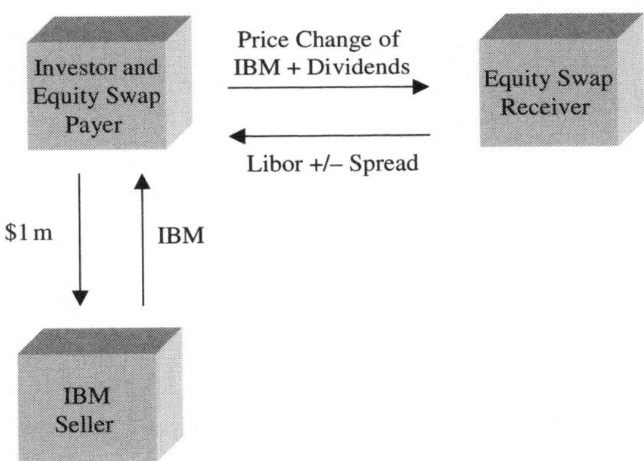

Figure 2.8: An investor swaps his $1 million investment in IBM into a Libor +/− spread return

The difference between a TROR and an equity swap

In an equity swap one party pays an equity return or equity index return. The other party pays an interest rate, usually Libor +/− a spread. Including the original equity investment, the equity swap structure is seen in figure 2.8.

In figure 2.8, the investor has no further exposure to IBM, since he passes the IBM return to the equity swap receiver. So what is the difference between a TROR and an equity swap? Not much. In a TROR the return of an interest rate asset, a bond, or a loan, is swapped into Libor; in an equity swap the return of an equity or equity index is swapped into Libor.

The relationship between a TROR and a Repo

Before we discuss the relationship between a TROR and a Repo, let's just explain how a Repo works. A Repo (Repurchase agreement) is simply a securitized loan. A1 borrows cash

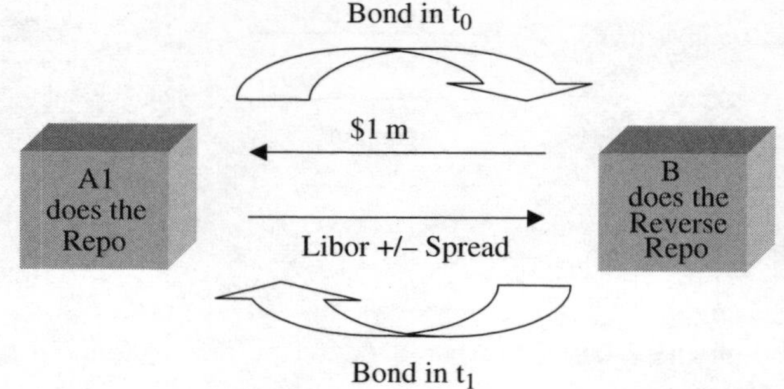

Figure 2.9: The structure of a Repo

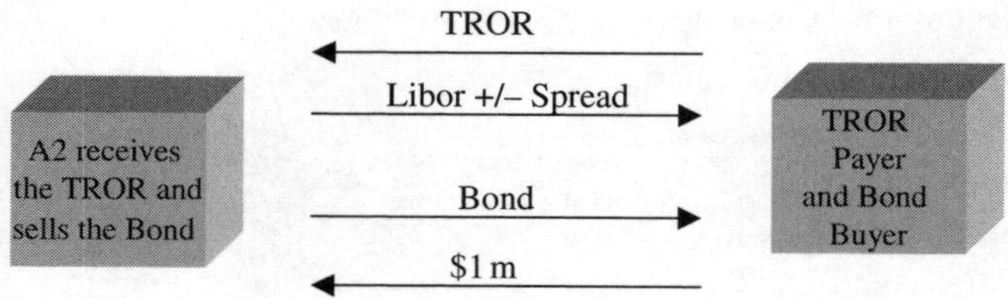

Figure 2.10: A2 receives the TROR and sells the bond to generate cash

from B and gives B bonds or other collateral as security. If A1 can't pay back the loan, B simply keeps the bonds. Graphically represented, a Repo can be seen in figure 2.9.

In figure 2.9, A1 pays an interest rate, the Libor +/− spread, since he borrows cash. If the bond should pay coupons during the period of the Repo, these are passed back to A1. Repos are quite popular, because cash borrowers often find lower interest rates in the Repo market than in the money market. Comparing Repos and TRORs, we find the following relationship:

$$\text{Repo} = \text{Receiving in a TROR} + \text{Sale of the bond} \tag{2.3}$$

Let's verify equation (2.3) graphically. The right side of equation (2.3) is represented in figure 2.10.

From figures 2.9 and 2.10 we can see that the risk profiles of A1 and A2 are identical. A1 borrows $1 million at Libor +/− spread. If we assume that A1 has borrowed the bond and lends it to B, A1 does not have exposure to the bond. The same risk profile applies to A2: He borrows $1 million at Libor +/− spread. The first (TROR) and third (bond) leg of A2 in figure 2.10 cancel out. As for A1, we assume that A2 has also borrowed the bond, which he sells in the market (leg 3 in figure 2.10).[10]

Naturally, if equation (2.3) is violated, arbitrage opportunities exist. If the Libor +/− spread is lower in the Repo than it is in the TROR market, an investor should do the Repo and pay in the TROR (hence receive the high Libor +/− spread) and buy the bond. If the

Libor +/− spread is higher in the Repo than it is in the TROR market, an investor should do a reverse Repo, receive in the TROR and sell the bond.

Key benefits of TRORs

Since a TROR is equal to a default swap plus market risk, TRORs have similar advantages as default swaps.

On a macroeconomic level, TRORs reduce the overall economic risk. Bond owners can pay in a TROR and pass the default risk, credit deterioration risk, and market risk to the TROR receiver. TROR receivers are often financial institutions, which aggregate the risk and reduce it with their expertise.

On a microeconomic level, TRORs eliminate or reduce the default risk, credit deterioration risk, and market risk for an individual bond owner, who pays in a TROR. Generally, TRORs allow taking a long or short position in an asset without explicit funding. In particular, shorting a bond is quite cumbersome in the cash market, but often conveniently possible in the TROR market. This removes the asset from the balance sheet, and thus reduces regulatory capital. From a speculative point of view TRORs offer high leverage, since a long or short position in an asset is taken without funding. Furthermore, since a TROR can be replicated by a Repo plus a sale of the underlying bond, arbitrage opportunities may exist.

Credit-spread Products

As seen in figure 2.1, credit-spread products can have the form of options, futures, and swaps. Credit-spread products have the same application as default swaps and TRORs: they are used to hedge, enhance yields, reduce cost, achieve arbitrage, or reduce regulatory capital. The most popular credit-spread products are credit-spread options, so let's discuss them first.

Credit-spread options

Let's first understand a credit-spread. It refers to the difference between the yield[11] of a risky bond and the yield of a risk-free bond, such as a Treasury bond:

$$\text{Credit-spread} = \text{Yield of risky bond} - \text{Yield of risk-free bond} \tag{2.4}$$

There are two types of standard options: calls and puts. A call is the right but not the obligation to purchase an underlying asset at a pre-agreed price called the strike price. A put is the right but not the obligation to sell an underlying asset at the strike price. In a credit-spread option, the underlying asset is the credit-spread in equation (2.4).

The reader should be careful with the terminology. In the field of exotic options, where spread options are standard instruments, a *call* on a spread has a payoff of max (spread (T)

– strike spread, 0), where T is the option maturity. However, in the field of credit derivatives, the payoff max (spread (T) – strike spread, 0) is referred to as a credit-spread *put*. Thus, a credit-spread put buyer profits if the spread widens, which means she profits if the yield of the risky bond increases or the price of the risky bond decreases. Let's list the payoffs to make things clear. Including a duration term, which is usually added to the payoff, and the notional amount N, we get:

$$\text{Payoff credit-spread put (T)} = \text{Duration} \times N \times \max[\text{Credit-spread (T)} - \text{Strike spread}, 0] \tag{2.5}$$

$$\text{Payoff credit-spread call (T)} = \text{Duration} \times N \times \max[\text{Strike spread} - \text{Credit-spread (T)}, 0] \tag{2.6}$$

where the credit-spread is defined in equation (2.4) and T is the option maturity. Duration plays a key role in understanding the payoff in equations (2.5) and (2.6) as well as the payoff in credit-spread forwards and swaps. So let's briefly discuss duration.

What is duration?

Duration measures how long it takes on average for an investor to get his money back. Hence, duration is expressed in time units, typically in years. For a zero coupon bond with a maturity of 5 years, an investor has to wait 5 years for his investment to return. Thus for zero-coupon bonds, the maturity is equal to the duration. For coupon bonds, the duration is shorter than maturity since some of the coupons are paid before maturity. Technically, duration measures how much an infinitesimal change in the bond's yield changes the percentage price of the bond. Let's derive this mathematically.

Derivation of Duration: A bond price can be expressed as the discounted value of all future cash flows as in the bond equation in note 11. Simplifying that equation, using c for all cash flows including the notional amount N, and using $(1 + y)^{-t} \cong e^{-yt}$, we get:

$$B = \sum_{t=1}^{T} c_t e^{-yt} \tag{2.7}$$

where T is the maturity of the bond, c are the coupons and the notional amount, e is Euler's number (e = 2.71828 . . .), and y is the annual continuously compounded[12] yield. Differentiating equation (2.7) partially with respect to y, using the condition if $B = e^{f(y)} \Rightarrow B' = f'(y)\, e^{f(y)}$ and since $f(y) = -yt \Rightarrow f'(y) = -t$, we get:

$$B' = \frac{\partial B}{\partial y} = \sum_{t=1}^{T} -tc_t e^{-yt}.$$

Dividing by B to derive a percentage change of the bond, we get the duration –D as:

$$-D = \frac{\partial B/B}{\partial y} = \sum_{t=1}^{T} -tc_t e^{-yt}/B, \quad \text{or} \quad D = \frac{\partial B/B}{\partial y} = \sum_{t=1}^{T} tc_t e^{-yt}/B. \tag{2.8}$$

In equation (2.8) we can see that the duration D is the weighted average of the times when the payments occur, t. The weights are $c_t e^{-yt}/B$. Note that the sum of the weights $\sum_{t=1}^{T} c_t e^{-yt}/B = 1$, as equation (2.7) states. Let's derive the duration in a numerical example.

Example 2.3: A 4-year bond with a price and notional amount of $100 has a coupon of 6%. It follows (from equation (2.7)) that the yield of the bond is 6%. The continuously compounded yield is ln (1 + 0.06) = 5.83%. What is the duration of the bond?

Table 2.1: Derivation of the duration of 3.6726 years[13]

Time t	Cash flows c_t	$c_t e^{-yt}$	weight $c_t e^{-yt}/B$	$tc_t e^{-yt}/B$
1	6	5.6602	0.0566	0.0566
2	6	5.3396	0.0534	0.1068
3	6	5.0372	0.0504	0.1512
4	106	83.9515	0.8395	3.3580
Sum		100.0000	1.0000	**3.6726**

Interpretation of Duration: In table 2.1, the bond owner has to wait on average 3.6726 years for his investment of $100 to be repaid. Also, following equation (2.8), for a 1% change in the yield, the relative change in the price of the bond will be approximately $3.6726. This is an approximate number, since it ignores second degree (convexity) and higher orders of the bond–yield function.

Now that we understand duration, we can better understand the payoff in equations (2.5) and (2.6). Since the duration is $-\frac{\partial B/B}{\partial y}$, the duration term in equations (2.5) and (2.6) effectively transforms the change in the yield of the bond ∂y into a change in the relative price of the bond $\partial B/B$. Since most investors want to protect against a price decrease not a yield increase, this does make sense. Let's look at a simple example, which explains equation (2.5).

Example 2.4: A credit-spread put option has a notional amount of $1 million. At option maturity the yield of a bond is 9%, the Treasury bond yield is 5% and the strike spread is 2%. The duration of the bond at option start was 3.67. What is the payoff of a credit-spread put option?

Following equation (2.5), it is 3.67 × $1,000,000 × [(9% – 5%) – 2%] = $73,400.

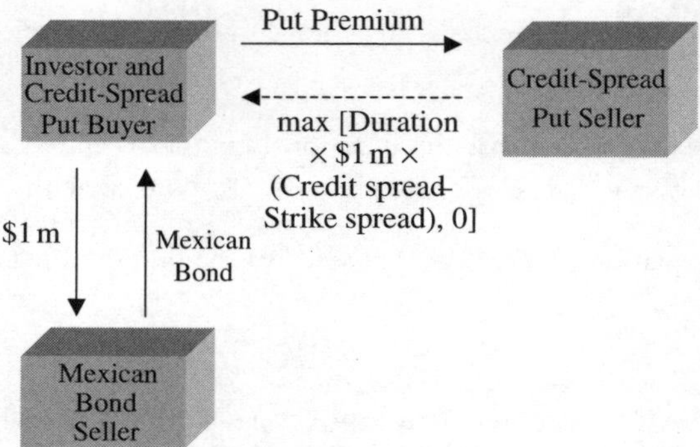

Figure 2.11: An investor hedging his $1 million Mexican bond investment with a credit-spread put

It should be mentioned that it would be appropriate to use the duration at option maturity. However, since this is an unknown at the option start, for simplicity reasons the duration at option start is used in equations (2.5) and (2.6).

The main applications of credit-spread options are hedging, speculation, arbitrage, and regulatory capital reduction. Since hedging is most often used in practice, let's look at an example.

Hedging with credit-spread options

Let's assume an investor owns a Mexican bond. He is worried that the bond might decrease in price or default. He can now buy a credit-spread put to protect against price deterioration and default risk. Graphically this can be seen in figure 2.11:

Let's look at this hedge with a credit-spread put in a numerical example.

Example 2.5: An investor owns a 4-year Mexican bond with a price of $100 and notional amount of $1,000,000 (the investor owns 10,000 bonds) and a coupon and a yield of 6%. The duration (see example 2.3) is 3.67 years. At option start the Treasury bond has a yield of 5%. The investor is afraid that the bond price will decrease in the next three months. As a hedge the investor buys a credit-spread put with a strike spread of 2%, a notional amount of $1,000,000, and 91 days to maturity. The premium derived on a Black-Scholes model for spread options with an assumed implied volatility of the spread of 150% is $3,523 (see www.dersoft.com/csobs.xls; see chapter 5 for a detailed discussion on Black-Scholes). If the bond price decreases to $80 at option maturity, the yield will increase to 13.06%.[14] Is the investor over-hedged or under-hedged?

The investor has lost 10,000 × ($100 − $80) = $200,000 on the decrease of the Mexican bond price. Let's assume the yield of the Treasury bond has not changed and

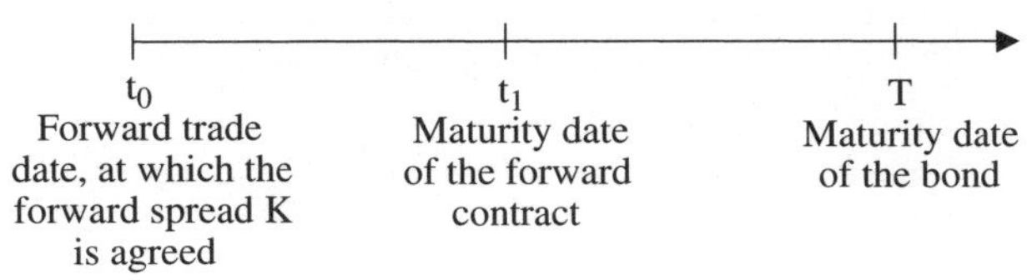

Figure 2.12: Structure of a credit-spread forward contract

is still 5% at option maturity. Following equation (2.5), the payoff on his credit-spread put is 3.67 × $1,000,000 × [(13.06% – 5%) – 2%] = $222,402. Comparing this number to the $200,000 the investor lost from the bond price decrease, we find that the investor is over-hedged. This mismatch is not surprising, since the original bond investment and the option hedge are different instruments, with different duration, convexity, and leverage. Without the duration term, the payoff would have been $1,000,000 × [(13.06% – 5%) – 2%] = $60,600, thus, the investor would have been strongly under-hedged.

We can conclude that credit-spread options hedge credit default risk and credit deterioration risk. An increase in one of these risks leads to a price decrease of the reference asset, which leads to an increase of the present value of the credit-spread put option. If an interest rate change leads to the same change in the yield of the risky bond and the yield of the risk-free bond, credit-spread options do not protect against market risk, since in this case the credit-spread remains unchanged. If an investor is *short* the reference asset and wants to hedge against a price increase, he can either buy a credit-spread call option or sell a credit-spread put option.

Credit-spread forwards

A forward is a contract between two parties to trade a certain asset at a future date, at a price which is determined today. In a credit-spread forward contract the underlying asset is a credit-spread, defined as in equation (2.4). The structure of a credit-spread forward contract on the credit-spread of a bond can be seen in figure 2.12.

The payoff of a credit-spread forward is similar to the payoff of a credit-spread option. The payoff at time t_1 is:

$$\text{Duration} \times N \times [K - S(t_1)] \qquad (2.9)$$

where duration is defined as in equation (2.8), N is the notional amount, K is the agreed spread at t_0 (expressed in percent) and $S(t_1)$ is the actual spread at t_1 (also expressed in percent).

The buyer of the credit-spread forward has a long bond position, i.e. the buyer hopes the relative risky bond price (relative to the Treasury bond price) will increase. In this case the credit-spread S will decrease. If $K > S(t_1)$, the buyer will receive the resulting payoff in equation (2.9) from the seller of the credit-spread contract. The seller of the credit-spread contract has a short bond position. He hopes the relative bond price will decrease. In this case, the spread S will increase. If $K < S(t_1)$, the seller will receive the resulting payoff in equation (2.9). Let's look at a simple example.

Example 2.6: An investor believes the credit quality of a bond will decrease and hence the relative price of the bond will decrease. He sells a credit-spread forward contract with an agreed spread K of 2%. The notional amount N is \$1,000,000 and the duration of the bond at trade date is 3.67.

The credit quality of the bond price, however, increases so that the yield spread decreases to 1%. What is the loss of the credit-spread forward seller?

Following equation (2.9), the credit-spread forward seller has to pay $3.67 \times \$1{,}000{,}000 \times (2\% - 1\%) = \$36{,}700$ to the credit-spread forward buyer at t_1.

Forwards versus futures

In example 2.6, we have assumed that the premium of the forward is zero. This is always the case for futures, but not necessarily for forwards. The difference between futures and forwards is that futures are standardized contracts that trade on an exchange. Forwards are traded OTC (over the counter) so not on an exchange and are flexible in determining the notional amount, maturity, forward price, and other features.

Futures have a zero premium, i.e. no cash is paid from the buyer to the seller or vice versa at the trade date. This is because a futures price at any time is the fair mid-market price that is derived by supply and demand in the market. So entering into a future contract does not bear an advantage for the buyer or seller, thus no upfront cash is exchanged. However, for a forward, the agreed spread, K, may not be the fair mid-market spread. If the spread, K, is higher than the current mid-market spread $S(t_0)$, the buyer has to pay the present value of the forward contract to the seller at the trade date, and vice versa.

As with credit-spread options, credit-spread forwards and futures protect against default risk and credit deterioration risk, since a change in either of these risks leads to a change in the market price of the reference asset, which leads to a change in the value of the forward or futures position. If an interest rate change leads to the same change in the yield of the risky bond and the yield of the risk-free bond, credit-spread forwards do not protect against market risk, since in this case the credit-spread remains unchanged.

Credit-spread swaps

To begin with, the reader should not confuse default swaps (DS), also termed credit default swaps (CDS), with credit-spread swaps. As mentioned above, a default swap is the most popular credit derivatives product and can be viewed as an insurance against default of the underlying asset, if the underlying asset is owned.

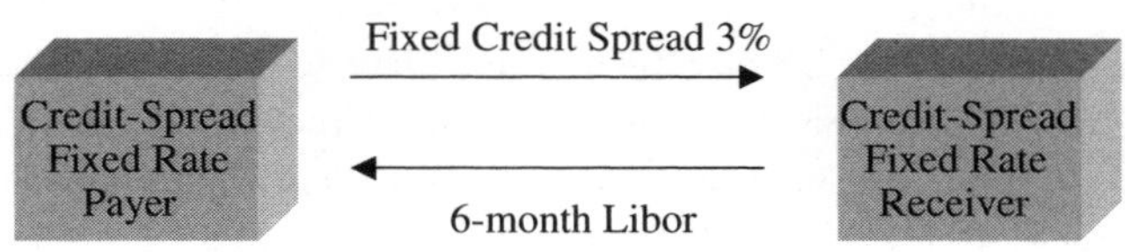

Figure 2.13: The structure of a credit-spread swap with a fixed credit-spread rate of 3% against 6-month Libor (both payments are made periodically)

Let's just define a swap: A swap is an agreement between two parties to exchange a series of cash flows. In a credit-spread swap, party A pays a fixed credit-spread rate, and party B pays the 6-month Libor, as seen in figure 2.13.

The fixed-rate payer in a credit swap has a short position in the underlying bond: if the bond price decreases and consequently the credit-spread increases, the present value of the credit-spread swap will increase in favor of the fixed-rate payer (if, for example, the mid-market credit-spread increases to 4%, however, the fixed-rate payer only pays 3%, creating a profit for the fixed-rate payer). The receiver in a credit-spread swap has a long bond position: If the bond price increases and the credit-spread decreases, the present value of the swap will decrease in favor of the fixed-rate receiver. Let's look at an example of a credit-spread swap.

Example 2.7: Party A (the credit-spread fixed rate payer in figure 2.13) believes a bond price will decrease over the next 2 years. Thus, party A enters into a 2-year credit-spread swap with party B (credit-spread fixed rate receiver in figure 2.13). Party A agrees to pay the current 3% yield-spread semi-annually, party B will pay a floating rate, the 6-month Libor (6ML), as seen in figure 2.14. Since the swap is traded at par (the fixed rate equals the market rate), the present value of the swap is zero.

If the notional amount is $1,000,000, the fixed-rate payer A will pay 3% × 500,000 = $15,000 every 6 months. The floating-rate payer B will pay the 6ML every 6 months. The fixing of each 6ML occurs 6 months before each payment. Therefore the first fixing is on the day the swap starts at t_0, the last fixing is at $t_{1.5}$.

Let's assume after 3 months the price of the bond has decreased and the credit-spread has increased to 5%. Assuming the spread curve is flat at 5%, the present value of the swap has increased to $28,541.[15] This is the profit of A, since the swap was done at par.

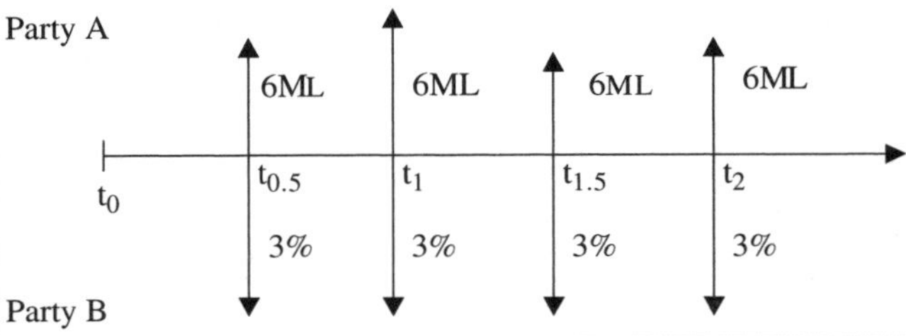

Figure 2.14: The structure of a 3% credit-spread swap against 6ML

It should be mentioned that credit-spread swaps and TRORs are quite similar instruments. In a TROR the total rate of return (price change + coupon) of a risky bond is exchanged, which is reflected in the bond's yield. In a credit-spread swap, the difference between the risky bond's current spread (current risky bond yield minus current Treasury bond yield) and the 6ML is exchanged. Thus, in a TROR a yield is exchanged against Libor, in a credit-spread swap a yield difference is exchanged against Libor.

As with credit-spread options and credit-spread forwards and futures, credit-spread swaps protect against default risk and credit deterioration risk. This is because a change in one of these risks leads to a change in the market price of the reference asset, which leads to a change in the present value of the credit-spread swap. If an interest rate change leads to the same change in the yield of the risky bond and the yield of the risk-free bond, credit-spread swaps do not protect against market risk, since in this case the credit-spread remains unchanged.

When to hedge and with what credit-spread product

When should an investor hedge his credit risk with a credit-spread option, credit-spread forward, and credit-spread swap? The answer is quite simple: if the investor is not so sure that the credit quality of the underlying asset will decrease, he should hedge with an option. This is because an option has limited downside, but unlimited upside potential. That is why an option requires a premium, and a forward and a swap do not, if traded at mid-market. Thus, if the credit quality increases, the investor will not exercise his credit-spread put and will participate in the price increase of the underlying asset.

However, if the investor is very sure that the credit quality of the underlying asset will decrease, it is cheaper to hedge with shorting a credit-spread forward or paying in a credit-spread swap. However, if the credit quality and the price of the reference asset unexpectedly increase, the investor will not profit from the asset price increase, since the hedge will produce an increasing loss with an increasing asset price.

Besides hedging, other applications of credit derivatives are speculation, arbitrage, cost reduction, convenience (e.g. keeping a good client relationship) and regulatory capital reduction. Before these applications are discussed in more detail in chapter 4, let's first look at how credit derivatives are embedded in bonds and loans, in synthetic structures tailored to investors' risk preferences.

Summary of Chapter 2

In this chapter, the different credit derivative products were discussed. They can be categorized as default swaps, total rate of return swaps, and credit-spread products.

Default swaps (DS), also termed credit default swaps (CDS), represent a position in the credit quality of a reference bond or loan. For default swaps, ISDA has provided standardized (master) contract templates in 1999, with an update in 2003, which has led to a sharp increase in default swap trading volume. Default swaps protect not only against default risk, but also against credit deterioration risk, if they are marked-to-market. However, default swaps do not protect against market risk, which for bonds and loans is primarily interest rate risk.

Total rate of return swaps (TRORs) create a non-funded long or short position in the total return of a reference bond or loan. TRORs protect against credit risk and market risk.

There are basically three types of credit-spread products: credit-spread options, credit-spread forwards, and credit-spread swaps. If an investor wants to hedge his credit exposure but at the same time wishes to participate in a potential increase in the credit quality of the underlying asset, he should hedge with a credit-spread option. If the investor is quite sure that the asset will decrease he should use a forward or swap as a hedge, since they require no premium if traded at mid-market.

Naturally the credit derivatives products are related. A TROR is equivalent to a default swap plus market risk. A TROR itself is quite similar to a standard asset swap or an equity swap. Since a Repo is equal to a TROR plus selling a bond, arbitrage opportunities may exist. TRORs and credit-spread swaps are also quite similar. In a TROR the yield of a bond is exchanged against Libor, in a credit-spread swap a yield difference is exchanged against Libor.

On a microeconomic level, the key benefit of all credit derivatives is hedging individual risks. On a macroeconomic level, credit derivatives can reduce the overall economic risk. Bond and loan owners can enter into a credit derivative and pass the default risk, credit deterioration risk, and in some cases also the market risk to the credit derivative seller. Credit derivative sellers are often financial institutions, which aggregate the risk and reduce it with their expertise. Thus, the overall risk in an economy can be reduced.

References and Suggestions for Further Readings

Basel Committee, "The New Basel Capital Accord," January 2001, http://www.bis.org/.

Das, S., "Credit Derivatives and Credit Linked Notes," *Credit Management*, September 2002, p. 25.

Euromoney, "Credit Derivatives: Applications for Risk Management," Euromoney Publications, 1998.

Hull, J., *Options, Futures, and Other Derivatives*, 5th edn, Prentice Hall, 2002.

ISDA: Definitions 1999, http://www.isda.org/.

Nelken, I., *Implementing Credit Derivatives*, McGraw-Hill, 1999.

Risk Books, *Credit Derivatives Applications for Risk Management, Investment and Portfolio Optimization*, Risk Publications, 1998.

Tavakoli, J., *Credit Derivatives: A Guide to Instruments and Applications*, 2nd edn, John Wiley & Sons, 2001.

Questions and Problems

Answers, available for instructors, are on the Internet. Please email gmeissne@aol.com for the site.

2.1 *Does a default swap hedge against (a) default risk, (b) credit deterioration risk, and (c) market risk? Discuss each point!*

2.2 *Does a TROR hedge against (a) default risk, (b) credit deterioration risk, and (c) market risk? Discuss each point!*

2.3 *Discuss the arbitrage relationship: Long a risk-free bond = Long a risky bond + Long a default swap. What features weaken this relationship?*

2.4 *Explain why these equations hold:*

Receiving in a TROR = short a default swap + long a risk-free asset, *and*
Paying in a TROR = long a default swap + short a risk-free asset.

2.5 *Explain the difference between a TROR and an asset swap. Explain the difference between a TROR and an equity swap!*

2.6 *Explain the following relationship graphically:*

Repo = Receiving in a TROR + Sale of the Bond, *and*
Reverse Repo = Paying in a TROR + Purchase of a bond

2.7 *Name the three types of credit-spread products. What is the difference between a credit-spread future and a credit-spread forward?*

2.8 *What are the payoff functions of a credit-spread put and call? Why is the put and call payoff reversed in the credit market compared to the exotic option market? Do you think the reversion is reasonable? Why is a duration term added in the payoff functions?*

2.9 *In which situation should an investor hedge her credit risk with a credit-spread option, credit-spread forward, and credit-spread swap?*

Notes

1 A put option gives the buyer (owner) the right to sell a reference obligation at a pre-agreed price, called strike price. The seller of a put has to buy the reference obligation at the strike price if the put buyer decides to exercise the put, i.e. if he decides to sell the reference obligation at the strike price.

2 A knock-in option is a type of barrier option. A knock-in option starts existing if a certain event occurs.

3 ISDA, www.ISDA.org, "1999 ISDA Credit Derivatives Definitions," p. 16; ISDA, www.ISDA.org, "2003 Definitions"

4 ISDA www.ISDA.org, "1999 ISDA Credit Derivatives Definitions," p. vi

5 ISDA www.ISDA.org, "1999 ISDA Credit Derivatives Definitions," p. 18

6 In a short squeeze, traders buy a financial asset to increase the price since they know the asset has to be bought back by other traders.

7 Marking-to-market means that the profit and loss of the portfolio is calculated at the end of the trading day. Financial institutions mark-to-market all assets in their trading books. The clearing house marks-to-market every asset that trades on an exchange.

8 The term "obligation" is used in the ISDA documentation, so we are applying it a lot in this book. Naturally, what is an obligation for the debtor is an asset for the creditor. So we will use the term "asset" instead of "obligation" if we are referring to the creditor.

9 In this case, leverage is measured as the relative change of the potential return divided by the relative change of invested cash.

10 Note that A2 will have to buy back the bond in order to return it to the lender. However, A2 has no exposure to the bond price, since it has a long exposure (via receiving in the TROR) and a short exposure (via short selling the bond). For example, if the bond price (for 10,000 bonds) has decreased from $100 to $70, A2 will make a profit of $30 on the buyback, however, it will have lost this price decrease by paying it in the TROR. For reasons of pedagogy, figure 2.9 does not include the repayment of the $1,000,000 loan of A1 at t_1, and figure 2.10 does not include A2's buyback of the bond.

11 The yield (also called yield to maturity, YTM) of a bond is the annual percentage profit of the bond, if the bond is purchased at the current market price and held to maturity, assuming the

bond does not default. Mathematically, the yield y is the interest rate in the discount factor $1/(1+y)^t$ that discounts all cash flows, the coupons c and the notional amount N, which occur at future times t, back to today. If T is the maturity of the bond, today's bond price B is $B = \sum_{t=1}^{T} \frac{c_t}{(1+y)^t} + \frac{N}{(1+y)^T}$. (For more on the yield, see www.dersoft.com/bond)

12 A continuously compounded interest rate is a rate, where the interest on interest is paid in infinitesimally short time units. An interest rate r can be transformed into a continuously compounded interest rate r_{cc} by equation $r_{cc} = \ln(1 + r/m)m$, where ln is the natural logarithm and m is the payment frequency of r per year.

13 For the duration derived with Excel see www.dersoft.com/bond.xls.

14 There is no closed form solution to calculate the yield of a bond. The yield of a bond can be calculated by iterative search procedures as Newton-Raphson, with a financial calculator, or with Excel. A simple calculation of the yield with Excel can be found at www.dersoft.com/bond.xls.

15 See www.dersoft.com/interestrateswap.xls

Chapter Three
Synthetic Structures

Es irrt der Mensch, so lang er strebt (Humans will err as long as they strive.) (Goethe)

Synthetic structures have enjoyed significant growth in recent years. This chapter will categorize them, analyze them, and point out the opportunities and risks for the issuer, intermediary, and investor. Let's start with a categorization of the types of synthetic structures as seen in figure 3.1.

The terminology within synthetic structures is far from clear or consistent among practitioners and academics. Especially the distinction between CLNs (credit-linked notes) and CDOs (collateralized debt obligations) has become increasingly blurry. One more reason to clarify things. Let's start with CLNs.

Credit-Linked Notes (CLNs)

A credit-linked note (CLN) in its simplest form is just a note (bond or loan) with an embedded credit feature. For example, a CLN issuer pays an above market coupon if a bond is not downgraded. If the bond is downgraded, the coupon payment reduces. If the issuer of the CLN owns the reference asset, the CLN structure can be seen in figure 3.2.

The motivation for the CLN issuer in figure 3.2 is clear: He has transferred the credit deterioration risk and default risk of his Mexican bond to the CLN buyer. The price for the risk transfer is the difference in the coupons in case of no downgrade and no default, 2%. The CLN issuer has additionally employed his view on the downgrade of the Mexican bond. The best-case scenario for the CLN issuer is if the Mexican bond is downgraded but does not default. In this case the CLN issuer makes a profit of 3%. In case of default, the Mexican bond owner and CLN issuer will receive the recovery rate from the Mexican bond seller and pass it to the CLN buyer.

The motivation for the CLN buyer in figure 3.2 is yield enhancement. The CLN buyer is willing to take the Mexican bond default risk and credit deterioration risk for a return of 10% in case the bond is not downgraded. The CLN buyer obviously believes that the probability of a downgrade of the Mexican bond is low.

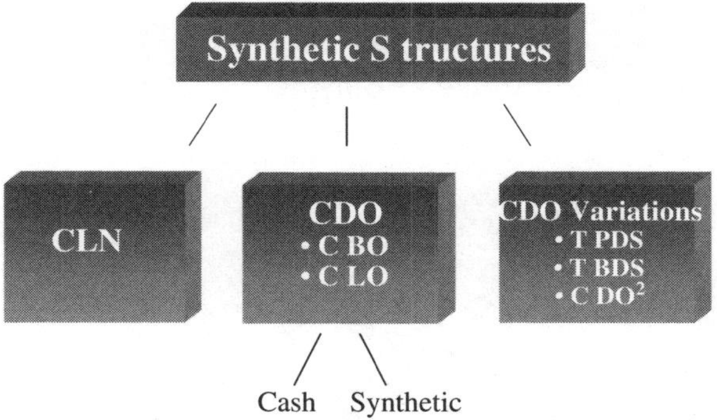

Figure 3.1: A broad overview of traded synthetics structures
CLN: credit-linked note; CDO: collateralized debt obligation; CBO: collateralized bond obligation; CLO: collateralized loan obligation; TPDS: tranched portfolio default swap; TBDS: tranched basket default swap; CDO^2: CDO squared, also called CDO of CDOs

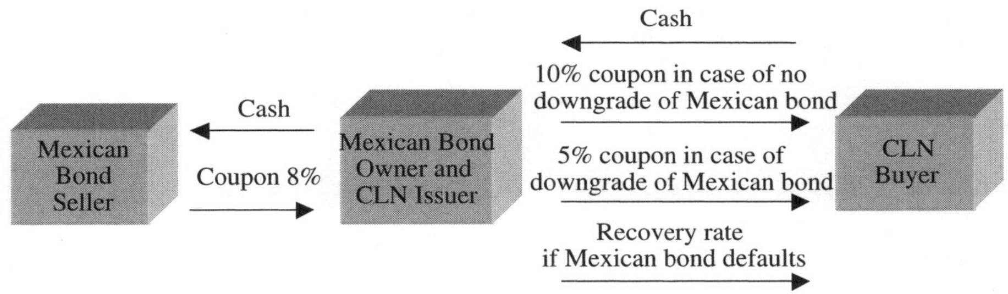

Figure 3.2: A bond owner transferring credit risk via a CLN

Note that the CLN buyer also has counterparty risk: If the CLN issuer defaults, the CLN buyer will not receive his coupon payments and his original cash investment back in full or in part. The CLN buyer is also exposed to correlation risk: The higher the correlation between the CLN issuer and the Mexican reference asset, the higher the risk for the CLN buyer. Due to these risks, investors can often find more attractive yields in the CLN market than yields for similarly rated bonds in the bond cash market.

Comparing the hedge of the CLN issuer with the hedge in a default swap (see figure 2.2 in which the default swap buyer has counterparty default risk), we realize that the CLN issuer has no counterparty risk, since the CLN buyer has transferred cash (has funded his investment). However, there is no free lunch: Due to the funded nature of the CLN, the CLN issuer usually has to pay a higher yield than in an equivalent default swap.

A benefit of CLNs is that certain market participants who are not allowed to participate in the derivatives market, due to off-balance-sheet restrictions or due to regulatory reasons, can gain access to this market through synthetic structures. A drawback of CLNs is that they are privately placed notes, and thus often quite illiquid. Therefore, investors may be advised to hold them to maturity.

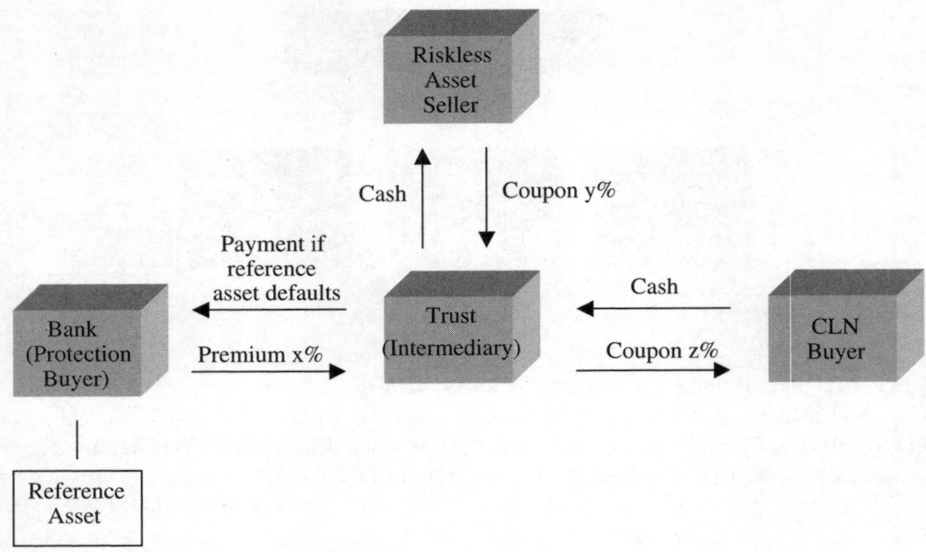

Figure 3.3: A synthetic credit-linked note

A more complex credit-linked note structure

The following structure offers a bank a hedge, the intermediary a fee income and an investor (the CLN buyer) a synthetic exposure to a reference asset, as seen in figure 3.3.

In the structure of figure 3.3, the bank (protection buyer) enters into a default swap, hedging his reference asset investment. The trust, which arranges the structure, makes a profit of x% + y% − z%. The trust does not have credit risk, since it has received the premium x% and the cash from the CLN buyer and has invested this in a risk-free asset. The CLN buyer receives an above-market coupon z, since he takes the counterparty risk of the trust.

Importantly, the CLN buyer also takes credit risk, since the coupons z and/or the repayment of his cash investment are linked to the credit performance of the reference asset. For example, the CLN buyer might get a lower coupon and/or only a partial repayment of his cash investment, if the credit rating of the reference asset decreases.

Collateralized Debt Obligations (CDOs)

As mentioned above, the distinction between credit-linked notes (CLNs) and collateralized debt obligations (CDOs) has become somewhat blurry. Nevertheless, there are some differences on which most practitioners and academics agree. First, CDOs are usually arranged by a special-purpose vehicle (SPV). SPVs, also called special-purpose entities (SPEs) or

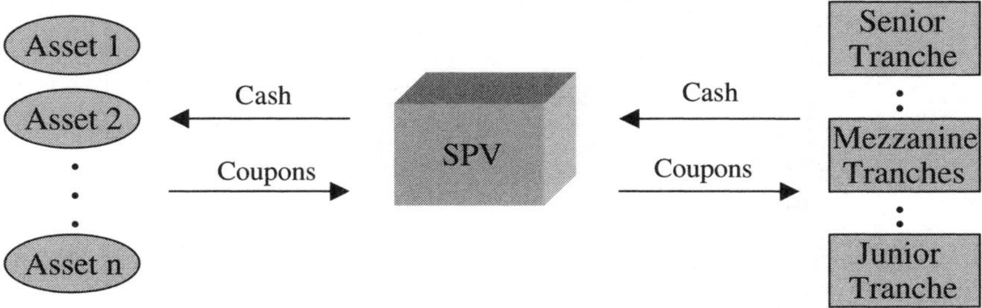

Figure 3.4: The structure of a cash CDO

special-purpose corporations (SPCs), are special entities of financial institutions and are usually triple-A rated. The financial institution and the SPV are mostly legally distinct, hence a credit quality deterioration of the financial institution does not affect the SPV. Second, CDOs usually provide credit exposure to a basket of up to 200 or more credits. Third, CDOs are usually tranched, providing the investor with a specific risk profile. Furthermore, CDOs can be either cash or synthetic. A typical cash CDO is shown in figure 3.4.

In figure 3.4 we see that the SPV has invested cash in a basket of n assets. It has then repackaged and allocated the assets into several tranches. The idea of tranching is not new, but stems from mortgage-backed securities (MBSs), where debtors can repay their mortgage anytime without penalty. In a MBS, the first repayments flow into the first tranche. After this tranche is full and first tranche investors have received their notional amount, the next repayments flow into the second tranche, and so on. Naturally, the junior (first) tranche in a MBS has the highest probability of repayment in a low interest rate environment, which leads to low reinvestment returns. Therefore the junior tranche pays the highest coupon.

In a CDO a similar principle applies. A default of any asset in the basket leads to a loss of coupon and notional amount for investors of the junior tranche, also called first-to-default tranche. If the tranche is full, additional defaults will lead to losses for the second tranche, and so on. Sometimes junior tranches work with a threshold: Only if more than x percent of assets in the basket have defaulted does a loss for investors in the junior tranche occur. Junior tranches of CDOs do not necessarily consist only of bonds and loans, but can also include equity (they are then termed equity CDOs).

Naturally, junior tranches incur the highest risk and receive the highest coupon, which can be as high as 30%. The criterion of success of a CDO is generally related to the success of selling the junior tranche, which is often quite difficult due to its high default risk. Consequently, SPVs are often required to keep the junior tranche in their own portfolio or their parent institution acquires it.

Mezzanine tranches, which incur losses if the junior tranche is complete, usually have credit ratings from single B to AA. Senior tranches, which are usually the largest of all tranches, are commonly rated AA or AAA. Often SPVs actively manage the assets in the CDO. The goal is to pay higher coupons in a CDO than the equivalent bonds pay in the cash market.

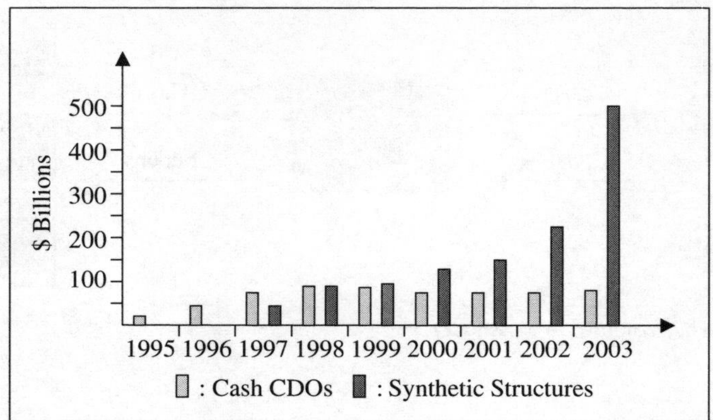

Figure 3.5: Trading volume of cash CDOs and synthetic structures in billions
Source: Bank of America: www.gtnews.com and Lang Gibson, *Asset Securitization Report*, January 13, 2004

Synthetic CDOs

Currently one the most popular structures are synthetic collateralized debt obligations, which were issued first in 1997. They have since surpassed cash CDOs in trading volume, as seen in figure 3.5.

The difference between cash CDOs and synthetic CDOs lies in the fact that the SPV in a synthetic CDO does not acquire the original assets in a standard cash transaction, but gains long credit exposure[1] to the assets via selling credit protection, e.g. default swaps. The SPV uses the cash from the sale of the tranches and the default swap premiums to purchase risk-free bonds, as seen in figure 3.6.

The rise in popularity of synthetic CDOs is primarily due to the fact that the ownership of the assets is not legally transferred to the SPV. Thus the assets do not appear on the balance sheet of the SPV. Furthermore, in a synthetic CDO the SPV has no operational risk[2] with respect to the original assets. For example, for legal or political reasons, the SPV in a *cash* CDO might not be able to enforce the coupon or notional payments.

In a synthetic CDO, as in a cash CDO, the default risk of the assets is transferred to the investors of the individual tranches, the junior tranche again incurring the first losses.

A two-currency, partly cash, partly synthetic CDO with embedded hedges

Synthetic structures can be fairly complex using a variety of financial innovations. For the reader who likes it complicated, let's look at a CDO which is partly cash and partly synthetic. Furthermore, some of the original assets are purchased in a foreign currency. However, the SPV wants to eliminate the currency risk and uses a cross currency swap as

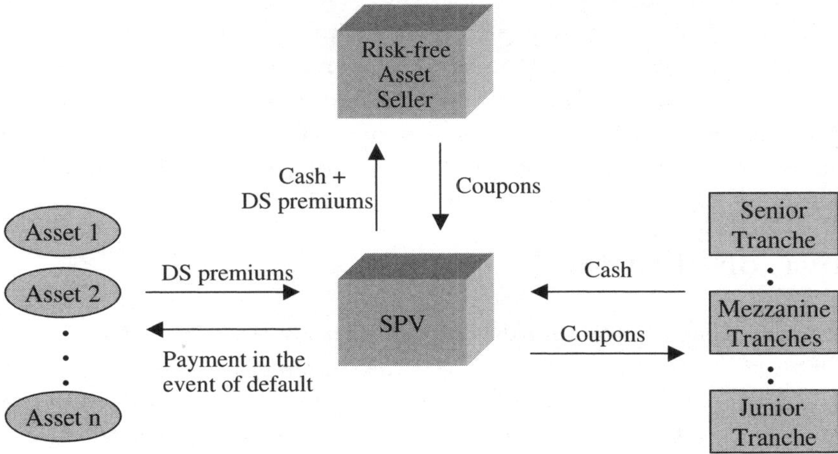

Figure 3.6: The structure of a synthetic CDO (DS = Default Swap)

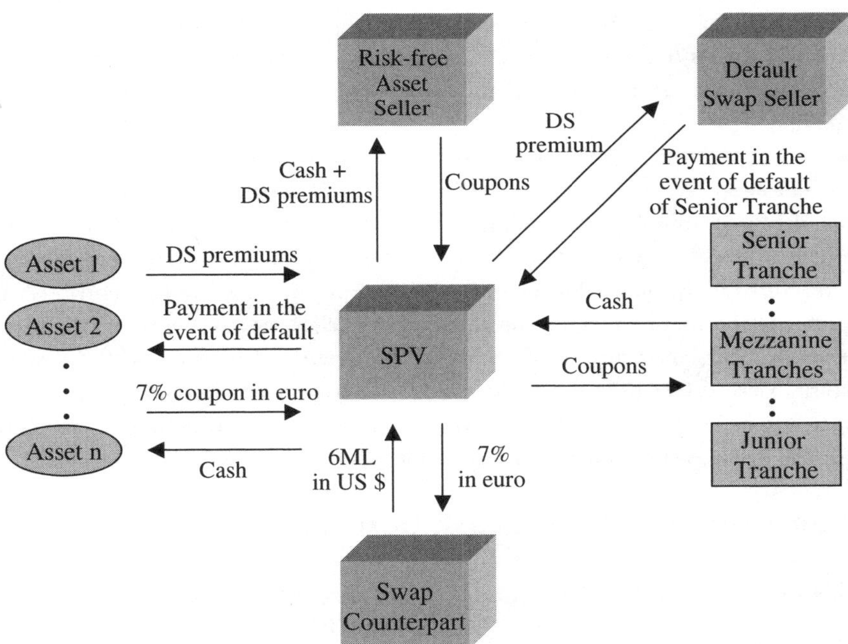

Figure 3.7: A partly cash, partly synthetic CDO with a cross currency swap hedge and a senior tranche hedge

a hedge. In a cross currency swap one party (SPV in figure 3.7), pays a fixed rate in a certain currency, e.g. Euro 7% and the other party (swap counterpart in figure 3.7) pays a floating rate in another currency e.g. 6 ML (6 month Libor) in US dollars. If the SPV owns a fixed rate bond, the SPV has swapped the Euro fixed rate income into a risk-free floating

US dollar income. At inception, cross currency swaps are typically traded at par (at a present value of zero), so no currency swap premium is exchanged at the trade date.

Furthermore, in figure 3.7 the SPV wants to increase the rating of the CDO by guaranteeing the notional amount of the senior tranche. Thus it purchases a default swap from a third party for the senior tranche. This will not be too expensive since the senior tranche is usually AA or AAA rated, thus the default probability is low. The whole structure can be seen in figure 3.7.

Motivation of CDOs

There are different motivations for the different participants within a CDO. For the SPV, the CDO is income-motivated: The SPV gets fees for placing, structuring, and managing the CDO. These fees can be quite substantial. They can reach up to 10% of the notional amount. SPVs can also make a profit on the difference between the generated income from the tranches and the default swap premiums and coupons of the risk-free asset. This type of CDO is termed an *arbitrage*[3] *CDO*.

The SPV can also initiate a CDO to achieve regulatory capital relief by removing an asset from their balance sheet. For example, an SPV might already own assets, and create a tranched CDO, thus transferring the credit risk to the investors of the tranches. This type of CDO is termed a *balance sheet CDO* and can extend a client's credit line and additionally raise funding.

The motivation for the owners of the assets (left side of figure 3.7) is laying off credit risk via a default swap without having to inform the original debtor, thus maintaining a good creditor–debtor relationship. Synthetic structures are also more convenient from an administrative point of view, since no physical transfer of the original asset takes place. Finally, synthetic structures are flexible, allowing customized credit risk transfer of an individual credit.

The motivation for the investors in the tranches (right side of figure 3.7) is primarily yield enhancement. The tranches often pay a higher return than assets with the same risk in the cash markets. However, the investor is advised to keep an eye on the usually high fees in CDOs. A further motivation for the investor is that a CDO allows them to access payoff profiles that would be difficult, if not impossible to create with cash products.

Market value CDOs and cash flow CDOs

A further categorization criterion of CDOs can be the way the SPV repays its investors. We differentiate two types: market value CDOs and cash flow CDOs.

In a market value CDO, the SPV pays its liabilities to the investor mainly by successively selling assets of the tranched portfolio. Market value CDOs are often actively managed, i.e. the SPV frequently buys and sells assets in the portfolio. The assets are usually liquid, containing more equity and revolving credits than a cash flow CDO. Due to its actively managed nature, the profitability of a market value CDO depends largely on the trading success of the SPV.

In a cash flow CDO, repayments to the investor are done mainly via coupon flows and notional amount repayments. Cash flow CDOs are often static (i.e. not actively managed).

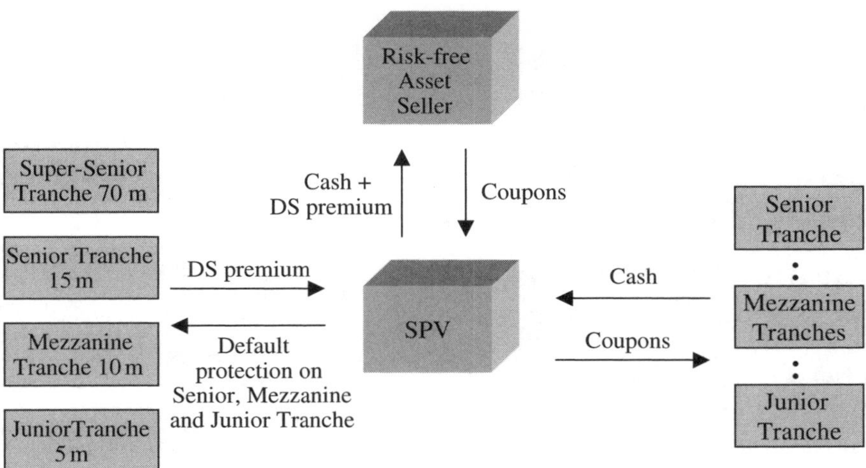

Figure 3.8: A tranched portfolio default swap (TPDS)

The profitability of cash flow CDOs depends mainly on the asset's ability to withstand defaults.

Tranched portfolio default swaps (TPDS)

Tranched portfolio default swaps (TPDSs) are fairly new synthetic structures with strong growth potential. They can be viewed as more flexible, customized CDOs. In a TPDS, the SPV can assume credit risk on certain tranches of reference assets (left side of figure 3.8). A TPDS often contains a super-senior tranche, which is AAA rated, and which is usually the largest of the tranches. Often the SPV assumes credit risk on all tranches except the super-senior tranche. Let's look at a TPDS in which this is the case in figure 3.8.

In figure 3.8, the SPV takes on the default risk on all assets, except the assets in the super-senior tranche. The loss risk from the initial tranches (left side of figure 3.8) is transferred partially or totally to the investors of the corresponding tranches (on the right side of figure 3.8). The advantage in a TPDS compared to a standard CDO is that in a TPDS, the SPV and the default swap buyer can trade default risk flexibly on a specific degree of risk. Investors willing to take risk will buy junior tranches, risk averse investors will prefer mezzanine or senior tranches.

Tranched basket default swaps (TBDSs)

Close cousins of TPDSs are tranched basket default swaps (TBDSs). TBDSs are a combination of N-to-default baskets and CDOs. The difference to a TPDS is that the attachment

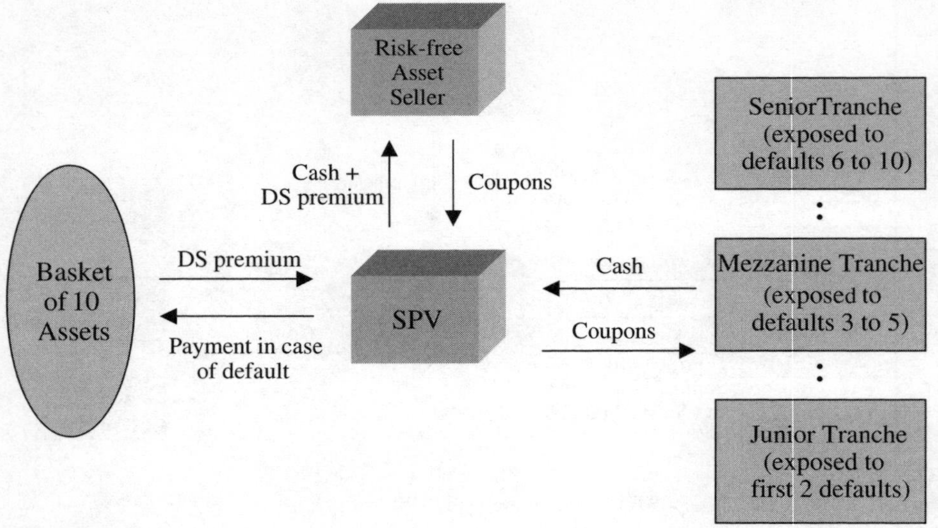

Figure 3.9: Example of a tranched basket default swap (TBDS)

point (i.e. the starting criteria for default in a tranche) in a TBDS is defined by a certain *number* of credits defaulting, not the amount of default. For example, if the attachment point "M" of the mezzanine tranche is 3 and the detachment point "N" is 5, the mezzanine investor is exposed to the third, fourth, and fifth default. (The first and second loss is covered by the junior tranche). Thus, if any 3 to 5 of the assets in the basket default, the mezzanine tranche investor is exposed, whereas in a TPDS the default exposure is linked to the amount of default. Let's look at a tranched basket default swap, in which the junior tranche is exposed to the first two defaults, the mezzanine tranche to the third, fourth and fifth default, and the senior tranche is exposed to defaults 6 to 10, as seen in figure 3.9.

In practice the basket of a TBDS can contain up to several hundred assets. The more assets in a basket and the more negative the default correlation of the assets, the higher the risk for the investor.

In a TPDS and TBDS typically only the specific tranche (right side of figures 3.8 and 3.9) is closed in case a credit event occurs, not the whole TPDS or TBDS structure. The leverage[4] in a CDO (and TPDS and TBDS) is usually expressed as the inverse of the first loss percentage. Thus the junior tranche in a 20% first loss structure takes on a leverage of 5 times, since 1/20% = 5.

CDO squared structures

A further recent and successful variation of CDOs are CDOs squared, also called CDO of CDOs. In a CDO squared structure an "outer CDO" exists, which is typically single tranched. Subordinated to the outer CDO are several tranches of "inner CDOs," whose

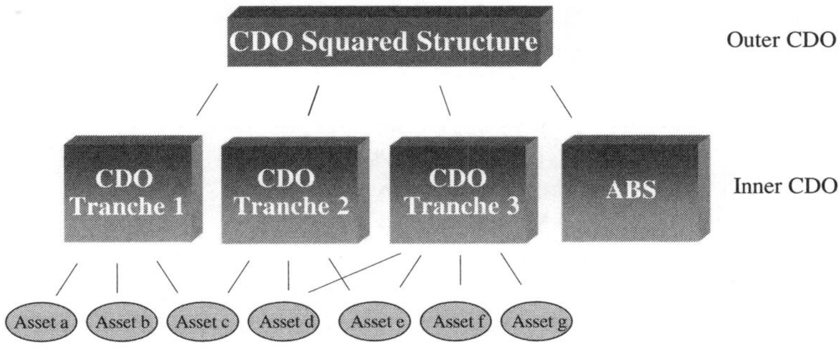

Figure 3.10: A CDO squared structure; in practice the number of tranches and ABSs is typically higher and the number of assets in a tranche can go up to 100 or more

assets often overlap. The inner CDO structure often also contains simple ABSs[5]. An example of a CDO squared transaction is seen in figure 3.10.

Each tranche of the CDO structure has an attachment point and detachment point. When the attachment point, typically defined as a loss amount, is breached, the loss is passed through to the outer CDO. The loss of each tranche is typically capped at a predefined loss level, the detachment point. Naturally, the lower the attachment point and the higher the detachment point of each tranche, the riskier the CDO squared structure.

The motive for CDO squared investors is the higher yield that CDO squared structures pay in comparison to standard CDO structures. The drawback of CDO squared structures is their complexity for the investor as well as the arranger. Default correlations for the numerous assets, which often overlap in the tranches, have to be calculated. The overlap can be as high as 30%, which increases the default correlation of the tranches. Rating agencies had to develop new Monte-Carlo based methodologies to rate CDO squared structures. The complexity of the CDO squared structures is attracting mainly well-educated investors.

Despite the relative complexity, CDO squared structures have been quite successful in the recent past. In December 2002, JP Morgan arranged "Quadrum," a $1.25 billion dollar structure for Australian bank Westpac. The deal was backed by mortgage-backed securities and standard CDOs on Westpac's balance sheet, and freed up capital for Westpac (since the investors bought the default risk). "Orange" and "Blue" were further successful CDO structures arranged by JP Morgan in 2003. The deals were mostly targeted to Japanese investors, who were interested in increasing their yield in the low Japanese yield environment.

Rating

Synthetic structures are constantly rated by rating agencies such as Standard & Poors, Moody's, and Fitch to inform investors about the credit quality of structures. Some of the synthetic structure ratings as well as valuable rating information can be accessed for free

Table 3.1: Rating system for long-term debt generated by S&P, www.standardandpoors.com, also used by Fitch (Moody's rating in brackets)

Rating category	**Credit quality**
AAA (Aaa)	Highest credit quality. The Issuer's capacity to meet its financial commitments is *extremely strong*.
AA (Aa)	Differs from AAA debt only to a small degree. The obligor's ability to pay interest and notional is *very strong*.
A (A)	Is more susceptible to adverse effects of changes in circumstances and economic conditions. Still, the obligor's capacity to meet its financial obligation is *strong*.
BBB (Baa)	Denotes *adequate* credit quality. However, unfavorable economic conditions and varying circumstances are more likely to lead to a weakened capacity on the part of the obligor to meet its financial commitments.
BB (Ba)	Denotes *somewhat weak* credit quality. The obligor's capacity to repay interest and notional is somewhat weak because of major uncertainties or exposure to unfavorable business or economic conditions.
B (B)	Denotes *weak* credit quality. The obligor currently has the capacity to meet its financial commitments on the obligation. But adverse business, financial, or economic conditions would likely impair capacity to repay interest and notional.
CCC (Caa)	A CCC rated obligation is *currently vulnerable* to non-payment, and is dependent upon favorable business and financial conditions for the obligor to meet its financial commitments on the obligation.
D (D)	The obligation is in *payment default*, or the obligor has filed for bankruptcy or bankruptcy protection. The "D" rating is used when interest or notional payments are not made on the date due, even if the applicable grace period has not expired.

Credits from AAA to BBB are considered investment grade or prime. Credits lower than BBB are typically termed junk or speculative grade

on the sites of the rating agencies: www.standardandpoors.com, www.moodys.com and www.fitchratings.com. The rating of the BISTRO, the first CDO launched in December 1997 by JP Morgan (which will be discussed below) can be found at www.moodys.com/moodys → Structured Finance → CDOs/Derivatives → Rating List.

Unfortunately, the rating categories differ from company to company. Even within one rating company a variety of different categories and scales exist, based on product, maturity, and geographical location. For an overview of S&P's various rating scales, see www.standardandpoors.com/ResourceCenter/NatRatScales.html.

Table 3.1 shows eight basic rating categories for rating long-term debt. It is used by Standard & Poors and Fitch. (Moody's rating scale is in brackets.)

The rating categories in table 3.1 are typically refined by adding + and − degrees to each category. Moody's refines its long-term debt rating by subcategories 1, 2, 3, in particular: Aaa, Aa1, Aa2, Aa3, A1, A2, A3, Baa1, Baa2, Baa3, Ba1, Ba2, Ba3, B1, B2, B3, Caa1, Caa2, Caa3, Ca, and D.

Table 3.2: Corporate recovery rates from 1970 to 2000

Security	Average recovery rate	Standard deviation
Senior secured bank loans	64.0%	24.4%
Senior unsecured bank loans	49.0%	28.4%
Senior secured bonds	52.6%	24.6%
Senior unsecured bonds	46.9%	28.0%
Senior subordinated bonds	34.7%	24.6%
Subordinated bonds	31.6%	21.2%
Junior subordinated bonds	22.5%	18.7%
Preferred stock	18.1%	17.2%

Source: Moody's Special Comment, "Default and Recovery Rates of Corporate Bond Issuers," David Hamilton, February 2001

Standard & Poors' *short-term* credit risk is categorized in A1, A2, A3, B, C, D (see www.standardandpoors.com/ResourceCenter). Moody's categorizes short-term debt with prime 1, prime 2 and prime 3, if the credit is investment grade and "not prime" for non-investment grade short-term credits.

The methodology of rating a synthetic structure depends on the type of the structure. Actively managed market value CDOs, which have a high turnover of assets and contain volatile equity tranches, are more difficult to value than static cash flow CDOs. Nevertheless, the crucial criteria for valuing any CDO are:

- Default probability of the assets in the CDO, often expressed as the weighted average rating factor (WARF);
- Credit deterioration risk (equal to migration risk if the assets are rated);
- Recovery rates (see below);
- Default correlation of the assets in a CDO;
- Expertise of the SPV managers;
- Overcollateralization (see below);
- Interest coverage (see below).

Recovery rates

Recovery rates vary strongly with respect to whether the economy is in a recession or boom. In the downturn of 2001, the average recovery rate fell to a low of 21% on defaulted bonds, down from 25% in 2000. This was actually substantially lower than the 27% average recovery rate in the recession 1990–1, indicating the severity of the later recession. The average recovery rate over the last 20 years was 40%. Recovery rates also vary strongly with respect to the seniority of the asset, as seen in table 3.2.

Principally, the higher the recovery rate of the assets in a CDO, the higher is the credit rating of the CDO. This is because assets which have defaulted are entered into the rating models with their recovery value, which usually reflects the market price. However, the market price of defaulted assets is often quite volatile and the bid-offer spread is usually quite large. Often the market bid for defaulted assets is so low ($10 or less for a par value of $100) that managers do not sell a defaulted asset at this price but hold it in hope of higher prices. However, marking-to-market a CDO requires that current market prices are input into the models. The effect on the models is typically minimal since the price is so low.

Coverage ratios

Coverage ratios are typically analyzed to help determine the credit quality of synthetic structures. The two most common ratios are *overcollateralization ratios* (OC ratios) and *interest rate coverage ratios* (IC ratios).

An overcollateralization ratio measures how many times the collateral (assets) in a synthetic structure can cover the liabilities that an SPV owes its investors. For a market value CDO, the overcollateralization ratio is:

$$\mathrm{OC} = \frac{\text{Total assets market value}}{\text{Liabilites par value}}.$$

For a cash flow CDO the overcollateralization ratio is calculated for each tranche, as:

$$\text{OC Senior Tranche} = \frac{\text{Total assets par value}}{\text{Senior tranche par value}}$$

$$\text{OC Mezzanine Tranche} = \frac{\text{Total assets par value}}{\text{Senior} + \text{Mezzanine tranche par value}}$$

$$\text{OC Junior Tranche} = \frac{\text{Total assets par value}}{\text{Senior} + \text{Mezzanine} + \text{Junior tranche par value}}.$$

Market value structures use the market value of assets, not the par value, in the OC ratio, since the assets are often sold at the market value and not kept until maturity. The opposite applies to cash flow structures. They use par values when calculating the OC ratio, since the assets in a cash flow structure are often held until maturity.

Another ratio, the interest rate cover ratio, is analyzed to determine the credit quality of a synthetic structure. It is derived by dividing the total interest rates to be received in a structure by the interest rate liability of each tranche, as in the OC ratios above. Note that OC Senior tranche > OC Mezzanine tranche > OC Junior tranche and IC Senior tranche > IC Mezzanine tranche > IC Junior tranche.

For the OC and IC ratios predefined levels exist, which are of a crucial nature. If the level is breached, cash flows are redirected from lower tranches to higher ranked tranches. This is done until the predefined levels are reinstated. If an SPV cannot reinstate predefined levels within a core period, the lowest tranche, and with it the synthetic structure, will be categorized as in default and will have to terminate.

Coverage ratio levels vary widely within synthetic structures. Naturally, lenient levels favor junior tranche holders, since cash flows are not redirected if the credit quality of the structure deteriorates to a small extent. Tight levels favor senior tranche holders, since for a rather small credit deterioration, cash flows are directed to the senior tranches in order to reinstate OC and IC levels. With the same logic, early defaults favor senior tranche holders, whereas later defaults favor junior tranche holders. Since synthetic structures often have a premature repayment of the investment, junior tranche holders might already have been repaid if the default occurs, at the expense of senior tranche holders.

Notching

With respect to rating, the aspect of notching has created controversy in the recent past. Notching involves automatically downgrading a single debt in a CDO that had not originally been rated. This leads to a downgrade of the entire CDO structure. Moody's and S&P downgrade debt that they have not originally rated by four notches. Fitch also notches, but to a lesser degree. Fitch accepts the credit rating of their competitors if the debt attains the same rating. If the ratings are different, they apply the lower of the two ratings. If only one competitor has rated the debt, Fitch reduces the rating by one notch if the debt is investment grade and by two notches if it is junk (below BBB).

Fitch, who opposes the notching policy of Moody's and S&P, claims that notching results in unfair competition, since investment managers often hire the market leaders Moody's and S&P to provide additional ratings.

Most importantly, the consequence of notching is a distorted lower credit rating and consequently lower price for CDOs that contain non-rated debt. This may be seen as an investment opportunity by some investors.

Successful Synthetic Structures

In December 1997, market leader JP Morgan launched the first synthetic structure termed BISTRO (Broad Index Securitized Trust Obligation). It was in the form of a synthetic collateralized loan obligation (CLO) introduced to the Japanese market with an initial notional amount of $163 million. The reference portfolio comprised debt of 65 Japanese banks, insurance firms, and semi-sovereign entities. The BISTRO is still today one of the most actively traded synthetic structures. In 2001, JP Morgan referenced over $46 billion of credit risk within the BISTRO structure, and transferred over $11 billion of it to the mezzanine tranche, which has the form of a credit-linked note. The initial structure of the BISTRO is seen in figure 3.11.

In the original BISTRO structure in figure 3.11, the originating bank buys protection on $10 billion of the Japanese loans. JP Morgan is the seller of the protection on the $10 billion but transfers the risk on the first $700 million losses to the SPV. The position of JP Morgan does not incur high default risk, since the 2. loss portfolio, on which JP Morgan took credit risk, was AAA rated.

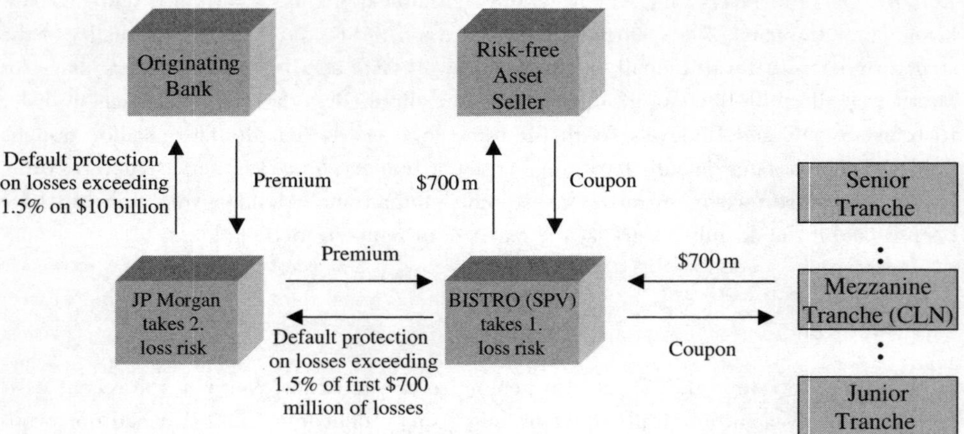

Figure 3.11: The original BISTRO structure

In the original BISTRO structure the reference portfolio ($10 billion) is substantially higher than the assets available to the investor ($700 million). This is a standard feature of synthetic structures.

One reason for JP Morgan to appear in the BISTRO structure is that the OECD status of JP Morgan provided regulatory capital relief for the originating bank. Any protection buyer has to hold regulatory capital due to the probability of default of the protection seller. If the originating bank had bought protection from the SPV directly, it would have had to hold 8% of the contract's notional amount as regulatory capital. Since the intermediary JP Morgan is an OECD member bank, the regulatory capital requirement reduced to 1.6%. However, this OECD advantage is eliminated in the new Basel II Accord (see chapter 4, in the section "Regulatory Capital Relief").

In 2001 the economic downturn led to credit downgrades of many synthetic structures. The BISTRO was no exception. Currently the various BISTRO issues have credit ratings from Aa1 to Ca; see www.moodys.com/moodys → Structured Finance → CDOs/Derivatives → Rating List.

Naturally the success of the BISTRO encouraged competitive banks to issue synthetic structures. In 2000 Europe's market leader Deutsche Bank issued a similar structure to the BISTRO, also with Japanese reference assets, termed J-Port (Japanese portfolio). Deutsche Bank claims the J-Port is a first purely investor demand driven structure. The key feature of the J-Port structure is its high diversification. The reference portfolio includes 20 debtors from 18 different industries. Consequently the default correlation is low (i.e. the probability of one default of one debtor triggering more defaults is small). This low default correlation helps to improve the credit rating of the J-Port.

A further variation of the original BISTRO is the Alpine structure issued by UBS Warburg. In this synthetic structure UBS Warburg credit-swapped a reference portfolio mostly of their own exposure, including interest rate and currency swaps and options into $750 million of notes for its investors. The Alpine structure included international reference exposure but also contained Japanese debt.

In 2000 JP Morgan and Deutsche Bank both claimed to have been the first to issue a synthetic structure on German Schuldschein debt. Schuldscheine are bilateral tradable loans issued by German regional and mortgage banks. They comprise about 5% of the German debt market.

JP Morgan launched the Clip (credit-linked investment protected note), which is a notional amount guaranteed at maturity and pays the typical high coupon on first-to-default debt. Reference assets comprise 50–100 debtors with a synthetically generated exposure of €500 million to €1 billion. About 75% of the original debt is in Schuldschein form. The Clip exposure can be up to 15 years, locking in the high yield of long maturities. However, the yields decrease with increasing defaults of the reference assets. To evaluate the risk of each Clip issue, JP Morgan offers its own optimization algorithm, which allows investors to calculate their individual risk-return profile.

Deutsche Bank created its own Schuldschein debt structure termed Repon (return enhanced portfolio note). In contrast to the Clip it contains a first loss equity tranche. Deutsche Bank reports sales of €12–13 billion of the Repon structure with a €2 billion first loss tranche.

In general, the synthetic CDO market has suffered from downgrades and defaults in the economic downturn of 2000 to 2003. Currently, investors are less willing to take high-risk first loss positions, so that SPV are often required to retain the first loss risk. This was also the case with Deutsche's Repon structure.

The rating of currently traded CDOs can be found at www.moodys.com → Structured Finance → CDOs/Derivatives → Rating List.

Investing in Synthetic Structures – A good idea?

The CDO market is still young; therefore only a few studies exist which analyze the performance of CDOs.

In the equity market, numerous studies have confirmed the disappointing truth that most fund managers cannot beat the market indexes. For example, a study by Robert et al. (2000) finds that for the 10-year period from 1988 to 1998, 86% of all 355 investigated fund mangers underperformed the Vanguard 500. After capital gains and dividend taxes, even 91% of the fund managers underperformed. For a 15-year period from 1983 to 1998, 95% underperformed, and for a 20-year period from 1978 to 1998, 86% underperformed.

These disappointing results should encourage investors to look into ETFs (exchange traded funds), also called index shares or i-shares. With ETFs, for example the diamonds DIA reflecting the DOW, or the cubes QQQ reflecting the NASDAQ, investors can assume exposure on a whole market index at a significantly lower cost than mutual funds charge. HOLDRS imply the same notional. The difference to ETFs is that HOLDRS reflect the performance of a certain market segment (e.g. retail sector, RTH, or biotechnology, BBT) and not an index. For more details see www.amex.com → ETFs or → HOLDRS.

Table 3.3: Comparison of the yield spread of CDOs and corporate bonds

Rating	CDO spread (in basis points)	Corporate bond spread (in basis points)	Difference (in basis points)
AAA	45	−8	53
AA	74	47	27
A	130	84	46
BBB	218	150	68
BB	665	353	312

Source: Gibson, "Synthetic Multi-Sector CBOs," September 2001

Table 3.4: Upgrades and downgrades of ABSs and CDOs compared to corporate bonds

Rating	ABS and CDOs		Corporations		Difference	
	Upgrades	Downgrades	Upgrades	Downgrades	Upgrades	Downgrades
Aaa	0.0%	0.3%	0.0%	9.5%	0.0%	−9.2%
Aa1	3.6%	10.8%	3.0%	16.5%	0.6%	−5.7%
Aa2	2.5%	1.6%	3.2%	15.0%	−0.7%	−13.4%
Aa3	2.7%	3.6%	3.0%	14.4%	−0.3%	−10.8%
A1	2.8%	1.0%	5.5%	12.0%	−2.7%	−11.0%
A2	4.7%	0.5%	6.2%	11.8%	−1.5%	−11.3%
A3	3.1%	3.6%	10.0%	12.8%	−6.9%	−9.2%
Baa1	2.2%	10.3%	10.8%	12.7%	−8.6%	−2.4%
Baa2	1.6%	2.7%	11.6%	10.8%	−10.0%	−8.1%
Baa3	1.7%	12.0%	14.7%	12.2%	−13.0%	−0.2%
Ba1	50.0%	12.0%	14.1%	12.0%	35.9 %	0.0%
Ba2	1.6%	8.1%	13.9%	12.7%	−12.3%	−4.6%
Ba3	0.0%	12.7%	10.7%	15.5%	−10.7%	−2.8%
B1	0.0%	17.9%	10.4%	14.1%	−10.4%	3.8%
B2	0.0%	7.7%	11.9%	16.7%	−11.9%	−9.0%
B3	0.0%	19.0%	11.9%	18.4%	−11.9%	0.6%
Average	4.8%	7.8%	8.8%	13.6%	−4.0%	−5.8%

Source: Gibson, L., "Synthetic Multi-Sector CBOs," September 2001

Do the CDO managers do an equally poor job as their colleagues in the equity market? It does not seem to be the case. A study by Lang Gibson (September, 2001) finds that high yield CDOs generate a significantly higher return than equally rated bonds, as seen in table 3.3.

A study by Fitch finds that the average default rate from 1989 to 2000 for all structured products was estimated to be 0.01%, a substantial difference from corporate bonds, which had a default rate of 0.77%.[6]

A further study by Gibson compares the migration of securitized structures and corporate bonds from 1986 to 2000. ABSs (asset-backed securities) and CDOs outperformed corporate bonds, especially for Aaa to A rated structures, as seen in table 3.4.

Altogether, the first analyses show a good performance of CDOs compared to standard bonds. Investors should keep an eye though on the high fees that SPVs often charge. These placement, structuring, and management fees together can be as high as 10% of the notional amount of the CDO.

Summary of Chapter 3

Synthetic structures have enjoyed enormous growth since their inception in 1997. Numerous varieties of structures exist, which can be broadly categorized as credit-linked notes (CLNs), collateralized debt obligations (CDOs), and basket structures such as tranched portfolio default swaps (TPDSs) and tranched basket default swaps (TBDSs), which can be viewed as customized CDOs.

A CLN in its simplest form is just a note (bond or loan) with an embedded credit feature. For example, a CLN pays a higher than market coupon in case of no credit event, but a lower than market coupon in case of a credit event.

CDOs are more complex structures than CLNs. They differ from CLNs in three ways. First, CDOs are usually arranged by a special purpose vehicle (SPV), which is usually triple-A rated. Second, CDOs usually provide credit exposure to a basket of up to 200 or more credits. Third, CDOs are usually tranched, providing the investor with a specific risk profile.

Synthetic CDOs are among the most popular synthetic structures. The difference between cash CDOs and synthetic CDOs lies in the fact that the SPV in a synthetic CDO does not acquire the original assets in a standard cash transaction, but gains credit exposure to the assets via default swaps. The rise in popularity of synthetic CDOs is primarily due to the fact that the SPV in a synthetic CDO does not legally own the underlying assets. Thus the assets do not appear on the balance sheet of the SPV.

With respect to the SPV's motivation, arbitrage CDOs and balance sheet CDOs can be differentiated. If the SPV is primarily interested in generating a profit on the difference between the generated income from the tranches and the default swap premiums and the coupons of the risk-free asset, the CDO is termed an arbitrage CDO. If the SPV's primary motivation is regulatory capital relief, the CDO is termed a balance sheet CDO.

Furthermore, market value CDOs and cash flow CDOs can be differentiated. In a market value CDO, which often contains an equity tranche, the SPV pays its liabilities to the investor mainly by successively selling assets of the tranched portfolio. In a cash flow CDO, repayments to the investor are done mainly via coupon flows and notional amount repayments.

Tranched portfolio default swaps (TPDSs) and tranched basket default swaps (TBDSs) are fairly new synthetic structures with strong growth potential. They can be viewed as more flexible, customized CDOs. In a TPDS, the SPV can assume credit risk on certain tranches of reference assets. A TPDS often contains a super-senior tranche, which is AAA rated, and which is usually the largest of the tranches. The difference between a TPDS and a TBDS is that in a TPDS the default exposure is linked to a certain amount of loss, whereas in a TBDS the default exposure is linked to a certain number of defaults. CDO squared structures, also termed CDOs of CDOs, are also fairly new structures. They offer higher yields than standard CDOs at the cost of higher complexity and higher default risk.

Synthetic structures are continuously rated by rating companies such as Standard & Poors, Moody's, and Fitch, to inform investors of the credit quality of a structure. Individual debt in synthetic structures which has not been originally rated is notched down by the rating agencies. This arbitrary downgrading (and consequently lower price) may be seen as an investment opportunity by some investors.

Coverage ratios, such as overcollateralization ratios (OC ratios) and interest rate coverage ratio (IC ratios) are analyzed to help determine the credit rating of synthetic structures. For the OC and IC ratios, predefined levels exist which are of crucial nature. If the level is breached and cannot be reinstated, the synthetic structure will be categorized as in default and will have to be terminated.

Recovery rates, which vary due to the economic situation and seniority of the bond, influence the price of a synthetic structure. This is because assets which have defaulted are entered into the pricing models with their recovery value, which usually reflects the market price.

Since JP Morgan launched the first synthetic structure, termed BISTRO in the form of a CLO (collateralized loan obligation) in 1997, numerous synthetic structures have been issued. Among the most successful were JP Morgan's own Clip structure, Deutsche Bank's J-Port and Repon, and UBS's Alpine structure.

First analyses show a good performance of synthetic structures compared to equally-rated bonds. Investors should keep an eye though on the high fees that SPVs often charge.

References and Suggestions for Further Readings

Barclays, "The Barclays Capital Guide to Cash Flow Collateralized Debt Obligations," http://www.securitization.net/pdf/barclays_cdoguide_090601.pdf.

Bomfim, A., "Understanding Credit derivatives and their potential to Synthesize Riskless Assets," http://www.federalreserve.gov/pubs/feds/2001/200150/200150pap.pdf.

Da Silva, M., "Synthetic Collateralized Debt Obligations and Credit-Linked Notes – A Rating Perspective," http://www.standardandpoors.com.

Deloitte & Touche Germany, "Conventional versus Synthetic Securitization – Trends in the German ABS Market," http://www.dttgsfi.com.

Fitch, "Synthetic CDOs: A growing market for credit derivatives," http://www.mayerbrown.com.

Gibson, L., "Structured Credit Portfolio Transactions," *Asset Securitization Report*, July 2001, vol. 1, issue 30, pp. 10–11.

Gibson, L., "Synthetic Credit Portfolio Transactions: The Evolution of Synthetics," http://www.gtnews.com/articles6/3918.pdf.

Gibson, L., "Synthetic Multi-Sector CBOs," *Asset Securitization Report*, October 2001, vol. 1, issue 37, pp. 14–16.

Hall-Barber, S., "Introduction to Credit Linked Notes," http://www.naic.org/1svo_research/documents/SVO_May01cc.pdf.

J.P. Morgan, *J.P. Morgan/Risk Magazine Guide to Risk Management*, Risk Waters Group, 2001.

Moody's, "Commonly Asked CDO questions: Moody's Responds," http://www.mayerbrown.com/cdo/publications/MoodysFAQCDOs1.pdf.

Nelken, I., *Implementing Credit Derivatives: Strategies and Techniques for using Credit Derivatives in Risk Management*, McGraw-Hill, 1999.

O'Kane, D., and R. McAdie, "Trading the Default Swap Basis," *Lehman Brothers internal paper,* March 2003.

Robert, A., A. Berkin and J. Ye, "How well have taxable investors been served in the 1980s and 1990s?" *The Journal of Portfolio Management,* Summer 2000, vol. 26, issue 4, pp. 84–94.

Rule, D., "The credit derivatives market: its development and possible implications for financial stability," http://www.bankofengland.co.uk/fsr/fsr10art3.pdf.

Questions and Problems

Answers, available for instructors, are on the Internet. Please email gmeissne@aol.com for the site.

3.1 *What is a synthetic structure in the credit markets? What types of synthetic structures exist?*

3.2 *What is the difference between a CLN (credit-linked note) and a CDO (collateralized debt obligation)?*

3.3 *Explain the function of an SPV (special-purpose vehicle) in a CDO. Why is an SPV typically AAA rated?*

3.4 *Explain the principle of tranching within a CDO. Relate that principle to MBSs (mortgage-backed securities).*

3.5 *What is the difference between a cash CDO and a synthetic CDO? Why have synthetic CDOs outgrown cash CDOs in the recent past?*

3.6 *Explain the difference between an arbitrage CDO and a balance sheet CDO.*

3.7 *What are motivations to enter into a CDO for the (a) original asset owner, (b) the SPV, and (c) the investor?*

3.8 *What is the difference between market value CDOs and cash flow CDOs?*

3.9 *How are tranched portfolio default swaps (TPDSs) and tranched basket default swaps (TBDSs) related to CDOs? What is the difference between TPDSs and TBDSs?*

3.10 *How do CDO squared structures get their name? What is the main reason for the difficulty of valuing CDO squared structures?*

3.11 *Name the main eight rating categories by Standard & Poors, Fitch, and Moody's, and discuss them each briefly. Find a financial institution that is AAA rated. What ratings do investment grade bonds have? What ratings do junk bonds have?*

3.12 *What factors determine the level of recovery rates? Do you think recovery rates are fairly constant in time and among industries?*

3.13 *Explain the principle of notching. Why is notching seen as an investment opportunity by some traders?*

Notes

1 See chapter 2, in the section "What is a default swap?" for an explanation of long credit exposure of a default swap seller.

2 See chapter 4 for a detailed discussion on operational risk.

3 Arbitrage is commonly defined as a risk-free profit, for example buying gold at $300 in London and simultaneously selling it at $302 in New York. However in trading practice, arbitrage is often defined more broadly as an *expected* profit. For example, in a "takeover arbitrage" the company that is acquired is purchased and the company that takes over is sold, expecting the spread to narrow.

4 Leverage is measured differently for different financial structures. For a company's capital structure it is measured by the debt-to-equity ratio. For derivatives, leverage is usually measured as elasticity, also called gearing. This measures the relative change of the derivative divided by the relative change of the underlying asset. (See www.dersoft.com/stockoption.xls for the calculation of leverage for calls and puts.)

5 ABSs, asset-backet securities, are claims (e.g. bonds) that are backed by expected cash flows (e.g. mortgages, loan repayments, rentals, royalty income, etc.).

6 Fitch, "Fitch Ratings' Approach to CDO Rating Actions," February 2002, www.Fitchratings.com.

Chapter Four
Application of Credit Derivatives

These instruments [credit derivatives] appear to have effectively spread losses from defaults to a wider set of banks. (Alan Greenspan)

There are numerous applications of the various credit derivatives products. We will categorize five types of applications:

1 Hedging;
2 Yield enhancement;
3 Cost reduction and convenience;
4 Arbitrage;
5 Regulatory capital relief.

Naturally, the above applications have interdependencies. A credit derivative or a credit derivative structure can involve several of the above applications. For example a simple default swap can hedge credit exposure and at the same time may reduce costs and provide regulatory capital relief. Nevertheless, let's discuss the applications from an individual point of view.

Hedging

Undoubtedly one of the strongest motivations for using credit derivatives is hedging. Hedging means reducing risk. More precisely, hedging is entering into a second trade in order to reduce the risk of an original trade. It should be mentioned that in this chapter, the discussion will be on the hedging of individual risks. The hedging of aggregate portfolio risks via diversification will be analyzed in chapter 6 on risk management.

There is a wide spectrum of users who apply credit derivatives to hedge. Commercial and investment banks, insurance companies, hedge funds, non-financial institutions, as well as individual investors apply credit derivatives to reduce credit risk. Let's first look how credit risk compares to other types of risk.

There are numerous types of risks that corporations face when they are doing business. Figure 4.1 shows an overview. Naturally, the risks in the figure also apply to individuals and sovereign entities which conduct business. Let's discuss these risks in more detail.

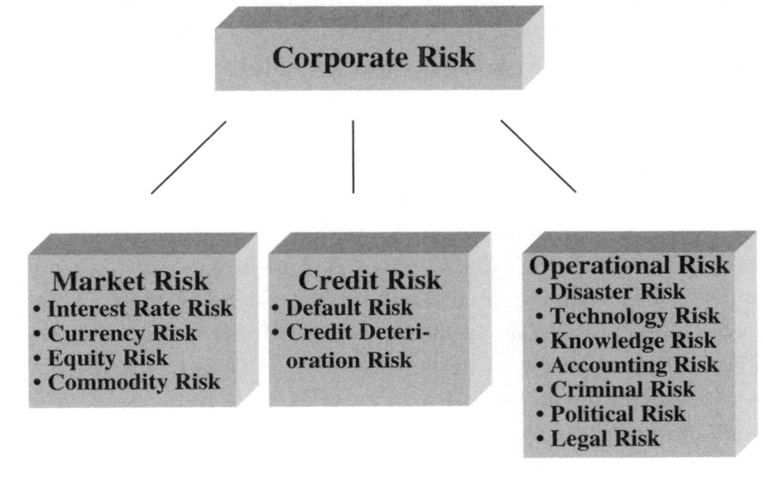

Figure 4.1: Broad categorization of types of risk

Market risk

Until the mid 1990s, the markets had been divided into four categories: The financial markets consisting of the fixed income market (also called bond market or interest rate market), the currency market, the equity market, and the commodity market. Since the mid 1990s, the credit market has emerged as a fifth actively traded market. For details on the state of the credit market see chapter 1. A further new market, the market for operational risk, is currently evolving.[1]

The underlying instruments for credit derivatives are usually bonds and loans, so credit derivatives are mostly exposed to the interest rate risk. But as discussed in chapter 3, synthetic structures often contain an equity tranche, so exposure to the equity market exists. Furthermore, synthetic structures may contain currency swaps and commodity swaps, so credit derivatives may have exposure to all existing market risks.

Market risk can conveniently be hedged with standard derivatives such as futures, swaps, and options. Hedging interest rate risk is accomplished with interest rate futures such as money market futures or longer-term Treasury bond futures. The interest rate swap market is also very liquid with maturities up to 30 years. Interest rate options for hedging Libor exposure are Caps and Floors. For hedging longer-term interest rate risk, bond options and swap options can be purchased and sold.[2]

In the interest rate market, currency market, equity market and the commodity market, liquidity risk and volatility risk exist.

Liquidity risk is the risk that due to low liquidity, the bid-offer spread is so wide that a trade would result in an uneconomical price. Occasionally a market can be totally illiquid, so that no trade is possible. Since the credit derivatives market is still young, the credit derivatives bid-offer spreads are often quite wide compared to established markets. This was also seen in chapter 1, where it was observed that the illiquidity of the QBI Futures and the QBI Options on Futures contract results in rather unusual trading: Traders enter bids and offers at anytime during a "pre-opening" period each day from 7:30 a.m. until 1:30 p.m. Chicago Time. Orders become "firm" i.e. cannot be canceled or modified between 1:20 p.m. and 1:30 p.m., when the orders are matched and executed.

Liquidity risk can also take the form of *asset liquidity risk*. Asset liquidity risk is the risk that the high trading activity of a company leads to an unfavorable change of the price of the traded asset. This was the case in the 1994 Metallgesellschaft crash, when the company bought long-term WTI[3] futures contracts and sold short-term futures contracts, leading to an unfavorable change of the shape of the future curve from backwardation to contango.[4] Asset liquidity risk also contributed to the bankruptcy of Long Term Capital Management (LTCM) in 1998, when the immense assets of LTCM made it impossible to liquidate the positions without moving the market.

Liquidity risk can also take the form of *funding liquidity risk*. Funding liquidity risk is the risk that a company cannot raise new funds to finance its debt. However, funding liquidity risk is not really a risk per se, but usually the consequence of prior mistakes and mismanagement.

Volatility risk is the risk that the volatility of the traded asset is so high, that the trade can lead to an unreasonable price. Volatility risk exists especially for bonds that have just defaulted. The volatility can reach up to 200%.[5]

Additionally, with respect to options, volatility risk is the risk that the implied volatility of the option contract changes unfavorably. Implied volatility risk or Vega risk is rather a trading risk that option traders face and less an operational risk. Nevertheless, let's explain it.

The implied volatility of the underlying asset is the figure that is input in the standard Black-Scholes[6] model to derive the price of an option. For standard options, implied volatility is actually the only parameter option traders can influence. There is a market consensus what the correct implied volatility of an option is. If an option trader has bought options, and the implied volatility decreases, the resulting lower option value will lead to losses of the option position, and vice versa. The implied volatility risk of options is measured by the Vega, as seen in equation (4.1):

$$\text{Vega(Call)} = \partial C/\partial V \quad \text{Vega(Put)} = \partial P/\partial V \tag{4.1}$$

where C is the call price, P is the put price, and ∂ is the partial differential operator. V is the implied volatility of the underlying asset, which for credit derivative calls and puts is the spread between the risky bond yield and the risk-free Treasury bond yield (see chapter 2). Thus, equation (4.1) answers the question of how much does the call or put price change if the implied volatility of the underlying spread changes by a very small amount.

It should be mentioned that implied volatility is a tradable asset. The VIX measures the implied volatility of eight options of the S&P 500 and the VXN measures the implied volatility of the options on the NASDAQ 100. Both VIX and VXN trade on the Chicago Board of Options Exchange (CBOE). For more details go to www.CBOE.com → Learning center → Advanced Concepts → CBOE volatility index VIX. For an example of how to exploit implied volatility distortions in the credit derivatives market, see example 4.10.

Credit risk

As already explained in the introduction, credit risk can be divided into default risk and credit deterioration risk. Default risk is the risk that an obligor does not meet part or his entire financial obligation. ISDA conveniently defines six credit events that trigger the default swap payments: Bankruptcy, Failure to pay, Obligation Acceleration, Obligation Default, Repudiation/Moratorium, and Restructuring.[7]

Credit deterioration risk is the risk that the credit quality of the debtor decreases. In this case, the value of the bonds or loans of the debtor will decrease, resulting in a financial loss for the creditor.

How are market risk and credit risk related?

The answer to how market risk and credit risk are related is given by the *specific credit–market risk*, which measures the impact of credit risk on market risk. For example, if the credit risk of a firm increases, typically expenses for the firm increase and the market price of the firm decreases; low-rated financial institutions usually have to pay higher interest rates to borrow money. Hence, a higher credit risk decreases the profitability of a firm and can increase the firm's vulnerability to market risk. In practice, specific risk is typically viewed and managed as credit risk.

Determining the degree of specific risk, i.e. what magnitude of the asset price deterioration is due to credit risk, is a question of duration and convexity (discussed in detail in chapter 2). If an asset decreases by more than duration and convexity imply, this portion is attributed to credit quality deterioration.

Having discussed the impact of credit risk on market risk, consequently we should ask the reverse question: is there an impact of market risk on credit risk? The answer is clearly "yes." If the value of a firm decreases due to market risk, the default risk will increase, and vice versa. How much market risk will influence credit risk depends on the degree of exposure that a company has to market risk and the current credit quality. Adverse movements in market risk tend to influence the credit quality of highly rated companies less.

As mentioned above, for bonds and loans market risk mainly comprises interest rate risk. Principally, any company is exposed to interest rate risk, since all future cash flows are discounted with the current yield curve. Hence any firm is exposed to market risk, which can diminish the credit standing of a firm.

There is sufficient empirical evidence that changes in market risk and changes in credit risk are correlated. Duffie (1998), as well as Das and Tufano (1996), and Longstaff and Schwartz (1995), find that credit-spreads tend to decrease if risk-free interest rates increase, and vice versa. Hence, in a prospering economy with rising interest rates, the probability of default decreases, and vice versa. This is in line with the original Merton model (see chapter 5): Rising interest rates tend to increase the rate of return of a firm's assets and hence decrease the probability of default.

As a consequence, the impact of credit risk on market risk and the impact of market risk on credit risk should be included in single asset risk management as well as in company-wide risk management.

Operational risk

The BIS (Bank for International Settlements) defines operational risk as "the risk of direct or indirect loss resulting from inadequate or failed internal processes, people and systems or from external events."[8] Another way of assessing operational risk is to define it as residual risk, i.e. all risk, which is not market risk or credit risk. The two definitions do not contradict each other.

As seen in figure 4.1, operational risk can be categorized as disaster risk, technology risk, knowledge risk, accounting risk, criminal risk, political risk, and legal risk. Let's look at these types of operational risk in more detail.

We will refer to any external damage of a company's property as *disaster risk*. Besides terrorist attacks or wars, disaster risk includes property damage stemming from natural catastrophes like earthquakes, hurricanes, floods, or fires. Disaster risk in the form of natural catastrophes can be hedged with traditional insurances. Insurances against terrorist attacks await appearance.

Technology risk is the risk that problems in a company's technology lead to a deterioration of the company's operation. Viruses can paralyze a company's computer system and consequently a company's operation. Hackers can damage a computer system by copying or deleting the code. Today, corporations use "fire walling" as a means to totally isolate the company's computer system from the outside. Technology risk is also the risk that a company's technological progress is inferior to that of the competition, thus leading to a demise in the company's competitive status.

Knowledge risk is the risk that a lack of knowledge leads to deterioration of a company's operation. Knowledge risk exists at every level of a company's hierarchy. It can comprise of mathematicians creating erroneous algorithms, programmers coding incorrectly or under-skilled risk managers misusing a company's risk management software. Knowledge risk can also comprise the upper management engaging in the wrong strategic decisions or settlement employees sending out erroneous statements. On April 26, 1986, in one of the most severe technical errors, technicians shut down all emergency systems of the Chernobyl atomic reactor in order to do testing. After a reactor meltdown and two explosions, the people of Chernobyl were exposed to radioactivity comparable to that of the Hiroshima bomb.

Accounting risk was brought to corporate America's attention in several severe accounting scandals in 2001 and 2002. Enron accountants had tried to hide financial problems with numerous special purpose entities (SPE), located in the Cayman Islands and other tax havens. As a result of their financial and operational mismanagement, Enron filed for Chapter 11 bankruptcy on December 2, 2001. In June 2002, WorldCom announced that the company needed to restate its financial statements, as its internal audit found that certain transfers from line cost expenses to capital accounts during 2001 and first quarter 2002 were not made in accordance with generally accepted accounting principles (GAAP). The total amount of these wrongful transfers was as high as $3.1 billion for 2001 and $797 million for first quarter 2002. On July 21, 2002 WorldCom had to file for reorganization under the Chapter 11 bankruptcy code.

Criminal action can naturally damage a company's operation. One of the most publicized criminal cases was that of Nick Leeson in 1995, who brought down Barings Bank, England's oldest merchant bank, due to excessive trading of Nikkei futures and options. After trying to hide his losses, Nick Leeson pleaded guilty to twelve crimes, of which four were for forgery, two were for amending prices, and six were for implementing cross trades, which reduced his variation margin.

Criminal action can also harm municipals, as in the famous 1994 Orange County case. Robert Citron, the treasurer of Orange County, had bought fixed reverse floaters,[9] speculating on decreasing interest rates. When interest rates increased, the fixed reverse floaters paid a below market interest rate. In December 1994 Orange County had to file for Chapter 11 bankruptcy. Robert Citron admitted misusing public money and falsifying statements and was sentenced to one year in prison, five years' probation, and a $100,000 fine.

In a recent case in spring 2002, David Duncan's admittance of destroying documents in the Enron bankruptcy filing devastated the name of Andersen Consulting. Most of Andersen's clients abandoned the company and its US risk consulting business was taken over by Robert Half International Inc. The demise of a company's reputation as a result of criminal or other internal misconduct is also referred to as reputational risk.

Political risk can arise if a new political government does not honor the obligations of the previous government, resulting in losses for the creditor. Political risk can also comprise of harmful fiscal policy measures by the administration, or wrongful monetary policy by the central bank.

Legal risk is the risk that legal measures harm a company's operation. In 1984, AT&T was ordered by court action to split its corporation into eight companies. Microsoft barely avoided the same fate in 2000, when Judge Jackson ruled the company had to be split into a company running the Windows operating system and a company running software applications. However, the ruling was overturned in November 2001. Legal risk can also involve a company doing business in an emerging country and encountering legal problems. It can be the case that the legal system in the emerging country is not developed enough or not willing to guarantee fair legal treatment of the foreign company.

It should be mentioned that the BIS has requested all internationally active banks to report operational value at risk (VAR) numbers by early 2007.[10]

Which credit derivative hedges which risk?

Hedging with default swaps

When introducing the credit derivatives products in chapter 2, we already partly discussed the crucial hedging aspect of default swaps. With respect to credit risk, credit deterioration risk, and market risk, we concluded: A default swap naturally hedges credit default risk. When marked-to-market, a default swap also hedges credit deterioration risk. However, default swaps do not protect against market risk (for bonds and loans, primarily interest rate risk), since the default swap value principally does not change if interest rates change (see chapter 2, section "Hedging with default swaps").

Default swaps and operational risk

To what extent does a default swap hedge against operational risk? The answer depends on the *specific operational–credit risk*. In other words, it depends on the degree of impact of the operational damage on the credit quality. This can be written as in equation (4.2):

$$R_{OC} = \Delta B/B \div \Delta E_o/E_o \tag{4.2}$$

where R_{OC} is the specific operational–credit risk (i.e. the impact of an operational event, measured by $\Delta E_o/E_o$, on credit quality, measured by $\Delta B/B$, all other variables constant); ΔB is the discrete change in the bond price; and ΔE_o is the discrete change in the company's outstanding equity as a result of the operational event.

Naturally ΔE_o is difficult to quantify. For example, the terrorist attack of September 11, 2001 resulted not only in a monetary loss, but also in a loss of lives and knowledge. In addition, the effect on the equity value can occur with a time lag and over an uncertain future period of time. Furthermore, determining the sole impact of an operational event on the equity value is difficult, since the equity value is influenced by many factors such as company performance, interest rate changes, political events, etc.

If the specific operational–credit risk in equation (4.2) is zero, the operational event does not impact the present value of the bond and consequently the default swap. Hence, the default swap will not hedge the operational risk. However, the higher is R_{OC}, the higher is the impact of the operational event on the credit quality. Thus, the higher is the degree of default swap hedge due to operational risk. Let's look at an example.

Example 4.1: An investor owns bonds of company X and has hedged the bonds with a default swap with a notional amount of $10,000,000. Accounting errors are found at company X, which lead to a downgrade of the company and to a decrease of the outstanding equity value, ΔE_o, of $1 billion. The bond falls from $100 to $85. This leads to an increase in the default swap present value by approximately 15%, assuming equation (2.1) holds. Consequently the operational impact on the bond is hedged by the increase in the default swap value.

Naturally, the equity value change of the operational event is only partially hedged, since the equity value of the company is much higher than the notional bond value, which is underlying the default swap. This is typically the case in reality.

Generally, it is more sensible to hedge operational exposure with a put on the stock price of the company than with a default swap on a bond of the company. This is because a stock price reflects the operational exposure more accurately than a bond price. For example, a bond trading below par, which is close to maturity will tend to gradually increase to its par value, even though an operational event has occurred, assuming the company is still relatively far away from bankruptcy.

Hedging with total rate of return swaps (TRORs)

With respect to hedging with TRORs, we have already concluded in chapter 2 that a TROR hedges default risk, credit deterioration risk, and in contrast to default swaps also market risk. For answering the question if a TROR hedges operational risk, a similar logic can be applied as for default swaps: If the operational damage leads to a decrease in the price of the reference asset, the TROR will provide a hedge for the TROR payer, since the TROR payer will receive the price decline from the TROR receiver (see figure 2.5). Example 4.2 describes the partial hedge of operational risk with a TROR.

Example 4.2: An investor is long 10,000 bonds of company X with a par value and current price of $100. Thus the investment is $1,000,000. To partially hedge his bond price exposure, the investor has entered into a TROR, where he pays the TROR on half his investment amount of $500,000. External auditors have found that traders of company X have overstated their profits. The company is downgraded and the bond falls from $100 to $75. Consequently the TROR receiver will pay $25 × 50,000 = $125,000 (plus the coupon minus Libor +/− spread) to the investor at the next payment date. Thus, the investor is compensated for half of his price losses in the amount of $25 × 100,000 = $250,000.

Hedging with credit-spread products

As pointed out in chapter 2, there are three main credit-spread products: credit-spread options, credit-spread forwards, and credit-spread swaps. In chapter 2 we concluded that all credit-spread products protect against credit risk and credit deterioration risk. We also concluded that the more certain a hedger is that the reference asset will change unfavorably, the more he should use premium-free credit-spread futures and swaps, rather than options, which incur a premium.

Do credit-spread products also protect against operational risk? To answer this question we can apply the same logic as in the previous section: If the operational damage leads to a decrease in the price of the reference asset, the credit-spread product will provide a hedge, since the present value of the credit-spread product will change in favor of the hedger. Let's look at a simple example.

Example 4.3: An investor has provided a 4-year loan of $1,000,000 to company X with no interest rate payments during the loan. The latest acquisition of company X has not met expectations and profits and revenue of company X are declining. Currently the 4-year Treasury yield is 5%. The yield difference between the yield of the loan (determined by a dealer poll) and the Treasury yield is 1.5%. The investor buys a credit-spread put on the loan to hedge against a further decline of the value of the loan. The credit-spread put has a 91-day maturity, and a strike-spread of 2%. Including the industry standard duration term in the pricing, in this case 4, it follows that the price of the credit-spread put, derived on a simple Black-Scholes model with a 150% implied volatility and a 5% risk-free interest rate is \$10,734.[11]

Due to the failed acquisition, the company is downgraded and the credit-spread between the loan and the Treasury bond (determined by a dealer poll) increases to 3%. As a consequence, the present value of the credit-spread put (assuming 10 days have passed since the option trade date) increases to \$46,991. Thus, the profit of the credit-spread hedge is \$46,991 − \$10,734 = \$36,257.

This amount should be compared to the loss from the downgrade of the loan to achieve the overall profit or loss. The present value of the loan has decreased from $\$1{,}000{,}000 / (1 + 0.065)^4 = \$777{,}323$ to $\$1{,}000{,}000 / (1 + 0.08)^{(4-10/365)} = \$736{,}581$, so by \$40,742. Thus the loan position and the credit-spread hedge resulted in a rather small loss of \$40,742 − \$36,257 = \$4,485.

To conclude our analysis of the hedging power of credit derivatives with respect to operational risk, we find that all credit derivatives provide at least a partial hedge against operational risk, if the operational damage leads to a decrease in the credit quality of the asset which is underlying the credit derivative. If this is the case, the present value of the credit derivatives will change in favor of the hedger.

Yield Enhancement

A second important motivation of credit derivatives is yield enhancement. The main users who apply credit derivatives to enhance yield are investment banks, hedge funds, third party asset managers, and individual investors and speculators.

There are numerous strategies to enhance yield with default swaps, TRORs and credit-spread products. We have already implicitly mentioned some of these strategies. For example in a first-to-default basket default swap, an investor receives an above market yield for assuming default risk on any debt in the basket. In fact, in most CDOs the investor receives an above market yield for assuming some degree of credit risk, depending on the specific tranche.

As might be expected, the yield appetite of investors is strongly related to the business cycle. In a boom with high employment, high stock prices, and low default rates, investors are often willing to take high degrees of risk, purchasing CDOs and first-to-default basket structures. However, during the 2000–3 economic downturn, investors turned quite risk-averse. This has diminished the success of many synthetic structures, often forcing the SPV to retain the first-loss tranche.

In the following we will suggest several yield enhancement strategies for different credit derivatives. Let's start with a covered credit-spread put selling strategy.

Covered credit-spread put selling strategy

Example 4.4: At the end of the Asian financial crisis in 1999, an investor owns a 5-year fixed-coupon $1,000,000 (US-denominated) Korean bond. He believes that Korea will further recover and that the credit-spread (between the Korean bond yield and the Treasury bond yield) will further decrease. Thus to increase his return, the investor sells a cash settled credit-spread put with a credit-spread strike equal to the current yield spread of 3% with a 1-year maturity and a notional amount of $1,000,000. With a 5% risk-free interest rate, a duration term of 3.67 and a 130% implied volatility, the investor receives the upfront put premium of $50,722.[12]

This is the additional income for the investor if the credit quality increases or remains unchanged. If however, the investor's perception is wrong and the credit-spread widens, the investor will incur losses, since the present value of the sold credit-spread put will increase. For example, should the credit-spread widen to 5% after 6 months, the present value of the put will have increased to $93,385.[13] Thus the investor's loss on the put is $93,385 − $50,722 = $42,663.

In example 4.4, the investor has two long positions: He is long the bond and additionally synthetically long the bond via selling the put (meaning he makes money if the credit-spread decreases, thus the Korean bond price increases). Thus, the investor is strongly exposed to a credit-spread widening (price decrease of the Korean bond). The term *covered* credit-spread put selling is therefore quite misleading.

Covered credit-spread call selling strategy

Example 4.5: At the start of the 2001 recession, an investor believes the economy will not improve within the next year. The investor owns a bond of a BBB-rated company. The investor believes the company will not do too well during the recession and hence the credit rating of the bond will not increase within the next year. To improve his return, the investor sells a physically settled one-year credit-spread call with a credit-spread strike of 3%, which is equal to the at-the-money forward spread.[14]

If the investor is correct and the spread increases or stays the same, he will keep the call premium as additional income. However, if the credit quality of the company unexpectedly improves and the credit-spread decreases, he will get exercised on the credit-spread call. The investor will then have to deliver the bond at the credit strike spread, which is smaller than the current market credit-spread. Thus the investor will incur an opportunity loss, since he did not participate in the price increase of his bond.

In example 4.5 the investor is covered, since he is long the bond and synthetically short the bond via the short credit-spread call. This strategy is similar to the covered call selling strategy of standard options. The difference is simply the underlying. In a credit-spread call, the underlying instrument is the credit-spread; in a standard covered call writing strategy, the underlying is the price of the asset.

Let's look at a yield enhancement strategy involving a credit-spread put-call collar.

Covered credit-spread collar strategy

Example 4.6: An investor owns a single-A rated bond of company X. The investor believes that credit quality of company X will probably decrease. He wants to hedge against this decrease and at the same time generate upfront cash. Hence, the investor buys a put on the credit-spread and finances the put by selling a credit-spread call. The investor chooses the spread strikes of the put and call fairly high, so that he receives a net premium (the higher the strike-spread, the higher the call premium and the lower the put premium). Thus the investor has collared his credit exposure: if the credit-spread increases above the strike spread of the put, he will sell the bond at the strike spread of the put. However, if the credit quality of the bond increases and the credit-spread decreases to a level lower than the call strike, the bond will be called at the strike of the call and the investor incurs an opportunity loss.

Let's look at a strategy in which an investor sells a covered credit-spread straddle.

Covered short credit-spread straddle strategy

Example 4.7: An investor has purchased 10,000 BBB-rated bonds with an 8% annual coupon with a remaining maturity of 5 years. The bond currently trades at the par value of \$100.

The bond spread has not fluctuated much in the last 3 months. The investor believes this low spread volatility will continue in the next 3 months. Thus, he sells a credit-spread straddle (a call and a put with the same strike). He chooses the strikes to be at-the-money. The current market spread is 3%, thus the strike spread is 3%. With a 91-day maturity, 110% implied volatility, a duration of 3.67 and a 5% risk-free interest rate, the call and put premium are \$23,529, thus the investor receives upfront \$47,058.[15] The reader should note that the investor has two long exposures to credit risk, the bond and the short put, and one short exposure to credit risk, the short call.

Scenario 1: In the next 3 months the low credit-spread volatility continues. At the end of three months, the company's credit-spread is at 3%. Thus, the investor is not exercised on the call or the put and keeps the \$47,058 as a profit.

Scenario 2: The company has done unexpectedly well and the credit-spread has decreased to 1.5%. Thus at option maturity the investor is exercised on the call and – assuming cash settlement – has to pay $(3\% - 1.5\%) \times 3.67 \times \$1{,}000{,}000 = \$55{,}050$. Thus the loss for the investor is $\$55{,}050 - \$47{,}058 \times (1 + 0.05)^{91/360} = \$7{,}408$ (the factor $(1 + 0.05)^{91/360}$ stems from the fact that the option premium was received 3 months ago and has been invested for 3 months). However, the decrease in the credit-spread of 1.5% has increased the bond price to \$106.23. Hence the overall profit for the investor is $(\$106.23 - \$100) \times 10{,}000 - \$7{,}408 = \$54{,}892$.

Hence, the strategy will generate profits if the credit quality remains unchanged or improves. If the credit quality decreases, the investor will encounter losses, which the reader can verify herself.

The next yield enhancement opportunity is derived from the range notes (also called fairways) of the mid 1990s. In a traditional range note, the owner would receive an above market coupon, but incurs a penalty if a certain variable, e.g. the 6 ML (6-Month Libor) would be outside a predetermined range. In a credit-spread range note, the investor incurs a penalty if the credit-spread is outside a predetermined range. This is equivalent to selling a series of forward credit-spread strangles. If the magnitude of the deviation of the forward credit-spread strangles from the predetermined range is irrelevant, the investor is short a series of digital strangles. Let's look at an example.

Example 4.8: An investor believes that the credit-spread volatility during the next year will be low. To exploit this view, the investor invests $1,000,000 in a single-B credit-spread range note with a credit-spread range of 2%–4%. The investor will receive an above market coupon of 8%. However, for every day that the note's credit-spread is outside the 2%–4% range the coupon will reduce by 0.03%. The note has a minimum coupon payment of 2%, thus is floored.

Scenario 1: The investor is correct and the credit-spread volatility during the next year is low. Only on 7 days was the credit-spread outside the 2%–4% range. Thus his annual coupon payments of 8% × $1,000,000 = $80,000 reduces by 7 × 0.0003 × 1,000,000 = $2,100.

Scenario 2: Due to a recurrence of the recession, credit-spreads have increased. During the next year the note's credit-spread is above 4% on 250 days. Thus the investor's coupon payments of $80,000 would reduce by 250 × 0.0003 × 1,000,000 = $75,000. However, since the coupon payments are floored at 2%, the investor receives $20,000 in coupon payments.

The examples 4.4 to 4.8 are currently popular yield enhancement strategies in the credit market. They involve owning an asset and enhancing the yield with a credit derivative. An investor can also simply speculate with credit derivatives, i.e. take a naked position in a credit derivative. For example, an investor, who believes the shape of the credit-spread curve is distorted, can engage in "yield curve plays." Let's look at an example which involves credit-spread forwards.

Credit-spread forward strategy to participate in a flattening of an inverted credit-spread curve

Example 4.9: An investor believes that due to the current recession the credit-spread forward curve for single-B rated debt is too inverted[16] and will flatten. More precisely, the investor believes that 2-year single-B forward credit-spreads, currently at 5% will decrease to 4.5% in one year's time, and the 10-year single-B forward credit-spread currently at 3% will increase to 3.5% in one year.

In order to exploit this credit-spread flattening view, the investor buys a credit-spread forward on the 2-year credit-spread at the current forward spread of 5%. The investor sells a credit-spread forward on the 10-year credit-spread at the current forward credit-spread of 3%. Since the investor enters into these credit-spread forward contracts at the current forward spread rate, the premiums of each of the forward transactions are zero. The notional amount for each forward is $1,000,000.

Scenario 1: The investor's expectation was correct and after 1 year the 2-year single-B credit-spread has decreased from 5% to 4.5%. Following equation (2.9) Duration × N × [K − S (t_1)], the payoff for the investor with an assumed duration of 1.7 is 1.7 × 1,000,000 × (5% − 4.5%) = $8,500. The investor was also correct on the view on 10-year single-B credit-spreads. They increased from 3% to 3.5%. With an assumed duration of 8.5, the investor receives 8.5 × 1,000,000 × (3.5% − 3%) = $42,500.

Scenario 2: The recession has worsened and the 2-year single-B credit-spread has widened by 2 percentage points, but the 10-year credit-spread increased by only 0.2 percentage points. The investor will lose 1.7 × 1,000,000 × (7% − 5%) = $34,000 on the long 2-year credit-spread forward. He will make 1,000,000 × (3.2% − 3%) × 8.5 = $17,000 on the short 10-year forward position. Thus, the investor incurs a total loss of $17,000.

A position of gaining from an anticipated flattening of the inverted credit-spread curve can also be created by selling an 8-year credit-spread with a 2-year forward start. If the credit-spread curve flattens, the 8-year credit-spread 2 years forward, which is determined by the 2-year and 10-year credit-spread, will increase, thus leading to a gain for the investor.

There are numerous other ways to speculate with a credit derivative. An investor can take a long or short position in any credit derivative, provided he can come up with the necessary margin to insure payment of potential losses. As a last example let's look at a "Vega play." The Vega was already explained in the section "Market risk."

Example 4.10: An investor believes that the credit market is currently overly nervous and consequently that implied volatility of credit-spread options is too high. He sells a naked straddle (a put and a call with the same strike without owning the underlying) with 3-month maturity on $1,000,000 on a BB-rated bond. The current credit-spread of the BB-rated bond is 2%. The straddle is at-the-money, thus the credit-spread straddle strike is 2%. With a duration value of 1.7, a 180% implied volatility and a 5% risk-free interest rate, the straddle premium is $23,294.[17]

Scenario 1: The investor's perception is correct. The credit market calms down and after 1 month implied credit-spread volatility has decreased to 130%. The current credit-spread for BB-rated bonds has decreased to 1.8%. As a result, the call premium is $5,791 and the put premium is $9,163. Thus the profit of the investor is $23,294 − (5,791 + 9,163) = $8,340 (ignoring the time value effect of receiving the $23,294 at an earlier time).

Scenario 2: The investor was wrong. After 1 month, implied volatility has increased to 200%. Additionally, the bond is downgraded and the bond's credit-spread has widened to 4%. As a result, the call premium is $4,094 and the put premium is $37,812. Thus, the investor incurs a loss of ($4,094 + $37,812) − $23,294 = $18,612.

Example 4.10 indicates that a short credit-spread straddle strategy has limited upside potential, which is the straddle premium. However, a short straddle strategy has unlimited downside risk. Therefore an investor who sells a naked straddle should have stop-loss limits in place. A stop-loss is a price at which a certain loss has accumulated and the position is closed to prevent further losses.

Cost Reduction and Convenience

Another important motivation of credit derivatives is simply that they can reduce cost when assuming or hedging different types of risk. Credit derivatives can also be more convenient than cash instruments with respect to maintaining a good client relationship, in terms of ease of trading, or from an administrative point of view. The cost reduction feature benefits the transactions of investment banks and hedge funds, while the convenience feature facilitates the business mainly of commercial lending institutions.

Cost reduction

We'll now look at several examples illustrating how to reduce costs with credit derivatives. Let's start with a low rated company with high funding costs.

Example 4.11: A non-rated hedge fund faces funding costs of Libor + 300 basis points.[18] The hedge fund is interested to assume exposure on a junk bond, which pays Libor + 400 basis points. Consequently, if the hedge fund would fund and purchase the junk bond in the cash market, the net income would be 100 basis points.

The hedge fund finds a bank which owns the junk bond and wants to buy a default swap on the bond at an annual premium of 200 basis points. Thus the hedge fund can assume exposure on the junk bond by selling a default swap at an income of 200 basis points, instead of 100 basis points when funding and buying the bond in the cash market. (The attentive reader recalls that the hedge fund as the seller of a default swap assumes a long position in the credit quality of the reference asset; see chapter 2, "What is a default swap?") One difference remains though: Had the hedge fund purchased the bond in the cash market, the hedge fund would have a long position in the credit quality *and* a long market position (the hedge fund would profit from a credit quality increase *and* a price increase of the bond due to interest rate decreases).

The bank, assuming it has funding costs of Libor flat, will make a profit of 200 basis points, since it receives Libor + 400 from the junk bond, finances the junk bond purchase at Libor flat and pays 200 basis points in the default swap. However, the bank is left with market risk and has counterparty risk, since the seller of the default swap is the non-rated hedge fund.

Let's look at another example, where credit derivatives are more efficient than cash instruments. Shorting bonds in the cash market is often quite cumbersome and expensive. An investor has to first borrow the bond in the Repo market and then try to sell it in the secondary cash market. A more convenient and often cheaper way to assume a short position in a bond is the TROR market, as in example 4.12.

Example 4.12: An investment bank believes that a Canadian Libor-flat paying bond is overpriced and plans to short it for 1 year. To short the bond in the cash market, the bank has to first borrow it in a reverse-Repo transaction. In the reverse Repo, the bank receives an assumed Libor − 20 basis points (compare figure 2.9). Let's assume the Canadian bond price has not changed within 1 year, hence the bank sells the bond at Libor flat. Thus, the investor's expense when borrowing the bond in the Repo market and shorting the bond in the cash market is 20 basis points.

For common names, such as Canada, the TROR market is typically quite liquid. Thus, if the investment bank wants to assume a short position in the Canadian bond, it can usually conveniently pay in a TROR. That means the investment bank pays the price increase plus the coupon, which in this example is Libor flat and receives Libor +/− spread (compare figure 2.5). If the investment bank can receive Libor plus a spread of 10 basis points in the TROR, it will have an advantage of 30 basis points compared to the cash market. For a short position of $10,000,000, the advantage is $10,000,000 × 0.0030 = $30,000.

Let's look at a similar example, in which shorting a bond is synthetically achieved by credit-spread options.

Example 4.13: Bank A wants to short a single-A rated bond. When borrowing the bond in the Repo market and then shorting it, the bank has to pay Libor + 30. However, Bank A can synthetically short the bond forward if it sells a credit-spread call and buys a credit-spread put with identical strikes of Libor + 25 and identical premiums. If the credit quality of the bond decreases (e.g. to Libor + 50), the bank will exercise the put and sell the bond at the favorable strike (the bank pays Libor + 25). If the credit quality increases and the bond improves (e.g. to Libor + 10), the bank will get exercised on the call and will have to sell the bond at the now unfavorable strike (pay again Libor + 25). Hence, the bank will pay Libor + 25 in the synthetic short position and achieve an advantage of 5 basis points compared to the cash shorting.

A slight disparity between the cash trade and the synthetic trade remains. The bank will receive the bond not today but at option maturity in the synthetic trade. However, this disparity is of small nature, since the option price incorporates the forward nature of the trade by discounting with – typically – the risk-free interest rate.

Let's look at another example, in which two banks simply exchange default swaps in order to diversify their risk. This can be achieved cost-neutral or even cost-saving as in example 4.14.

Example 4.14: Let's assume Bank A has a $100,000,000 short position in a default swap with company X, and Bank B has a $100,000,000 short swap default position with company Y. Both banks want to reduce their high exposure to an individual company. Thus, Bank A and Bank B can simply agree to exchange part of their short default swap positions. Bank A sells $50,000,000 of their short default swap on company X to Bank B, and Bank A buys $50,000,000 of Bank B's short default swap position on company Y. Assuming Bank A and B, as well as company X and Y, are equally rated, this exchange can be done cost-neutral (i.e. no exchange of cash between bank A and bank B). In this case, both banks have diversified their risk without extra cost, as in figure 4.2.

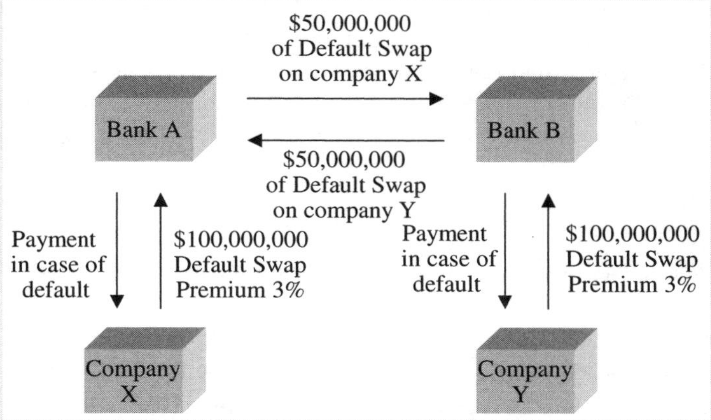

Figure 4.2: Cost-neutral exchange of short default swap positions to increase diversification

In the following example an investment bank can achieve the required return on capital with shorting a credit-spread put.

Example 4.15: The required return on capital of an investment bank for a BBB rated bond is Libor + 50 basis points. However, by purchasing the bond in the cash market, the return is

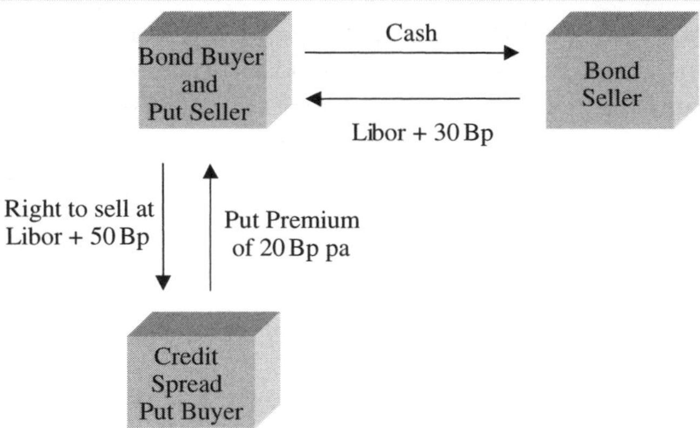

Figure 4.3: A bond buyer, enhancing his yield by selling a credit-spread put

only Libor + 30 basis points. To achieve the required Libor + 50 basis points, the investment bank can purchase the bond and sell a credit-spread put on the loan for 20 basis points annually at a strike of Libor + 50 basis points.

Scenario 1: The credit quality of the bond does not decrease and the investment bank will receive the required Libor + 50 basis points annually on the loan.

Scenario 2: The credit quality of the bond decreases and the investment bank will be exercised on the put and will have to buy additional units of the bond. It will receive the required bond strike of Libor + 50 basis points. However, the credit quality of the bond is presently lower than Libor + 50, for example Libor + 100, otherwise the put buyer would not have exercised the put. There is no free lunch.

Convenience

Using credit derivatives rather than cash trades can also be more convenient from a variety of perspectives.

Shorting a bond in the TROR market is more convenient from an administrative point of view, since the bond does not have to be borrowed in the Repo market and then sold in the cash market. The administrative cost of a credit derivatives transaction is also often lower than that of a cash trade. Shorting the bond in the cash market might also be difficult for certain companies due to legal, tax, and accounting regulations.

Moreover, some bonds and often loans do not trade actively in the secondary market. Hence, a default swap, a TROR, or a credit-spread product might be the only way to assume or hedge risk on illiquid bonds and loans.

Most importantly, credit derivatives can maintain a good bank–client relationship. Suppose an investment bank reaches its credit limits for a client. Without credit derivatives, it would have to sell the credit in the often rather illiquid secondary cash market. If the client discovers the sell, he will most likely be upset about his debt resurfacing. It might also be required that customer consent is necessary to transfer the debt and the customer refuses to give that consent. If selling the debt is not possible, the bank would have to reject further lending to the client, naturally harming its bank–client relationship.

Credit derivatives can solve the problem. A bank can simply hedge the credit of a questionable client with a default swap, effectively writing it off their balance sheet and opening new credit facilities for the client. In most cases, the client does not even notice that his credit line was full and had to be synthetically extended. Thus, the use of credit derivatives can discreetly maintain a good bank–client relationship.

Arbitrage

As already discussed in chapter 3, arbitrage is commonly defined as a risk-free profit. For example, a trader who buys one ounce of gold at $300 in London and simultaneously sells it at $302 in New York, makes a risk-free profit of $2 per ounce (excluding the 2-day delivery risk from the London seller). However, in trading practice, arbitrage is often defined more broadly as an *expected* profit, also termed "risk-arbitrage." For example in a "takeover arbitrage" the company that is acquired is purchased and the company that takes over is sold, expecting the spread to narrow. In this analysis, we will define arbitrage narrowly as a risk-free profit.

Since a certain financial expertise and accessibility to information are required to do arbitrage, mainly professional institutions such as investment banks and hedge funds are the ones that are able to perform arbitrage with credit derivatives. The cause for arbitrage lies in the fact that many credit derivates and credit derivatives structures can be replicated with cash instruments. Let's have a look.

In the following two examples, if equation (2.1b), Return on risk-free bond = Return on risky bond – Default swap premium (p.a.), is not satisfied, arbitrage opportunities exist.

Example 4.16: Due to the crisis in Argentina, Argentine yields are inflated. If the Argentine bond yield is 27%, the Argentine default swap premium 20%, and the Treasury bond yield 5%, an investor can achieve an arbitrage by buying the Argentine bond, buying the default swap, and shorting the Treasury bond. The arbitrage would be 2% on the notional amount as seen in figure 4.4.

Note that, as discussed in chapter 2, equation (2.1) is only an approximation. Hence, for the arbitrage to work, the following assumptions have to hold: (a) no counterparty risk in the default swap; (b) market risk (interest rate risk) affects the Argentine bond and the Treasury bond to the same extent (this is quite a strong assumption, since the Argentinean bond price, although denominated in US dollars, should also be a function of Argentinean interest rates); (c) no accrued interest; (d) no liquidity risk; (e) no additional cost for shorting the Treasury bond.

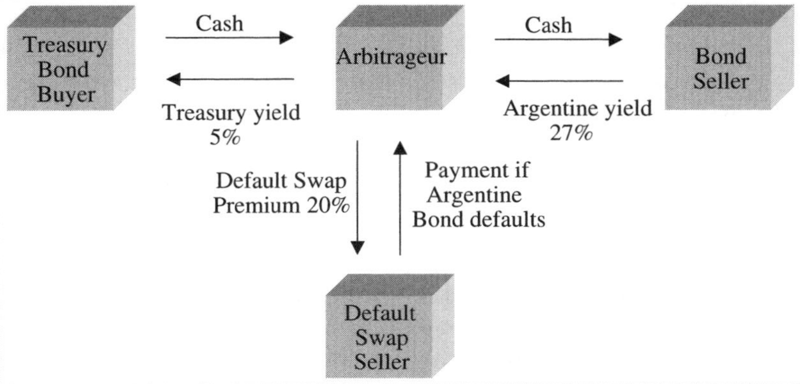

Figure 4.4: An investor exploiting an inflated Argentine bond yield to achieve an arbitrage of 2%

If the Argentine default swap market is distorted, i.e. excess demand for Argentine default swaps has led to high default swap premiums, the following arbitrage is possible. In example 4.17 the cash flows of example 4.16 are reversed.

Example 4.17: Due to the crisis in Argentina, default swap premiums on Argentine bonds are inflated. If the Treasury bond yield is 5%, the Argentine bond yield 24%, and the Argentine default swap premium 20%, an investor can achieve an arbitrage by shorting the Argentine bond, shorting the default swap, and buying the Treasury bond. The arbitrage would be 1% on the notional amount, as seen in figure 4.5.

Note that we have made the similar simplified assumptions as in example 4.16: (a) no counterparty risk in the default swap; (b) market risk (interest rate risk) affects the Argentine bond and the Treasury bond to the same extent; (c) no accrued interest; (d) no liquidity risk; (e) no additional cost for shorting the Argentinean bond.

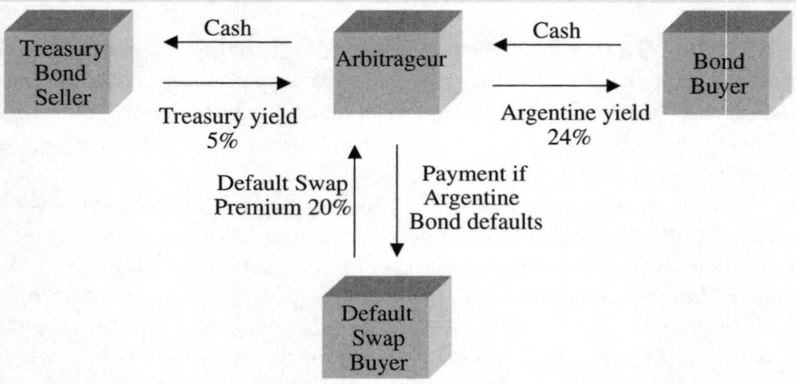

Figure 4.5: An investor exploiting an inflated Argentine default swap premium to achieve an arbitrage of 1%

A similar type of arbitrage is seen in example 4.18, in which the favorable funding of a bank is utilized.

Example 4.18: An AAA rated company has a funding of Libor − 30. The AAA company purchases a double-BB rated asset with a coupon of Libor + 70.[19] It hedges the default risk with a default swap and pays – due to its AAA rating – a low annual premium of 40 basis points. Graphically, this can be seen in figure 4.6.

The AAA rated bank is left with the default risk of the default swap seller and the default risk of the BB-rated bond issuer. The correlation of the defaults of the default swap seller and the BB-rated issuer is of importance, and will be discussed in detail in chapter 5 on pricing.

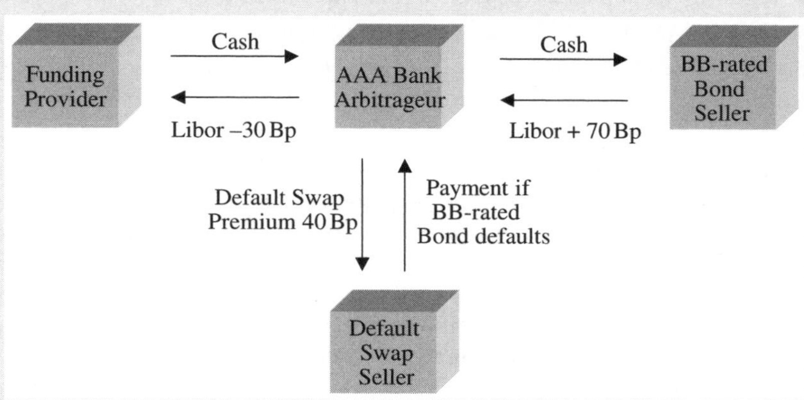

Figure 4.6: An arbitrageur exploiting his low funding cost to achieve an arbitrage of 60 basis points

In the following example, an arbitrageur exploits her favorable funding in connection with a TROR.

Example 4.19: An A-rated bank has a funding cost of Libor + 20 and purchases a loan on Yahoo, which pays Libor + 70. If the bank can pay net 40 basis points in a TROR, it makes an arbitrage of 10 basis points, as seen in figure 4.7.

In this example the A-rated bank is left with counterparty risk of the TROR receiver and Yahoo. The arbitrageur is also exposed to basis risk: If the positive value change of the loan in the cash market is less than the value change in the TROR, the arbitrageur will incur a mark-to-market loss. However, arbitrageurs will step in and receive in the TROR and short the loan in the cash market, thus reducing the basis.

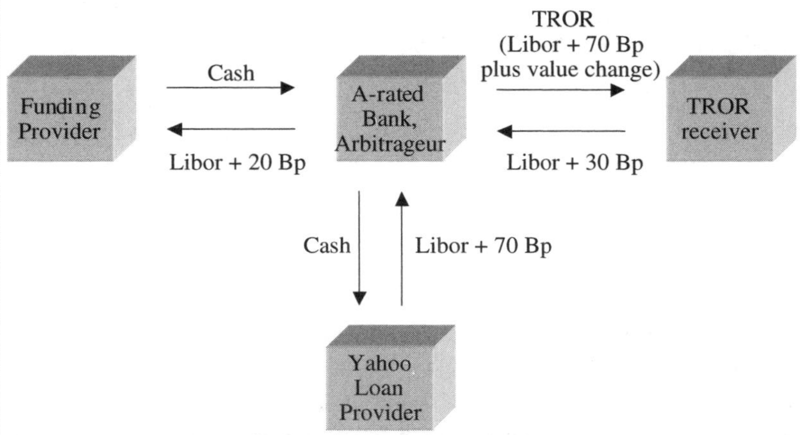

Figure 4.7: An arbitrageur exploiting her favorable funding in connection with a TROR to achieve an arbitrage of 10 basis points

In the following example, an arbitrageur can exploit the inequality of equation (2.2), TROR = Default swap + Market risk, to achieve a profit.

Example 4.20: An AA rated bank can achieve a low default swap premium of 20 basis points on a BBB-rated reference asset. If the bank receives Libor + 30 in a TROR on the same asset and shorts a Treasury bond future in order to assume short market risk, the bank achieves an arbitrage of 10 basis points, as seen in figure 4.8.

The bank is left with counterparty risk in the TROR and the default swap. The bank is also exposed to TROR–default swap basis risk, since it receives in a TROR and pays in the default swap. The bank is also left with TROR–Treasury futures risk: if the price increase in the TROR is smaller than the price decrease of the Treasury future, the bank will incur a mark-to-market loss. However, arbitrageurs will step in, pay in the TROR and buy the future, which will reduce the basis.

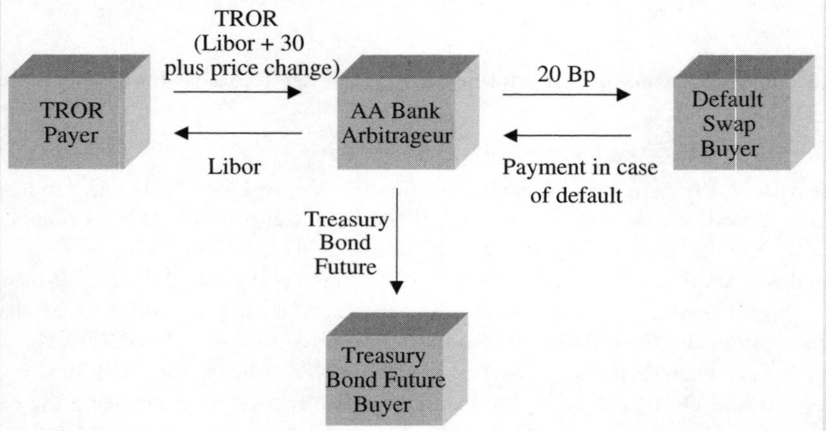

Figure 4.8: An AA-rated bank exploiting a low default swap premium relative to a TROR to achieve an arbitrage of 10 basis points

In the following example an arbitrageur exploits the inequality of equation (2.3), Repo = Receiving in a TROR + Sale of the Bond.

Example 4.21: Due to its AA rating, an investment bank can pay Libor + 30 in a TROR, sell the TROR underlying bond, and receive Libor + 50 in a reverse Repo, as seen in figure 4.9.

The arbitrage is 20 basis points, since the first and third horizontal legs in figure 4.9 cancel out. Hence the arbitrageur is left with receiving $1 million against Libor + 30 basis points and paying $1 million and receiving Libor + 50 in the reverse Repo. The arbitrageur is left with counterparty risk of the TROR payer.

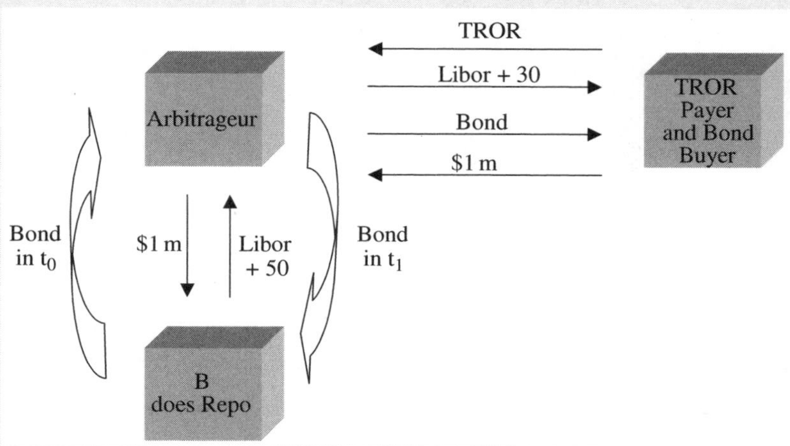

Figure 4.9: An arbitrageur doing a reverse Repo, receiving in a TROR and selling the bond to achieve an arbitrage of 20 basis points

If the TROR Libor spread is higher than the Libor spread in the Repo, arbitrage with the reverse flows to those in the figure 4.9 is possible. An arbitrageur can pay the spread in a Repo, buy the bond and receive the high Libor spread in a TROR.

The next example shows how it is possible to exploit the fact that, with puts and calls, a synthetic short (or long) position in the underlying asset can be created.

Example 4.22: In the credit-spread option market, credit-spread puts are often slightly more expensive than credit-spread calls, since puts protect against credit deterioration, thus demand is high. Hence, an investor can sell a 1-month credit-spread put and buy a 1-month credit-spread call at a high identical strike of 60 basis points above Libor, whereby the premiums add up to zero. In addition, the investor can sell the underlying bond 1-month forward at Libor + 50 basis points, hence achieving an arbitrage of 10 basis points, as seen in figure 4.10.

The investor is left with counterparty risk of the call seller, who in case of its default and a credit quality increase of the bond will not be able to meet his obligation to sell the bond at the strike of Libor + 60 basis points.

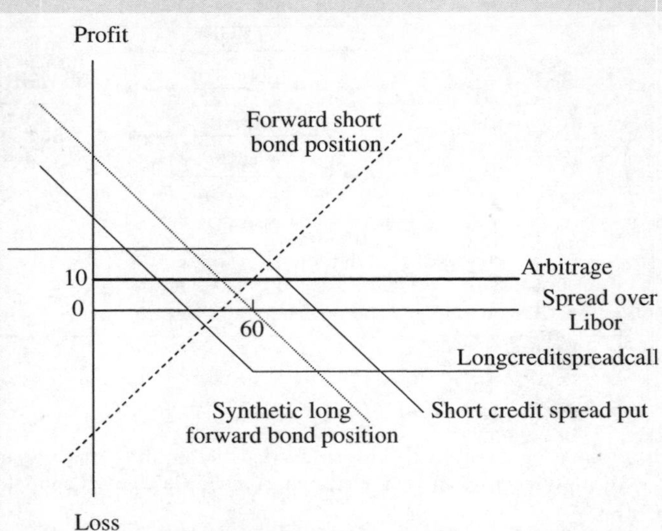

Figure 4.10: An investor creating a synthetic long position via selling a credit-spread put and buying a credit-spread call. Together with a forward short position he achieves an arbitrage of 10 basis points.

The reader might get bored with all the arbitrage examples. So here is the last one. It exploits the similarity between an equity put option and a default swap.

Example 4.23: A hedge fund can buy a far out-of-the-money put on the stock of company X with a strike of \$100 for 5 basis points. The hedge fund can also sell a default swap for an upfront premium of 5 basis points. The maturity and notional amount of the equity put and the default swap are identical.

Scenario 1: The price of company X remains roughly unchanged. In this case, the hedge fund does not incur a profit or a loss, since the put and the default swap lose time value to a similar extent.

Scenario 2: The credit of company X deteriorates (improves). In this case, the value of the put and the default swap increase (decrease) by about the same amount.

Scenario 3: Company X defaults and the stock price goes to zero. Let's assume the recovery rate is 15%. The hedge fund receives \$100 on the put. However, the hedge fund pays out only \$100 − \$15 = \$85 on the default swap, achieving an arbitrage of \$15.

With the relative value play in example 4.23, the hedge fund exploits its view on the potential recovery rate. The hedge fund can also utilize the similarity between equity puts and default swaps on its views of the future price spread between puts and default swaps.

In example 4.23 the hedge fund is left with systematic risk: If interest rates decrease and stock prices increase, the put price may decline by more than the default swap

Table 4.1: Minimum risk weights of the 1988 Basel Accord

Issuer	**Risk Weight (to be multiplied by 8%)**
OECD[22] governments	0%
(Plus guarantees or claims collateralized by an OECD government)	
OECD incorporated banks	20%
(Plus guarantees or claims collateralized by an OECD incorporated bank)	
Loans secured by mortgage	50%
Corporations and non-OECD governments and incorporated banks	100%

premium. In example 4.23 we have also assumed that the equity put pays the full intrinsic value ($100) in case of default. This is not always the case in reality. Certain put contracts include a clause which only pays a percentage amount of the intrinsic value in case of default.

Regulatory Capital Relief

So far we discussed four applications of credit derivatives: hedging, yield enhancement, cost reduction and convenience, and arbitrage. As the last application, we will discuss how financial and non-financial institutions can reduce their regulatory capital with credit derivatives. Let's first look at some basic elements of banking regulation.

In 1988 the Basel Committee on Banking Supervision[20] of the BIS[21] established the Basel Accord. The key element of the accord is the capital adequacy ratio, which requires banks to hold a minimum of 8% capital against the notional amount of risky assets appearing on their balance sheet. The 1988 Basel Accord has since been established in over 100 countries with minor adjustments to account for national laws and regulations.

The capital adequacy framework of the 1988 Accord established four risk-categories, which were created to reflect the risk of the borrower. The categories and their risk-weighting – all to be multiplied by 8% – are shown in table 4.1.

The risk categories in table 4.1 are naturally quite broad and lead to a misallocation of capital. For example, Mexico as a member state of the OECD but only single-A rated, enjoys a 0% risk weighting, in contrast to Singapore, which as a non-OECD member but despite its AAA rating has a risk weight of 100% (× 8%). Thus capital is misallocated towards OECD countries. The degree of differentiation in table 4.1 is also quite low. AAA and CCC rated OECD incorporated banks fall in the same 20% risk weight category.

Under the Basel 1988 Accord, credit derivatives have been used to exploit the distortion of risk weights to reduce capital requirements: A bank can enter into a credit derivative (e.g. buy a default swap) to substitute the risk weight of the issuer with the risk weight of the credit derivative seller. Naturally OECD banks are often chosen as protection sellers because of their low risk weights. As a consequence, protection buyers are often willing to

Table 4.2: Minimum risk weights in the new Basel Accord for assets of sovereigns and banks (to be multiplied by 8%)

	AAA to AA–	**A+ to A–**	**BBB+ to BBB–**	**BB+ to B–**	**Below B–**	**Unrated**
Sovereigns	0%	20%	50%	100%	150%	100%
Banks Option 1	20%	50%	100%	100%	150%	100%
Banks Option 2						
>3 months	20%	50%	50%	100%	150%	50%
<3 months	20%	20%	20%	50%	150%	20%

pay a higher premium if the seller is an OECD bank, leading to an unfair trading advantage of OECD banks.

Highly rated, non-OECD debt (e.g. Singapore) incurs the largest disparity between economic and regulatory capital. Due to the high rating, the lending income is quite low and due to the non-OECD status the capital requirement is high. Consequently, these credits are often the ones that banks wish to hedge. The hedge provides high regulatory capital relief due to the non-OECD status. If additionally the default swap seller is highly rated (e.g. Deutsche Bank), the capital requirement for the protection buyer is low.

In light of the obvious shortcomings of the 1988 Basel Accord, the Basel Committee has proposed a new more detailed capital adequacy framework called Basel II, which will replace the 1988 Basel I Accord. The latest version was published in October 2002 with a supplement in April 2003.[23] Let's have a look at the basic elements.

The Basel II Accord

The Basel II Accord is a consultative, preliminary document, principally designed for internationally active banks. It is intended to "align capital adequacy assessment more closely with the key elements of banking risks and to provide incentives for banks to enhance their risk measurement and management capabilities." The purpose of the new accord is to "contribute to a higher level of safety and soundness in the financial system."[24] The Basel Committee is explicitly asking for comments and feedback on their proposal.

The new accord consists of three pillars. Pillar 1 sets the new minimum capital requirements for market risk, credit risk, and operational risk. Pillar 2 focuses on the supervisory review process. Pillar 3 determines the disclosure obligations of the banks for market, credit, and operational risk. Let's look at the new minimum capital requirements of the banks in pillar 1.

The new minimum capital requirements set out in pillar 1 are summarized in table 4.2 and table 4.3. As in the 1988 Accord, each weight is multiplied by the minimum capital ratio 8%.

Table 4.3: Minimum risk weights in the new Basel Accord for corporations (to be multiplied by 8%)

	AAA to AA–	A+ to A–	BBB+ to BB–	Below BB–	Unrated
Corporations	20%	50%	100%	150%	100%

The risk weights for sovereigns (table 4.2 row 1) are determined by the Basel Committee. To derive the risk weights for banks, national supervisors have two options.

Option 1 (table 4.2 row 2) is derived by assigning one risk category less favorable (i.e. higher) than the sovereign rating (table 4.2 row 1), whereby the possible risk categories are set as 0%, 20%, 50%, 100%, and 150%. However, risk weights of banks rated BB+ to B– and unrated banks are capped at 100%. The risk weight for banks with a B- and worse rating is equal to the sovereign rating of 150%, since 150% is the highest category.

Option 2 allows banks to choose an external rating assessment. Let's assume these risk weights are as in row 3 in table 4.2. It then follows that for maturities below 3 months, banks may apply a risk weight one category more favorable than for maturities above 3 months, with a minimum risk weight at 20%. However, this treatment does not apply to risk weights in the 150% category. In this case, the risk weight remains 150%.

For corporations, 5 instead of 6 risk brackets are established table (4.3).

The risk weights in tables 4.2 and 4.3 are definitely a welcome refinement of the old accord. Nevertheless the somewhat cumbersome nature with many exceptions lacks stringency.

Furthermore, a weakness in tables 4.1 and 4.2 is that the unrated risk weight is usually lower than that of the lowest rated bracket. This might encourage corporations with declining credit to choose not to re-rate in order to gain the lower risk weight of the non-rated bracket. The Basel Committee has addressed this problem and has proposed that supervisors should require a higher risk weight than 8% if a corporate tries to exploit the lower risk weight of unrated corporations.

A further drawback is that many foreign companies are not rated, so that their risk weight would be naturally that in the unrated bracket although their default risk varies strongly.

Standardized versus IRB approach

The Basel Committee refers to the risk weight approach in tables 4.2 and 4.3 as the *standardized approach*. This approach is intended to neither raise nor lower the regulatory capital compared to the 1988 Accord. The Basel Committee also proposes an *internal rating based (IRB) approach*. In this approach in option 2, banks can internally choose a rating from a certain external agency, e.g. Standard & Poors, Moody's, or Fitch. The internal rating based approach is divided into the *foundation* and the *advanced* approach.

In the foundation IRB approach, banks that meet robust supervisory standards will internally derive the probability of default of an obligor. Additional risk factors such as exposure given default and loss given default are derived with the help of the standardized supervisory estimates.

The advanced IRB approach is available for financial institutions that meet more rigorous regulatory standards. Under the advanced IRB approach banks have more freedom to determine the various components of risk. However at this point in time, the Basel Committee is stopping short of allowing banks to calculate their own capital requirements based on their own models. Nevertheless, the Basel Committee "hopes to see more banks moving from the standardized approach to the IRB approach."[25]

It is important to mention that the standardized as well as the IRB approach are designed for assets in the banking book and not the trading book of a financial institution. Let's just clarify the difference.

Banking book versus trading book

The *banking book* constitutes the account where a bank's conventional transactions such as loans, bonds, deposits, and revolving credit facilities are recorded. On average, most of these instruments are of a long-term nature and are intended to be held until maturity. Thus, since they are not traded on a regular basis, most tend to be quite illiquid. In addition, assets held in the banking book are recorded at their historical costs and any profits or losses are therefore not accounted for until the instruments are either sold or reach maturity.

A *trading book* comprises instruments that are explicitly held with trading intent or in order to hedge other positions in the trading book. They tend to be traded frequently and are short-term in nature, usually less than 6 months. In addition, instruments eligible to be held in the trading book have to be marked-to-market on a daily basis and thus any profit or loss is accounted for immediately in the profit and loss account. Thus the major differences between the two books are their respective valuation techniques, the relative maturity of the assets held, and the specific intent with which they are held.[26]

Instruments held in the trading book tend to require smaller capital charges than positions held in the banking book, which naturally provides incentives for banks to record as many transactions as possible in the trading book. The reasons for the differentials in capital charges are linked to the differences described above.

First, whereas the daily marking-to-market of trading book instruments allow for the immediate recognition of market risk, this feature is not included in the banking book due to its use of historical cost accounting. Therefore, since any potential losses are not accounted for until the asset is sold, exposures are considered more risky when held in the banking book.

Second, the short-term nature and higher liquidity of positions held in the trading book imply lower risk and therefore merit lower capital charges.

Risk weights for positions hedged by credit derivatives in the banking book

The above-mentioned distinction between the banking book and trading book is crucial for determining the risk weight for credit derivatives exposure. For credit derivatives that hedge exposure in the banking book, the New Basel Capital Accord specifies the risk weight r^* for the buyer of a credit derivative as:

$$r^* = w \times r + (1 - w) \times g \tag{4.3}$$

where

w: weight applied to the underlying exposure (w is set at 0.15 for all credit derivatives recognized as giving protection)
r: risk weight of the underlying obligor
g: risk weight of the protection seller.

Including the notional amount N, the total amount of capital required for protection is N × r*:

$$N \times r^* = N[w \times r + (1 - w) \times g]. \tag{4.4}$$

Let's show in an example how the capital requirement of a hedged position is reduced in the new accord.

Example 4.24: Under the old accord the risk weight of a sovereign BBB-rated, non-OECD obligor is 100% (see table 4.1). Thus the capital requirement for a \$1,000,000 investment under the old accord is \$1,000,000 × 100% × 8% = \$80,000.

Under the new accord the risk weight of any sovereign BBB-rated obligor is r = 50% (see table 4.2). The risk weight of a BB-rated default swap selling bank is g = 100% (see table 4.3). Following equation (4.3) the total risk weight (bond plus default swap hedge) under the new accord using a default swap as a hedge is r* = 15% × 50% + (1 − 15%) × 100% = 0.925 and the capital requirement is \$1,000,000 × 0.925 × 8% = \$74,000.

If the default swap selling bank is an AAA-rated bank (20% risk weight, see table 4.2) the total risk weight under the new accord is r* = 15% × 50% + (1 − 15%) × 20% = 0.245 and the capital requirement is a mere \$1,000,000 × 0.245 × 8% = \$19,600.

Example 4.24 shows the reduction of required capital under the new accord when credit derivatives are utilized. The reduction is especially high for non-OECD debt and high rated protection sellers.

The w-factor in equations (4.3) and (4.4) is designed to capture any type of residual operational risk (e.g. legal risk or criminal risk) that makes the protection unenforceable. In the recent past, the w-factor has encountered heavy criticism, especially from the ISDA (International Swap and Derivatives Association, see www.ISDA.org). As a consequence, in September 2001, the Basel Committee reconsidered their standing on the w-factor saying: "After further consideration, the Capital Group believes the most effective way forward would be to treat this residual risk under the proposed framework's second pillar, i.e. the supervisory review process, rather than using the w-factor under the first pillar, i.e. minimum capital requirements."[27]

The elimination of the w-factor would eliminate the residual risk in the calculation of the risk weight of credit derivatives, thus reducing equation (4.3) to:

$$r^*_{w=0} = g. \tag{4.5}$$

Thus the new risk weight for credit derivatives $r^*_{w=0}$ would be merely the counterparty risk of the protection seller g. From equation (4.3) we can see that this increases or decreases the new risk weight $r^*_{w=0}$ compared to the old r^*, depending on the relationship r (risk weight of the underlying obligor) and g (risk weight of the protection seller). For $r < g$, it follows that the new weight $r^*_{w=0}$ is higher than the old r^*, and vice versa. For $g = r$ it follows that the old and new risk weight are identical $r^*_{w=0} = r^*$.

Risk weights for positions hedged by credit derivatives in the trading book

Credit derivatives are typically short-term and are often used for trading purposes. Thus the new Basel Committee regulations for the trading book will apply to many credit derivatives held by banks. For positions in the trading book that are hedged by default swaps and credit linked notes, the Basel Committee grants partial capital relief.

If the default swap or credit linked note exactly hedges the underlying position in terms of maturity, notional amount, and currency, an 80% risk offset is granted to the transaction with the higher capital charge, while the side with the lower capital charge receives no capital relief. Transaction in this case means the underlying position *and* the hedge. Thus, if a bond were hedged with a default swap, the bondholder and default swap buyer would be granted the capital relief, since this transaction has the credit exposure and consequently the capital charge. Let's look at an example.

Example 4.25: A bank owns a BB-rated sovereign bond with a notional amount of \$1,000,000. The bank decides to hedge the credit risk with buying a default swap. The underlying of the default swap is the BB-rated bond and the default swap has the same notional amount, maturity, and currency as the bond. The sovereign bond and default swap is marked-to-market, thus managed in the trading book of the bank.

The BB-rated sovereign bond has a risk weight of 100% (see table 4.2). Thus the capital charge without utilizing the Basel II offset for hedged positions is \$1,000,000 × 100% × 8% = \$80,000.

Using the new Basel II regulation, the default swap grants an 80% risk offset. Thus the capital requirement reduces to \$80,000 − (\$80,000 × 80%) = \$16,000.

For TRORs that hedge a trading book position, a 100% offset is granted, if the TROR matches the position exactly with respect to the underlying asset, maturity, notional amount and currency. This is reasonable, since a TROR, in contrast to a default swap, also hedges market risk.

For transactions where there is no mismatch with respect to the notional amount, but there is a mismatch in currency or maturity, the capital charge is applied only to the side with the higher capital requirement.

The BIS minimum capital requirement for combined credit, market, and operational risk

In January 2001, the BIS defined a combined credit, market, and operational risk requirement.[28] It is calculated as total capital divided by credit risk plus 12.5 times the sum of market risk plus operational risk, as seen in equation (4.6):

$$\frac{\text{Total capital (tiers 1 and 2)}}{\text{Credit risk} + 12.5 \times (\text{Market risk} + \text{Operational risk})}. \tag{4.6}$$

The resulting ratio of equation (4.6) cannot be less than 8%. Tier 1 capital in equation (4.6) is defined as core capital, including permanent shareholders' equity and disclosed reserves. Tier 2 capital is limited to 100% of Tier 1 capital. The fact that in equation (4.6) only market risk and operational risk, but not credit risk is weighted with 12.5, has a technical reason: The market risk charge and operational risk charge are calculated directly on the underlying assets, whereas credit risk is calculated on the already risk-weighted assets. Let's look at a simple numerical example of equation (4.6).

Example 4.26: Bank X has combined Tier 1 and Tier 2 capital of $3 billion. Bank X also has risk-weighted assets compiled for credit risk of $10 billion, a market risk charge of $1 billion, and an operational risk charge of $2 billion. Following equation (4.6), we derive

$$\frac{3}{10 + 12.5 \times (1+2)} = 6.32\%.$$

Since the BIS has set the combined minimum ratio at 8%, the ratio in this example is too low. Hence the bank has to either increase its Tier 1 or Tier 2 capital, or reduce its credit, market or operational risk requirement via reducing these risks. The risks can be reduced by either selling risky assets, entering into trades that net the original trades, or, as discussed in detail, with derivatives.

Summary of Chapter 4

In chapter 4, the various applications of credit derivatives in practice were discussed. We categorized five types of applications: hedging, yield enhancement, cost reduction and convenience, arbitrage, and regulatory capital relief.

Hedging various types of risk is one of the major applications of credit derivatives in practice. In terms of risk we can distinguish three main areas: market risk, credit risk, and operational risk.

Default swaps hedge credit risk, however, not market risk. Whether default swaps hedge operational risk depends on the impact of the operational damage on the credit quality. The higher the impact, the higher is the operational risk hedge that default swaps provide.

TRORs provide a hedge against credit risk as well as market risk. TRORs also provide an operational risk hedge if the operational damage leads to a price decrease of the reference asset.

Credit-spread products, which are comprised of credit-spread options, credit-spread forwards, and credit-spread swaps, all hedge credit risk. They do not hedge against market risk, if the interest rate movements do not alter the credit-spread. As with default swaps, credit-spread products provide a hedge against operational risk, if the operational damage leads to a price change of the reference asset.

Yield enhancement is another popular application of credit derivatives. There are many ways to achieve an additional return. Most CLN and CDO structures provide the investor with an above market yield in return for assuming credit exposure on a certain credit.

Other popular yield enhancement strategies are *covered credit-spread put selling strategy* to exploit a static or an increase in credit quality, *covered credit-spread call selling* to participate in a static or slight decrease in credit quality, *shorting a digital credit straddle* to exploit a ranged credit quality, a *credit-spread forward strategy* exploiting a possible flattening or steepening of the credit curve, or *selling a credit-spread straddle* in order to participate in a decrease of the credit-spread implied volatility.

It should be mentioned that many of the mentioned yield enhancement strategies incur high downside risk. Thus an investor should have a stop-loss to limit potential losses.

Cost reduction and **convenience** are further motivations to use credit derivatives. Cost reduction can often be achieved when the cash market is quite illiquid and shorting bonds and loans is expensive. Often it is cheaper to conveniently short a credit in the TROR market than borrowing it in the Repo market and selling it in the secondary cash market. This is especially true for institutions with a bad credit rating. Credit derivatives can eliminate or reduce their high funding disadvantage.

Companies can also reach their required return on investment by shorting credit derivatives. Furthermore, companies can conveniently enhance their diversification by swapping credit derivatives, often at zero cost.

A further benefit of credit derivatives is maintaining a good bank–client relationship. If the credit line of a client is full, the bank might sell the credit in the cash market and the client might be upset seeing his credit resurfacing. Even worse, the bank might inform the client that no further credit is available. However, by purchasing protection on the credit the bank can discreetly hedge the exposure and extend the credit line, maintaining a good bank–client relationship.

Arbitrage is a further motivation for using credit derivatives. In this book arbitrage is defined narrowly as a risk-free profit. Thus we are excluding strategies such as "risk-arbitrage" or "take-over arbitrage," which include the possibility of a loss.

Arbitrage opportunities exist because cash instruments or other credit derivatives can replicate many credit derivatives. If the equation Return on risk-free bond = Return on risky bond − Default swap premium is not satisfied, arbitrage exists. If the Return on risk-free bond < Return on risky bond − Default swap premium, an investor can buy the risky bond, buy a default swap, and short the Treasury bond to achieve a risk-free profit.

If Return on risk-free bond > Return on risky bond − Default swap premium, an investor can short the risky bond, short the default swap, and buy the Treasury bond. The main assumptions underlying this type of arbitrage are that market risk affects the risky and the risk-free bond to the same extent, there is no additional cost for shorting bonds, and we abstract from counterparty risk of the default swap seller.

Further arbitrage opportunities exist if the equation TROR = Default swap + Market risk and the equation Repo = Receiving in a TROR + Sale of the Bond are not satisfied. Arbitrage also exists if an investor can achieve a synthetically long (short) position with a credit-spread put and call, which has a higher return than a cash forward short (long) position. Hedge funds have recently made use of the close relationship between equity puts and default swaps to exploit their views on the potential recovery rate to achieve arbitrage.

Regulatory capital relief can be achieved with credit derivatives. The Basel II capital accord, which is currently being assessed by practitioners and academics, is scheduled to be implemented in 2007. The accord sets new risk weights for sovereigns, banks and corporations based not on OECD membership as in the old accord, but based on external and internal ratings. The Basel Committee encourages the implementation of the internal rating based approach, which to a certain extent allows banks to determine default probabilities, loss given default, and other components of risk, based on their own internal models.

The Basel Accord specifies capital requirements for positions in the banking book and the trading book of a financial institution. Since the trading book requires lower capital charges, financial institutions will try to book most of the credit derivatives in the trading book.

With respect to the banking book, the capital group of the Basel Committee has recently decided to abandon the controversial w-factor. It was designed to capture residual operational risk, which would make the protection unenforceable. As a result of the elimination of the w-factor, the risk weight for a buyer of protection is simply the risk weight of the protection seller.

With respect to the trading book, the new Basel Accord grants an 80% capital relief for exposure hedged by default swaps and credit linked notes, if the maturity and notional amount of the exposure are exactly matched. For TRORs, which in contrast to default swaps also protect against market risk, a 100% risk offset is granted, if the underlying position is exactly matched.

References and Suggestions for Further Readings

Andres, U. and M. Sandstedt, "An operational risk scorecard approach," *Risk Magazine*, January 2003, pp. 47–50.

Basel Committee, "The New Basel Capital Accord," January 2001, http://www.bis.org/.

Basel Committee, "Overview of the New Basel Capital Accord," January 2001, http://www.bis.org/publ/bcbsca02.pdf.

Basel Committee, "Quantitative Impact Study 3, Technical Guidance," October 2002, http://www.bis.org/.

Basel Committee, "Working Paper on the Treatment of Asset Securitizations," http://www.bis.org/publ/bcbs_wp10.pdf.

Bennett, O., "Moody's Offers LGD Calculator," *Risk Magazine,* August 2001, p. 8.

Cruz, M., *Modeling, measuring and hedging operational risk*, Wiley, 2002.

Das, S., *Credit Derivatives and Credit Linked Notes*, John Wiley & Sons (Asia) Pte Ltd.: Singapore, 2000.

Das, S. and P. Tufano, "Pricing Credit Sensitive Debt When Interest Rates, Credit Rating and Credit Spreads are Stochastic," *Journal of Financial Engineering*, 5(2), 1996, pp. 161–98.

Deloitte & Touche Germany, "Conventional versus Synthetic Securitization – Trends in the German ABS Market," May 2001, http://www.dttgsfi.com/publications.pdf.

Duffie, D., "First-to-default valuation," Working Paper, Stanford University, 1998.

European Central Bank (n.d.), "Fair Value Accounting in the Banking Sector," http://www.ecb.int/pub/pdf/notefairvalueacc011108.pdf.

Fitch, "Synthetic CDOs: A Growing Market for Credit Derivatives," http://www.mayerbrown.com/cdo/publications/wsyn0206.pdf.

Gibson, L., "Structured Credit Portfolio Transactions," *Asset Securitization Report*, July, 2001, vol. 1, issue 30, pp. 10–11.

Jarrow, R. and S. Turnbull, "The Intersection of market and credit risk," *Journal of Banking & Finance*, 24, 2000, pp. 271–99.

J.P. Morgan, *The J.P. Morgan's Guide to Credit Derivatives*, Risk Publications, 1999.

Longstaff, F. and E. Schwartz, "A Simple Approach to Valuing Risky Fixed and Floating Rate Debt," *The Journal of Finance*, no. 3, July 1995, pp. 789–819.

Meissner, G., *Trading Financial Derivatives*, Simon and Schuster, 1998.

Meissner, G., *Outperform the Dow*, Wiley, 2000.

Nelken, I., *Implementing Credit Derivatives: Strategies and Techniques for using Credit Derivatives in Risk Management*, McGraw-Hill, 1999.

Risk Books, *Credit Derivatives: Applications for Risk Management, Investment and Portfolio Optimization*, Risk Books, 1998.

Rule, D., "Risk Transfer between Banks, Insurance Companies and Capital Markets: an Overview," http://www.bankofengland.co.uk/fsr/fsr11art4.pdf.

Standard & Poor, "Implications of Basel II for Bank Analysis," http://www.gtnews.com/banking/home.html.

Questions and Problems

Answers, available for instructors, are on the Internet. Please email gmeissne@aol.com for the site.

4.1 *Name five applications of credit derivatives. What do you consider the most important application of credit derivatives for the financial markets?*

4.2 *Name the three types of risk that are currently differentiated. How are market risk and credit risk related?*

4.3 *Does (a) a default swap, (b) a TROR, (c) a credit-spread option hedge operational risk? Discuss each point.*

4.4 *Explain why the term "covered" credit-spread put selling is somewhat misleading. Do you believe it is currently a good idea to do a covered credit call selling strategy?*

4.5 *Do you think a naked short credit-spread straddle strategy is currently a good strategy? What is the maximum loss of this strategy? What additional trade should an investor implement, when using a naked short credit-spread straddle strategy?*

4.6 *Show in an example how credit derivatives can be cheaper than using cash instruments.*

4.7 *One of the main benefits of credit derivatives is maintaining a good bank–client relationship. Explain why.*

4.8 *Show an arbitrage opportunity with (a) a default swap, (b) a TROR, (c) a credit-spread option. Discuss each point individually.*

4.9 *What is the purpose of the capital adequacy ratio? Discuss the equation:*

$$\frac{\text{Total Capital (Tier 1 and 2)}}{\text{Credit Risk} + 12.5 \times (\text{Market Risk} + \text{Operational Risk})} \geq 8\%.$$

4.10 *What is the difference between the standardized approach and the IRB approach in the new Basel II Accord? Do you think it is reasonable that the Basel Committee has set different capital ratios for the banking book and the trading book?*

Notes

1 For a good introduction to the operational risk market see Cruz, M., *Modeling, measuring and hedging operational risk*, Wiley, 2002.

2 For hedging interest rate risk with derivatives see Meissner, G., *Trading Financial Derivatives*, 1998, chapters 3, 5, and 10.

3 WTI stands for West Texas Intermediate. WTI is a type of oil that can be delivered under the light crude oil futures contract.

4 Backwardation stands for a decreasing futures curve, i.e. short-term future prices are higher than long term future prices. The opposite applies to contango.

5 For calculating volatility see Meissner, G., *Outperform the Dow*, Wiley 2000, pp. 151ff.

6 For a standard Black-Scholes model valuing options on credit-spreads see www.dersoft.com/csobs.xls.

7 ISDA, www.ISDA.org, Article IV, p. 16.

8 BIS, *The New Basel Capital Accord*, www.BIS.org, January 2001, p. 94.

9 A fixed reverse floater pays an interest rate of x% – 6 ML (6-Month Libor). Thus if the 6 ML increases, the interest rate payments of the fixed reverse floater will reduce.

10 Basel Committee of Banking Supervision, "Quantitative Impact Study 3, Technical Guide," www.BIS.org, pp. 6ff; see section "Regulatory capital relief' in this chapter; for a detailed discussion on VAR, see chapter 6.

11 See www.dersoft.com/csobs.xls.

12 See www.dersoft.com/csobs.xls.

13 See again www.dersoft.com/csobs.xls.

14 An at-the-money forward spread is a spread at which the strike spread is equal to the forward spread. The forward spread is the spread that the model determines as the fair spread at option maturity.

15 See www.dersoft.com/csobs.xls.

16 For single-B and lower rated debt, the default probability is typically higher in the short run than in the long run, thus the credit-spread curve is usually inverted; see also table 5.4.

17 See once more www.dersoft.com/csobs.xls.

18 One basis point is equal to 1/100 of a percentage point.

19 A floating rate bond or loan has a par price at the fixing date and a close to par price between fixing dates, since it pays the current market Libor rate of the fixing date. The spread over Libor reflects the credit risk.

20 The Basel Committee on Banking Supervision is a committee of the BIS and was established in 1975. It functions as a supervisory authority, establishing the regulatory framework for financial institutions. The 12 member states are Belgium, Canada, France, Germany, Italy, Japan, Luxembourg, the Netherlands, Sweden, Switzerland, the UK and the US. The committee usually meets in Basel, Switzerland.

21 The BIS (Bank for International Settlements) was founded in 1930 and is owned by central banks. The BIS is an international organization, which fosters cooperation among central banks and other agencies in pursuit of monetary and financial stability.

22 Organization for Economic Cooperation and Development, see www.OECD.org.

23 BIS, "The New Basel Accord," October 2002, www.BIS.org; BIS, "Quantitative Impact Study 3, Technical Guidance," www.BIS.org, April 2003.

24 BIS, "Overview of the New Basel Accord," www.bis.org.

25 See BIS, "Overview of the New Basel Accord," www.bis.org.

26 For more details on the banking and trading book see European Central Bank, "Fair Value Accounting in the Banking Sector," at www.ecb.int/pub/pdf/notefairvalueacc011108.pdf.

27 www.bis.org.

28 BIS, "Overview of the New Basel Accord," January 2001, #63, www.BIS.org; and BIS "Quantitative Impact Study 3, Technical Guidance," www.BIS.org, October 2002, #22.

Chapter Five

The Pricing of Credit Derivatives

Patience is a minor form of despair, disguised as a virtue. (Ambrose Bierce)

The pricing of most credit derivatives is more complex than that of equity, commodity, interest rate, or foreign exchange derivatives. One reason for the higher complexity is that the market price for the underlying variable (i.e. the bond or loan) is often not easily observable. This is especially true for loans, which typically do not trade in a secondary market. Even if substantial research is conducted, measuring the credit quality of a debtor can be difficult, since credit quality criteria such as quality of the management or intangible assets are difficult to quantify.

However, if the underlying company is rated by an agency, traders can use the rating of the agency as a proxy for the value of the debt. Nevertheless, this might be problematic, since different rating agencies sometimes derive different ratings for the same debt. In addition, published ratings are often outdated, since agencies are not able to analyze the underlying debt on a timely basis.

Pricing credit derivatives is also problematic because defaults are rare events. Especially, since a company typically only defaults once, empirical data on the default of a solvent company is typically unavailable. To overcome this obstacle, it is often assumed that companies in the same credit category and sector display similar default dynamics and properties.

In addition, there are numerous causes for default. There can be internal causes such as mismanagement, incompetence, or fraud; and external causes such as a recession or stiff competition. Typically default is caused by a combination of factors, whose correlation has to be integrated into the pricing model.

Furthermore, with credit derivatives, the counterparty risk is an important pricing element, since the default of the underlying debt typically leads to a large settlement payment of the protection selling counterparty. Ideally, the correlation between the default risk of the counterparty and the default risk of the underlying debt should be considered in the pricing process. Furthermore, the correlation between credit risk, market risk, and operational risk should be recognized when pricing credit derivatives. All this makes pricing credit derivatives not an easy venture.

Credit Derivatives Pricing Approaches

Various approaches to price credit derivatives exist. They can be categorized as (a) traditional models or (b) structural models – which are comprised of (b1) firm value models and (b2) first-time passage models, and (c) reduced form models.

Traditional models value credit risk based on historical data. A risky bond price is derived by observing default rates of past losses or downgrades of bonds with comparable credit rating and seniority. Beside the obvious constraint of projecting historical data into the future, these data-fitting approaches often abstract from the economic situation. This is problematic since default and recovery rates are dependent on the business cycle (i.e. whether the economy is in a recession or boom).

In this context, Altman (1989) in an often-cited article, found that investors appear to be highly risk-averse: When taking into account past default rates, the return of an investment in risky bonds was significantly higher than the return on Treasury bonds.[1] This implies that investors are not risk-neutral but require a high-risk premium when investing in risky bonds. Part of the low risky bond price can be explained by the lower liquidity of risky bonds and by the anticipation of a recession, which would increase downgrade and default probabilities.

Structural models derive the value of credit risk by analyzing the capital structure of the company. Robert Merton in 1974 in a seminal paper laid the groundwork for structural models. The Merton model is mathematically identical with the original Black-Scholes model,[2] however the variables are redefined.[3] The basic concept of the Black-Scholes-Merton model underlies structural credit risk models as well as *reduced form credit risk models*. Before we discuss the Black-Scholes-Merton as well as structural and reduced form models in detail, let's observe some simple approaches to generating the probability of default.

Simple approaches

Let's first have a closer look at some basic pricing features of credit derivatives. Table 5.1 shows the input variables for deriving the price of a credit derivative.

Integrating all of the issues in table 5.1 into a single pricing model is not a trivial task. Currently no pricing model is accepted as a benchmark model as, for example, the Black-Scholes model for standard options. In the following, let's look at the most popular credit derivative, a default swap and how the default swap premium is usually derived in trading practice.

The default swap premium derived from asset swaps

As already discussed in chapter 2, asset swaps and default swaps are quite similar instruments (compare figure 2.7). The asset swap spread reflects the credit quality difference between the underlying asset and a risk-free Libor flat asset. Equally, the default swap premium reflects the credit quality difference between the risky asset and a risk-free asset, expressed as a difference in the yields (compare equation (2.1a) and (2.1b) and figure 2.4).

Table 5.1: Inputs for deriving a credit derivatives price

Input variables for deriving the price of a credit derivative	
1)	Default probability and credit deterioration probability of the reference asset
2)	Default probability and credit deterioration probability of the credit derivatives seller
3)	Correlation between 1) and 2)
4)	Volatility of the underlying reference asset
5)	Volatility of the credit derivatives seller
6)	Correlation between 4) and 5)
7)	Maturity of the credit derivative
8)	Expected recovery rate of the reference asset
9)	Expected recovery rate of the credit derivatives seller
10)	Return of the reference asset (e.g. coupon of the reference bond)
11)	Risk-free interest rate term structure used to discount future cash flows
12)	Default probability of the credit derivatives buyer in case of periodic credit derivative premium[4]
13)	Expected recovery rate of the credit derivatives buyer in case of periodic credit derivative premium
14)	Correlation between the default probability of the credit derivatives buyer and the reference asset in case of periodic credit derivatives premium
15)	Market risks (as interest rate risk, currency risk, commodity risk, and stock price risk) and the correlation between market risk and credit risk
16)	Operational risks (e.g. legal risks, documentation risks, or settlement risks), which might endanger the enforceability of the payoff and the correlation between operational risk and credit risk
17)	Liquidity of the credit derivative
18)	Liquidity of the underlying reference asset
19)	BIS risk weight of the credit derivatives seller
20)	Urgency of protection (e.g. is an immediate credit deterioration expected or does the protection free up credit lines to enable further business with a client)
21)	Transaction costs

As a consequence, default swap traders often use the asset swap spread as a benchmark for deriving the default swap premium. The equality of the asset swap spread and the default swap premium can be shown with an arbitrage argument similar to the one in example 4.18.

In figure 5.1, 'x' represents the asset swap spread. Let's assume identical currency, maturity, and notional amounts for the funding, the investment in the A-rated asset, and the default swap. From figure 5.1 we can see that the no-arbitrage condition for the investor, assuming he finances at Libor flat, is $d = x$.

In the default swap market, the difference $d - x$ is called the basis. A long basis trade means buying the reference asset and buying protection as in figure 5.1. A short basis trade means shorting the asset and shorting default protection. If $d > x$, the basis is termed positive, if $d < x$, the basis is negative.

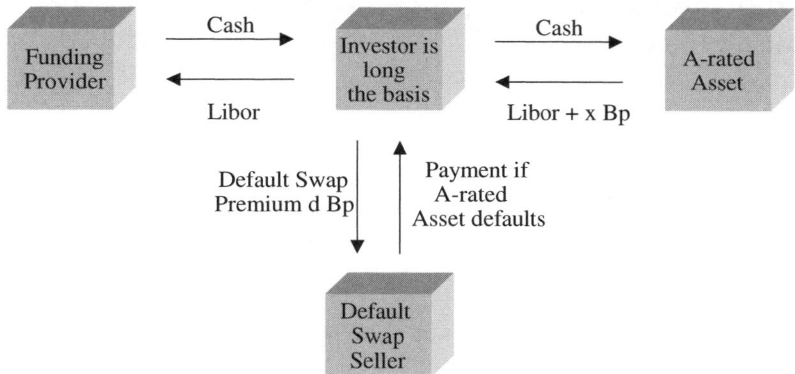

Figure 5.1: An investor buying an asset and hedging the credit risk with a default swap (Bp = basis points)

As pointed out, in an arbitrage-free environment, the no-arbitrage condition for Libor flat funding is d = x. However, in trading practice there are some features, which can increase or decrease the basis.

Features that increase the basis (default swap premium d – asset swap spread x)

1. *Natural market:* The default swap market has grown into the natural market to hedge credit risk. Especially for 3- to 5-year maturities many credit hedgers use the liquid default swap market rather than the asset swap market, driving default premiums up.
2. *Convertible bond arbitrage:* Hedge funds and other financial institutions strip the credit risk from the convertible bond and hedge it with default swaps to concentrate on managing the equity option.
3. *The delivery option:* In a default swap the delivery option allows the protection buyer to choose delivery from a pre-defined pool of assets, which increases the value of default swaps compared to asset swaps
4. *Default criteria:* Default criteria are clearly defined in the ISDA 1999 definitions, which facilitate trading. Also, default swap payments may be triggered by events, which do not constitute default in the cash market.

Features that decrease the basis (default swap premium d – asset swap spread x)

1. *Counterparty risk:* The default swap buyer is exposed to higher counterparty credit risk than the asset swap payer, since in an asset swap two cash flows of similar value are exchanged on a regular basis.
2. *Marking-to-market in default:* In case of default, it is typically quite difficult to mark-to-market an asset swap. Default swaps are designed to function in a default, so their marking-to-market is typically easier to achieve. This might drive asset swap spreads up, since the asset swap fixed rate payer, who will suffer a financial loss in the event of default, might want to be compensated for the higher uncertainty with receiving a higher spread.

Deriving the default swap premium using arbitrage arguments

We already derived an important arbitrage argument in chapter 2, which is used in trading practice to help determine the price of a default swap. The relationship was expressed in equation (2.1):

Return on risk-free bond = Return on risky bond − Default swap premium (p.a.). (2.1b)

Solving equation (2.1b) for the default swap premium, we get:

Default swap premium (p.a.) = Return on risky bond − Return on risk-free bond. (5.1)

Equation (5.1) can only serve as an approximation, as already discussed when examining equation (2.1) in chapter 2. Equation (5.1) abstracts from several features, which have to be included in the pricing of a defaults swap. We have listed these inputs in table 5.1. One of the most important points – and which is not included in equation (5.1) – is counterparty risk (i.e. the risk that the default protection seller defaults). As mentioned above, counterparty risk is an important feature, since in the case of default a typically large payment is due from the protection seller. In addition, the correlation between counterparty default risk and default risk of the underlying asset is of importance, since the default protection buyer will incur a loss in the amount of his reference asset value plus the default swap premium (minus the recovery rate of the reference asset issuer and the counterparty), if both the protection seller and the underlying asset default. These issues will be discussed later in this chapter.

"I price it where I can hedge it:" Pricing default swaps using hedging arguments

In the following, we will derive a price range for a default swap premium based on hedging considerations. Let's just recall the basic structure of a default swap, as seen in figure 5.2.

Since bank A has bought the default swap on a bond, it is short the credit risk of the bond (bank A's present value of the default swap will increase, if the bond price decreases due to credit deterioration). Thus to hedge the long default swap position, bank A has to go long the bond. If the funding for bank A is Libor + w and the bond pays Libor + x, the hedge of bank A can be seen in figure 5.3.

In figure 5.2, bank B is short the default swap, thus has a long bond position. Thus to hedge it, bank B has to short the bond. If bank B borrows the bond in the Repo market, the hedge can be seen in figure 5.4.

In a Repo the interest rate paid is usually sub-Libor, since the cash lender bank B has very little risk, since it receives the bond as collateral. This is why bank B only receives Libor − y.

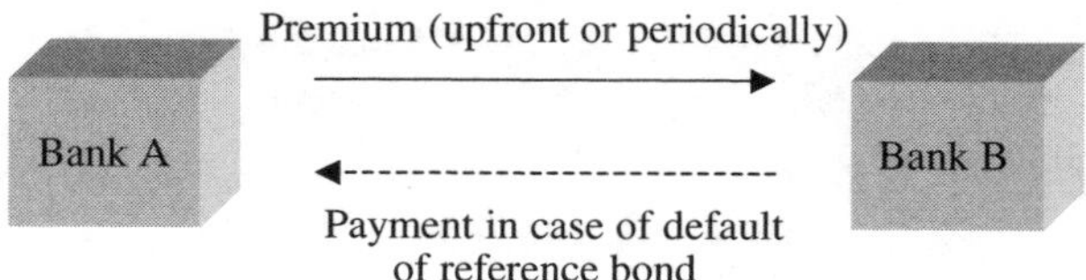

Figure 5.2: A standard default swap transaction

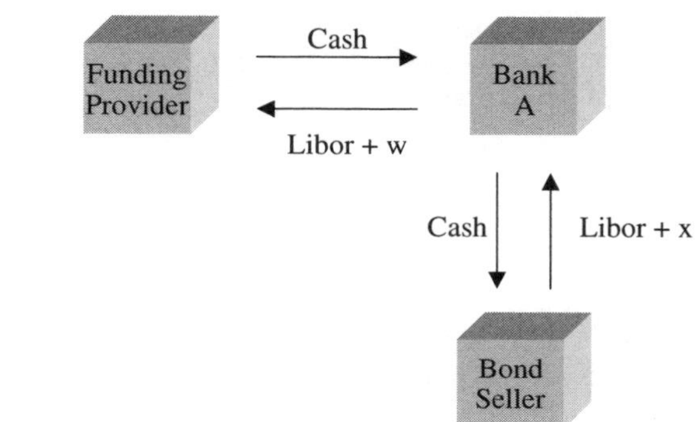

Figure 5.3: Bank A hedges a long default swap position by going long the underlying bond (Bank A's income is x − w)

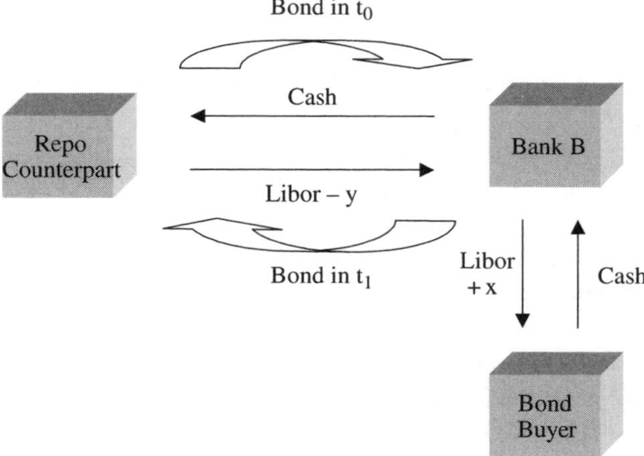

Figure 5.4: Bank B hedges a short default swap position by borrowing the bond in the Repo market and shorting it;[5] bank B's cost is x − (−y) = x + y

From figures 5.3 and 5.4 we can conclude that the income of the hedge for bank A is x − w. The cost for bank B is x + y. Hence, if the default swap price is derived on the basis of hedging costs, the price of the default swap lies between x − w and x + y. Let's look at an example.

Example 5.1: Bank A is long a default swap, bank B is short the default swap. To hedge their position, bank A has to go long the underlying bond, bank B has to borrow the bond in the Repo market and short it.

Bank A's funding cost is Libor + 50. The bond pays Libor + 200. Bank B's interest rate received in the Repo is Libor − 30. Thus w = 50, x = 200 and y = 30. Therefore the default swap price lies between 200 − 50 = 150 basis point and 200 + 30 = 230 basis points.

Note that if the banks A and B agree on a price of 200 basis points, they will both lose money on the deal: Bank A pays 200 basis points for the default swap and receives 150 basis points in the hedge. Bank B receives 200 basis points from selling the default swap, but pays 230 basis points in the hedge.

The reasons why both banks might still enter into the default swap transaction, are the following:

- Bank A might be willing to pay a high price for the default swap, since the default swap might free credit lines to enable further credits to the client;
- Bank B might be a speculator and be willing to sell the default swap for 200 basis points;
- The default swap might increase the diversification for bank A and bank B;
- The low rating of bank A or bank B might make the default swap attractive relative to funding the transaction in the cash market;
- Due to low liquidity in the cash market, the default swap might still be more attractive than a cash deal;
- The off-balance-sheet feature might make the default swap more attractive than a cash transaction.

It is important to mention, that the profit of the hedged position for bank A and bank B depends on the funding cost and the interest rate paid in the Repo. In the above example 5.1, the breakeven default swap premium for both banks is 230 basis points if the funding cost of bank A is Libor − 30.

If the funding cost of bank A is even lower than Libor − 30 and the interest paid in the Repo is higher than Libor − 30, one or both banks can achieve a profit on their hedged position. For example, if the funding of bank A is Libor − 40 and the interest rate paid in the Repo is Libor − 20, a default swap premium of 230 basis points leads to a profit of 10 basis points for bank A and bank B.

Deriving the default probability and the upfront default swap premium on a binomial model

Deriving the probability of default of the underlying debt is one of the most important features when pricing credit derivatives. In the following, we will present a simple binomial model to find the risk-neutral probability of default.

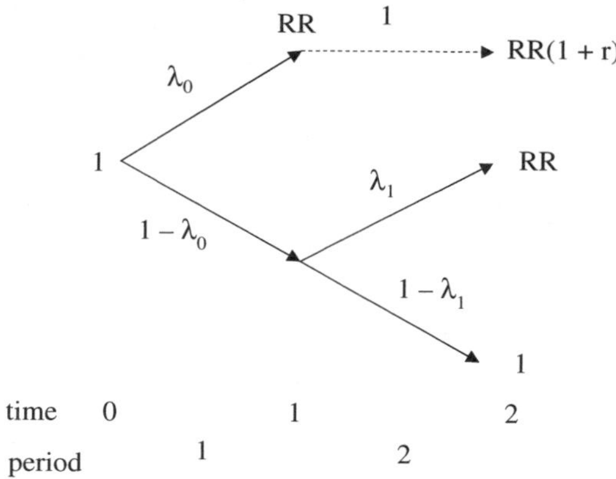

Figure 5.5: A two-period tree of risky debt with a notional amount of 1
λ_t = risk-neutral default probability in period t − 1;[6] RR = recovery rate (exogenous); r = risk-free interest rate.

Risk-neutrality is an important concept when pricing derivatives. If investors are risk-neutral, they do not require a compensation for taking risk. As a consequence, the expected return on all securities (including derivatives) is the risk-free interest rate. Hence, the present value of any security can be derived by discounting all future cash flows with the risk-free interest rate. The concept of risk-neutrality will be discussed in more detail in the section "Basic Properties of the Black-Scholes-Merton model," and "When to use martingale probabilities, when to use historical probabilities" in the presentation of the Jarrow-Lando-Turnbull 1997 model.

The binomial price tree of a two-period risky debt with a notional amount of 1 can be found in figure 5.5.

In figure 5.5 we can see that the value of the debt is set to 1 at time 0. At time 1 the debt has either defaulted with probability λ_0 and the debt will have a value of the recovery rate RR, or the debt will have not defaulted with probability $1 - \lambda_0$. It is assumed that the debt, if it has defaulted, will stay in default. Thus at time 2, the debt, if it has defaulted in time 1, will stay in default with a probability of 1 (dashed line in figure 5.5). Hence the received recovery rate RR at time 1 will increase to RR(1 + r) at time 2.

If the debt has not defaulted at time 1, it can either default at time 2 with probability λ_1, in which case the value of the debt is RR at time 2. If the debt does not default at time 2, the debt will mature with a value of 1 with a probability of $1 - \lambda_1$.

Let's now include the annual return of a risk-free debt r and an annual default swap premium of s in the tree. For a \$1 investment in the risk-free debt an investor receives 1 + r at the end of period 1. Also, if we solve equation (2.1b), Return on risk-free asset r = Return on risky asset − Default swap premium (p.a.) s, for the risky bond return we get:

Return on risky asset = Return on risk-free asset r + Default swap premium (p.a.). s

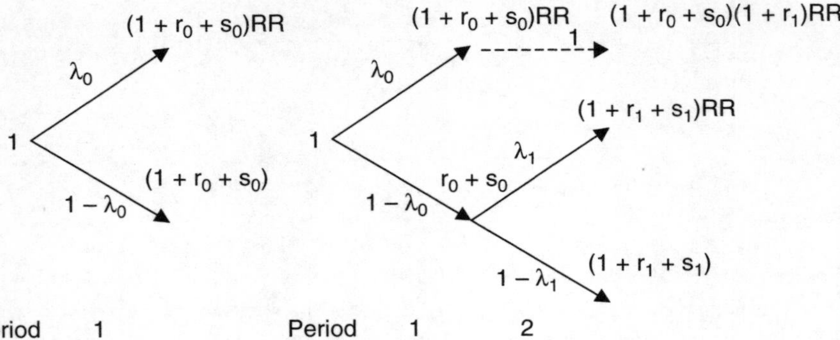

Figure 5.6: Cash flows of a one-period and a two-period risky debt issue with a notional amount of 1

λ_t: risk-neutral default probability in period $t-1$; RR: recovery rate (exogenous); r: risk-free interest rate; s: default swap premium.

Thus the risky investment of \$1 will grow to $1 + r + s$ at the end of period 1. If we include these cash flows, we derive for a one-period debt and a two-period debt issue the binomial trees as in figure 5.6.

We can now find the risk-neutral probability of default during period 1, λ_0, by using the risk-neutral relationship that the expected return of the risk-free debt, $1 + r_0$, must be equal to the expected return of the default probability weighted risky debt. From the one-period tree in figure 5.6, we derive the returns at the end of period 1:

$$1+r_0 = \lambda_0 RR(1+r_0+s_0)+(1-\lambda_0)(1+r_0+s_0). \tag{5.2}$$

Dividing equation (5.2) by $(1 + r_0)$, we find another intuitive interpretation from equation (5.2a):

$$1=[\lambda_0 RR(1+r_0+s_0)+(1-\lambda_0)(1+r_0+s_0)]/(1+r_0). \tag{5.2a}$$

Equation (5.2a) reflects the risk-neutral pricing principle: all expected cash flows $[\lambda_0 RR(1 + r_0 + s_0) + (1 - \lambda_0)(1 + r_0 + s_0)]$ are discounted with the risk-free rate r_0, to derive the (given) present value of 1.

Solving equation (5.2) or (5.2a) for the risk-neutral probability of default in period 1, λ_0, we derive:

$$\lambda_0 = \frac{s_0}{(1+r_0+s_0)(1-RR)} \tag{5.3}$$

The values of r_0 and s_0 can be found in the market. However, to derive λ_0, we have to also determine the recovery rate RR. This can be done by observing the recovery rate of previously defaulted debt with identical seniority in the same sector as the underlying debt. Let's look at deriving the probability of default in an example.

Example 5.2: The 1-year risk-free interest rate r = 5%, the 1-year default swap premium s = 3%, and the recovery rate is assumed to be RR = 60%. What is the risk-neutral probability of default in period 1? It is:

$$\lambda_0 = \frac{0.03}{(1+0.05+0.03)(1-0.6)} = 6.94\%.$$

In order to derive λ_1, the risk-neutral default probability in period 2, we can equate the risk-free return at time 2, $(1 + r_0)(1 + r_1)$, to the probability weighted payoff of the risky debt in period 1 and 2. The reader should notice that r_1 is the *forward* interest rate from time 1 to time 2.[7] Correspondingly λ_1 is the default probability in period 2, so also a forward variable, which is realized at time 2. Thus, from the two-period tree in figure 5.6 we derive:

$$\begin{aligned}(1+r_0)(1+r_1) = {} & \lambda_0 RR(1+s_0+r_0)(1+r_1) + \\ & (1-\lambda_0)[(r_0+s_0)(1+r_1)+\lambda_1 RR(1+r_1+s_1)+(1-\lambda_1)(1+r_1+s_1)].\end{aligned}$$

In the above equation derived from figure 5.6, we compare all values at time 2. Hence the first term λ_0 RR $(1 + s_0 + r_0)$ $(1 + r_1)$ reflects the fact that if default occurs at time 1, the investor receives RR $(1 + s_0 + r_0)$ with probability λ_0 and can invest this return at the risk-free interest rate r_1. The term $(r_0 + s_0)(1 + r_1)$ reflects the fact that looking from time 0, the proceeds at time 1 in case of no default $(r_0 + s_0)$ are certain and thus can be reinvested at the risk-free rate r_1.

Solving for the risk-neutral default probability in period 2, λ_1, we get:

$$\lambda_1 = \frac{\left(\dfrac{(1+r_0)(1+r_1)-\lambda_0 RR(1+r_0+s_0)(1+r_1)}{(1-\lambda_0)}\right)-(r_0+s_0)(1+r_1)-1-r_1-s_1}{RR(1+r_1+s_1)-1-r_1-s_1}. \tag{5.4}$$

Example 5.3: The 1-year risk-free interest rate r_0 is 5% and the forward risk-free interest rate r_1 from time 1 to time 2 is 6%. The default premium for the first year is 3% and the forward default swap premium from time 1 to time 2 is 3.5%. The recovery rate is assumed to be 60%. What is the probability of default in period 2? Following equation (5.4) it is

$$\lambda_1 = \frac{\left(\dfrac{\begin{array}{c}(1+0.05)(1+0.06)-0.0694\times 0.6\times \\ (1+0.05+0.03)(1+0.06)\end{array}}{(1-0.0694)}\right)-(0.05+0.03)(1+0.06)-1-0.06-0.035}{0.6\times(1+0.06+0.035)-1-0.06-0.035}$$

$$=7.99\%.$$

See www.dersoft.com/ex53.xls for this example.

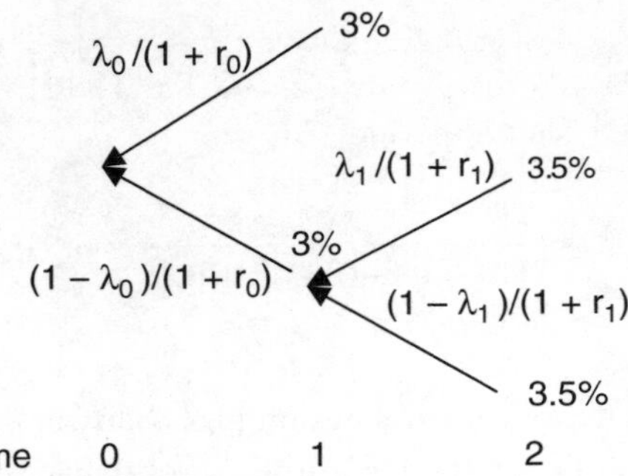

Figure 5.7: Probability weights and discount factors in a two-period tree

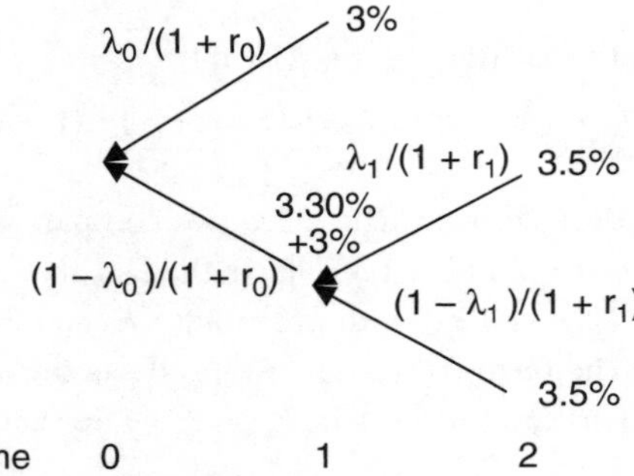

Figure 5.8: Probability weights and discount factors in a two-period binomial tree including the discounted value of the default swap premiums of time 2

Naturally, the risk-neutral default probabilities for a more than 2-period model can be derived by iteratively extending equations (5.3) and (5.4). A multi-period model can be found at www.dersoft.com/binomialdefaultmodel.xls.

To derive the upfront default swap premium, we have to weight the default swap premiums with their risk-neutral probability of occurrence and discount these with the risk-free interest rate. For our 2-period tree this can be seen in figure 5.7.

Following figure 5.7, we find the value of the default swap premiums at time 1 with $\lambda_1 = 7.99\%$ and $r_1 = 6\%$ as $3.5\% \times 0.0799 / (1 + 0.06) + 3.5\% \times (1 - 0.0799) / (1 + 0.06) = 3.30\%$. Integrating this value in figure 5.7 gives the result shown in figure 5.8.

Following figure 5.8, the upfront default swap premium at time 0 of the two-period default swap is $[(3\% + 3.30\%)(1 - 0.0694) / (1 + 0.05)] + [3\% \times 0.0694 / (1 + 0.05)] = 5.78\%$.

It should be mentioned that in figure 5.6 and equations (5.2) to (5.4) we assumed that the recovery rate RR is applied to the notional amount of 1 *and* the coupon r + s, hence to 1 + r + s. It is also reasonable to assume that the recovery rate only applies to the notional amount of 1. In this case figure 5.6 would simplify to figure 5.9.

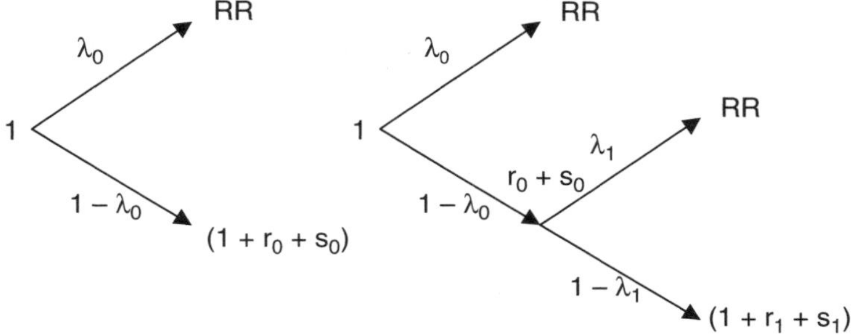

Figure 5.9: Cash flows of one-period and two-period binomial risky debt with a notional amount of 1 assuming the recovery rate is only paid to the notional amount

Equation (5.2) would then read (5.2b) $1 + r_0 = \lambda_0 \text{ RR} + (1 - \lambda_0)(1 + r_0 + s_0)$ and equation (5.3) would read (5.3a) $\lambda_0 = \frac{s_0}{(1 + r_0 + s_0 - \text{RR})}$.

In the following, before we price credit derivatives in the Black-Scholes-Merton environment, let's look at some basic properties of this approach.

Basic Properties of the Black-Scholes-Merton model

A *stochastic process* describes the uncertain course that a variable follows through time. In 1973 Fischer Black, Myron Scholes, and Robert Merton transferred a stochastic process from physics to finance: the *generalized Wiener process*. According to this concept a variable grows with an average drift rate μ. Superimposed on this growth rate is a stochastic term, which adds volatility to the process.

If the relative change of a variable follows a generalized Wiener process, this is typically referred to as a *geometric Brownian motion*. Applied to stock prices, we derive that the relative change of a stock price S, dS/S, follows a path with an average expected growth rate μ, which is comprised of the expected stock price change plus the dividend. Superimposed on this growth rate is a noise term, which consists of the expected volatility of the stock σ multiplied with a Wiener process dz:

$$dS/S = \mu dt + \sigma dz \tag{5.5}$$

where

dS: change in the stock price S

μ: drift rate, which is the expected stock return (price change + dividends)

dt: infinitely short time period

σ: expected volatility of the stock price S

dz: $\varepsilon\sqrt{dt}$, where ε is a random drawing from a standardized normal distribution. All drawings are independent from each other.

μ dt in equation (5.5) is the expected return during period dt. σ dz is the stochastic part of the relative change of S.

The discrete version of equation (5.5) is

$$\Delta S/S = \mu\Delta t + \sigma\Delta z. \tag{5.6}$$

Let's look at equation (5.6) in an example.

Example 5.4: The present stock price is \$150, next year's expected return is 20%, the annual expected volatility is 30%. The sample drawing from a standardized normal distribution results in +1. What is the expected stock price in one day (= 1/365) due to the geometric Brownian motion?

Due to equation (5.6), the one-day change of the stock is $\Delta S = \$150 \times [(0.2 \times 1/365) + 0.3 \times 1 \times \sqrt{1/365}] = \$2.44$.

Thus, the stock price after one day is assumed to be \$150 + \$2.44 = \$152.44.

Since this stock price prediction is partly determined by a random drawing from a normal distribution, this prediction methodology is called a *random walk* process. If a price follows a random walk process, this means that due to the random nature of the process, principally no above market return trading strategy can be formulated.

This is consistent with the *efficient market hypothesis*, which says that all information about a stock is already incorporated in the current stock price. As a consequence, the past information of a stock price is irrelevant and the future process of a stock price depends only on its value at the beginning of the period. This property is also referred to as the *Markov property*. This property denies the essential hypothesis of technical analysis, which suggests that the future stock price can be derived from the past pattern of the stock price.

If a generalized Wiener process has no drift rate, thus $\mu = 0$, this is typically referred to as a *martingale*. A martingale has the convenient property that the expected value E of a random variable X at a future time t is equal to the current value of the variable: $E(X_t) = X_0$. Using this logic, a zero-coupon bond is not a martingale, since it will increase in time to its notional amount, assuming no default. Hence for a zero coupon bond we derive $E(X_t) > X_0$. It may also be argued that stock prices are not martingales, since stock prices increase on average in time. In the Black-Scholes-Merton environment the expected stock growth rate is the risk-free interest rate r, which is the growth rate of all assets, including derivatives.

Martingales are often compared to a "fair game." For example when playing roulette the probability of winning when betting on black is always 18/37 (assuming there are 18 black, 18 red, and 1 green (the zero) possibility) independent of what the previous outcome was. With the same logic the game blackjack is not a martingale, since the outcome of a game depends on the previous cards, assuming the cards are not put back into the stack.

Martingales also have convenient mathematical properties. Let's define θ as a *trading strategy* for security X, $\theta > 0$ representing a long position in X, and $\theta < 0$ representing a short position in X. We can now express a portfolio of θ units in X as a stochastic integral $\int_0^t \theta_s dx_s$. This is a martingale if X is a martingale, thus we can derive complex continuous martingales from simpler martingales. Since $\int_0^t \theta_s dx_s$ is a martingale, we can derive the convenient property from equation $E(X_t) = X_0$ that $E\left(\int_0^t \theta_s dX_s\right) = 0$.

We further assume that a *money market account* exists, which has a notional amount of \$1 at time zero and which grows with the risk-free interest rate r. Assuming reinvestment at r_k, the price of the money market bond for discrete time periods and discrete r is $M_t = \prod_{k=1}^{t-1}(1+r_k)$. For discrete time and with continuously compounded r, $M_t = \exp\left(\sum_{k=1}^{t-1} r_k\right)$.[8] For continuous time and a continuously compounded r we get $M_t = \exp\left(\int_0^t r(s)ds\right)$. The purpose of introducing the risk-free money market account is to fund the trading strategy θ. If an investor needs to borrow cash for the strategy, he can short the money market bond B_t to receive the cash. We will abstract from additional cost for borrowing B. The money market bond is often used as a *numeraire*, i.e. the unit in which profit and loss are measured. Principally any tradable asset with a strictly positive price process can serve as a numeraire.

While an investment in the money market grows with the risk-free interest rate r, a risky asset grows with the expected return of the risky asset μ, consider equations (5.5) and (5.6). The relationship between r and μ was expressed first by William Sharpe in his famous paper in 1966.[9] Sharpe stated that an investor wants to be compensated for taking risk, the risk being expressed as the volatility of the invested asset i, σ_i. The compensation for the risk is reflected in the excess return of the asset i, $\mu_i - r$:

$$\chi_i = \frac{\mu_i - r}{\sigma_i} \tag{5.7}$$

where χ is the Sharpe ratio, often referred to as the *market price of risk*. In a risk-neutral world, where investors are indifferent to risk, every asset grows with the same expected rate, which is the risk-free interest rate r. If we apply Sharpe's concept, the expected growth rate, solving equation (5.7) for r, is $\mu_i - \chi_i\sigma_i$.

Arbitrage is – as in chapter 4 – again narrowly defined as a risk-free profit. Formally, arbitrage exists if the trading strategy θ increases the wealth W with probability P of 1: If $W_0 = 0 \Rightarrow W_t > 0$ with $P = 1$ and $t > 0$. A trading strategy is called *self-financing* if the change in wealth W is solely derived by borrowing in the money market and/or from gains and losses of the trading strategy.

With the help of Ito's lemma,[10] Black, Scholes, and Merton found the famous partial differential equation (PDE) for valuing a derivative D:

$$D = \frac{\partial D}{\partial t}\frac{1}{r} + \frac{\partial D}{\partial S}S + \frac{1}{2}\frac{\partial^2 D}{\partial S^2}\frac{1}{r}\sigma^2 S^2 \tag{5.8}$$

where r is the risk-free interest rate, S is the price of the underlying asset (e.g. the stock price), and σ is again the volatility of the underlying asset.

For every derivative that satisfies the PDE (5.8), a dynamic, self-financing trading strategy can be created that replicates the derivative. For example, a long put can be replicated by selling the delta amount of the underlying. This property is also referred to as *completeness*. If the PDE (5.8) is satisfied, going long the derivative and short the portfolio or vice versa, is *arbitrage-free*, arbitrage in this case being defined narrowly as a risk-free profit.

Also – arguably luckily – the variable μ drops out during the process of creating the PDE. Therefore, no variable regarding the risk-preference of an investor is present. Thus, the PDE is *risk-neutral*. This means that the expected growth rate of all securities (including derivatives) under the risk-netural probability measure is the risk-free interest rate. If a security is expected to grow by more than the risk-free rate, investors will buy it and hence increase the price and reduce the rate of return to the risk-free rate, and vice versa.

Since a derivative is a *contingent claim* on an underlying security based on the specified input parameters, the Black-Scholes-Merton framework is called the arbitrage-free, risk-neutral, contingent claim pricing methodology.

One equation that satisfies the PDE, equation (5.8), is the famous Black-Scholes equation for valuing European style options.[11] For a call C:

$$C = SN(d_1) - Ke^{-rT}N(d_2) \tag{5.9}$$

where

$$d_1 = \frac{\ln\left[\frac{S}{Ke^{-rT}}\right] + \frac{1}{2}\sigma^2 T}{\sigma\sqrt{T}} \quad \text{and} \quad d_2 = d_1 - \sigma\sqrt{T}$$

where N: cumulative standard normal distribution; S: stock price; K: strike price; ln: natural logarithm; σ: volatility of the underlying asset, in this case the stock price; T: option maturity expressed in years; r: risk-free continuously compounded interest rate.

After having discussed the Black-Scholes-Merton framework, we will introduce two approaches to value credit-spread options on slightly modified Black-Scholes equations.

Valuing credit-spread options on a modified Black-Scholes equation where the credit-spread is modeled as a single variable

As discussed in chapter 2, a credit-spread option is an option on the difference between the yield of a risky asset and the yield of a risk-free asset. A credit-spread is defined as in equation (2.4):

Credit-spread = Yield of risky bond − Yield of risk-free bond.

We defined the payoff of a credit-spread put and a credit-spread call at option maturity T in equations (2.5) and (2.6) as:

$$\text{Payoff credit-spread put (T)} = \text{Duration} \times N \times \max(\text{Credit-spread (T)} - \text{Strike spread}, 0) \quad (2.5)$$

$$\text{Payoff credit-spread call (T)} = \text{Duration} \times N \times \max(\text{Strike spread} - \text{Credit-spread (T)}, 0) \quad (2.6)$$

where duration is defined in equation (2.8) as $D = -\frac{\partial B/B}{\partial y} = \sum_{t=1}^{T} tc_t e^{-yt}/B$, N is the notional amount of the swap, and the strike spread as in equations (2.5) and (2.6) is determined at option start.

One of the simplest approaches to value a credit-spread option is to model the credit-spread as a single variable S. We then apply a slight modification of the original Black-Scholes equation (5.9). In equation (5.9), the variable S grew with the risk-free interest rate r. This is not a reasonable assumption for a credit-spread. Setting the growth rate of the credit-spread to zero, we derive equation (5.9a)

$$C = e^{-rT}[SN(d_1) - KN(d_2)] \quad (5.9a)$$

where

$$d_1 = \frac{\ln\left(\frac{S}{K}\right) + \frac{1}{2}\sigma^2 T}{\sigma\sqrt{T}} \quad \text{and} \quad d_2 = d_1 - \sigma\sqrt{T}$$

where S is now the current credit-spread and σ is the annual volatility of this spread. All other variables are as defined in equation (5.9). Equation (5.9a) is also used to value options on futures where S in equation (5.9a) is the current futures price. It should be mentioned that the modified equation (5.9a) does not satisfy the PDE, equation (5.8). Hence, no self-financing replicating strategy can be created.

Let's look at an example of pricing a credit-spread option with equation (5.9a).

Example 5.5: Given is a current credit-spread of 3.30% and a strike spread of 3%. The notional amount is \$1,000,000, the duration is 3.67, and the option maturity is 1 year. The risk-free interest rate is 5% and the annual volatility of the credit-spread is 150%. What is the credit-spread put option premium?

The reader should first recall that the payoffs in the credit-spread market are reversed, as expressed in equation (2.5) and (2.6) and discussed in chapter 2. So to value a put we have to use equation (5.9a) and we derive for

$$d_1 = \frac{\ln\left(\frac{0.033}{0.03}\right) + \frac{1}{2}1.5^2 \times 1}{1.5\sqrt{1}} = 0.8135 \quad \text{and} \quad d_2 = 0.8135 - 1.5\sqrt{1} = -0.6865.$$

N(0.8135) = 0.7921 and N(−0.6865) = 0.2462; see table A.1 in the appendix or use the Excel function normsdist(0.8135) = 0.7921 and normsdist(−0.6865) = 0.2462).

From equation (5.9a) we derive $e^{-0.05\times 1}(0.033 \times 0.7921 - 0.03 \times 0.2462) = 0.0178$. Multiplying this with the constant factors duration and notional amount we derive the credit-spread put price as 0.0178 × 3.67 × \$1,000,000 = \$65,326. Compare www.dersoft.com/csobs.xls for this derivation as well as for the derivation of the credit-spread call price.

The simple approach of equation (5.9a) has some serious drawbacks. First, since the spread is modeled as a single variable, due to the log-normality assumption, the credit-spread cannot be negative. While this assumption is reasonable for a credit-spread between a risky asset and a risk-free asset, it is clearly not reasonable for a spread between two risky assets. Second, due to the single variable approach, the individual features of the underlying two yields such as yield level, yield volatility, and the yield correlation are not inputs of the model. Naturally, all drawbacks of the Black-Scholes approach apply, such as constant volatility, constant interest rates, and the inability to price American style options. Counterparty default risk is also not included in the approach.

Valuing credit-spread options on a modified Black-Scholes equation as an exchange option

Two counterparties may agree to simply exchange the yield of a risky asset and the yield of a risk-free asset. Hence the payoff is:

$$\max(y_2 - y_1, 0) \tag{5.10}$$

where

y_2: yield of the risky asset

y_1: yield of the risk-free asset.

The payoff in equation (5.10) reduces to $y_2 - y_1$, assuming that the risky bond cannot have a lower yield than the risk-free bond. The reader should note that since there is no strike in the payoff definition of equation (5.10), a distinction between call and put is not reasonable.

An option with a payoff of equation (5.10) is a frequently traded exotic option, termed an *exchange option*. William Margrave was the first to derive a closed form solution to value exchange options on a modified Black-Scholes equation.[12]

In order to value a credit exchange option on the basis of the Margrave model, we have to add the credit industry standard duration term of the risky asset 2, D(2) and the notional amount N. We then receive the payoff:

$$D(2)\,N\max(y_2 - y_1, 0)$$

and the resulting valuation equation for the credit exchange option $'E$ is:

$$'E = e^{-rT} D(2) N[y_2 N(d_1) - y_1 N(d_2)] \tag{5.11}$$

where

$$d_1 = \frac{\ln\left[\frac{y_2}{y_1}\right] + \frac{1}{2}\sigma^2 T}{\sigma\sqrt{T}} \quad \text{and} \quad d_2 = d_1 - \sigma\sqrt{T}$$

and σ: volatility of y_2/y_1, $\sigma = \sqrt{\sigma_1^2 + \sigma_2^2 - 2\rho\sigma_1\sigma_2}$, where

σ_1: yield volatility asset 1

σ_2: yield volatility of asset 2

ρ: correlation coefficient of the yields y_1 and y_2.

The exchange option value $'E$ has a negative dependence on the correlation coefficient ρ, $\partial E/\partial \rho < 0$. This is an expected result, since the more negative the correlation coefficient ρ, the higher will be the volatility of the difference between the two yields, and consequently the higher the expected payoff and option value. Furthermore, intuitively, the exchange option value $'E$ has a positive dependence on both the yield volatility of the asset 1 and asset 2, σ_1 and σ_2.

Example 5.6: The current yield of a risk-free asset 1, y_1, is 5% and the current yield of a risky asset 2, y_2, is 7%. The option maturity T is one year, the duration of the risky asset 2, D(2) is 3.67, and the notional amount N is $1,000,000. The risk-free interest rate r is 4%, the yield volatility of asset 1, σ_1, is 20% and the yield volatility of asset 2, σ_2, is 50%. The yield correlation coefficient is 0.5. What is the price of a credit-spread option with a payoff D(2) N $\max(y_2 - y_1, 0)$?

Following equation (5.11), the volatility is $\sigma = \sqrt{0.2^2 + 0.5^2 - 2 \times 0.5 \times 0.2 \times 0.5}$ = 43.59%.

$$d_1 = \frac{\ln\left[\frac{0.07}{0.05}\right] + \frac{1}{2}0.4359^2 \times \sqrt{1}}{0.4359 \times 1} = 0.9899 \text{ and } d_2 = 0.9899 - 0.4359 \times \sqrt{1} = 0.5540.$$

N(0.9899) = 0.8389 and N(0.5540) = 0.7102. Hence the credit exchange option value is:

$$e^{-0.05 \times 1} \times 3.67 \times \$1{,}000{,}000[0.07 \times 0.8389 - 0.05 \times 0.7102] = \$81{,}032.$$

A model which prices credit-spread options as an exchange option can be found at www.dersoft.com/csoex.xls.

The valuation approach of equation (5.11) is an improvement on equation (5.9a) since it includes the individual yield volatilities and the yield correlation. However, equation (5.11) does not include counterparty default risk and has, due to the Black-Scholes framework, constant volatilities and no mean reversion of interest rates.

Valuing credit-spread options on a term-structure based model

A term structure of interest rates describes the uncertain path that interest rates take through time. The interest rate that is modeled is the *short rate*, also called *instantaneous rate*, which applies to an infinitesimally short period of time. The short rate process is usually displayed in the form of a discrete or continuous binomial or trinomial model.

One of the first term structure models is the Cox-Ross-Rubinstein (CRR) (1979) model. The model is sometimes credited to Rendleman-Bartter (1980). Some sources (e.g. Smithson 1992) mention Sharpe (1978) as the original author, who outlined the basics of the concept of the CRR model.

The CRR model can be expressed as:

$$dr/r = \mu dt + \sigma dz \tag{5.12}$$

where

r: short-term interest rate

μ: expected growth rate

σ: expected volatility of r

dz: Wiener process, as discussed in equation (5.5) and example 5.4.

Equation (5.12) states that the relative change in the short rate r, dr/r, is comprised of two terms. The first term μ dt represents the expected average growth rate of r. The second term, σdz, adds the volatility, also called "noise" to the process. The higher the volatility σ, the greater the possibility that dr/r will deviate from the expected growth path μ.

The attentive reader will notice that equation (5.5) expressing stock price behavior and equation (5.12) expressing interest rate behavior are mathematically identical. Hence Cox, Ross, and Rubinstein model the short rate the same way that stock prices are often modeled in finance.

Other more complex term structure models for the short rate are Vasicek (1977), Cox-Ingersoll-Ross (1985), or the no-arbitrage models of Ho-Lee (1986), Black-Derman-Toy (1990), and Hull-White (1990). Heath, Jarrow and Morton (1992) model an entire term structure of instantaneous forward rates, while Brace, Gatared, and Musiela (Libor market model) (1997) model an entire term structure of forward Libor rates.

We will now value a credit-spread option on the Hull-White trinomial model.[13] The model is expressed as:

$$dr = [\theta(t) - ar]dt + \sigma dz \tag{5.13}$$

where

θ: function chosen so that the model fits the current term structure
a: mean reversion of r
other variables as defined in equation (5.12).

The key equations in the Hull-White model are:

$$P_{m+1} = \sum_{j=-n_m}^{n_m} Q_{m,j} e^{[-(\alpha_m + j\Delta R)\Delta t]}. \tag{5.14}$$

Solving equation (5.14) for α_m we derive:

$$\alpha_m = \frac{\ln \sum_{j=-n_m}^{n_m} Q_{m,j} e^{-j\Delta R \Delta t} - \ln P_{m+1}}{\Delta t}. \tag{5.15}$$

Furthermore:

$$Q_{m+1,j} = \sum_{k} Q_{m,k} q(k,j) e^{[-(\alpha_m + k\Delta R)\Delta t]} \tag{5.16}$$

where

P_{m+1}: zero coupon bond maturing at time m + 1
n_m: number of nodes on each side of the central node at time $m\Delta t$
Q_m: present value of a security at time m that pays \$1 if node (i,j) is reached and zero otherwise
R*: discrete interest rate for time Δt on a tree that is evenly spaced and has a zero slope
R: discrete interest rate for time Δt on a tree that matches the current term structure
α: variable that transforms an evenly spaced zero slope tree with interest rates R* into a tree that matches the upward (or downward) slope of the term structure with interest rates R – hence $\alpha(t) = R(t) - R^*(t)$
i: horizontal parameter of node (i,j)
j: vertical parameter of node (i,j)
q (k,j): probability of moving from node (m,k) to node (m + 1,j); the summation is taken over all values of k for which the probability is non-zero.

In an iterative, forward inductive process, first the $Q_{m,j}$ values are derived with equation (5.14) and the input of the market given zero bond price P_m. The value for α_m is then derived with equation (5.15). The value of α_m is then used to transform R into R* via $\alpha(t) = R(t) - R^*(t)$. In the next time step the values for $Q_{m+1,j}$ are derived, which give α_{m+1}, and so on.

The concept of a 3-period trinomial tree can be seen in figure 5.10. A model of the Hull-White trinomial tree can be found at www.dersoft.com/hwtri.xls.

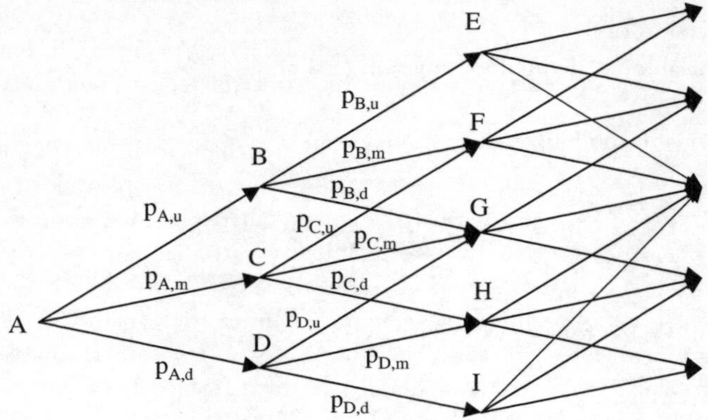

Figure 5.10: Three-period Hull-White trinomial tree
$p_{X,u}$, $p_{X,m}$, $p_{X,d}$: risk-neutral probability of moving from node X up, middle, and down, respectively; probabilities on the same level are identical, for example $p_{A,u} = p_{C,u} = p_{G,u}$; $p_{A,m} = p_{C,m} = p_{G,m}$ and $p_{A,d} = p_{C,d} = p_{G,d}$ (compare with figure 5.11).

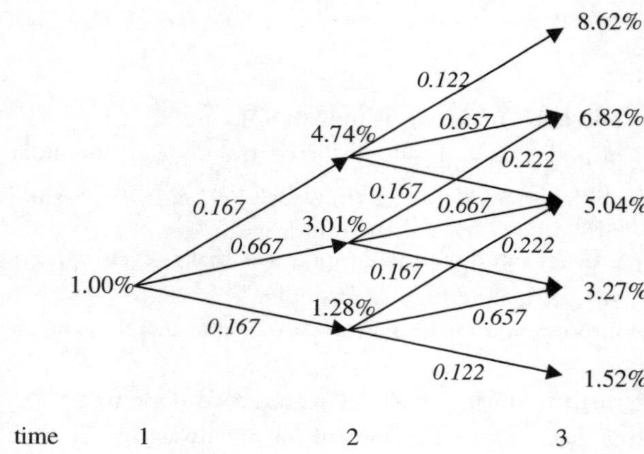

Figure 5.11: Hull-White two-period credit-spread tree with a 1%, 2%, and 3% credit-spread for year 1, 2, and 3 respectively and a mean reversion of 0.1 and volatility of 1% (spread rates are expressed as continuously compounded one-year rates)

Let's now evaluate a credit-spread option on the Hull-White tree. We first have to create a credit-spread tree. Let's assume an issuer has a bond with a 1-year credit-spread of 1%, the two-year credit-spread of 2%, and the 3-year credit-spread of 3%. Using these data in combination with the Hull-White trinomial model with $\Delta t = 1$ year, and the parameters 0.1 for the mean reversion a, and 1% for the volatility σ, we derive figure 5.11. The Hull-White trinomial model to evaluate credit-spread puts and calls can be found at www.dersoft.com/csohw.xls.

We can now use standard discrete option valuation techniques to value a credit-spread option.

Example 5.7: Given is a two-year credit-spread put option with a payoff as in equation (2.5): Duration × N × max[credit-spread (T) − strike spread, 0]. For the option price derivation we can currently ignore the constant factors Duration and N and implement them later.

Let's look at a credit-spread put option with a strike spread of 3% and an option maturity at time t = 2. At option maturity, the value of the option is just the intrinsic value: max[credit-spread (T) − strike spread, 0]. Hence for node E (see figures 5.10 and 5.11) we derive max(8.62% − 3%, 0) = 0.0562. For the other nodes we derive F = 0.0382, G = 0.0204, H = 0.0027 and I = 0. We now have to discount these values at time 2 weighted by their probabilities back to time 1. Let's assume the risk-free interest rate from time 1 to time 2 is 5%. (In a more sophisticated analysis we could apply an interest rate term structure tree to have different discount factors for each probability.)

$$\text{Node B} = e^{-(0.05\times 1)} \times [0.0562 \times 0.122 + 0.0382 \times 0.657 + 0.0204 \times 0.222] = 0.0347$$

$$\text{Node C} = e^{-(0.05\times 1)} \times [0.0382 \times 0.167 + 0.0204 \times 0.667 + 0.0027 \times 0.167] = 0.0194$$

$$\text{Node D} = e^{-(0.05\times 1)} \times [0.0204 \times 0.222 + 0.0027 \times 0.657 + 0 \times 0.122] = 0.0060$$

Finally we have to discount the option values from time 1 back to time 0. Let's assume the interest rate from time 0 to time 1 is 4%. For the credit-spread put option value at time 0 we derive:

$$\text{Node A} = e^{-(0.04\times 1)} \times [0.0347 \times 0.167 + 0.0194 \times 0.667 + 0.006 \times 0.167] = 0.0190 \text{ or } 1.90\%.$$

To derive the credit-spread put option price in equation (2.5) Duration × N × max[credit-spread (T) − strike spread, 0], we have to add the duration and notional amount. If the duration is 3.67 and the notional amount is \$1,000,000, the credit-spread put option price is 3.67 × \$1,000,000 × 0.0190 = \$69,730.

See www.dersoft.com/ex57 for this example.

In order to value a credit-spread *call* option with a payoff as in equation (2.6), Duration × N × max[strike spread − credit-spread (T), 0] only a minor change to the evaluation in example 5.7 has to be done. The only difference is the intrinsic value at the last node, which in the case of a credit-spread call is max[strike spread − credit-spread (T), 0]. Then the same analysis as for a put (as in example 5.7) can be applied to derive the present value of the credit-spread call option. A credit-spread call with the inputs of example 5.7 comes out to 0.03%.

A simple spreadsheet for a put and call of example 5.7 can be found at www.dersoft.com/ex57.xls. As mentioned above, for a complete Hull-White trinomial model to evaluate credit-spread options, see www.dersoft.com/csohw.xls.

The advantage of using a term structure model is that we can incorporate the mean reversion of credit-spreads in the model. Also, the credit-spreads fit the initial term structure of credit-spreads in the market and we can evaluate American style credit-spread options. The drawback of the term structure approach is again that the individual features of the risky and risk-free bond, i.e. the individual yield level, yield volatility, and the yield correlation, are not inputs of the model.

After having derived the credit-spread option price with two modified Black-Scholes approaches and a term structure model, let's now look at the valuation of credit derivatives on a group of models termed *structural models*.

Structural Models

Structural models derive the probability of default by analyzing the capital structure of a firm, especially the value of the firm's assets compared to the value of the firm's debt. Structural models can be divided into *firm value models* and *first-time passage models*. In firm value models, bankruptcy occurs when the asset value of a company is below the debt value at the maturity of the debt T. In first-time passage models, bankruptcy occurs when the asset value drops below a pre-defined, usually exogenous barrier, allowing for bankruptcy before the maturity of the debt. Structural models have close ties to the Merton 1974 model. Let's have an in-depths look at it.

The original 1974 Merton model

In 1974 Robert Merton in a seminal paper created a firm value model to estimate a company's value of debt and the probability of default.[14]

The Merton call

Merton combined the simple equation, shareholders' equity (E) = company's assets (V) − company's liabilities (D), with the Black-Scholes option pricing framework. Merton's model is mathematically identical with the original Black-Scholes equation (5.9) for valuing a call. However, the variables are reinterpreted:

$$E_0 = V_0 N(d_1) - De^{-rT} N(d_2) \tag{5.17}$$

where

$$d_1 = \frac{\ln\left[\frac{V_0}{De^{-rT}}\right] + \frac{1}{2}\sigma_V^2 T}{\sigma_V \sqrt{T}} \quad \text{and} \quad d_2 = d_1 - \sigma_V \sqrt{T}$$

where E_0 is the current value of equity, V_0 is the current value of assets, D is the debt to be repaid at time T, N is the cumulative standard normal distribution, r is the risk-free continuously compounded interest rate, σ_V is the expected volatility of the asset, and T is the option maturity, measured in years.

Equation (5.17) states that equity holders have a claim on the assets of a company: If the asset value V increases, the equity value E will increase with unlimited upside potential; on the downside, if the debt D exceeds the assets V, the company will go bankrupt. In this case the equity holders will take the remaining assets to repay part of the debt, the equity value being zero. This unlimited upside potential and limited downside risk is an essential option criteria and is reflected in the time value as seen in figure 5.12.

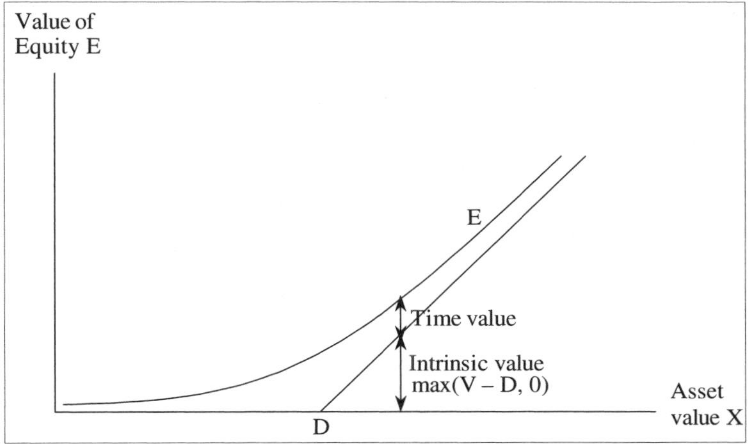

Figure 5.12: Intrinsic value and time value of Merton's credit model

In figure 5.12, the intrinsic value is max(V − D, 0). This intrinsic value plus the time value equals the value of the equity.

A well known property of the Black-Scholes model is that the risk-neutral probability of exercising a call option is $N(d_2)$. Therefore, the probability of not exercising the option is $N(-d_2)$. Not exercising the equity option means that the debt D is bigger than the assets V. This is the case of bankruptcy. Therefore, the probability of default in the Merton framework is $N(-d_2)$. Let's derive this default probability in a numerical example.

Example 5.8: The assets of company X are currently worth \$1,300,000. In 90 days company X has to repay \$1,000,000 in debt. The expected volatility of the assets is 30% and the risk-free interest rate is 5%. What is the probability of default in 90 days on the basis of the Merton model?

The probability of default is:

$$N(-d_2) = N\left(-\frac{\ln\left[\frac{V_0}{De^{-rT}}\right] + \frac{1}{2}\sigma_V^2 T}{\sigma_V\sqrt{T}} + \sigma_V\sqrt{T}\right)$$

$$= N\left(-\frac{\ln\left[\frac{1,300,00}{1,000,000 \times e^{-0.05\times 90/365}}\right] + \frac{1}{2}0.3^2 \times 90/365}{0.3\times\sqrt{90/365}} + 0.3\times\sqrt{90/365}\right)$$

$= N(-1.7695) = 3.84\%.$[15]

The Merton model can be found at www.dersoft.com/Mertonmodel.xls.

The Merton Put

The value of credit risk and the probability of a company's default in Merton's model can also be found by expressing credit risk with the help of a put option on the assets of the company: The equity holders can hedge the credit risk by buying a put on the assets with strike D, the put seller being the asset holders. In case of default, i.e. $V < D$, the equity holders will deliver the assets to the asset holders, the loss for the asset holders being $D - V$. Thus, the put option can be expressed as in equation (5.18)

$$P_0 = -V_0 N(-d_1) + De^{-rT} N(-d_2) \tag{5.18}$$

where

$$d_1 = \frac{\ln\left[\frac{V_0}{De^{-rT}}\right] + \frac{1}{2}\sigma_V^2 T}{\sigma_V \sqrt{T}} \quad \text{and} \quad d_2 = d_1 - \sigma_V \sqrt{T}$$

where P_0 is the current value of a put option on the company's assets V with strike D, and other variables are as defined in equation (5.9).

The equity holders will exercise the put option in equation (5.18) at time T if $D > V$. In the Merton model, this is the case of bankruptcy. Thus, the probability of exercising the put, which is $N(-d_2)$, is again the probability of default.

Rewriting equation (5.18) as $P_0 = \left(-\frac{N(-d_1)}{N(-d_2)} V_0 + De^{-rT}\right) N(-d_2)$ results in an intuitive interpretation of the default risk: The term $\frac{N(-d_1)}{N(-d_2)} V_0$ reflects the amount retrieved of the asset value V_0 in case of default, thus the recovery value. The term De^{-rT} is the present value of the debt, thus $\left(-\frac{N(-d_1)}{N(-d_2)} V_0 + De^{-rT}\right)$ is the present value of the loss in the event of default. Multiplying $\left(-\frac{N(-d_1)}{N(-d_2)} V_0 + De^{-rT}\right)$ with the probability of default $N(-d_2)$ gives the present value of the default risk, which equals the put value P_0.

The put option in equation (5.18) serves as a basis to find a closed form solution for the value of the underlying risky bond B. We can start by expressing B_0 as the debt D to be repaid at time T discounted by e^{-rT} minus the value of the credit risk, which is the put in equation (5.18):

$$B_0 = D_T e^{-rT} - [-V_0 N(-d_1) + D_T e^{-rT} N(-d_2)].$$

Using simple algebra and $1 - N(-d_2) = N(d_2)$ results in the value of the risky bond of:

$$B_0 = D_T e^{-rT} N(d_2) + VN(-d_1) \tag{5.19}$$

where

$$d_1 = \frac{\ln\left[\frac{V_0}{De^{-rT}}\right] + \frac{1}{2}\sigma_V^2 T}{\sigma_V \sqrt{T}} \quad \text{and} \quad d_2 = d_1 - \sigma_V \sqrt{T}.$$

The reader should keep in mind that deriving the risky bond price (and return) is crucial since we can derive the default swap premium from equation (5.1), Default swap premium (p.a.) = Return on risky bond − Return on risk-free bond, once we have derived the risky bond return. However, the reader should keep the restrictions of the simple equation (5.1) in mind, which are, among others, that counterparty risk is not included and we assume that interest rate changes affects the risky and risk-free bond to the same extent.

Merton's model using equity as proxy

One drawback of Merton's elegant model is that we need the asset value V and the asset volatility σ_V as inputs. Both parameters are not easily available in practice. However the equity value E and the equity volatility σ_E are observable. Using equation (5.17) and equation (5.20) derived from Ito's lemma:

$$E_0 = \frac{N(d_1)V_0\sigma_V}{\sigma_E} \tag{5.20}$$

we have two equations with two unknowns to solve for, V and σ_V.

Example 5.9: The equity of company X is currently worth \$2,000,000. In one year, company X has to repay \$1,800,000 in debt. The volatility of the equity is 80% and the risk-free interest rate is 5%. What is the probability of default in 1 year on the basis of the Merton model using equity volatility as a proxy?

Solving equations (5.17) and (5.20) iteratively, we derive the value of assets V_0 = \$3,693,544 and the volatility of the assets as σ_V = 44.45%. Inputting these values into equation (5.17), it follows that $d_2 = 1.5073$ and $N(-d_2) = 1 - N(d_2) =$ 6.59%. Thus, the probability of default in 1 year is 6.59%.

The reader may also verify equation (5.19) $B_0 = D_T e^{-rT} N(d_2) + VN(-d_1)$. The bond value B_0 comes out to be $1{,}800{,}000 \times e^{-0.05\times 1} \times 0.9341 + 3{,}727{,}549 \times 0.0255 =$ \$1,693,544. This is identical with the present value of the debt $D_0 = V_0 - E_0 =$ \$3,693,544 − 2,000,000 = \$1,693,544.

The Merton model using equity volatility can be found at http://www.dersoft.com/Mertonequity.xls.

An interesting feature of the Merton model is that equity holders will benefit from an increase in volatility of the assets. In this case, the time value of equity will increase (see figure 5.12).

As mentioned above, the path-breaking Merton model serves as a basis for structural and reduced form models that value credit risk. However, the model is quite simple in a number of respects. It principally only allows default at the maturity of the debt T, and the debt can only take the form of zero-coupon bonds. Coupons as well as different seniorities cannot be handled. There is only one bankruptcy event, which occurs when the asset value falls below the value of the debt at maturity of the debt. Other bankruptcy events such as illiquidity, restructuring of debt, or a moratorium are not taken into account.

Due to the simplicity of the Merton model, it is not surprising that empirical testing of the default probability $N(-d_2)$ or the bond price equation (5.19) have overall not produced good results.[16] Nevertheless, the Merton model has served as an excellent basis for developing more realistic, complex models.

Extensions of the Merton model: first-time passage models

The Merton model uses the arbitrage-free Black-Scholes-Merton environment to derive the probability of default. The model principally only observes two points in time: today and option maturity. As a consequence the model can only evaluate European style options, i.e. options that can only be exercised at option maturity. The model does not apply to American style options, thus premature exercise is not accounted for. Therefore the original Merton model principally only evaluates the possibility of default at option maturity T, which corresponds to the maturity date of the debt.

This drawback was addressed by numerous authors and has led to the emergence of *first-time passage models*. These models define a typically exogenous default boundary in units of the asset value V, V_d. If the value of the assets V falls below the boundary V_d, the company is forced to restructuring or bankruptcy. Hence, default can occur at any time during the period of the debt. Let's have a closer look at first-time passage models.

The Black-Cox 1976 model

One of the first to discuss first-time passage models were Black and Cox in 1976.[17] Black and Cox suggest an exogenous exponential default boundary of $V_d = ke^{-\gamma(T-t)}$, where k and γ are exogenous constants. If the asset value V drops below V_d during time t to T, the asset holders can force the company into bankruptcy or restructuring. The mandatory bankruptcy or restructuring, expressed as a *safety covenant* of the asset holders, is an important feature of the model. It protects asset holders from further deterioration of the company's assets. In that sense a high value of k and a low value of γ forces early bankruptcy or restructuring and principally protects asset holders.

Besides safety covenants, Black and Cox also investigate subordination arrangements and restrictions for the equity holders to finance interest and dividend payments. All three provisions tend to increase the value of the risky bond.

Black and Cox also find a closed form solution for the risky bond B, which includes (continuous) dividends, a, to the stockholders:

$$B = Ne^{-rT}[N(z_1) - y^{2\theta-2}N(z_2)] + Ve^{-aT}[N(z_3) + y^{2\theta}N(z_4) + y^{\theta+\xi}e^{aT}N(z_5) + y^{\theta-\xi}e^{aT}N(z_6) - y^{\theta-\eta}N(z_7) - y^{\theta-\eta}N(z_8)] \quad (5.21)$$

where N is the notional amount of the bond, r the continuously compounded interest rate, T the maturity of the bond, and N cumulative normal standard distribution and:

$y = ke^{-\gamma T}/V$; k and γ exogenous

V: asset value

$\theta = (r - a - \gamma + 0.5\sigma^2)/\sigma^2$

a: continuously compounded dividends

σ^2: variance of the return of the firm

$$\delta = (r - a - \gamma - 0.5\sigma^2)^2 + 2\sigma^2(r - \gamma)$$

$$\xi = \sqrt{\delta}/\sigma^2$$

$$\eta = \sqrt{\delta - 2\sigma^2 a}/\sigma^2$$

$$z_1 = [\ln V - \ln PA + (r - a - 0.5\sigma^2)T]/\sqrt{\sigma^2 T}$$

$$z_2 = [\ln V - \ln PA + 2\ln y + (r - a - 0.5\sigma^2)T]/\sqrt{\sigma^2 T}$$

$$z_3 = [\ln V - \ln PA - (r - a - 0.5\sigma^2)T]/\sqrt{\sigma^2 T}$$

$$z_4 = [\ln V - \ln PA + 2\ln y + (r - a + 0.5\sigma^2)T]/\sqrt{\sigma^2 T}$$

$$z_5 = [\ln y + \xi\sigma^2 T]/\sqrt{\sigma^2 T}$$

$$z_6 = [\ln y - \xi\sigma^2 T]/\sqrt{\sigma^2 T}$$

$$z_7 = [\ln y + \eta\sigma^2 T]/\sqrt{\sigma^2 T}$$

$$z_8 = [\ln y - \eta\sigma^2 T]/\sqrt{\sigma^2 T}.$$

The asset process in the Black-Cox model is $dV/V = (\mu - c)dt + \sigma_1 dz_1$, where c is the payout of the risky bond. The underlying interest rate process and the recovery rate are rather simple. Interest rates do not follow a stochastic process but are assumed constant at a rate r, and the recovery rate is simply set to the asset value V at the time of default.

The Kim, Ramaswamy, and Sundaresan 1993 model

Kim, Ramaswamy, and Sundaresan (1993)[18] use a simpler default boundary but a more realistic stochastic interest rate process than Black and Cox. Default is triggered if the asset value drops below an exogenous constant w. The interest rate process follows the risk-neutral Cox-Ingersoll-Ross model:[19] $dr = a(b - r)dt + \sigma_1\sqrt{r}dz_1$, where r = interest rate, a = mean reversion factor, b = long term average of r, σ_1 = volatility of r, dz = Wiener process as defined in equation (5.5). In the Cox-Ingersoll-Ross model, interest rates mean-revert with rate a to the long-term average of rates, b. Since the interest rate r is taken to the square root, the model has the convenient property that interest rates cannot get negative.

The default boundary in the Kim-Ramaswamy-Sundaresan model is $1/(c\gamma)$, where c is the coupon rate and γ is the cash outflow of the firm. Thus the default boundary is endogenous but not time-dependent as in the Black-Cox model. The recovery rate is the minimum of the asset V and the face value of the debt D, if default occurs at maturity of the debt D: $RR(T) = \min(V, D)$. If however, default occurs before the debt maturity T, the recovery rate is the minimum of an exogenous recovery rate expressed in percent of a risk-free bond and the asset value: $RR(t < T) = \min(wP, V)$, where w is the exogenous recovery rate, P is the price of the risk-free bond.

Using a generalized Wiener process of the form $dV/V = (\mu - \gamma)dt + \sigma_2 dz_2$ for the asset value process V, where μ is the usual expected rate of return of V, and γ equals the payout of the firm, Kim, Ramaswamy, and Sundaresan derive a partial differential equation for coupon bonds B:

$$B = \frac{1}{2}\sigma_1^2 V^2 \frac{\partial^2 B}{\partial V^2} + \rho\sigma_1\sigma_2\sqrt{r}V\frac{\partial V}{\partial r \partial V} + \frac{1}{2}\sigma_2^2 r\frac{\partial^2 B}{\partial r^2} + a(b-r)\frac{\partial B}{\partial r} + (r-\gamma)V\frac{\partial B}{\partial V} - rB + c \tag{5.22}$$

where c is the coupon of the risky bond B.

Equation (5.22) has no closed form solution. However, Kim, Ramaswamy, and Sundaresan test it numerically and derive significantly better results in deriving realistic default swap premiums than the original Merton model.

The Longstaff-Schwartz 1995 model

In an often-cited paper, Longstaff and Schwartz (1995)[20] suggest a first-time passage model with an exogenous and constant default boundary k and an exogenous and constant recovery rate w. For the interest rate process, Longstaff and Schwartz use the well-known Vasicek model:[21] $dr = a(b - r)dt + \eta\sigma_1 dz_1$, where r = interest rate, a = mean reversion factor, b = long-term average of r, η = exogenous constant, σ_1 = volatility of r, and dz = Wiener process as defined in equation (5.5). The asset value also follows a generalized Wiener process as in equation (5.5): $dV/V = \mu dt + \sigma_2 dz_2$.

With the help of the closed form solution for a zero-coupon bond derived in the Vasicek model, Longstaff and Schwartz find a solution for the price of risky zero-coupon bonds and floating rate bonds. The equation for the risky zero-coupon bond B is:

$$B(V, k, r, T) = P(r, T) - wP(r, T)Q(V, k, r, T) \tag{5.23}$$

where B = Price of a risky bond; k = boundary for asset value V, if $V < k$ restructuring or default occurs; r = risk-free interest rate, T = maturity of risky bond B; P = Price of a risk-free bond; w = 1 − recovery rate; and

$$Q = \sum_{i=1}^{n}\left(N(\alpha_i) - \sum_{j=1}^{i-1} q_j N(\beta_{i,j})\right)$$

where

$$\alpha_i = \frac{-\ln X - M(iT/n, T)}{\sqrt{S(iT/n)}}$$

and

$$\beta_{ij} = \frac{M(jT/n, T) - M(iT/n, T)}{\sqrt{S(iT/n) - S(jT/n)}}$$

where

$$M(t,T)=\left(\frac{a-\rho\sigma\eta}{b}-\frac{\eta^2}{b^2}-\frac{\sigma^2}{2}\right)t+\left(\frac{\rho\sigma\eta}{b^2}+\frac{\eta^2}{2b^3}\right)e^{-bT}e^{(bt-1)}$$
$$+\left(\frac{r}{b}-\frac{a}{b^2}+\frac{\eta^2}{b^3}\right)(1-e^{-bt})-\left(\frac{\eta^2}{2b^3}\right)e^{-bT}(1-e^{-bt})$$
$$S(t)=\left(\frac{\rho\sigma\eta}{b}+\frac{\eta^2}{b^2}+\sigma^2\right)t-\left(\frac{\rho\sigma\eta}{b^2}+\frac{2\eta^2}{b^3}\right)(1-e^{-\beta t})+\left(\frac{\eta^2}{2b^3}\right)(1-e^{-2bt})$$

where a and b are parameters of the risk-free bond from the Vasicek model, ρ is the instantaneous correlation coefficient between the Wiener processes dz_1 and dz_2, and the passage of time integral Q(V,k,r,T) is the limit of Q(V,k,r,t,n) as $n \rightarrow \infty$.

Equation (5.23) is quite intuitive. P(r,T) is the value of the risk-free bond. Subtracted from P(r,T) is the discount for the risk of the bond B, which consists of two terms: wP(r,T) is the amount of the write-down in case of default, which is weighted with the probability of default Q(V,k,r,T).

However, the closed form solution (5.23) is obviously quite cumbersome and it is difficult to calibrate the parameters w, α, β, η, σ, and ρ so that the credit-spreads found in the market are matched.

Longstaff and Schwartz test their model with a simple linear regression of the form $\Delta s = a + b\Delta y + cI + \varepsilon$, where s is the credit-spread, y is the yield of the 30-year Treasury bond and I is the return of the firm's equity or asset index.

Key findings of Longstaff and Schwartz are that $b < 0$ and $c < 0$. $b < 0$ implies that credit-spreads decrease when the risk-free Treasury rate increases. This appears counterintuitive but can be explained by the fact that a higher interest rate means a higher growth rate μ of the asset value V. As a consequence of the higher asset value the probability of default is lower, and with it the credit-spreads.

The inverse relationship between long term risk-free interest rates and credit-spread is stronger for firms with lower credit quality. This is intuitive since a strong growth in the asset value V can improve the asset-liability relationship of a low rated firm to a significant degree.

$c < 0$ implies that the higher the value of assets or equity the lower the credit-spread. This is an anticipated result. Again the inverse relationship is higher for lower rated firms.

Drawbacks of the Longstaff-Schwartz model are the complex parameter calibration of the numerous parameters for the bond equations, and the fact that the underlying Vasicek model for interest rates is generally not arbitrage-free.

The Briys-de Varenne 1997 model[22]

In 1997, Briys and de Varenne addressed shortcomings of the Black-Cox, Kim-Ramaswamy-Sundaresan, and Longstaff-Schwartz models. In these models, the payoff to bondholders in case of bankruptcy may be larger than the firm's asset value. In this respect, payoff demands of the equity holders are not taken into account. Consequently, Briys and de Varenne suggest a default boundary and recovery rate, which guarantee that the payoff to bondholders at the time of default is realistic with respect to demands from the equity holders, and cannot be higher than the firm's asset value.

The default boundary is set at $V_d = kFP$, where k is an exogenous constant, F is the face value of the risky bond and P is the price of the risk-free bond. If $k = 1$, there is no risk for the bondholders since default is triggered at a value of FP. Hence, assuming $P = 1$, bond holders will receive the face value of the bond F. The other extreme is $k = 0$. In this case there is no exogenous default boundary V_d and the model corresponds to the original Merton model, where the default boundary is $V_T < D$.

To guarantee that bondholders can receive the payoff as defined in the model, Briys and de Varenne address the issue of the *strict priority rule*. The strict priority rule states that bondholders receive all of the remaining assets in case of bankruptcy and stockholders receive nothing. Let f_1 $(0 \leq f_1 \leq 1)$ and f_2 $(0 \leq f_2 \leq 1)$ be fractions of the remaining assets at default, f_1 denotes the fraction of the asset value if default occurs before maturity, f_2 denotes the fraction of the assets if default occurs at maturity. If $f_1 = f_2 = 1$, the strict priority rule applies, since the fraction paid to the bondholders is constant in time, i.e. there is no bargaining process between the equity holders and the asset holders in time. In reality, though, the strict priority rule often does not apply, thus $f_1 \neq f_2$.

Interest rates in the Briys-de Varenne model follow the stochastic process $dr = a(t)[b(t) - r_t]dt + \sigma_1(t)dz_1$. This resembles closely the extended Vasicek or Hull-White model of $dr = a(b - r_t)dt + \sigma_1 dz_1$. The difference lies in the fact that Briys and de Varenne model the mean reversion, a, the long term average, b, and the volatility, σ_1, as deterministic functions of time a(t) and $\sigma(t)$, which was discussed by Hull and White in 1990.[23]

For the assets of the company, Briys and de Varenne choose the stochastic process $\frac{dV}{V} = r\,dt + \sigma\left[\rho dz_1 + \sqrt{1-\rho^2}\,dz_2\right]$, where ρ is the correlation between the assets and the interest rates.

Following these assumptions, a closed form solution for the price of the risky bond B is derived:

$$B = FP(0,T)\left[1 - \mathrm{Put}(\ell_0, 1) + \mathrm{Put}\left(q_0, \frac{\ell_0}{q_0}\right) - (1-f_1)\ell_0\left(N(-d_3) + \frac{N(-d_4)}{q_0}\right) - (1-f_2)\ell_0\left(N(d_3) - N(d_1) + \frac{N(d_4) - N(d_6)}{q_0}\right)\right] \tag{5.24}$$

where

$$d_1 = \frac{\ln \ell_0 + \Phi(T)/2}{\sqrt{\Phi(T)}} = d_2\sqrt{\Phi(T)}$$

$$d_3 = \frac{\ln q_0 + \Phi(T)/2}{\sqrt{\Phi(T)}} = d_4\sqrt{\Phi(T)}$$

Table 5.2: Key features of the original Merton model in comparison with first-time passage models

Model	**Asset process**	**Interest rate process**	**Closed form solution for risky bond**	**Default Boundary**	**Recovery Rate**
Merton 1974	$dV/V = \mu\, dt + \sigma\, dz$	constant r	yes eq. (5.19)	$V_T = D_T$	$N(-d_1)/N(-d_2)$
Black-Cox 1976	$dV/V = (\mu - c)\, dt + \sigma_1\, dz_1$	constant r	yes eq. (5.21)	$V_d = ke^{-\gamma T}$	V
Kim, Ramaswamy & Sundaresan 1993	$dV/V = (\mu - \gamma)\, dt + \sigma_2\, dz_2$	CIR: $dr = a(b - r)dt + \sigma_1\sqrt{r}\, dz_1$	no, see eq. (5.22)	$V_d = c/\gamma$	before T: min(wP, V) at T: min (V, D)
Longstaff-Schwartz 1995	$dV/V = \mu\, dt + \sigma_2\, dz_2$	Vasicek: $dr = a(b - r)dt + \eta\sigma_1\, dz_1$	yes eq. (5.23)	$V_d = k$	w
Briys-de Varenne 1997	$dV/V = rdt + \sigma\,[\rho dz_1 + \sqrt{1-\rho^2}dz_2$	Hull-White: $dr = a(t)\,[b(t) - r_t]\, dt + \sigma_1(t)\, dz_1$	yes eq. (5.24)	$V_d = kFP$	before T: f_1V_d at T: f_2V_T

$$d_5 = \frac{\ln q_0^2 + \Phi(T)/2}{\sqrt{\Phi(T)}} = d_6\sqrt{\Phi(T)}$$

$$\Phi(T) = \int_0^T \left[(\rho\sigma_V + \sigma_P(t,T))^2 + (1-\rho^2)\sigma_V^2\right]dt$$

$$\ell_0 = \frac{V_0}{FP(0,T)} \quad \text{and} \quad q_0 = \frac{V_0}{kFP(0,T)}$$

$$\text{Put}(\ell_0, 1) = -\ell_0 N(-d_1) + N(-d_2) \quad \text{and} \quad \text{Put}\left(q_0, \frac{\ell_0}{q_0}\right) = -q_0 N(-d_5) + \frac{\ell_0}{q_0} N(-d_6).$$

Equation (5.24) is quite intuitive: assuming the face value of the risky bond F = 1, the term FP(0,T) is the price of the risk-free bond. Deducted from FP(0,T) is the standard Merton put $(\ell_0,1)$, which reflects the default risk of the bond B. Added to FP(0,T) is a $\text{Put}\left(q_0, \frac{\ell_0}{q_0}\right)$, which mirrors the safety covenant, i.e. that bondholders can trigger default in the event of V_d = kFP(0,T). The terms including f_1 and f_2 reflect the strict priority rule. In case the strict priority rule applies, i.e. $f_1 = f_2 = 1$, the terms cancel out. Additionally, if $q_0 = \ell_0$, implying k = 1, the two put options cancel out and the bond B is risk-free, B = FP(0,T), as derived above.

Table 5.2 sums up the crucial features of the original Merton model and the first time passage models.

Critical appraisal of first-time passage models

The major achievement of first-time passage models is that unlike in the original Merton model, default before the maturity of the debt at time T is possible. However, several significant drawbacks remain. First, with the exception of the Kim-Ramaswamy-Sundaresan model, the default boundary involves an exogenous constant. Furthermore, the recovery rate of the models, with the exception of the Black-Cox model, also involves an exogenous constant. Consequently the default boundary and recovery rate are difficult to determine for practical purposes.

In addition, the closed form solutions for the risky bond price, equations (5.21) through (5.24) are quite complex and the calibration of the numerous parameters to match market credit-spreads is difficult in trading practice. Other shortcomings of the first-time passage models include the fact that some underlying stochastic processes for the asset value (e.g. CIR and Vasicek) are generally not arbitrage-free. Altogether, these drawbacks have so far limited the use of first-time passage models in credit risk practice.

Reduced Form Models

So far we have discussed two of the three basic concepts that derive the value of credit risk: traditional models (which use historical data) and structural models (which use the evolution of the asset-liability structure of a company to derive the value of credit risk).

Let's now discuss the third approach termed *reduced form models* also called *intensity models*. They are called reduced form, since they abstract from the explicit economic reasons for the default, i.e. they do not include the asset-liability structure of the firm to explain the default.

Rather, reduced form models use debt prices as a main input to model the bankruptcy process. Default is modeled by a stochastic process with an exogenous *default intensity* or *hazard rate*, which multiplied by a certain time frame, results in the risk-neutral default probability, also called pseudo- or martingale default probability. The value of hazard rate is derived by calibration of the variables of the stochastic process. Since reduced form models only model the timing of the default not the severity, the recovery rate is usually exogenous. Let's discuss several crucial reduced form models used in today's credit risk practice.

The Jarrow-Turnbull 1995 model[24]

Jarrow and Turnbull were one of the first to derive the value of credit risk and to price credit derivatives in the arbitrage-free reduced form model environment.

Jarrow and Turnbull combine a process for risk-free interest rates and a bankruptcy process of the risky debt to derive default probabilities and credit derivatives prices. The two processes are assumed to be independent from each other.

Let's define P as the price of the risk-free zero-coupon bond with notional amount 1 and maturity at time 2. π_0 is risk-neutral probability of an interest rate increase. This brings us to the interest rate tree in figure 5.13.

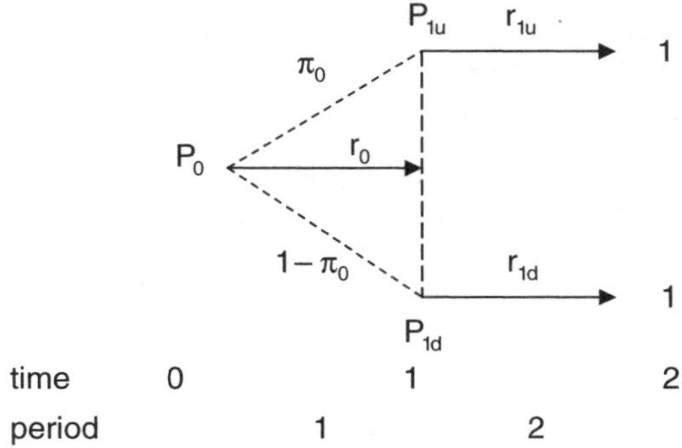

Figure 5.13: Risk-free interest rate tree in the Jarrow-Turnbull model
r = risk-free interest rate, P = risk-free zero-coupon bond price

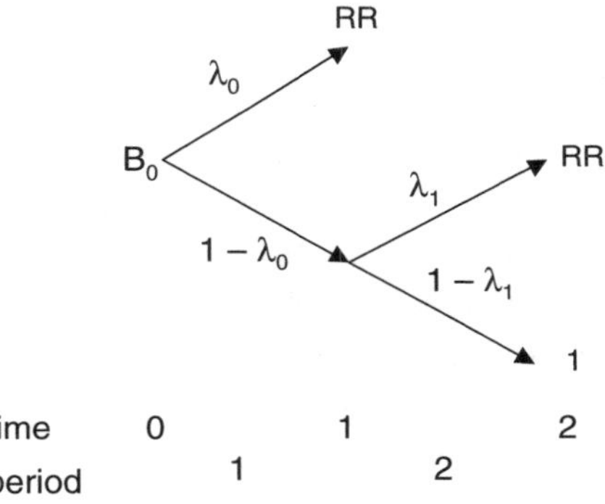

Figure 5.14: Bankruptcy process of risky bond B in the Jarrow-Turnbull model

The risk-free bond price at time t with maturity T, is $P_{t,T} = 1/(1 + r_{t,T})$. Since $r_{1u} > r_{1d}$, it follows that $P_{1d} > P_{1u}$.

Let B be the price of a risky zero-coupon bond with a notional amount of 1 and maturity at time 2. Let λ be the risk-neutral probability of default,[25] 1-λ the risk-neutral probability of survival, and RR the recovery rate in case of default. Thus, we derive the default process for the risky bond B in figure 5.14.

Combining figures 5.13 and 5.14, we get the quadruple tree in figure 5.15.

In figure 5.15, $B_{t,T}$ is the price of the risky bond at time t with maturity T. The recovery rate RR is exogenous and assumed independent from the bankruptcy process, and the interest rate process. r_1 is the risk-free forward interest rate from time 1 to time 2.

At time 1, the risky bond price takes the recovery value RR in case of default. If in default, it is assumed that the bond stays in default, thus the probability 1 from time 1 to time 2. The recovery rate RR is invested with the risk-free forward rate r_{u1} or r_{d1}, thus values $RR(1 + r_{1u})$ or $RR(1 + r_{1d})$ at time 2. In case of no default at time 1, the bond can take prices $B_{1,2,c}$ and $B_{1,2,d}$. $B_{1,2,c} < B_{1,2,d}$ since interest rates have increased in case of $B_{1,2,c}$ with probability π_0.

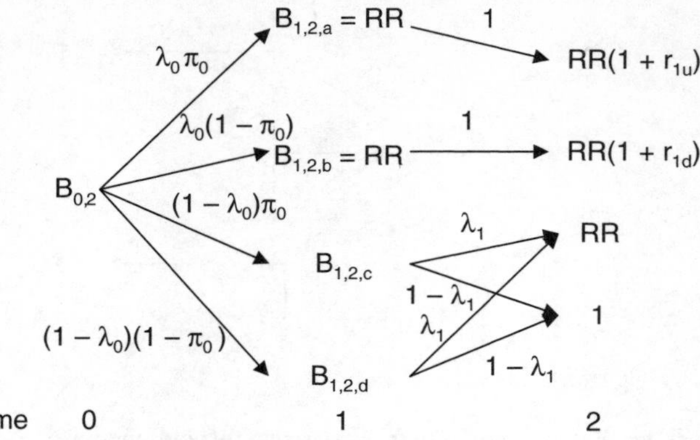

Figure 5.15: A combined interest rate and bankruptcy process

The reader should note that π_1 and $1 - \pi_1$ are not necessary in the 2-period tree, since the probabilities π_0 and $1 - \pi_0$ determine the interest rates from time 1 to time 2. The values for r and π can be generated by any short-rate model: Ho-Lee (1986); Cox-Ingersoll-Ross (1985); Vasicek (1977); Hull-White (1990); or Black-Derman-Toy (1990).

Jarrow and Turnbull show that their model is complete, i.e. that the derivatives can be replicated by primary products. In addition, the unique, risk-neutral or pseudo-probabilities λ and π guarantee that the prices P and B are martingales, thus the model is arbitrage-free. Furthermore, the Markov property allows displaying the combined interest rate and bankruptcy tree as a recombining tree.

Jarrow and Turnbull use a foreign exchange rate analogy to model the risky bond price B. The risky bond price at any time t with maturity T, $B_{t,T}$, is equal to the risk-free bond price $P_{t,T}$ multiplied with the "exchange rate" e, which is 1 in case of no default and equal to the recovery rate RR in case of default. Thus $B_{t,T} = P_{t,T}e_t$. If $E(e_T)$ is the expected payoff at time T, the risky bond price can be expressed as

$$B_{t,T} = P_{t,T}E(e_T). \tag{5.25}$$

Equation (5.25) states that the risky bond price is the expected payoff $E(e_T)$ discounted by the risk-free price $P_{t,T}$.

The probability of default

In the Jarrow-Turnbull model, the risk-neutral probability of default in period 1, realized at time 1, λ_0, can be derived separately from the interest rate process, since it is assumed that the interest rate process and the bankruptcy process are independent. Hence, from figure 5.14, for a one-period debt with a notional amount of \$1, we get:

$$B_{0,1} = P_{0,1}[\lambda_0 RR + (1 - \lambda_0)1]. \tag{5.26}$$

Equation (5.26) states that the risky bond price with maturity 1, $B_{0,1}$, is derived as the probability weighted values at time 1, discounted with the risk-free bond $P_{0,1}$. Solving equation (5.26) for λ_0 gives:

$$\lambda_0 = \frac{1 - \dfrac{B_{0,1}}{P_{0,1}}}{1 - RR}. \tag{5.27}$$

For the risk-neutral default probability in period 1, realized at time 2, λ_1, we receive from figure 5.14:

$$B_{0,2} = P_{0,1}\lambda_0 RR + P_{0,2}(1-\lambda_0)[\lambda_1 RR + (1-\lambda_1)].^{26} \tag{5.28}$$

Solving equation (5.28) for the risk-neutral default probability at time 2, λ_1, we get:

$$\lambda_1 = \frac{\dfrac{B_{0,2} - P_{0,1}\lambda_0 RR}{P_{0,2}(1-\lambda_0)} - 1}{RR - 1}. \tag{5.29}$$

This derivation of λ_0 and λ_1 is quite similar to that of the binomial tree in equations (5.3) and (5.4). The difference is that in the binomial tree in equations (5.3) and (5.4), the nature of the risky bond was incorporated via the swap premium s, whereas Jarrow and Turnbull use the bond price B to incorporate the risk. Also, in equations (5.3) and (5.4) all values were compared at time 2, not at time 0, as in equations (5.26) to (5.29). Also, in the binomial tree we used the spot interest rate r_0 and the forward rate r_1 to derive future values. In equation (5.26) to (5.29) we discount with the risk-free zero bond price P. Furthermore, in the binomial tree in equations (5.3) and (5.4), the swap premium s is effectively a coupon, whereas in the Jarrow-Turnbull equations (5.26) to (5.29) the underlying risky and risk-free bonds have no coupon.

Let's now derive the probability of default in the Jarrow-Turnbull model in an example.

Example 5.10: Let's assume that the probability of default in period 1 was derived with equation (5.27) as 4%. The risk-free bond prices for bonds with maturity 1 and 2 are 99 and 98 respectively. The risky bond price with maturity 2 is 91. The recovery rate is assumed to be 30%. What is the probability of default in period 2, realized at time 2, in the Jarrow-Turnbull model?

Following equation (5.29) it is:

$$\frac{\dfrac{91 - 99 \times 0.04 \times 0.3}{98 \times (1-0.04)} - 1}{0.3 - 1} = 6.48\%.$$

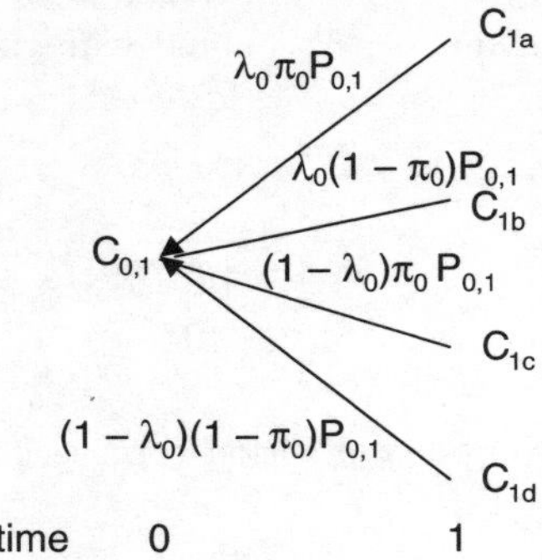

Figure 5.16: Deriving the call price at time 0 with maturity 1, $C_{0,1}$, in the Jarrow-Turnbull model

Pricing options in the Jarrow-Turnbull model

The call and put option price in the Jarrow-Turnbull model can easily be derived on the basis of the quadruple tree in figure 5.15. As in a standard binomial model, we first derive the underlying price tree, in this case the zero-coupon bond price tree. We then create an option price tree and discount back from the last node to find the present value of the option.

We have already derived the bond price tree for a bond with a notional amount of 1 and a maturity of 2 in figure 5.15. The bond prices $B_{1,2,a}$ and $B_{1,2,b}$ in case of default at time 1, regardless whether interest rates have gone up or down, are RR. The bond prices $B_{1,2,c}$ and $B_{1,2,d}$ in figure 5.15 are:

$$B_{1,2,c} = P_{1,2,u}[\lambda_1 RR + (1 - \lambda_1)] \tag{5.30}$$

$$B_{1,2,d} = P_{1,2,d}[\lambda_1 RR + (1 - \lambda_1)]. \tag{5.31}$$

$P_{1,2,u}$ is the risk-free forward bond price from time 1 to time 2 in case of an interest rate increase in period 1; $P_{1,2,d}$ is the risk-free forward bond price from time 1 to time 2 in case of an interest rate decrease in period 1. Recall that $P_{t,T} = 1/(1 + r_{t,T})$ and $P_{1,2,u} < P_{1,2,d}$.

Pricing a call: Having derived the bond prices, we can now build the option tree to derive the option price. Let's start with a call. The call price tree for a call with maturity 1 and an underlying bond with maturity bigger than time 1 is seen in figure 5.16.

Since time 1 is the maturity of the call, the call price at time 1 is simply the intrinsic value $\max(B_{t,T} - K, 0)$, where K is the strike price. Thus $C_{1,a} = \max(B_{1,2,a} - K, 0)$ as is $C_{1,b} = \max(B_{1,2,b} - K, 0)$, $C_{1,c} = \max(B_{1,2,c} - K, 0)$, and $C_{1,d} = \max(B_{1,2,d} - K, 0)$. From figure 5.16, we can see that the call price at time 0 is equal to the call at time 1, discounted with $P_{0,1}$ and weighted with the default probability λ_0 and the interest rate probability π_0:

$$C_{0,1} = [\lambda_0 \pi_0 C_{1a} + \lambda_0(1 - \pi_0)C_{1b} + (1 - \lambda_0)\pi_0 C_{1c} + (1 - \lambda_0)(1 - \pi_0)C_{1d}]P_{0,1}. \tag{5.32}$$

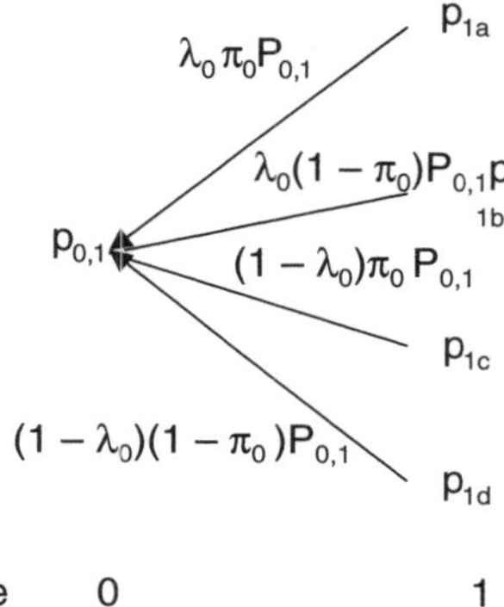

Figure 5.17: Deriving the put price at time 0 with maturity 1, $p_{0,1}$, in the Jarrow-Turnbull model

Example 5.11: Let's assume from the term-structure based model we have derived that $\pi_0 = 0.6$, $P_{0,1} = 0.94$, $P_{1,2,u} = 0.93$, and $P_{1,2,d} = 0.96$ where $P_{1,2,u}$ is the forward price from time 1 to time 2 in case of an upward move of interest rates, and $P_{1,2,d}$ is the forward price from time 1 to time 2 in case of a downward move of interest rates. Let's further assume that as in example 5.10, the probability of default in period 1, λ_0 is 4% and the probability of default in period 2 λ_1 is 6.48%. The recovery rate is assumed to be 40%. What is the price of a call with a strike of 0.85 and a maturity of time 1 on a bond with maturity at time 2 derived on the 2-period Jarrow-Turnbull binomial tree?

We first derive the prices $B_{1,2}$. From figure 5.15 we derive that $B_{1,2,a} = B_{1,2,b} = RR = 0.4$. From equation (5.30), $B_{1,2,c} = 0.93 \times (0.0648 \times 0.4 + (1 - 0.0648)) = 0.8938$, and from equation (5.31) $B_{1,2,d} = 0.96 \times (0.0648 \times 0.4 + (1 - 0.0648)) = 0.9227$. We can now derive $C_{1,a} = \max(0.4 - 0.85, 0) = 0$; $C_{1,b} = \max(0.4 - 0.85, 0) = 0$; $C_{1,c} = \max(0.8938 - 0.85, 0) = 0.0438$; and $C_{1,d} = \max(0.9227 - 0.85, 0) = 0.0727$. Following equation (5.25), we derive the call price as:

$$C_{0,1} = [0.04 \times 0.6 \times 0 + 0.04 \times (1-0.6) \times 0 + (1-0.04) \times 0.6 \times 0.0438 + (1-0.04) \times (1-0.6) \times 0.0727] \times 0.94 = 0.04995 \text{ or } 5.00\% \text{ of the notional amount of the bond of } 1.$$

Naturally, the Jarrow-Turnbull model can be extended to multi periods. A multi-period model of the Jarrow-Turnbull approach can be found at www.dersoft.com/jt.xls.

Pricing a put: Pricing a put within the Jarrow-Turnbull framework is similar to pricing a call. The only difference is the intrinsic value at maturity of the option. For a put, the intrinsic value is $\max(K - B_{t,T}, 0)$. Using the same technique as in figure 5.16 we can derive the tree shown in figure 5.17.

From figure 5.17 we derive equation (5.33) for a put p:

$$p_{0,1} = [\lambda_0 \pi_0 p_{1a} + \lambda_0 (1 - \pi_0) p_{1b} + (1 - \lambda_0) \pi_0 p_{1c} + (1 - \lambda_0)(1 - \pi_0) p_{1d}] P_{0,1}. \quad (5.33)$$

Let's derive the put price in a numerical example.

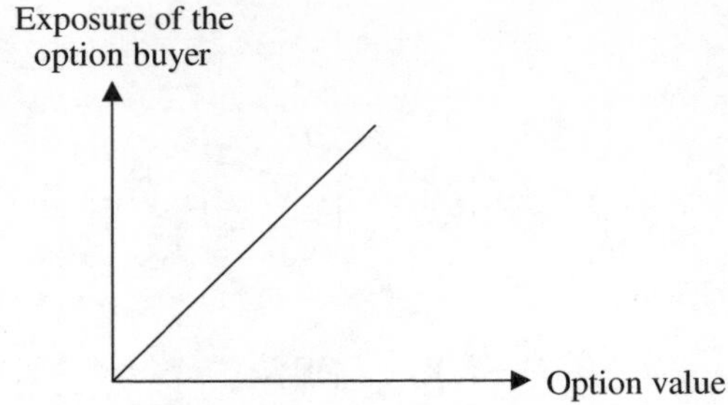

Figure 5.18: Credit exposure of an option buyer with respect to the option value

Example 5.12: Let's use the data from example 5.11. The probability of an upward move of interest rates in period 1 is $\pi_0 = 0.6$, $P_{0,1} = 0.94$, $P_{1,2,u} = 0.93$, and $P_{1,2,d} = 0.96$, where $P_{1,2,u}$ is the forward price from time 1 to time 2 in case of an upward move of interest rates, and $P_{1,2,d}$ is the forward price from time 1 to time 2 in case of a downward move of interest rates. The probability of default in period 1, λ_0 is 4% and the probability of default in period 2 λ_1 is 6.48%. The recovery rate is assumed to be 40%. What is the price of a put with a strike of 0.95 and a maturity of time 1 on a bond with maturity at time 2 derived in the 2-period Jarrow-Turnbull binomial tree?

From figure 5.11 we derive that $B_{1,2,a} = B_{1,2,b} = RR = 0.4$. From equation (5.30), $B_{1,2,c} = 0.93 \times (0.0648 \times 0.4 + (1 - 0.0648)) = 0.8938$ and from equation (5.31) $B_{1,2,d} = 0.96 \times (0.0648 \times 0.4 + (1 - 0.0648)) = 0.9227$. We can now derive $p_{1,a} = \max(0.95 - 0.4, 0) = 0.5500$; $p_{1,b} = \max(0.95 - 0.4, 0) = 0.5500$; $p_{1,c} = \max(0.95 - 0.8938, 0) = 0.0562$ and $p_{1,d} = \max(0.95 - 0.9227, 0) = 0.0273$. Following equation (5.33), we derive the put price as:

$$\begin{aligned} p_{0,1} &= [0.04 \times 0.6 \times 0.5500 + 0.04 \times (1-0.6) \times 0.5500 + \\ &\quad (1-0.04) \times 0.6 \times 0.0562 + (1-0.04) \times (1-0.6) \times 0.0273] \times 0.94 \\ &= 0.060963 \text{ or } 6.10\% \text{ of the notional amount of the bond of 1.} \end{aligned}$$

Pricing vulnerable options in the Jarrow-Turnbull model: In an option contract, the option buyer has counterparty risk, i.e. the risk that the option seller defaults. In that case, the option seller might not be able to meet his obligation to pay the intrinsic value to the option buyer. Figure 5.18 shows the credit exposure of the option buyer.

The option *seller* has no counterparty risk if the option premium is paid upfront. Hence, there is no future obligation from the option buyer to the option seller. An option that includes the aspect of default of the option seller in the valuation is termed *vulnerable option*.

The vulnerable option price in the Jarrow-Turnbull model can be derived easily: The value of the vulnerable option at time t with maturity T, $C_{t,T,V}$, can be expressed as the default-free option $C_{t,T}$ multiplied by the expected value of the bankruptcy process of the risky option seller, $E(e_{T,V})$. Thus we derive:

$$C_{t,T,V} = C_{t,T}E(e_{T,V}). \tag{5.34}$$

$e_{T,V}$ will be equal to 1 in case the vulnerable option seller has not defaulted at time T; $e_{T,V}$ will be equal to the recovery rate if the vulnerable option seller has defaulted at time T. Let's assume that the bankruptcy process of the payoff ratio e_V is independent from the risk-free interest rate process and the default process of the underlying asset. Hence, the option price at time 0 and with maturity 1 is simply the discounted price of the option at time 1:

$$C_{0,1,V} = (C_{1,1}/P_{0,1})E(e_{1,V})$$

or

$$C_{0,1,V} = C_{0,1}E(e_{1,V}).$$

Using equation (5.25) $B_{t,T} = P_{t,T}E(e_T)$, where $B_{t,T}$ is a zero-coupon bond issued by the option seller, we derive the value of the vulnerable option as:

$$C_{0,1,V} = (C_{0,1}B_{0,1})/P_{0,1}. \tag{5.35}$$

Since $B_{0,1}/P_{0,1} \leq 1$, the vulnerable option will always be lower than or equal to an option not including option seller default risk.

Example 5.13: The current bond price of the option seller with maturity 1 is at \$0.90 and the risk-free bond price with the same maturity is \$0.99. In example 5.11 we have derived a call price at time 0 with maturity time 1 excluding counterparty risk of 5.00%. What is the value of a corresponding vulnerable call? Following equation (5.35) with $B_{0,1} = 0.9$ and $P_{0,1} = 0.99$, we derive $C_{0,1,V} = 0.0500 \times 0.90/0.99 = 4.54\%$. Thus, the value of the default risk is 5.00% − 4.54% = 0.46%, or 0.46%/5.00% = 9.2% of the non-vulnerable call value.

Pricing non-vulnerable and vulnerable interest rate swaps in the Jarrow-Turnbull model

Contrary to an option, *both* swap counterparts in a swap have default risk. This is because both counterparts promise to make future payments. If company A has entered into a swap with company B, company A has default risk if the present value of the swap is positive from company A's point of view. Graphically this can be expressed as in figure 5.19.

If the present value of the swap is negative for company A, there is no credit risk for company A, since the swap represents a liability and not an asset.

Pricing non-vulnerable swaps: Let's start our analysis with pricing a non-vulnerable swap. We first have to find the discount factors to discount the future cash flows. In previous analyses, we have used the value of the risk-free bond P to discount. However, in a swap, it is more appropriate to find the discount factors from the swap curve.

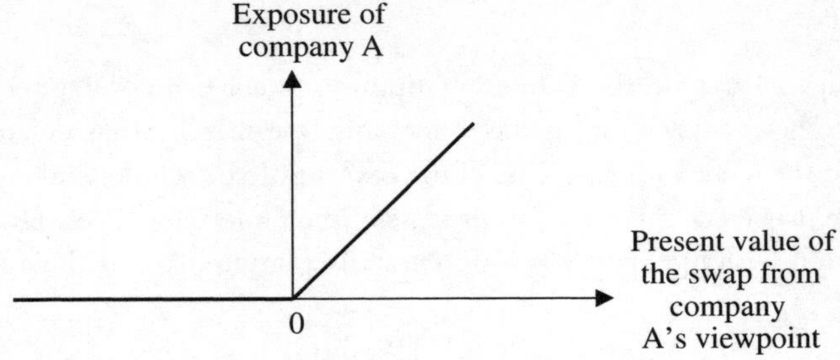

Figure 5.19: Credit exposure of a swap with respect to the value of the swap

Let's assume the 1-year swap rate is 4.60% and the two-year swap rate is 4.64%. The one year swap rate is a zero-rate (no coupons are paid until year 1), so we can derive the discount factor at time 1 easily as $df_1 = 1/(1 + r_1)$. With a 1-year swap rate of 4.60% we derive $df_1 = 1/(1 + 0.046) = 0.956023$. For the 2-year discount factor, assuming the swap rates are paid annually, we have to incorporate the fact that the rate is paid at time 1. We can use equation (5.36):[27]

$$df_n = \frac{df_0 - r_n \sum_{i=1}^{n-1} df_i (t_i - t_{i-1})}{1 + r_n (t_n - t_{n-1})}. \tag{5.36}$$

For the 2-year discount factor $n = 2$. With $r_2 = 4.64\%$ we derive:

$$df_n = \frac{1 - 0.0464 \times 0.956023 \times 1}{1 + 0.0464 \times 1} = 0.913265.$$

The forward swap rate from time 1 to time 2, $r_{1,2}$, can be derived from $df_1/df_2 - 1$. Thus we obtain $r_{1,2} = (0.956023/0.913265) - 1 = 4.68\%$.

Having derived all discount factors, we can now calculate the swap price. It is the difference between the discounted floating cash flows and the discounted fixed cash flows.

Example 5.14: The 1-year swap rate is 4.60% and the 2-year swap rate is 4.64%. What is the present value of a 2-year swap if the fixed rate is 4.64%? All rates are paid annually. The notional amount of the swap is 1. Figure 5.20 shows this diagrammatically.

In a standard swap, the fixing of the floating payment is done one period prior to the payment. Hence in figure 5.20, the payment of 4.6% at time 1 is fixed today, therefore known. (It is actually not precisely known, when the swap is down in the morning hours before the fixing.) The only stochastic cash flow in figure 5.20 is the floating cash flow at time 2.

Using the previously derived results, the fixed side of the swap has a present value

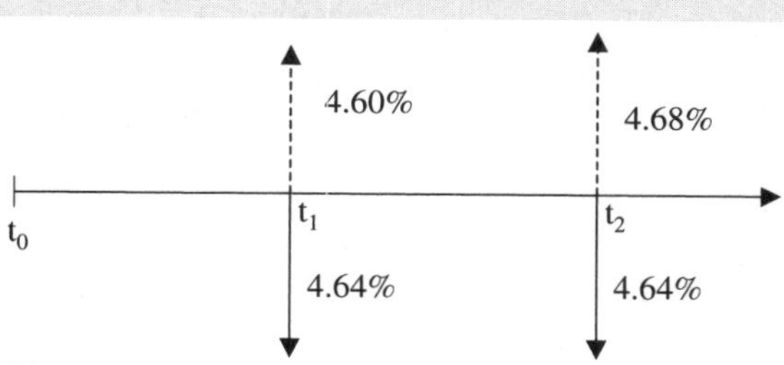

Figure 5.20: A swap with fixed cash flows of 4.64% and floating cash flows of 4.6% and an anticipated cash flow at time 2 of 4.68%

of $0.0464 \times 0.956023 + 0.0464 \times 0.913265 = 0.0867$. The present value of the floating side is $0.046 \times 0.956023 + 0.0468 \times 0.913265 = 0.0867$. Thus the swap has a present value of zero. This is the expected result, since the fixed rate in the swap 4.64% is equal to the swap rate of the maturity of the swap 4.64% (and the forward floating rate of 4.68% is the fair forward rate, which is assumed in swap valuation). This is also referred to as "par swaps value at par."

Pricing vulnerable swaps: A vulnerable swap is a swap which incorporates the possibility of default of the swap counterpart. Let's assume company A is paying a floating rate and is receiving a fixed rate in a swap with company B. If company B (or A) defaults, all future payments are null and void. Let e* be the payoff in default, then e* at time t, e^*_t, is zero with probability λ_{t-1}, and e^*_t is 1 with probability $1 - \lambda_{t-1}$. Let $E_0(e^*_t)$ be today's expected value of the payoff at time t. We can then write the value of the two-period vulnerable swap with annual payments and a notional amount of 1, V_{swap}, from the viewpoint of the floating rate payer company A as:

$$Vswap_0 = df_1[rfixed_1 - rfloating_1]E_0(e^*_1) + df_2[rfixed_2 - rfloating_2]E_0(e^*_2) \tag{5.37}$$

where rfixed represents the fixed cash flows, rfloating represents the floating cash flows, and the df terms are the discount factors.

Example 5.15: Let's assume the 1-year swap rate is 4.60% and the 2-year swap rate is 4.64%. The fixed rate of the swap is 7%. All rates are expressed as annual rates and paid annually. The notional amount of the swap is 1. The probability of default of company B in period 1, λ_0, is 4% and the probability of default in period 2, λ_1, is 6.48%. The discount factors, as derived above, are $df_1 = 0.956023$ and $df_1 = 0.913265$. What is the value of the vulnerable swap for the viewpoint of the floating rate payer A? Following equation (5.37) it is:

$$\begin{aligned} Vswap_0 = {} & 0.956023 \times (0.07 - 0.0460) \times (1 - 0.04) + 0.913265 \\ & \times (0.07 - 0.0468) \times (1 - 0.04) \times (1 - 0.0648) = 4.11\%. \end{aligned}$$

Ignoring default risk of counterpart B, the swap would have a value of:

$$0.956023\times(0.07-0.0460)+0.913265\times(0.07-0.0468)=4.41\%.$$

Thus, the value of the credit risk is 0.30% of the notional amount. Hence, for a $100,000,000 swap, the value of credit risk is $300,000.

The Jarrow-Turnbull 1995 model in combination with an underlying Cox-Ross-Rubinstein (CRR) interest rate process can be found at www.dersoft.com/jt.xls.

Critical appraisal of the Jarrow-Turnbull 1995 model

The Jarrow-Turnbull 1995 model was one of the first reduced form models that incorporated credit risk in the pricing algorithms of derivatives in a no-arbitrage martingale framework. It is a path breaking article that serves as a basis for most, more elaborate reduced form models used in today's trading practice.

The shortcomings lie in the basic approach of the model: the direct economic reasons for default, i.e. the company's specific asset-liability structure or the company's liquidity are not part of the analysis. Rather, bond prices are the major input, assuming that bond prices can serve to reflect the credit risk of the debtor and to derive default probabilities. However, it has been shown that bond prices overestimate a company's probability of default quite substantially (see e.g. Altman 1989). In addition, bond prices are often quite illiquid, resulting in difficulties in determining a fair mid-market price.

Furthermore, it is assumed that the interest rate process and the default process are independent. Also, the default intensity is assumed constant, thus default is equally likely over the life of the debt. Last, the recovery rate of the model does not depend on the model variables, but is exogenous.

These shortcomings were addressed in extensions of the model, as in the Jarrow-Lando-Turnbull 1997 model.

The Jarrow-Lando-Turnbull 1997 model[28]

In 1997, Jarrow, Lando, and Turnbull derive default probabilities and valuation methods for credit derivatives not from rather illiquid bond prices, but on the basis of historical transition probabilities. The analysis is done within the arbitrage-free martingale framework. However, Markov properties are not mandatory since the martingale transition probabilities, also termed risk-neutral- or pseudo-probabilities, may depend on historical data up to the present. Let's first look at a historical default matrix, as shown in table 5.3.

We can deduce the annual default probability from table 5.3. We simply take the difference in the cumulative default probability for each entry. Doing so, we derive table 5.4.

From table 5.4 we can see that the historical default probability stays constant or increases slightly in time for highly rated credit. However, for low credits such as Caa, the probabil-

Table 5.3: Average global cumulative historical default rates with respect to time (numbers in %)

Year	**1**	**2**	**3**	**4**	**5**	**6**	**7**	**8**	**9**	**10**
Aaa	0	0	0	0.04	0.12	0.21	0.3	0.4	0.52	0.64
Aa	0.02	0.03	0.07	0.16	0.26	0.36	0.46	0.57	0.65	0.73
A	0.02	0.09	0.22	0.36	0.51	0.68	0.86	1.07	1.31	1.56
Baa	0.22	0.61	1.08	1.69	2.25	2.81	3.38	3.94	4.58	5.26
Ba	1.28	3.51	6.09	8.76	11.36	13.74	15.66	17.6	19.46	21.29
B	6.51	14.16	21.03	27.04	32.31	36.73	40.97	44.33	47.17	50.01
Caa	23.83	37.12	47.43	55.05	60.09	65.22	69.26	73.88	76.50	78.54

Source: Moody's Investor Service, April 2003

Table 5.4: Average global annual default rates with respect to time (numbers in %)

Year	**1**	**2**	**3**	**4**	**5**	**6**	**7**	**8**	**9**	**10**
Aaa	0	0	0	0.04	0.08	0.09	0.09	0.10	0.12	0.12
Aa	0.02	0.01	0.04	0.09	0.10	0.10	0.10	0.11	0.08	0.08
A	0.02	0.07	0.13	0.14	0.15	0.17	0.18	0.21	0.24	0.25
Baa	0.22	0.39	0.47	0.61	0.56	0.56	0.57	0.56	0.64	0.68
Ba	1.28	2.23	2.58	2.67	2.60	2.38	1.92	1.94	1.86	1.83
B	6.51	7.65	6.87	6.01	5.27	4.42	4.24	3.36	2.84	2.84
Caa	23.83	13.29	10.31	7.62	5.04	5.13	4.04	4.62	2.62	2.04

Source: Moody's Investor Service, April 2003

ity of a default decreases with increasing time. This is reasonable, since for a company with a bad rating, the coming years are the most crucial ones. Once they have passed, it can be assumed that the probability of default declines.

Tables 5.3 and 5.4 only express the probability of a certain credit to move to default, i.e. to move to credit state D. Jarrow, Lando, and Turnbull use a *transition matrix* in their analysis. A transition matrix Λ shows the historical transition probability of a credit in state i to move to a credit in state j, within a certain time frame, thus

$$\Lambda = \begin{pmatrix} \lambda_{11} & \lambda_{12} \ldots \lambda_{1D} \\ \lambda_{21} & \lambda_{22} \ldots \lambda_{2D} \\ \vdots & \\ \lambda_{D-1,1} & \lambda_{D-1,2} \ldots \lambda_{D-1,D} \\ 0 & 0 \quad\quad 1 \end{pmatrix}$$

where the transition probabilities $\lambda_{ij} \geq 0$ for all i, j. The probability of default for a certain credit state i, $\lambda_{i,D}$, is in the last column of Λ. The probability of survival for a bond in rating

Table 5.5: One-year historical transition matrix of year 2002 (numbers in %)

		Rating at year-end								
		Aaa	**Aa**	**A**	**Baa**	**Ba**	**B**	**Caa**	**Default**	**WR**
Initial	Aaa	86.82	7.75	0	0	0	0	0	0	5.43
Rating	Aa	1.38	82.23	12.12	0.14	0	0	0	0	4.13
	A	0	2.18	82.83	8.86	1.01	0.47	0.08	0.16	4.43
	Baa	0.17	0.17	2.46	79.47	7.55	2.04	1.87	1.19	5.09
	Ba	0	0.18	0.18	2.39	72.38	13.26	2.03	1.47	8.10
	B	0	0	0.14	0.41	2.71	72.9	9.76	4.88	9.21
	Caa	0	0	0	0	0.34	3.42	56.85	27.74	11.64

Source: Moody's Investor Service, April 2003. WR represents companies that had been rated initially but are not rated at year-end

class i, $Q_i = \sum_{j \neq D} q_{i,j} = 1 - \lambda_{i,D}$. The probability of remaining in the same credit state is on the diagonal and is $\lambda_{i,i} = 1 - \sum_{\substack{j=1 \\ i \neq j}} \lambda_{i,j}$.

The last row in Λ expresses that a credit that has defaulted stays in default. Hence, the transition probability 0, and the probability to stay in default is 1. Let's look at a transition matrix in practice, table 5.5.

In table 5.5, 82.83 reflects the probability of a credit, let's assume a bond, which is currently rated A to stay in A; 0.47 reflects the probability of a bond that is currently rate A to migrate to B; 0.14 is the probability of a bond currently rated B to move to A.

Transforming historical default probabilities into martingale probabilities

In the following we will show that it is necessary to transform the historical default probabilities derived from a transition matrix into risk-neutral martingale probabilities in order to satisfy no-arbitrage conditions. We will discuss when to use historical probabilities and when to use martingale probabilities and the associated problems at the end of this section.

Let's assume we have four rating classes, A, B, C, and default D. Let s_{01A}, s_{01B}, and s_{01C} be the credit-spread (the excess yield, so the difference between the yield of the risky bond and the yield of the risk-free bond) from time 0 to time 1 for a risky bond currently in rating class A, B, and C, respectively. Let's assume $s_{01A} = 0.01$, $s_{01B} = 0.015$, and $s_{01C} = 0.02$, hence in matrix form we can write:

$$s_{01} = \begin{pmatrix} 0.01 \\ 0.015 \\ 0.02 \end{pmatrix}.$$

Let s_{02A}, s_{02B}, and s_{02C} be the spread from time 0 to time 2 for a bond currently in rating class A, B, and C, respectively. Let's assume $s_{02A} = 0.02$, $s_{02B} = 0.025$, and $s_{02C} = 0.03$, hence:

$$s_{02} = \begin{pmatrix} 0.02 \\ 0.025 \\ 0.03 \end{pmatrix}.$$

Let's further assume the one-year historical transformation matrix is

$$\Lambda = \begin{pmatrix} & A & B & C & D \\ A & 0.7 & 0.15 & 0.10 & 0.05 \\ B & 0.1 & 0.6 & 0.2 & 0.2 \\ C & 0.05 & 0.15 & 0.65 & 0.15 \\ D & 0 & 0 & 0 & 1 \end{pmatrix}.$$

Hence 0.7 is the probability of a bond currently rated A to stay in A; 0.2 is the probability of a bond currently rated B to be downgraded to C; 0.05 in the 2nd column and 4th row is the probability of a bond currently rated C to move to A. Let's further assume the risk-free continuously compounded interest rate from time 0 to time 1, $r_{01} = 5\%$ and the risk-free continuously compounded interest rate from time 0 to time 2, $r_{02} = 6\%$. The recovery rate RR is assumed to be 40%.

In a risk-neutral environment, we can express the risky zero-coupon bond price B at time t with maturity T and notional of $1 as the value of the discounted expected future cash flow of 1. We discount with the risk-free interest rate r plus the swap spread s:

$$B_{t,T} = E_t\left[e^{-(r_{t,T}+s_{t,T})T}\right] \tag{5.38}$$

where E_t is the risk-neutral expectation value at time t, and s is the excess yield of the risky asset.

For a bond with a notional of $1 that matures at time 1, the payoff at time 1 will be $1 if the bond finishes in rating class A, B, or C. The payoff will be the recovery rate RR, if the bond defaults. Including the historical default probabilities from the transition matrix, we can express the bond price B at time 0 with maturity 1, which is rated A, B_{01A} as:

$$B_{01A} = e^{-(r_{01}+s_{01})} \equiv e^{-r_{01}} \begin{pmatrix} 1 & 1 & 1 & RR \end{pmatrix} \begin{pmatrix} A \to A \\ A \to B \\ A \to C \\ A \to D \end{pmatrix} \tag{5.39}$$

where $A \to A$ is the historical probability of a bond currently in rating class A to stay in A; $A \to B$ is the historical probability of a bond currently in rating class A to move to B; etc.

It is important to note that equation (5.39) is usually not satisfied in reality. With our numerical values above, we get:

$$B_{01A} = e^{-(0.05+0.01)} \neq e^{-r_{01}}(1 \quad 1 \quad 1 \quad 0.4)\begin{pmatrix} 0.7 \\ 0.15 \\ 0.1 \\ 0.05 \end{pmatrix}$$

or

$$e^{-(0.05+0.01)} = 0.9418 \neq e^{-0.05}(1 \quad 1 \quad 1 \quad 0.4)\begin{pmatrix} 0.7 \\ 0.15 \\ 0.1 \\ 0.05 \end{pmatrix}$$

$$= e^{-(0.05)} \times (1 \times 0.7 + 1 \times 0.15 + 1 \times 0.1 + 0.4 \times 0.05) = 0.9227.$$

Hence, in order to satisfy the no-arbitrage condition (5.39), we have to transform the historical transition probabilities into risk-neutral martingale probabilities, which satisfy condition (5.39).

In order to find the martingale probabilities λ_m, we have to adjust the historical probabilities λ with a factor η. η can be interpreted as a risk premium or risk adjustment. We can then rewrite equation (5.39) for a bond currently rated in class A as:

$$B_{01A} = e^{-(r_{01}+s_{01})} = e^{-r_{01}}(1 \quad 1 \quad 1 \quad RR)\begin{pmatrix} 1-(1-(A \to A))\eta_A \\ (A \to B)\eta_A \\ (A \to C)\eta_A \\ (A \to D)\eta_A \end{pmatrix}. \tag{5.40}$$

Generalizing the right side of equation (5.40) for a bond at time t with maturity T and solving for the risk adjustment of that bond in rating class i, η_i (we assume i = {A, B, C, D}), we get:

$$\eta_i = \left\{1 - \left(\frac{e^{r_{t,T}}}{e^{(r_{t,T}+s_{t,T})}}\right)^T\right\} \frac{1}{(1-RR)\lambda_{iD}} \tag{5.41}$$

where $\lambda_{i,D}$ is the probability of default of a bond in rating class i.[29]

Example 5.16: Given is the risk-free spot interest rate $r_{01} = 0.05$, the risk spread of a risky bond in class A, $s_{01A} = 0.01$, class B, $s_{01B} = 0.015$, and class C, $s_{01C} = 0.02$. The recovery rate is assumed to be 40%. The historical transition matrix is given as:

$$\Lambda = \begin{pmatrix} & A & B & C & D \\ A & 0.7 & 0.15 & 0.10 & 0.05 \\ B & 0.1 & 0.6 & 0.2 & 0.1 \\ C & 0.05 & 0.15 & 0.65 & 0.15 \\ D & 0 & 0 & 0 & 1 \end{pmatrix}.$$

What are the risk-neutral martingale transition probabilities? We first have to derive the risk premiums λ_i. Following equation (5.41) we get:

$$\eta_A = \left\{1 - \left(\frac{e^{0.05}}{e^{(0.05+0.01)}}\right)^1\right\} \frac{1}{(1-0.4)(0.05)} = 0.3317$$

$$\eta_B = \left\{1 - \left(\frac{e^{0.05}}{e^{(0.05+0.015)}}\right)^1\right\} \frac{1}{(1-0.4)(0.1)} = 0.2481$$

$$\eta_C = \left\{1 - \left(\frac{e^{0.05}}{e^{(0.05+0.02)}}\right)^1\right\} \frac{1}{(1-0.4)(0.15)} = 0.2200.$$

We now multiply the 1st row of the historical transition matrix with the risk adjustment for a bond in rating class A, 0.3317, the second row with the risk adjustment of a bond in class B, 0.2481, and the third row for the class C bond with 0.2200. On the diagonal we apply the adjustment to $1-(1-(i \rightarrow i))$. Hence, we derive the martingale transition matrix of:

$$\Lambda_m = \begin{pmatrix} & A & B & C & D \\ A & 0.9005 & 0.0498 & 0.0322 & 0.0166 \\ B & 0.0248 & 0.9008 & 0.0496 & 0.0248 \\ C & 0.0110 & 0.0330 & 0.9230 & 0.0330 \\ D & 0 & 0 & 0 & 1 \end{pmatrix}.$$

Using these martingale probabilities, the no-arbitrage condition (5.39) is satisfied. For example, for the bond in class A we derive:

$$B_{01A} = e^{-(0.05+0.01)} = e^{-0.05}(1 \quad 1 \quad 1 \quad 0.4)\begin{pmatrix} 0.9005 \\ 0.0498 \\ 0.0322 \\ 0.0166 \end{pmatrix} \text{ or}$$

$$e^{-(0.05+0.01)} = e^{-0.05} \times [1 \times 0.9005 + 1 \times 0.0498 + 1 \times 0.0322 + 0.4 \times 0.0166] = 0.9418.$$

The reader may verify equation (5.40) for the bond in rating class B and C her/himself.

Martingale probabilities for period two

To calculate the risk adjustment and martingale probabilities for period 2, we first derive the historical transition matrix for period 2. Rating agencies usually provide transition probabilities just for a 1-year time frame. If we assume that time spent in one class is exponentially distributed and probabilities can be extrapolated, the historical transition probabilities from time 0 to time 2, Λ_{02}, are simply the transition matrix of period 1 multiplied by itself: $\Lambda_{02} = \Lambda_{01} \times \Lambda_{12}$. Using the values above we get:

$$\begin{pmatrix} & A & B & C & D \\ A & 0.7 & 0.15 & 0.10 & 0.05 \\ B & 0.1 & 0.6 & 0.2 & 0.1 \\ C & 0.05 & 0.15 & 0.65 & 0.15 \\ D & 0 & 0 & 0 & 1 \end{pmatrix} \times \begin{pmatrix} & A & B & C & D \\ A & 0.7 & 0.15 & 0.10 & 0.05 \\ B & 0.1 & 0.6 & 0.2 & 0.1 \\ C & 0.05 & 0.15 & 0.65 & 0.15 \\ D & 0 & 0 & 0 & 1 \end{pmatrix} =$$

$$\Lambda_{02} = \begin{pmatrix} & A & B & C & D \\ A & 0.51 & 0.21 & 0.165 & 0.115 \\ B & 0.14 & 0.405 & 0.26 & 0.195 \\ C & 0.0825 & 0.195 & 0.4575 & 0.265 \\ D & 0 & 0 & 0 & 1 \end{pmatrix}.$$

Using equation (5.41), we derive the risk adjustments from time 0 to time 2:

$$\eta_{02A} = \left\{1 - \left(\frac{e^{0.06}}{e^{(0.06+0.02)}}\right)^2\right\} \frac{1}{(1-0.4)(0.115)} = 0.5683$$

$$\eta_{02B} = \left\{1 - \left(\frac{e^{0.06}}{e^{(0.06+0.025)}}\right)^2\right\} \frac{1}{(1-0.4)(0.195)} = 0.4168$$

$$\eta_{02C} = \left\{1 - \left(\frac{e^{0.06}}{e^{(0.06+0.03)}}\right)^2\right\} \frac{1}{(1-0.4)(0.265)} = 0.3663.$$

We now multiply the first row of the historical transition matrix Λ_{02} with the risk adjustment for a bond in rating class A, 0.5683, the second row with the risk adjustment of a bond in class B, 0.4168, and the third row for the class C bond with 0.3663. On the diagonal we apply the adjustment to 1 − (1 − (i → i)). Hence, we derive the martingale transition matrix for time 0 to time 2 of:

$$\Lambda_{02m} = \begin{pmatrix} & A & B & C & D \\ A & 0.7215 & 0.1193 & 0.0938. & 0.0654 \\ B & 0.0584 & 0.7520 & 0.1084 & 0.0813 \\ C & 0.0302 & 0.0714 & 0.8013 & 0.0971 \\ D & 0 & 0 & 0 & 1 \end{pmatrix}.$$

The martingale probabilities in matrix Λ_{02m} guarantee that the no-arbitrage condition (5.39) is satisfied. For example for a bond currently in rating class B we derive:

$$B_{02B} = e^{-(r_{02}+s_{02})\times 2} = e^{-(r_{02}\times 2)}(1 \quad 1 \quad 1 \quad RR)\begin{pmatrix} B \rightarrow A \\ B \rightarrow B \\ B \rightarrow C \\ B \rightarrow D \end{pmatrix}.$$

This condition is satisfied since:

$$B_{02B} = e^{-(0.06+0.025)\times 2} = e^{-(0.06\times 2)} \times (1\times 0.0584 + 1\times 0.7520 + 1\times 0.1084 + 0.4\times 0.0813)$$
$$= 0.8437.$$

Pricing vulnerable derivatives using martingale probabilities

In the earlier section (equations 5.34 and 5.35), we derived the vulnerable option price with the help of the risky bond price B_{tT} as $C_{01V} = C_0B_{01}/P_{01}$. The approach using risk-neutral martingale probabilities is quite similar. We can use the cumulative default probability of the debtor (which is implicitly incorporated in the risky bond price B), multiply it with the loss given default (1 − RR) and discount back to today. Deducting this from the non-vulnerable call price $C_{t,T}$, we find the vulnerable call price $C_{t,T,V}$ as:

$$C_{t,T,V} = C_{t,T} - \left[e^{-r_{t,T}T}\lambda_{t,T,D}(1-RR)\right] \tag{5.42}$$

where $\lambda_{t,T,D}$ is the cumulative risk-neutral default probability of the counterparty from time t to T, and RR is the recovery rate. The term $\lambda_{t,T,D}(1 - RR)$ represents the default-probability weighted loss given default.

Example 5.17: Let's assume the non-vulnerable call price of a call with maturity T = 2 was derived as 8.00%. Let's further assume that the call seller is currently rated single B and his risk-neutral martingale default probability within 2 years is 0.0813 (see matrix Λ_{02m}). The recovery rate is assumed to be 40%. What is the value of a vulnerable call, if the 2-period risk-free spot interest rate r_{02} is 6%?

Following equation (5.42), the vulnerable call price is:

$$C_{02V} = 0.08 - \left[e^{-(0.06\times 2)} \times 0.0813 \times (1-0.4)\right] = 3.67\%$$

Hence the non-vulnerable call price is significantly reduced by 8.00% − 3.67% = 4.33% or 4.33%/8.00% = 54.08% of its no-default value.

The principle of equation (5.42) can be used for any derivatives such as forwards, futures, and swaps. Thus generalizing equation (5.42), we can write:

$$D_{t,T,V} = D_{t,T} - \left[e^{-r_{t,T}T}\lambda_{t,T,D}(1-RR)\right] \tag{5.43}$$

where $D_{t,T,V}$ is any derivative such as an option, forward, future, or swap, in which the counterpart has, on a netted basis, a future obligation.

Equation (5.43) shows that the vulnerable derivative $D_{t,T,V}$ will be equal to the non-vulnerable derivative $D_{t,T}$ in case the default probability of the counterpart $\lambda_{t,T,D}$ is zero. The same logic applies to the recovery rate. In the (theoretical) case it is 100%, the vulnerable derivative $D_{t,T,V}$ will be again equal to the non-vulnerable derivative $D_{t,T}$, independently of the probability of default $\lambda_{t,T,D}$. The Jarrow-Lando-Turnbull 1997 model can be found at www.dersoft.com/jlt.xls.

When to use martingale probabilities, when to use historical probabilities

When discussing traditional models at the beginning of this chapter, we have already mentioned an inconsistency in the credit market. In practice, risky bond prices tend to overestimate the probability of default significantly (see e.g. Altman, 1989). This phenomenon can be partly explained by the illiquidity of risky bonds, especially when they are close to default. Also, the probability of a future recession may be incorporated in the risky bond valuation, thus lowering their price.

It can also be argued that investors are principally risk-averse, requiring a risk premium that is higher than that of the risk-neutral approach, which derives a risky bond price as the default-probability weighted, discounted value of all future cash flows (see condition 5.39). It can also be argued that many investors do not have the necessary information, i.e. the transition and the default probabilities, in order to derive the risk-neutral price of a risky asset.

So when should we use historical or historically based probabilities, and when should we use risk-neutral martingale probabilities? The answer depends on the nature of the analysis: In a credit VAR (value at risk)[30] analysis, which calculates potential future losses due to credit risk, we should apply historical default probabilities. When pricing and hedging credit derivatives, martingale probabilities should be used. This would be consistent with the general usage arbitrage-free pricing methodologies, which are employed by pricing desks in banking practice.

Critical appraisal of the Jarrow-Lando-Turnbull 1997 model

In the 1995 Jarrow-Turnbull model, default probabilities and credit derivatives prices were derived on the basis of rather illiquid bond prices. In their 1997 model, Jarrow, Lando, and Turnbull replaced bond prices as the main input and apply historical transition probabilities as the basis for their analyses. In today's practice, many investment banks and insurance companies apply the 1997 model and its extensions to price and hedge credit derivatives.

One specific shortcoming of the model is that the default probability $\lambda_{i,D}$ can become bigger than 1. This is especially the case for longer maturities T. Equation (5.41)

$$\eta_i = \left\{1 - \left(\frac{e^{r_{t,T}}}{e^{(r_{t,T}+s_{t,T})}}\right)^T\right\}\frac{1}{(1-RR)\lambda_{iD}},$$

reduces to

$$\lambda_{iD} = \left\{1 - \frac{1}{e^{s_{t,T}T}}\right\} \frac{1}{(1-RR)\eta_i}.$$

For this equation to be smaller than 1, we require that $\frac{1}{e^{s_t T}} > 1 + \eta_i(RR - 1)$. This condition may not be satisfied for large s, T, η, and RR. (See www.dersoft.com/jlt.xls.)

General shortcomings of the model lie again in the fact that the ultimate reason of default, the asset-liability structure or the liquidity of a company, is not part of the analysis. Also, as in the 1995 model, the interest rate process and the bankruptcy process are assumed independent. Furthermore, the recovery rate RR is exogenously given.

Naturally, the nature of the transition matrix also bears problems. Jarrow, Lando, and Turnbull assume that bonds in the same credit class have the same yield spread. This is not necessarily the case as pointed out by Longstaff and Schwartz (1995). Rather, the rating–yield relationship is similar within sectors, which suggests conducting sector analyses, rather than aggregating data generally among counterparties.

A crucial problem is that ratings are often done infrequently and may not be recent enough to reflect current counterparty risk. In addition, Standard & Poors currently only rates about 8,000 companies in the US, and only about 1% of all companies worldwide. Nevertheless, the number of rated companies should increase in the future, allowing a widespread usage of the model and its extensions.

Other Reduced Form Models

Other significant reduced form models that have received recognition are Brennan-Schwartz (1980); Iben-Litterman (1991); Longstaff-Schwartz (1995); Das-Tufano (1996); Duffee (1996); Schoenbucher (1997); Henn (1997); Duffie-Singleton (1997); Brooks-Yan (1998); Madan-Unal (1998); Duffie-Singleton (1999); Duffee (1998); Das-Sundaram (2000); Hull-White (2000a); Wei (2001), Martin-Thompson-Brown (2001); Duffie-Lando (2001); and Jarrow-Yildirim (2002). For a survey article comparing the default swap evaluation equations of the Jarrow-Turnbull (1995), Brooks-Yan (1998), Duffee (1998), Das-Sundaram (2000), and Hull-White (2000a) models, see Cheng (2001).

Discussing all these models is beyond the scope of this book. Nevertheless let's look at crucial features of some of them.

Duffie and Singleton (1999)

Duffie and Singleton express the risky bond price B at time t with maturity T based on equation (5.38) $B_{t,T} = E_t[e^{-(r_{t,T}+s_{t,T})T}]$. In the Duffie-Singleton model, the swap spread $s_{t,T}$ equals approximately $\lambda_{t,T}(1 - RR)$. This result can be derived by a simple binomial tree for a zero-coupon bond with maturity at time 1 and a notional amount of \$1, as shown in figure 5.21.

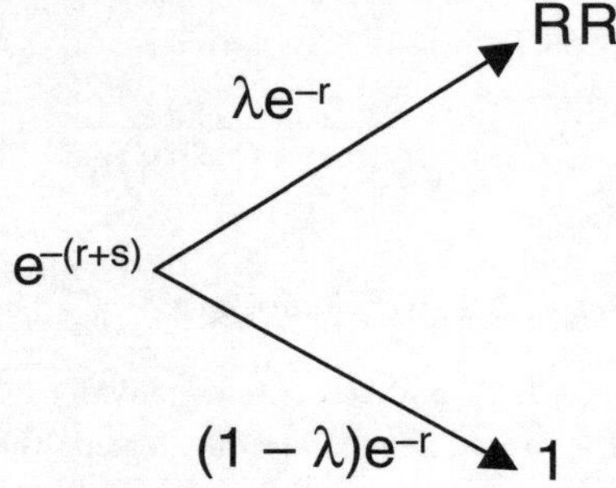

Figure 5.21: Deriving the swap spread s

In figure 5.21, r is the risk-free interest rate, s is the swap spread, λ is the *hazard rate*, which multiplied by time periods for default of 1 equals the risk-neutral probability of default. RR is the recovery rate.

From figure 5.21 we derive:

$$e^{-(r+s)} = \lambda e^{-r}RR + (1-\lambda)e^{-r}. \tag{5.44}$$

Solving equation (5.44) for s, using $e^x \approx 1 + x$, we get $s \approx \lambda(1 - RR) + \lambda r(1 - RR)$. Duffie and Singleton prove that the term $\lambda r(1 - RR)$ can be neglected for a continuous time setting. Hence, the interest rate process drops out and we can write for a default swap spread from time t to time T, $s_{t,T}$:

$$s_{t,T} \approx \lambda_{t,T}(1-RR) \tag{5.45}$$

where all variables are viewed at time t.

Equation (5.45) shows the intuitive approximate relationship between the swap spread s and the hazard rate λ: If the recovery rate RR is zero, $s_{t,T} \approx \lambda_{t,T}$. Hence the spread s approximately compensates the investor for the default risk λ. The relationship in equation (5.45) is often termed *credit triangle*, since two of the three variables are sufficient to generate the third.

The model may include a liquidity premium ℓ for the risky asset. In this case the swap spread is simply:

$$s_{t,T} \approx \lambda_{t,T}(1-RR) + \ell \tag{5.46}$$

where ℓ is a fractional value of the risky bond.

Duffie and Singleton show that any risky claim B with a notional amount N, for different interest rates r and swap spreads s at various times j, and time units of 1, with maturity $t + \Gamma$, can be expressed as:

$$B_{t,t+\Gamma} = E_t\left[e^{-\sum_{j=0}^{\Gamma-1}(r_{t+j}+s_{t+j})} N_{t+\Gamma} \right]. \tag{5.47}$$

Hence, one crucial finding of the Duffie-Singleton model is that any risky claim B can be priced by discounting the notional amount N with the default-adjusted process r + s. Equation (5.47) is an extension of equation (5.38).

In equations (5.44) to (5.46), the recovery rate RR is applied to the expected market value of the risky bond at the time of default, termed *recovery of market value RMV*, hence $E_d(RMV_{d+1}) = RR_d E_d(B_{d+1})$, where d + 1 is the time of default. In contrast, in the Jarrow-Turnbull 1995 and Jarrow-Lando-Turnbull 1997 model, the recovery value is a fraction of the risk-free bond price at the time of default. Brennan-Schwartz (1980), Longstaff-Schwartz (1995), and Duffee (1998) apply a simpler assumption with respect to the payoff in default. They assume that creditors at the time of default receive the recovery rate multiplied with the notional amount of the risky bond.

Das and Sundaram (2000)

Das and Sundaram express the risky bond price from time t to time t + Δt, with a notional amount of \$1, $B_{t,t+\Delta t}$ as:

$$B_{t,t+\Delta t} = e^{-(r_{t,t}+s_{t,t})\Delta t} = e^{-r_{t,t}\Delta t}[(1-\lambda_t)+\lambda_t RR] \tag{5.48}$$

where $r_{t,t}$ and $s_{t,t}$ are *instantaneous* rates (i.e. rates for infinitesimally small time periods) and λ_t is the risk-neutral default probability from time t to t + Δt. As pointed out earlier in this chapter, the hazard rate multiplied by a certain time frame, here Δt, results in the risk-neutral default probability.

In equation (5.48), for a risk-neutral default probability of $\lambda_t = 0$, the bond will pay the notional of \$1; for a risk-neutral default probability of 1, the bond will pay the recovery rate RR. Equation (5.48) is identical to equation (5.44) for t = 0 and Δt = 1. With respect to the recovery value at default, Das and Sundaram apply the recovery market value (RMV) approach of Duffie and Singleton. Hence the payoff in default, RMV, is the recovery rate multiplied with the expected value of the risky bond: $E_d(RMV_{d+1}) = RR_d E_d(B_{d+1})$, as above.

For the risk-free interest rate process, Das and Sundaram choose the Heath-Jarrow-Morton (HJM) (1992) term structure of forward rates. Hence, the risk-free forward interest rate viewed at a future time t + Δt, running from time T to T + Δt, $r_{t+\Delta t,T}$, is given by:

$$r_{t+\Delta t,T} = r_{t,T} + \alpha_{t,T}\Delta t + \sigma_{t,T} X_1 \sqrt{\Delta t} \tag{5.49}$$

where $0 \le t \le t + \Delta t \le T$. The variable α is the drift rate (average growth rate) of the risk-free interest rate r, σ is the volatility of r, and X_1 is a random variable. Equivalent to equation (5.49), the equation for the forward swap spread s, viewed at a future time t + Δt, running from time T to T + Δt, $s_{t+\Delta t,T}$, is given by:

$$s_{t+\Delta t,T} = s_{t,T} + \beta_{t,T}\Delta t + \upsilon_{t,T} X_2 \sqrt{\Delta t}. \tag{5.50}$$

The variable β is the drift of the swap rate s, υ is the volatility of s, and X_2 is a random variable.

In the Das-Sundaram model the drift rate α is expressed as a function of the volatility σ. In addition, a recursive relation expressing α and β as functions of σ and υ can be derived. These functionalities facilitate the implementation of the model, which is expressed as a quadruple tree as in Jarrow-Turnbull (1995).

The Das-Sundaram model allows for four states of correlation between the risk-free interest rate r and the swap spread s at each node of the quadruple tree. This is attained by the variables X_1 and X_2 in equations (5.49) and (5.50). X_1 and X_2 can each take the values −1 and 1, hence the joint distribution of X_1 and X_2 is:

$$(X_1, X_2) = \begin{cases} (+1,+1), & \text{w.p.}(1+\rho)/4 \\ (+1,-1), & \text{w.p.}(1-\rho)/4 \\ (-1,+1), & \text{w.p.}(1-\rho)/4 \\ (-1,-1), & \text{w.p.}(1+\rho)/4 \end{cases} \tag{5.51}$$

where ρ is the correlation coefficient between X_1 and X_2. ρ is principally constant for the time frame of the credit derivative, but can vary at each node at the cost of higher computational complexity.

The recovery rate in the Das-Sundaram model is not exogenous as in most reduced form models, but derived as:

$$RR = \frac{1}{\lambda_a} e^{-(s_{t,t}-\eta_{t,t})\Delta t} - 1 + \lambda_a \tag{5.52}$$

where λ_a is the actual or historical probability, $s_{t,t}$ is the instantaneous swap spread and η is the *risk premium*, which is used to transform actual probabilities λ_a into risk-neutral probabilities λ, via:

$$\lambda = \lambda_a \left[\frac{1 - e^{-(s_{t,t})\Delta t}}{1 - e^{-(s_{t,t}-\eta_{t,t})\Delta t}} \right]. \tag{5.53}$$

The risk premium η is assumed to be a fraction of the swap spread s, hence $\eta_{t,t} = \pi s_{t,t}$, where π is a constant.

In the Heath-Jarrow-Morton model, as in any term structure model, a whole interest rate curve is represented at any node. We will denote the forward risk-free interest rate curve with R and the forward spread curve with S. In order to scale the risk-neutral probability λ to values between 0 and 1, Das and Sundaram choose a simple logit function:

$$\lambda(S, R) = \frac{1}{e^x + 1} \quad \text{where} \quad x = a + bF + cS. \tag{5.54}$$

Following equations (5.48) to (5.54), the quadruple tree shown in figure 5.22 is derived.

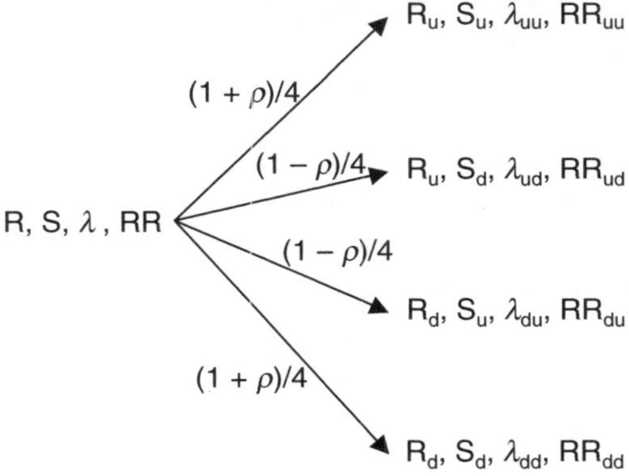

Figure 5.22: Quadruple tree of the Das-Sundaram model

In figure 5.22, R_u, R_d refer to $X_1 = 1$, $X_1 = -1$ respectively. S_u, S_d refer to $X_2 = 1$, $X_2 = -1$ respectively. λ_{uu} refers to the state R_u, S_u; λ_{ud}, λ_{du}, and λ_{dd} are defined respectively. R_{uu} refers to state R_u, S_u; RR_{ud}, RR_{du}, and RR_{dd} are defined respectively.

On the basis of equations (5.48) to (5.54), default swaps, European style and American style credit-spread options, as well as average credit-spread options can be priced. The inputs are R, S, the volatility of R and S, σ and υ, as well as the parameters a, b, c, π and the correlation coefficient ρ. The model (written in Visual Basic) can be found at www.dersoft.com/DasSundaram.exe.lnk. The reader should note that in the program we followed Das and Sundaram's notation of a credit-spread option. Here the payoff of a call is $\max(0, s_{T,T} - K)$ and the put payoff is $\max(K - s_{T,T}, 0)$, where K is the strike spread. These are the standard payoff definitions in the exotic options market for spread options. However, these payoffs are different from the payoff conventions in the credit derivatives market, where the call and put payoffs are opposite and a duration term is added; see equations (2.5) and (2.6).

Hull and White (2000)[31]

Hull and White derive a closed form solution for a default swap spread using swap valuation techniques. Hull and White incorporate the accrued interest of the reference asset, that a default swap buyer pays at the time of default in case of cash settlement. Also, the accrual payment of the default swap premium that a default swap buyer has to pay at the time of default is included in the analysis (for details on the accrued interest on the reference asset and the accrued interest on the swap premium, see chapter 2, "The default swap premium" and "Cash versus physical settlement").

In a standard default swap, the settlement amount of the default swap buyer is usually defined as the nominal amount N minus the recovery value RR, which may include the accrued interest, a, of the reference obligation. Hence we can express the expected settlement amount, also called claim amount, as:

$$N[1-(RR+RRa)]. \tag{5.55}$$

In example 2.1 in chapter 2, we had derived the claim amount. However, we had used equation N[1 – (RR + a)] instead of N[1 – (RR + RRa)]. Which of these two equations is more appropriate, is a question of the terms of the specific default swap contract. Hull and White apply equation N[1 – (RR + RRa)], since here the accrued interest, a, incorporates the default event in form of the recovery rate RR.

To derive the expected value of the claim amount of equation (5.55), we have to multiply by the risk-neutral probability of default λ, since the claim will be paid only in default. Discounting back to t_0 with the risk-free interest rate r, we derive the expected present value of the claim amount for a swap with a notional amount of N = 1 as:

$$\int_0^T (1-RR-RRa)\lambda_t e^{-rt}dt. \tag{5.56}$$

The value of the default swap *payments* of the default swap buyer can be expressed as the integral over all payments in case of default plus all payments in case of no default. Hence, we derive:

$$\int_0^T s\lambda_t(u_t+g_t)dt + s\left[1-\int_0^T \lambda_t dt\right]u_T \tag{5.57}$$

where s: swap premium; λ: risk-neutral probability of default of the reference asset; u: present value of all swap premium payments at rate \$1 between zero and time t; g: present value of accrual payments of the swap premium s paid at time t; T: swap maturity.

From equation (5.56) and (5.57) we derive the value of the default swap from the view of the default swap buyer as:

$$\int_0^T (1-RR-RRa)\lambda_t e^{-rt}dt - \int_0^T s\lambda_t(u_t+g_t)dt - s\left[1-\int_0^T \lambda_t dt\right]u_T. \tag{5.58}$$

In order to find the equilibrium swap premium s_e, which gives the default swap a zero value, we have to set equation (5.58) to zero and solve for s. This will give us the value of s_e as:

$$s_e = \frac{\int_0^T [1-(RR+RRa)]\lambda_t e^{-rt}dt}{\int_0^T \lambda_t(u_t+g_t)dt + \left[1-\int_0^T \lambda_t dt\right]u_T}. \tag{5.59}$$

Hull and White (2001)

Hull and White extended equation (5.59) to include the possibility of default of either the default swap buyer or the default swap seller. As mentioned earlier, this type of default swap is also termed a *vulnerable* default swap. The reader should note that the default swap buyer usually has significantly higher counterparty exposure since the claim amount is typically much higher than the periodic default swap premiums. In case of an upfront default swap premium, only the default swap buyer has counterparty default risk, since the default swap buyer has no future obligation to the default swap seller.

To account for the possible default of the counterparty, only one term has to be added to equation (5.59), and two variables have to be redefined. Define:

λ_t^*: risk-neutral probability of default of the reference asset at time t and no earlier default of the counterparty

ϕ_t: risk-neutral probability of default of the counterparty at time t and no earlier default of the reference entity

π_t: risk-neutral probability of no default by the counterparty or the reference asset during the life of the swap

As it is standard in a default swap, it is assumed that there is an accrual payment, g, on the swap premium from the default swap buyer in case of default of the reference asset. However, there is no such payment in case the counterparty defaults. With these assumptions we can express the equilibrium value of a vulnerable default swap $s_{e,v}$ as:

$$s_{e,v} = \frac{\int_0^T [1-(RR+RRa)]\lambda_t^* e^{-rt} dt}{\int_0^T \left[\lambda_t^*(u_t+g_t)+\phi_t u_t\right]dt+\pi u_T}. \tag{5.60}$$

Note that for the case of no counterparty default risk i.e. $\phi_t = 0$, equation (5.60) is mathematically identical with (5.59). For the possibility of counterparty risk, $\phi > 0$, it follows from equations (5.59) and (5.60) that the swap value decreases, i.e. $s_{e,v} < s_e$.

Using default correlations to value default swaps

The approach above uses the risk-neutral probabilities λ_t^* and ϕ_t, which reflect the timing of default events, as well as π_t, which gives the joint probability of no default. A different approach of valuing a default swap is to derive the joint probability of default of the reference entity and the counterparty via a correlation coefficient and then alter the swap premium s. This approach will be discussed now.

The *default correlation* of the reference entity and the counterparty naturally is an important feature in the valuation of a default swap. The higher this correlation, the lower the value of the default swap: Only if both the reference entity and the counterparty default, will the default swap buyer be left with a huge loss. Hence, any default swap buyer should ensure that the default correlation between the reference entity and the default swap seller is low before entering into the default swap.

The probability of a joint default can be expressed easily. Let's first start with some basic statistics: If two companies' default probabilities are independent, the joint probability of default is simply the product of the individual default probabilities. So if the default probability of company r, λ^r, is 2% and the default probability of company c, λ^c, is 3%, the joint probability of default, in case the default probabilities of the companies are independent, is 0.006%. If two companies' default correlation (usually derived from the equity correlation) is $\rho(\lambda^r, \lambda^c)$, the joint probability of default $\lambda^r \cap \lambda^c$ can be shown to be:

$$\lambda(r \cap c) = \rho(\lambda^r, \lambda^c)\sqrt{\left[\lambda^r - (\lambda^r)^2\right]\left[\lambda^c - (\lambda^c)^2\right]} + [\lambda^r \lambda^c]. \tag{5.61}$$

From equation (5.61) we can see that for a default correlation $\rho(\lambda^r,\lambda^c)$ of zero, the joint default probability $\lambda(r \cap c)$ is indeed the product of the individual default probabilities of λ^r and λ^c as stated above. We can also derive from equation (5.61), that the higher the correlation of default probabilities $\rho(\lambda^r, \lambda^c)$, the higher the joint probability of default $\lambda(r \cap c)$, thus the higher the expected loss. Therefore, assumptions about correlations are a key feature in the valuation of credit derivatives.

Hull and White (2001) derive an analytic approximation for a default swap premium, which incorporates the default correlation between the reference entity and the default swap counterparty. Define:

λ^r:	Probability of default of reference entity r during the life of the default swap
λ^c:	Probability of default of the counterparty c during the life of the default swap
$\lambda(r \cap c)$:	Joint probability of default of the reference entity r and the counterparty c during the life of the default swap (derived from equation (5.61))
g_c:	proportional reduction in the present value of the expected payoff (1 − RR − RRa) due to counterparty default
h_c:	proportional reduction in the present value of the expected swap premium payments s due to counterparty default
s:	default swap premium assuming no counterparty default risk
s_v:	default swap premium including counterparty default risk (v for vulnerable)

If the reference entity defaults first, there will be the payoff of a standard default swap, 1 − RR − RRa. However, if the counterparty defaults first, there will be no payoff.

A small value of g_c and a high value of h_c increase the default swap value. Hence, the relationship between s and s_v can be expressed as:

$$s_v = s\frac{1 - g_c}{1 - h_c}. \tag{5.62}$$

In equation (5.62) s is the standard default swap premium, hence s incorporates the probability of default of the reference entity.

Let's first look at the proportional reduction of the expected payoff g. For g to occur, first the reference entity has to default (so that the payoff 1 − RR − RRa is due) and conditionally on this default, the counterparty has to default. The attentive statistics student recalls that this conditional default probability can be expressed as:

$$\lambda^c | \lambda^r = \lambda(r \cap c)/\lambda^r. \tag{5.63}$$

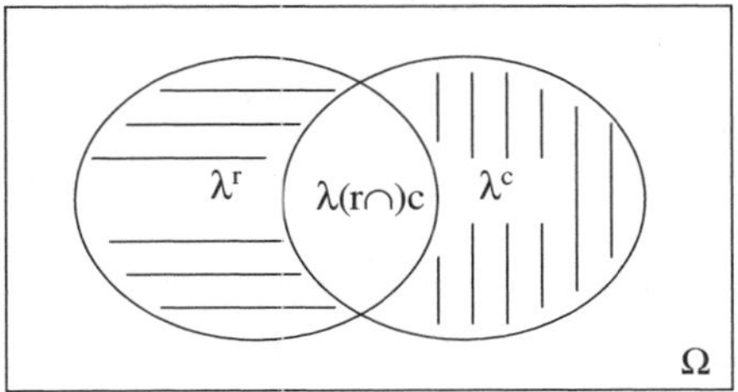

Figure 5.23: Risk-neutral default probability of reference entity r, λ^r, risk-neutral default probability of counterparty c, λ^c, and the joint default probability $\lambda(r \cap c)$

Equation (5.63) reads: The probability of counterparty c defaulting conditional on the default of the reference entity r, $\lambda^c \mid \lambda^r$, equals the joint probability of default of c and r, $\lambda(r \cap c)$, divided by the probability of default of r, λ^r. Hull and White assume that there is a 50% chance that the reference asset defaults first and then the counterparty defaults before having paid the payoff $1 - RR - RRa$. Only in this case will there be a reduction of the payoff reflected by g. Hence we get:

$$g = 0.5\lambda(r \cap c)/\lambda^r. \tag{5.64}$$

Let's now look at the expected proportional reduction h of the swap payments of the default swap buyer due to counterparty default risk. This reduction h will occur if the counterparty defaults or the reference entity defaults. However, we have already incorporated the reference entity default risk in the standard swap premium s. Hence, we have to exclude the reference entity default risk and only incorporate counterparty default effects. Displaying first the default probabilities, we get figure 5.23.

The probability of counterparty c defaulting and not the reference entity r defaulting can be derived from the addition law of basic probability theory:

$$\lambda(r \cup c) = \lambda^r + \lambda^c - \lambda(r \cap c). \tag{5.65}$$

Equation (5.65) reads: The probability of the reference entity r or the counterparty c defaulting, $\lambda(r \cup c)$, equals the probability of default of r plus c, $\lambda^r + \lambda^c$, minus the joint probability of default $\lambda(r \cap c)$. Equation (5.58) can easily be verified from figure 5.23.

From equation (5.65) we can derive the probability of counterparty c defaulting but not the reference entity r defaulting, $\lambda(c \cap \bar{r})$ (vertically shaded area in figure 5.23) as:

$$\lambda(c \cap \bar{r}) = \lambda(r \cup c) - \lambda^r = \lambda^c - \lambda(r \cap c). \tag{5.66}$$

As mentioned above, we presently only consider the case where the counterparty defaults before the reference asset defaults. Only this case has to be considered here, since the reference asset defaulting first is already incorporated in the standard swap premium s. Assuming there is 50% chance that the counterparty defaults first, the term $\lambda^c - \lambda(r \cap c)$ reduces to 0.5 $[\lambda^c - \lambda(r \cap c)]$.

So far we have investigated $\lambda(c \cap \bar{r})$, the vertically shaded area in figure 5.23. We now have to additionally consider the term $\lambda(r \cap c)$, since it is part of the counterparty default risk. In this case, Hull and White assume that when both default with the counterparty defaulting first, the payments of the default swap buyer will reduce by one third. Altogether this results in a proportional reduction of the swap premium payments h of:

$$h = 0.5[\lambda^c - \lambda(r \cap c)] + 0.5\lambda(r \cap c)/3 = 0.5\lambda^c - \lambda(r \cap c)/3. \quad (5.67)$$

Combining equations (5.62), (5.64), and (5.67), we derive the vulnerable swap premium s_v as:

$$s_v = s\frac{1 - 0.5\lambda(r \cap c)/\lambda^r}{1 - 0.5\lambda^c + \lambda(r \cap c)/3}. \quad (5.68)$$

Example 5.18: The joint probability of default of the reference entity and the counterparty was derived (e.g. with equation (5.61)) as 10%. The default probability of the reference entity r is 20% and the default probability of the counterparty c is 30%. What is the default swap premium, assuming the default swap premium without counterparty default risk was derived as 5%?

Following equation (5.68), we derive:

$$s_V = 0.05\frac{1 - 0.5 \times 0.1/0.2}{1 - 0.5 \times 0.3 + 0.1/3} = 4.25\%.$$

Hence, the incorporation of counterparty default risk reduces the swap premium by 0.05 – 0.0425 = 0.75 percentage points or 0.0075/0.05 = 15.00% of its no-counterparty risk value.

Kettunen, Ksendzovsky, and Meissner (KKM) (2003)

KKM derive the default swap premium with a combination of two easily implementable discrete binomial trees. One tree represents the default swap premium payments, the other the default swap payoff in case of default.

In the following, the model will be presented in three parts:

1 The model excluding counterparty default risk
2 The model including counterparty default risk, which is not correlated to reference asset default
3 The model including reference entity–counterparty default correlation

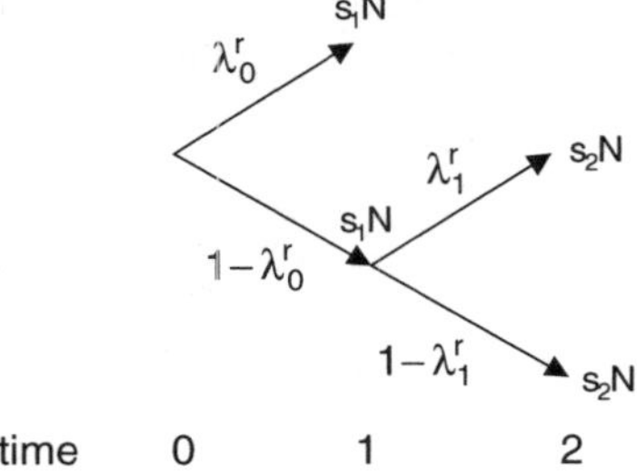

Figure 5.24: Discrete-time binomial model where the premium is paid at the end of a default period

1. The KKM model excluding counterparty default risk

Define:

λ_t^r: exogenous, risk-neutral probability of default of reference entity r, during time t to t + 1, which is expressed in years as $\Delta\tau_t$, viewed at time 0, given no earlier default of the reference entity r
s_t: default swap premium to be paid at time t
N: notional amount of the swap
r_t: risk-free interest rate from time 0 to time t + 1
τ_t: time between time 0 and time t, expressed in years
$\Delta\tau_t$: time between t and t + 1, expressed in years
RR_r: exogenous recovery rate of the reference entity
a: accrued interest on the reference obligation from the last coupon date until the default date.

A tree where the premium is paid at the end of a default period: Let's look first at the default swap premium tree. The discrete times t represent default swap premium payment dates. A simplified version of the default swap premium tree can be seen in figure 5.24.

The risk-neutral default probability λ^r is derived by calibration of the model. Including discount factors, we obtain the present value of the swap premium payments from figure 5.24 as:

$$\left[\lambda_0^r s_1 N + \left(1-\lambda_0^r\right)s_1 N\right]e^{-r_0\tau_1} + \left\{\left(1-\lambda_0^r\right)\left[\lambda_1^r s_2 N + \left(1-\lambda_1^r\right)s_2 N\right]\right\}e^{-r_1\tau_2} \tag{5.69}$$

where τ_t is the time between 0 and t expressed in years and r_t is the risk-free interest rate from time 0 to time t + 1.

Canceling several terms in equation (5.69) and generalizing for T periods we derive the present value of the default swap premiums as:

$$s_1 N e^{-r_0\tau_1} + \sum_{t=2}^{T}\left[s_t N e^{-r_{t-1}\tau_t}\prod_{u=0}^{t-2}\left(1-\lambda_u^r\right)\right]. \tag{5.70}$$

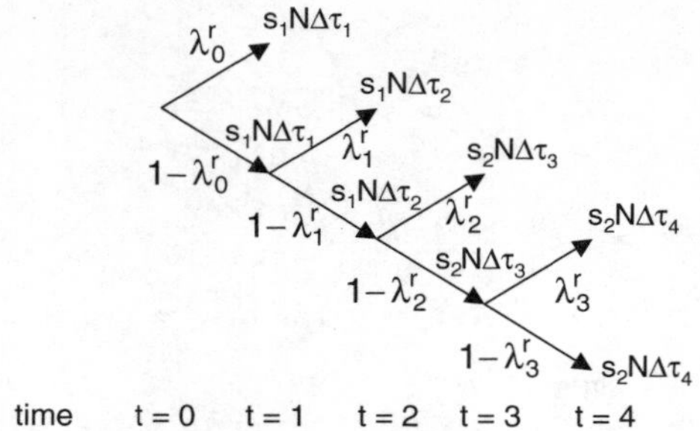

Figure 5.25: A tree with two premium payment dates at time t = 2 and t = 4 and four risk-neutral default probabilities λ_0 to λ_3

The first term of equation (5.70), s_1 N, is not weighted by a default probability. This is because in either default or no default at time 1, the premium payment s_1 N will be paid. It is typical in reality that in case of default, the default swap buyer will make a final (accrual) swap premium payment to the default swap seller.

A tree with more default periods than premium payment dates: In the simple tree in figure 5.24, the number of risk-neutral default probabilities is identical with the number of premium payment periods. The number of possible default periods can be easily increased. For example, if a user wants to double the number of default probabilities, the tree will look as in figure 5.25.

In figure 5.25, $\Delta\tau_t$ represents the time between t and t + 1, expressed in years. We assume that in case of default of the reference entity, the default swap buyer will make an accrual payment on his default swap premium $sN\Delta\tau_t$ at the end of the default period. Hence $sN\Delta\tau_t$ is paid at time t + 1, for default between time t and time t + 1. The exact time of default between times t will be determined by a random number generator in a programmed model, see section "The KKM model in combination with the Libor Market Model (LMM)," below.

In figure 5.25 we have 4 periods in which default can occur. If we have a two-year default swap with annual premium payments, it follows that $\Delta\tau_t = 0.5$. However, the length of the time periods in figure 5.25 may differ. Hence $\Delta\tau_x$ may be unequal to $\Delta\tau_y$.

As shown in figure 5.25, it is assumed that at the time of default, the default swap premium buyer will make a final accrual payment of the default swap premium $sN\Delta\tau_t$, which is typically the case in reality.

Integrating discount factors, we can derive the present value of the swap premium payments from figure 5.25 as:

$$
\begin{aligned}
&[\lambda^r_0 s_1 N\Delta\tau_0 + (1-\lambda^r_0) s_1 N\Delta\tau_0]e^{-r_0\tau_1} \\
&\quad + \{(1-\lambda^r_0)[\lambda^r_1 s_1 N\Delta\tau_1 + (1-\lambda^r_1) s_1 N\Delta\tau_1]\}e^{-r_1\tau_2} \\
&\quad + \{(1-\lambda^r_0)(1-\lambda^r_1)[\lambda^r_2 s_2 N\Delta\tau_2 + (1-\lambda^r_2) s_2 N\Delta\tau_2]\}e^{-r_2\tau_3} \\
&\quad + \{(1-\lambda^r_0)(1-\lambda^r_1)(1-\lambda^r_2)[\lambda^r_3 s_2 N\Delta\tau_3 + (1-\lambda^r_3) s_2 N\Delta\tau_3]\}e^{-r_3\tau_4}.
\end{aligned} \tag{5.71}
$$

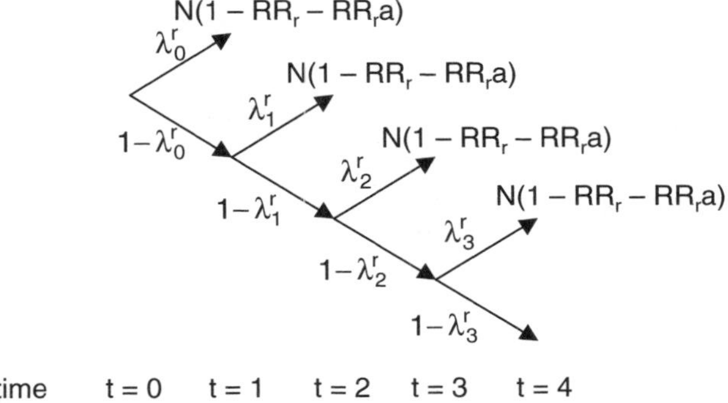

Figure 5.26: Binomial tree of the default swap payoff

If we set the swap premium s constant in time, i.e. $s_1 = s_2 = s_3 \ldots$, and cancel several terms in equation (5.71), we get for T time periods:

$$sN\Delta\tau_0 e^{-r_0\tau_1} + \sum_{t=2}^{T}\left[sN\Delta\tau_{t-1}e^{-r_{t-1}\tau_t}\prod_{u=0}^{t-2}\left(1-\lambda_u^r\right)\right]. \tag{5.72}$$

Let's now look at the process for the payoff that the default swap buyer receives from the default swap seller in case of default of the reference asset. This payoff in practice is typically $N - NRR_r - NRR_ra$ or $N(1 - RR_r - RR_ra)$, where N is the notional amount, RR_r is recovery rate of the reference entity, and a is accrued interest on the reference obligation from the last coupon date until the default date.

The payoff is paid only in the event of default. Using the grid points from figure 5.25, we can build a tree as in figure 5.26.

Integrating discount factors, we derive the present value of the expected payoff from figure 5.26 as:

$$\begin{aligned}&\lambda_0^r N(1-RR_r-RR_ra)e^{-r_0\tau_1}+\left(1-\lambda_0^r\right)\lambda_1^r N(1-RR_r-RR_ra)e^{-r_1\tau_2}\\&+\left(1-\lambda_0^r\right)\left(1-\lambda_1^r\right)\lambda_2^r N(1-RR_r-RR_ra)e^{-r_2\tau_3}\ldots\end{aligned} \tag{5.73}$$

Generalizing equation (5.73), we get for the present value of the expected payoff:

$$\lambda_0^r N(1-RR_r-RR_ra)e^{-r_0\tau_1}+\sum_{t=2}^{T}\left[N(1-RR_r-RR_ra)_t\lambda_{t-1}^r e^{-r_{t-1}\tau_t}\prod_{u=0}^{t-2}\left(1-\lambda_u^r\right)\right]. \tag{5.74}$$

Combining equations (5.72) and (5.74), we derive the present value of the default swap from the viewpoint of the default swap buyer as:

$$\begin{aligned}&\lambda_0^r N(1-RR_r-RR_ra)e^{-r_0\tau_1}+\sum_{t=2}^{T}\left[N(1-RR_r-RR_ra)_t\lambda_{t-1}^r e^{-r_{t-1}\tau_t}\prod_{u=0}^{t-2}\left(1-\lambda_u^r\right)\right]\\&-sN\Delta\tau_0 e^{-r_0\tau_1}+\sum_{t=2}^{T}\left[sN\Delta\tau_{t-1}e^{-r_{t-1}\tau_t}\prod_{u=0}^{t-2}\left(1-\lambda_u^r\right)\right].\end{aligned} \tag{5.75}$$

Setting equation (5.75) to zero and solving the equation for the default swap premium s, we get:

$$s = \frac{\lambda_0^r N(1 - RR_r - RR_r a)e^{-r_0\tau_1} + \sum_{t=2}^{T}\left[N(1 - RR_r - RR_r a)_t \lambda_{t-1}^r e^{-r_{t-1}\tau_t} \prod_{u=0}^{t-2}(1 - \lambda_u^r)\right]}{N\Delta\tau_0 e^{-r_0\tau_1} + \sum_{t=2}^{T}\left[N\Delta\tau_{t-1} e^{-r_{t-1}\tau_t} \prod_{u=0}^{t-2}(1 - \lambda_u^r)\right]}. \tag{5.76}$$

The swap premium s in equation (5.76) is the *fair* or *mid-market* default swap premium, since it gives the swap a value of zero. The fair default swap premium s multiplied with $\Delta\tau$ is paid at each time t, starting at t + 1 until T or default, whichever occurs sooner.

Example 5.19: Given is a default swap with a notional amount N of \$1,000,000, and an assumed recovery rate of the reference entity RR_r of 40%. The swap terminates in 1 year (time 2). The default swap premiums are paid annually and the probability of default λ in 6 months (time 1) is 10% and in 1 year (time 2) is 30%. The accrued interest, a, of the underlying bond from the last bond coupon date to time 1 will be 1% and to time 2, 4%. The 6-month and 1-year interest rates are 5% and 6%, respectively. What is the annual default swap premium s?

Following equation (5.76), the numerator is:

$$1{,}000{,}000 \times (1 - 0.4 - 0.4 \times 0.01) \times e^{(-0.05\times 0.5)} \times 0.1$$
$$+1{,}000{,}000 \times (1 - 0.4 - 0.4 \times 0.04) \times e^{(-0.06\times 1)} \times 0.3 \times (1 - 0.1) = 206{,}626$$

and the denominator is

$$1{,}000{,}000 \times 0.5 \times e^{(-0.05\times 0.5)} + 1{,}000{,}000 \times 0.5 \times e^{(-0.06\times 1)} \times (1 - 0.1) = 911{,}449$$

Hence the swap premium is 206,626/911,449 = 22.67%.

See www.dersoft.com/ex519.xls for this example.

2. The KKM model including counterparty default risk, which is not correlated to reference asset default

Counterparty default risk is the risk that a counterparty does not honor its obligation. As mentioned earlier, this type of default swap is also termed a *vulnerable* default swap. Counterparty default risk can be easily integrated in the model as derived so far. In the default swap (consider figure 2.2) the default swap buyer has counterparty default risk, since the default swap seller has a potential future obligation in the amount of $N(1 - RR_r - RR_r a)$ to the default swap buyer. This type of risk is included in the Kettunen, Ksendzovsky, and Meissner model.

In a standard default swap (consider figure 2.2), the default swap seller also has counterparty default risk, if the swap premium s is paid periodically, and additionally if the default swap premium s is an above market premium. (If the swap premium s is a below market premium, the default swap will have a negative present value for the default swap seller, so there is no risk; consider figure 5.19.) This type of counterparty default risk is not included in the Kettunen, Ksendzovsky, and Meissner model. Naturally, if the default swap premium is paid upfront, the default swap seller has no counterparty default risk, since the default swap buyer has no future obligation.

In this section we are excluding the correlation between the default of the reference asset and the counterparty. If the default probability of two entities is not correlated, the joint probability of default is simply the multiplication of the individual default probabilities. So if the default probability of the reference entity r, λ^r, is 2% and the default probability of counterparty c, λ^c, is 3%, the joint probability of default, in the case where the default probabilities are independent, is 0.006%. Formally: $\lambda(r \cap c) = \lambda^r \times \lambda^c$. This property will be applied in this section.

In order to include counterparty default risk, both trees, the payoff tree as well as the swap premium payment tree, will expand to a quadruple tree. Let's start with the payoff tree.

The default swap payoff tree: Define:

λ_t^c: exogenous, risk-neutral probability of default of counterparty c, during time t to t + 1, which is expressed in years as $\Delta\tau_t$, viewed at time 0, given no earlier default of the counterparty c

RR_c: Exogenous recovery rate of the counterparty

$S_f(t)$: Fair value of the default swap at time t excluding counterparty risk (i.e. the swap value including the notional amount that gives the default swap a present value of zero).

We assume that if both reference entity and the counterparty default, with probability $\lambda^r\lambda^c$, the standard payoff in case of default of the reference asset will be reduced by the recovery rate of the counterparty. Hence the payoff will be $N(1 - RR_r - RR_r a)RR_c$. There will be no payoff if neither the reference entity nor the counterparty default, probability $(1 - \lambda^r)(1 - \lambda^c)$. There will be the standard payoff $N(1 - RR_r - RR_r a)$ if only the reference entity defaults, probability $\lambda^r(1 - \lambda^c)$. We assume that if only the counterparty defaults, probability $(1 - \lambda^r)\lambda^c$, the counterparty will pay the time t value of the default swap, $S_f(t)$, multiplied by the recovery rate of the counterparty, $S_f(t)\ RR_c$. This can be represented as in figure 5.27.

Including discount factors, we derive from figure 5.27 the present value of the payoff of a two-period default swap as:

$$\begin{aligned}
&[\lambda_0^r\lambda_0^c N(1-RR_r-RR_r a)RR_c+(1-\lambda_0^r)(1-\lambda_0^c)N\times 0+\lambda_0^r(1-\lambda_0^c)N(1-RR_r-RR_r a)\\
&\quad+(1-\lambda_0^r)\lambda_0^c S_f(1)RR_c]e^{-r_0\tau_1}\\
&\quad+(1-\lambda_0^r)(1-\lambda_0^c)[\lambda_1^r\lambda_1^c N(1-RR_r-RR_r a)RR_c+(1-\lambda_1^r)(1-\lambda_1^c)N\times 0\\
&\quad+\lambda_1^r(1-\lambda_1^c)N(1-RR_r-RR_r a)+(1-\lambda_1^r)\lambda_1^c(S_f(2)RR_c)]e^{-r_1\tau_2}.
\end{aligned} \tag{5.77}$$

Generalizing equation (5.77) for T periods, we derive:

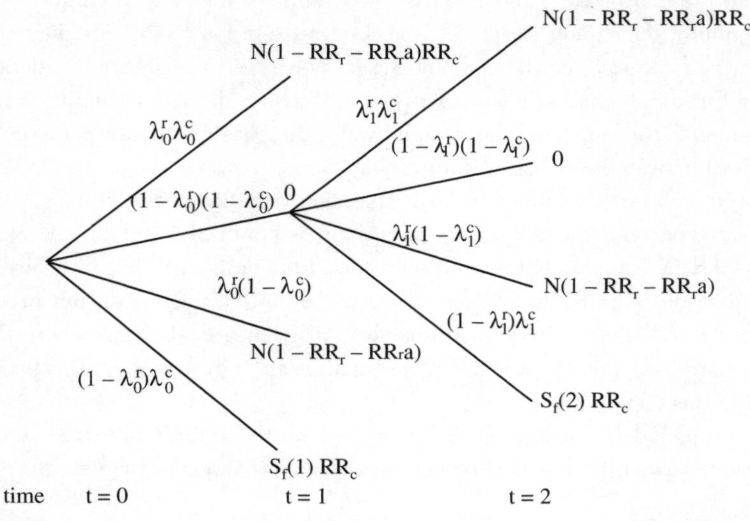

Figure 5.27: Two-period payoff tree of a default swap including counterparty default risk

$$\sum_{t=1}^{T}\{[\lambda_{t-1}^{r}\lambda_{t-1}^{c}N(1-RR_r-RR_r a)RR_c+\lambda_{t-1}^{r}(1-\lambda_{t-1}^{c})N(1-RR_r-RR_r a)+$$

$$(1-\lambda_{t-1}^{r})\lambda_{t-1}^{c}S_f(t)RR_c]e^{-r_{t-1}\tau_t}\prod_{u=0}^{t-2}(1-\lambda_u^{r})(1-\lambda_u^{c})\}. \tag{5.78}$$

The default swap premium payment tree: Let's now look at the default swap premium payment tree. In the case of no default of the reference entity or the counterparty, probability $(1-\lambda^r)(1-\lambda^c)$, the standard swap premium payment $sN\Delta\tau_t$ will apply. The same swap premium $sN\Delta\tau_t$ will be paid in case of the default of the reference asset and no default of the counterparty, probability $\lambda^r(1-\lambda^c)$.

In case of both the reference entity and the counterparty defaulting, probability $\lambda^r\lambda^c$, the final swap premium payment of the default swap buyer depends on the national bankruptcy law and the specific terms of the default swap contract. Principally three scenarios exist.

Scenario 1: The default swap buyer makes no final accrual payment and receives the payoff $N(1-RR_r-RR_r a)RR_c$.

Scenario 2: The default swap buyer makes a final accrual payment of the minimum of his obligation and the payment of the default swap seller: min $[sN\Delta\tau, N(1-RR_r-RR_r a)RR_c]$. This scenario nets the obligations in case of $sN\Delta\tau \geq N(1-RR_r-RR_r a)RR_c$ and gives a payoff of $N(1-RR_r-RR_r a)RR_c - sN\Delta\tau$ in case of $N(1-RR_r-RR_r a)RR_c \geq sN\Delta\tau$.

Scenario 3: The default swap buyer makes a final accrual payment of $sN\Delta\tau$. However, this payment may be higher than the reduced, recovery rate dependent, final payment of the default swap seller $N(1-RR_r-RR_r a)RR_c$.

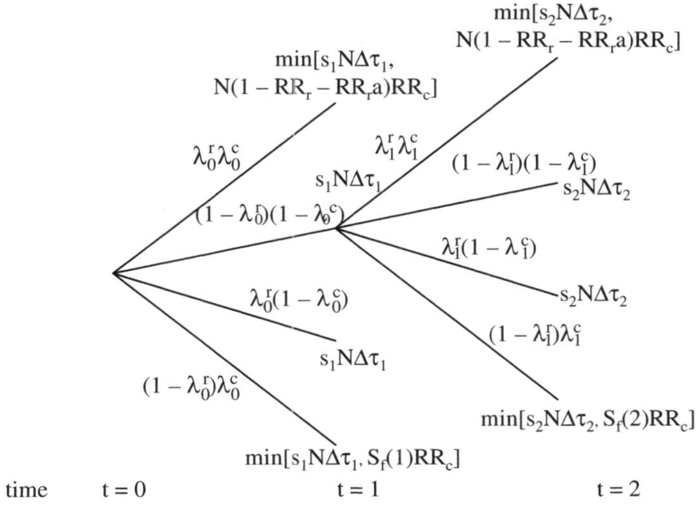

Figure 5.28: Two-period swap premium tree of a default swap including counterparty default risk

In case of the counterparty defaulting but not the reference entity, probability $(1 - \lambda^r)\lambda^c$, the final swap premium payment of the default swap buyer depends again on the national bankruptcy law and the specific terms of the default swap contract. Principally the modified three scenarios are now:

Scenario 1: The default swap buyer makes no final accrual payment and receives the payoff $N(1 - RR_r - RR_r a)RR_c$.

Scenario 2: The default swap buyer makes a final accrual payment of the minimum of his obligation and the payment of the default swap seller: min $[sN\Delta\tau, S_f(t)\, RR_c]$. This scenario nets the obligations in case of $sN\Delta\tau \geq S_f(t)\, RR_c$ and gives a payoff of $S_f(t)\, RR_c - sN\Delta\tau$ in case of $Ns_f(t)\, RR_c \geq sN\Delta\tau$.

Scenario 3: The default swap buyer makes a final accrual payment of $sN\Delta\tau$. However, this payment may be higher than the reduced, recovery rate dependent, final payment of the default swap seller $S_f(t)\, RR_c$.

Of all scenarios, scenarios 2 and 3 reflect best the international and US bankruptcy law. Scenario 1 is based on a "walk away clause," that allows the solvent party to cease payments but receive the recovery rate of the defaulting party. Most derivatives contracts do not include such a clause. Scenario 2 is based on netting agreements, which are a standard provision of the legal documentation of OTC derivatives, making scenario 2 a realistic choice. However, also scenario 3 can be considered realistic: Often solvent parties honor their obligation to their defaulting counterparty, even though the defaulting counterparty cannot honor its obligations. This is done for public relations reasons.

In the following analysis, we will apply scenario 2: Hence, we derive the swap premium payment tree as seen in figure 5.28.

From figure 5.28 we get for the present value of the swap premium payments:

$$\{\lambda_0^r\lambda_0^c \min[sN\Delta\tau_0, N(1-RR_r-RR_ra)RR_c]+(1-\lambda_0^r)(1-\lambda_0^c)s_1N\Delta\tau_0+\lambda_0^r(1-\lambda_0^c)s_1N\Delta\tau_0$$
$$+(1-\lambda_0^r)\lambda_0^c \min[sN\Delta\tau_0, S_f(1)RR_c]\}e^{-r_0\tau_1}$$
$$+(1-\lambda_0^r)(1-\lambda_0^c)\{\lambda_1^r\lambda_1^c \min[s_1N\Delta\tau_1, N(1-RR_r-RR_ra)RR_c]+(1-\lambda_1^r)(1-\lambda_1^c)s_1N\Delta\tau_1$$
$$+\lambda_1^r(1-\lambda_1^c)s_1N\Delta\tau_1+(1-\lambda_1^r)\lambda_1^c \min[s_1N\Delta\tau_1, S_f(2)RR_c]\}e^{-r_1\tau_2}. \tag{5.79}$$

Assuming a constant swap premium s, i.e, $s_1 = s_2 = s_3 \ldots$, generalizing equation (5.79) for T periods and simplifying the notation by using $\min[sN\Delta\tau_{t-1}, N(1 - RR_r - RR_ra)RR_c] \equiv \min[x_t]$ and $\min[sN\Delta\tau_{t-1}, S_f(t)RR_c] \equiv \min[y_t]$, we derive:

$$\sum_{t=1}^{T}\{[\lambda_{t-1}^r\lambda_{t-1}^c \min[x_t]+(1-\lambda_{t-1}^r)(1-\lambda_{t-1}^c)sN\Delta\tau_{t-1}+\lambda_{t-1}^r(1-\lambda_{t-1}^c)sN\Delta\tau_{t-1}$$
$$+(1-\lambda_{t-1}^r)\lambda_{t-1}^c \min[y_t]]e^{-r_{t-1}\tau_t}\prod_{u=0}^{t-2}(1-\lambda_u^r)(1-\lambda_u^c)\}. \tag{5.80}$$

From equations (5.78) and (5.80) we derive the value of the default swap from the viewpoint of the default swap buyer as:

$$\sum_{t=1}^{T}\{[\lambda_{t-1}^r\lambda_{t-1}^cN(1-RR_r-RR_ra)RR_c+\lambda_{t-1}^r(1-\lambda_{t-1}^c)N(1-RR_r-RR_ra)$$
$$+(1-\lambda_{t-1}^r)\lambda_{t-1}^cS_f(t)RR_c]e^{-r_{t-1}\tau_t}\prod_{u=0}^{t-2}(1-\lambda_u^r)(1-\lambda_u^c)\}$$
$$-\sum_{t=1}^{T}\{[\lambda_{t-1}^r\lambda_{t-1}^c \min[x_t]+(1-\lambda_{t-1}^r)(1-\lambda_{t-1}^c)sN\Delta\tau_{t-1}+\lambda_{t-1}^r(1-\lambda_{t-1}^c)sN\Delta\tau_{t-1}$$
$$+(1-\lambda_{t-1}^r)\lambda_{t-1}^c \min[y_t]]e^{-r_{t-1}\tau_t}\prod_{u=0}^{t-2}(1-\lambda_u^r)(1-\lambda_u^c)\}. \tag{5.81}$$

Setting equation (5.81) to zero and solving for the fair default swap premium s, which gives the default swap a value of zero, we derive:

$$s=\frac{\begin{gathered}\sum_{t=1}^{T}\{[\lambda_{t-1}^r\lambda_{t-1}^cN(1-RR_r-RR_ra)RR_c+\lambda_{t-1}^r(1-\lambda_{t-1}^c)N(1-RR_r-RR_ra)\\ +(1-\lambda_{t-1}^r)\lambda_{t-1}^cS_f(t)RR_c]e^{-r_{t-1}\tau_t}\prod_{u=0}^{t-2}(1-\lambda_u^r)(1-\lambda_u^c)\}\end{gathered}}{\begin{gathered}\sum_{t=1}^{T}\{[\lambda_{t-1}^r\lambda_{t-1}^c \min[x_t]/s+(1-\lambda_{t-1}^r)(1-\lambda_{t-1}^c)N\Delta\tau_{t-1}+\lambda_{t-1}^r(1-\lambda_{t-1}^c)N\Delta\tau_{t-1}\\ +(1-\lambda_{t-1}^r)\lambda_{t-1}^c \min[y_t]/s]e^{-r_{t-1}\tau_t}\prod_{u=0}^{t-2}(1-\lambda_u^r)(1-\lambda_u^c)\}\end{gathered}}. \tag{5.82}$$

Equation (5.82) with $\lambda^c = 0$ is identical to equation (5.76), which is the equation for the fair default swap premium excluding counterparty default risk. Equation (5.82) with RR_c

$=0$ and $\lambda^c > 0$ results in a default swap premium that is lower than the default swap premium without counterparty risk of equation (5.76), which satisfies the no-arbitrage condition with respect to counterparty default risk. A high recovery rate of the counterparty RR_c can, however, result in a default swap premium s that is higher than the default swap premium excluding counterparty default risk. This is the case in scenario 1, because the swap premium payments cease, but due to the high recovery rate of the counterparty the payoff will increase and with it the default swap value and consequently the premium s.

It is also interesting to note that the default swap premium s is negatively related to the recovery rate of the reference entity, hence $\partial s/\partial RR_r \leq 0$. This is because the recovery rate is deducted from the payoff, which is $N(1\text{-}RR_r\text{-}RR_r a)$. Hence with a higher recovery rate RR_r, the value of the default swap and with it the default swap premium s decreases. However, the swap premium has a positive dependence on the recovery rate of the counterparty: $\partial s/\partial RR_c \geq 0$. This is because a default swap buyer is willing to pay a higher default swap premium s, if the payoff will be higher due to a higher recovery rate RR_c.

Let's explain equation (5.82) in an example.

Example 5.20: Let's alter example 5.19 and include counterparty default risk. In example 5.19 we had a default swap with a notional amount N of \$1,000,000 and an assumed recovery rate of the reference asset RR_r of 40%. The swap terminates in 1 year (time 2). The default swap premiums are paid annually and the probability of default λ of the reference asset in six months (time 1) is 10% and in 1 year (time 2) is 30%.

The accrued interest, a, of the underlying bond from the last bond coupon date to time 1 will be 1% and to time 2, 4%. The 6-month and 1-year interest rates are 5% and 6%, respectively.

In order to include counterparty default, we first derive the fair value of the above default swap without counterparty default risk at time 1 of 22.67% (see www.dersoft.com/ex520.xls). Furthermore we assume that the probability of default λ^c of the counterparty in 6 months (time 1) is 20% and in 1 year 40% (time 2). What is the default swap premium s including counterparty default risk for an assumed recovery rate of the counterparty RR_c is 5%?

Following equation (5.82) the numerator is:

$$\begin{aligned}
&[0.1\times 0.2\times 1{,}000{,}000\times(1-0.4-0.4\times 0.01)+0.1\times(1-0.2)\times 1{,}000{,}000\times\\
&\quad(1-0.4-0.4\times 0.01)+(1-0.1)\times 0.2\times 1{,}000{,}000\times 0.2267\times 0.05]\times e^{-0.05\times 0.5}\\
&\quad+\{[0.3\times 0.4\times 1{,}000{,}000\times(1-0.4-0.4\times 0.01)+0.3\times(1-0.4)\times 1{,}000{,}000\times\\
&\quad(1-0.4-0.4\times 0.01)+(1-0.3)\times 0.4\times 1{,}000{,}000\times 0.3504\times 0.05]\times e^{-0.06\times 1}\}\\
&\quad(1-0.1)\times(1-0.2)=126{,}055
\end{aligned}$$

Following equation (5.82) we derive for period 1, min[x] = min[100,000, 29,800] = 29,800 and min[y] = min[100,000, 5,960] = 5,960 and for period 2, min[x] = min[100,000, 29,200] = 29,200 and min[y] = min[100,000, 17,520] = 17,520 (see www.dersoft.com/ex520.xls).

Hence, the denominator in equation (5.82) is:

$$[0.1\times0.2\times29{,}800/0.2000+(1-0.1)\times(1-0.2)\times500{,}000+0.1\times(1-0.2)\times500{,}000 +(1-0.1)\times0.2\times5{,}960/0.2000]\times e^{-0.05\times0.5}+[0.3\times0.4\times29{,}200/0.2000 \times(1-0.3)\times(1-0.4)\times500{,}000+0.2\times(1-0.4)\times500{,}000+(1-0.2)\times0.4 \times17{,}920/0.2000]\times e^{-0.06\times1}(1-0.1)\times(1-0.2)=630{,}195$$

Hence, the default swap premium including counterparty default risk is 126,055/630,195 = 20.00%. So including counterparty default risk, the default swap premium has decreased from 22.67% (see example 5.19) to 20.00% or by (22.67 – 20.00) / 22.67 = 11.77%. For scenario 1, the decrease of the default swap premium is 6.32% and for scenario 3, 32.74%.

3. The KKM model including reference entity–counterparty default correlation

So far we have assumed that the risk-neutral default probability of the reference entity λ^r and the risk-neutral default probability of the counterparty λ^c are not correlated. As stated above, the joint probability of two entities defaulting is simply the multiplication of the individual default probabilities, if the companies' default is not correlated. Formally: $\lambda(r \cap c) = \lambda^r \times \lambda^c$. Also note that $\lambda(\bar{x}) = 1 - \lambda^x$.

If the default probabilities of the reference entity r and the counterparty c are correlated, we apply equation (5.61):

$$\lambda(r\cap c)=\rho(\lambda^r,\lambda^c)\sqrt{[\lambda^r-(\lambda^r)^2][\lambda^c-(\lambda^c)^2]}+[\lambda^r\lambda^c] \qquad (5.61)$$

where $-1 \leq \rho(\lambda^r, \lambda^c) \leq 1$ is the correlation coefficient, which can be derived from equity correlation. The individual risk-neutral default probabilities λ^r and λ^c are derived by calibrating the model.

The probability of neither the reference asset nor the counterparty defaulting, i.e. $\lambda(\bar{r} \cap \bar{c})$ can be derived from the addition law of basic probability theory (see figure 5.23):

$$\lambda(r\cup c)=\lambda^r+\lambda^c-\lambda(r\cap c). \qquad (5.65)$$

From equation (5.65) it follows that:

$$\lambda(\bar{r}\cap\bar{c})=1-\lambda(r\cup c)=1-[\lambda^r+\lambda^c-\lambda(r\cap c)]. \qquad (5.83)$$

From equation (5.65) we can also derive the probability of the reference entity r defaulting and not the counterparty c, $\lambda(r \cap \bar{c})$ (see figure 5.23 horizontally shaded area):

$$\lambda(r\cap\bar{c})=\lambda^r-\lambda(r\cap c). \qquad (5.84)$$

Note that equation (5.84) with zero correlation, is equal to $\lambda^r(1 - \lambda^c)$ from part 2 of this section, which excluded correlation altogether. In case of zero correlation $\rho(\lambda^r, \lambda^c) =$

0, and from equation (5.61) it follows that $\lambda(r \cap c) = \lambda^r\lambda^c$. Substituting this into the right side of equation (5.84), we derive $\lambda^r - \lambda^r\lambda^c$ or $\lambda^r(1 - \lambda^c)$.

Naturally, the probability of the counterparty c defaulting and not the reference entity r, $\lambda(c \cap \bar{r})$, (see vertically shaded area in figure 5.23), is:

$$\lambda(c \cap \bar{r}) = \lambda^c - \lambda(r \cap c). \tag{5.85}$$

Example 5.21: Let's alter example 5.20 to include a default correlation between the reference entity and the counterparty. The default probability of the reference asset for the next year is 10% and for the counterparty 20%. Let's assume from equity correlation, the default correlation $\rho(r,c)$ is 0.5.

For period 1 we derive: From equation (5.61) the probability of joint default $\lambda(r \cap c) = 0.5 \times \sqrt{\left[0.1-(0.1)^2\right]\left[0.2-(0.2)^2\right]} + [0.1 \times 0.2] = 8\%$. From equation (5.83) the probability of both the reference entity and the counterparty not defaulting is $\lambda(\bar{r} \cap \bar{c}) = 1 - \lambda(r \cup c) = 1 - [0.1 + 0.2 - 0.08] = 78\%$. The probability of the reference entity r defaulting and not the counterparty c, $\lambda(r \cap \bar{c})$, is, following equation (5.84), $\lambda(r \cap \bar{c}) = 0.1 - 0.08 = 2\%$. The probability of counterparty c defaulting and not the reference entity r, $\lambda(c \cap \bar{r})$, is $\lambda(c \cap \bar{r}) = 0.2 - 0.08 = 12\%$.

For period 2, we have from example 5.19, $\lambda^r = 30\%$ and $\lambda^c = 40\%$. We assume the same correlation coefficient as in period 1, 0.5. Using the same equations (5.61), (5.83) to (5.85), we derive for period 2: $\lambda(r \cap c) = 23.22\%$, $\lambda(\bar{r} \cap \bar{c}) = 53.22\%$, $\lambda(r \cap \bar{c}) = 6.78\%$, and $\lambda(c \cap \bar{r}) = 16.78\%$.

Using these probabilities instead of the non-correlated default probabilities $\lambda^r\,\lambda^c$, $(1 - \lambda^r)(1 - \lambda^c)$, $(1 - \lambda^r)\lambda^c$ and $\lambda^r(1 - \lambda^c)$, we derive for scenario 2 a default swap premium of 6.81%, and 8.20% and 5.89% for scenarios 1 and 3, respectively (see www.dersoft.com/ex521.xls). When excluding this reference entity–counterparty default correlation (example 5.20) we had derived a default swap premium of 20.00% for scenario 2, and 21.24% and 15.25% for scenario 1 and 3 respectively. Hence, we realize the significant impact of the default correlation.

See www.dersoft.com/ex521.xls for this example.

The KKM model in combination with the Libor Market Model (LMM)

The Kettunen-Ksendzovsky-Meissner (KKM) model can be easily combined with any interest rate term structure based model. Before we show how it is combined with the Libor Market Model (LMM), let's first discuss basic properties of the LMM model.

The Libor Market Model

The Libor Market Model[32] falls into the framework of the Heath-Jarrow-Morton (HJM) 1992 term structure model.[33] The main weakness of the HJM model is that interest rates are expressed as instantaneous rates, i.e. for infinitesimally short periods of time. These rates are not observable in the market. In the LMM model, interest rates can be conveniently expressed as discrete forward rates.

Hull and White (2000a) show that a one-factor Libor Market Model can be discretized as

$$F_k(t_{j+1}) = F_k(t_j)\exp\left[\left(\sum_{i=j+1}^{k}\frac{\Delta\tau_i F_i(t_j)\Lambda_{i-j-1}\Lambda_{k-j-1}}{1+\Delta\tau_i F_i(t_j)} - \frac{\Lambda_{k-j-1}^2}{2}\right)\Delta\tau_j + \Lambda_{k-j-1}\in\sqrt{\Delta\tau_j}\right] \quad (5.86)$$

where

$F_k(t)$: forward interest rate between time k and k + 1, seen at time t, with compounding of $\Delta\tau_i$

$\Delta\tau_i$: time between horizontal nodes i and i + 1, expressed in years

ε: random drawing from a standard normal distribution

Λ_k: forward rate volatility term for time t_k to t_{k+1}. Assuming $\Delta\tau$ is constant, Λ can be derived iteratively using:

$$\Lambda_{k-1} = \sqrt{k\sigma_k^2 - \sum_{v=0}^{k-2}\Lambda_v^2} \quad (5.87)$$

where σ_k is a caplet's volatility between time t_k and t_{k+1}.

Figure 5.29 shows a non-recombining one-factor five-period LMM model. At each node, an entire interest rate curve is generated. The number displayed highest at each node represents the spot rate, the number displayed second highest represents the one-period forward rate, etc.

Pricing Default Swaps on the KKM model on the basis of the LMM model

Kettunen, Ksendzovsky, and Meissner (2003) derive the value of the European-style default swap including reference asset–counterparty default correlation using a Monte-Carlo implementation of the LMM model via the following steps:

1 The default probability of the reference asset is simulated by a one-factor LMM model. Hence, in equations (5.86) and (5.87), the forward interest rates and their volatilities are replaced by the forward default probabilities of the reference asset and its volatilities.

2 The default probability of the counterparty is also simulated by a one-factor LMM model. Hence, in equations (5.86) and (5.87), the forward interest rates and their volatilities are replaced by the forward default probabilities of the counterparty and its volatilities.

3 The default correlation between the reference asset and the counterparty is integrated into the model with equations (5.61), (5.83), (5.84), and (5.85).

4 A random number between 0 and 1 is generated to dictate which of the four different default scenarios occurs: No default $\lambda(\bar{r} \cap \bar{c})$, only reference asset default $\lambda(r \cap \bar{c})$, only counterparty default $\lambda(c \cap \bar{r})$, or both reference asset and counterparty default $\lambda(r \cap c)$. If either the reference asset or the counterparty or both default, a random number between 0 and 1 is generated and multiplied with the length of the time step to simulate the exact default time in the specific time step.

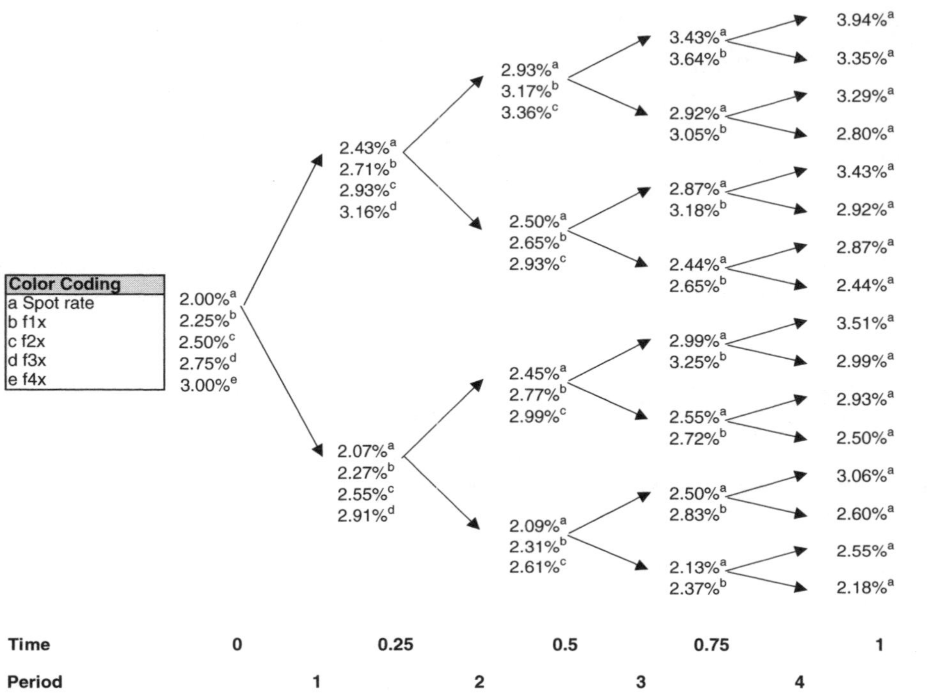

Figure 5.29: One-factor LMM model for 3-month interest rates with a 2% spot rate input and forward rate inputs of 2.25%, 2.5%, 2.75%, and 3% for periods 2, 3, 4, 5, respectively; caplet volatility inputs are 16%, 17%, 16%, and 15% for periods 2, 3, 4, 5, respectively
The model can be found at www.dersoft.com/lmmtree.xls

5 The payoff and the premium payment of the default swap are calculated taking into account the specific default scenario. Table 5.6 presents the payoffs and premium payments when the observed time step is one year, the coupon of the reference asset is paid annually, and the premium of the default swap is paid annually.[34]

6 The payoff (if other than zero) is discounted back to time zero using the interest rate term structure (that is modeled using LMM). The premium payment of the default swap is also discounted back to time zero using the interest rate term structure (that is modeled using LMM) and added to the previously discounted premium payments.

7 If there is no default during the time step and the maturity of the default swap is not reached, steps 1 to 6 are repeated until maturity or default is encountered. (See table 5.6 column "How to proceed.")

8 The accumulated discounted payoffs are divided by the accumulated discounted premium payments to derive the swap premium s, following equation (5.82), which includes the default correlation between the reference asset and the counterparty of equations (5.61) and (5.83) to (5.85). The swap premium s is derived as the average of all trials.

9 The steps 1 to 8 are repeated until the desired accuracy is achieved (recommended at least 100,000 times).

Table 5.6: Payoffs and premium payments for the four default scenarios

Default scenario	Payoff	Premium payment	Paid at	How to proceed
$\lambda(\bar{r} \cap \bar{c})$	–	sN	t_{k+1}	Continue to next time step (if not maturity)
$\lambda(r \cap \bar{c})$	$(1 - RR_r - RR_r cT_d)N$	sNT_d	T_d	Stop trial
$\lambda(c \cap \bar{r})$	$S_f(T_d)\ RR_c$	$Min(sNT_d, S_f(T_d)RR_c)$	T_d	Stop trial
$\lambda(c \cap r)$	$(1 - RR_r - RR_r cT_d)RR_c N$	$Min[sNT_d, (1 - RR_r - RR_r cT_d)\ RR_c N]$	T_d	Stop trial

where

RR_c: Exogenous recovery rate of the counterparty
RR_r: Exogenous recovery rate of the reference entity
T_d: Randomly simulated default time between the last node and the consecutive node, expressed in years
$S_f(T_d)$: Fair value of the default swap from the time the default swap was issued until the time of reference asset default without the possibility of counterparty default. $S_f(T_d)$ includes the notional amount N
a: Accrued interest on the reference asset from the last coupon date until the default date, hence $a = c\,T_d$, where c = coupon of the reference asset
s: Default swap premium
N: Notional amount of the swap

A visual basic program that follows the previously mentioned nine steps is available at www.dersoft.com/dslmmkkm.xls. The program requires the inputs:

- Forward interest rates and caplet volatilities;
- Forward default probabilities of the reference asset and reference asset volatilities;
- Forward default probabilities of the counterparty and counterparty volatilities;
- Default correlation between the reference asset and counterparty;
- Recovery rate of the reference asset;
- Recovery rate of the counterparty;
- Maturity of the default swap;
- Coupon of the reference asset and coupon payment frequency;
- Default swap premium payment frequency;
- Length of time step (0.25, 0.5, and 1 year are currently available).

The program provides a 95% confidence interval for the simulated result so that the accuracy of the result can be evaluated.

It is interesting to note that the model derives a zero value for the default swap premium, if the correlation coefficient $\rho(\lambda^r, \lambda^c)$ is 1, the default probabilities and the default volatilities of the reference asset and the counterparty are identical, and the recovery rates are zero. In this case, if the reference asset defaults, the counterparty will default, making the default swap useless. The reader can easily verify this feature when using the model.

Pricing TRORs

So far we have discussed several models that evaluate default swaps and credit-spread options. We have not explicitly mentioned how to price TRORs. The reason is simple. TRORs can be evaluated on the basis of default swaps. In chapter 2 we had derived equations (2.2a) and (2.2b):

Receiving in a TROR = Short a default swap + Long a risk-free asset
Paying in a TROR = Long a default swap + Short a risk-free asset

Consequently, in order to price a TROR, we can simple derive the price of a default swap and add a long or short position of a risk-free asset.

Further research in valuing credit derivatives

In the options market, the Black-Scholes equation and its modifications have been widely accepted as the benchmark model. No such model currently exists for pricing and hedging credit derivatives. Currently structural models and reduced form models compete to establish dominance in the market. An approach such as the one of Duffie and Lando (2001) that includes structural as well as reduced form elements could prove successful. Kamakura has already launched a hybrid Jarrow-Merton default probability model, which includes elements of structural and reduced form models.[35]

Further research will also focus on integrating most or all of the crucial input variables (see table 5.1) in credit derivatives models. Research will also focus on relaxing many of the restrictions that exist with current credit derivatives models. In a recent article Jarrow and Yildirim (2002) derive a model in which the process for interest rates and the process for default are correlated. Valuing exotic default swaps such as yield curve swaps, differential swaps, or Libor in arrears swaps and index amortizing swaps, as well as exotic types of options such as barrier options, lookback options, or average options also await exploration.

Summary of Chapter 5

Numerous input variables and their correlations are necessary to price a credit derivative. Among the most crucial inputs are the default probability of the reference asset and the default probability of the counterparty, and the reference asset–counterparty default correlation.

The two main approaches to value credit derivatives are *structural models* and *reduced form models* (also termed *intensity models*). Both models have their roots in the seminal Merton 1974 contingent claim methodology, though structural models have closer ties to Merton.

Structural models endogenize the bankruptcy process by modeling assets and liabilities of a company as in the Merton model. Structural models can be divided into *firm value models* and *first-time passage models*. In firm value models bankruptcy occurs when the asset value of a company is below the debt value at the maturity of the debt. In first-time passage models, bankruptcy occurs when the asset value drops below a pre-defined, usually exogenous barrier, allowing for bankruptcy before the maturity of the debt.

Reduced form models abstract from the explicit economic reasons for the default (i.e. they do not assess the asset–liability structure of the firm to explain the default). Rather, reduced form models use debt prices as a main input to model the bankruptcy process. Default is modeled by a stochastic process with an exogenous *default intensity* or *hazard rate*, which, multiplied by a certain time frame, results in the risk-neutral default probability also called *pseudo-* or *martingale default probability*. The value of the hazard rate is derived by calibration of the variables of the stochastic process.

Numerous types of structural and reduced form models exist, focusing on different aspects of the default process. Current research concentrates on the creation of a coherent combination of structural and reduced form models.

References and Suggestions for Further Reading

Albanese, C., G. Campolieti, O. Chen, and A. Zavidonov, "Credit barrier models," 2002, Working paper, University of Toronto.

Altman, E. "Measuring Corporate Bond Mortality and Performance," *Journal of Finance*, 44, 1989, pp. 909–21.

Bélanger, A., S. Shreve, and D. Wong, "A unified model for credit derivatives," 2001, *Working paper*, Carnegie Mellon University.

Black, F. and J. Cox, "Valuing Corporate Securities: Some Effects of Bond Indenture Provisions," *The Journal of Finance*, 31, May 1976, pp. 351–67.

Black, F., E. Derman, and W. Toy, "A One Factor Model of Interest Rates and Its Applications to Treasury Bond Options," *Financial Analysts Journal*, January/February 1990, pp. 33–9.

Black, F. and M. Scholes, "The Pricing of Options and Corporate Liabilities," *Journal of Political Economy*, 81, May–June 1973, pp. 637–54.

Brace, A., D. Gatarek, and M. Musiela, (BGM) "The Market Model of Interest Rate Dynamics," *Mathematical Finance*, 7, no. 2, 1997, pp. 127–55.

Brennan, M. and E. Schwartz, "Analyzing Convertible Bonds," *Journal of Financial and Quantitative Analysis*, 15(4), 1980, pp. 907–29.

Briys, E. and F. de Varenne, "Valuing Risky Fixed Rate Debt: An Extension," *Journal of Financial and Quantitative Analysis*, vol. 32, no. 2, June 1997, pp. 239–48.

Brooks, R. and D. Y. Yan, "Pricing Credit Default Swaps and the Implied Default Probability," *Derivatives Quarterly*, Winter 1998, pp. 34–41.

Cheng, W., "Recent Advances in Default Swap Valuation," *The Journal of Fixed Income*, 1, 2001, pp. 18–27.

Clewlow, L. and C. Strickland, *Implementing Derivatives Models*, Wiley, Chichester, 1998.

Cox, J., J. Ingersoll, and S. Ross, "A Theory of the Term Structure of Interest Rates," *Econometrica*, 53, 1985, pp. 385–407.

Cox, J., S. Ross, and M. Rubinstein, "Option Pricing: A Simplified Approach," *Journal of Financial Economics*, 7(3), 1979, pp. 229–63.

Crouhy, M., D. Galai, and R. Mark, "Credit risk revisited," *Risk Magazine*, March 1998, pp. 41–4.

Das, S. and K. Sundaram, "A Direct Approach to Arbitrage-Free Pricing of Credit Derivatives," *Management Science*, January 2000, vol. 46, issue 1, pp. 46–63.

Das, R. and P. Tufano, "Pricing Credit-Sensitive Debt when Interest Rates, Credit Ratings and Credit Spreads are Stochastic," *Journal of Financial Engineering*, 5(2), 1996, pp. 161–98.

Duffee, G., "On measuring credit risks of derivative instruments," *Journal of Banking and Finance*, 20, 1996, pp. 805–33.

Duffee, G., "The Relation Between Treasury Yields and Corporate Bond Yield Spreads," *Journal of Finance*, 53(6), 1998, pp. 2225–41.

Duffie, D. and D. Lando, "Term Structures of Credit Spreads with Incomplete Accounting Information," *Econometrica*, 69(3), 2001, pp. 633–64.

Duffie, D. and K. Singleton, "An Econometric Model of the Term Structure of Interest-Rate Swap Yields," *Journal of Finance*, 52(4), 1997, pp. 1287–321.

Duffie, D. and K. Singleton, "Modeling Term Structures of Defaultable Bonds," *Review of Financial Studies*, 12, 1999, pp. 687–720.

Esteghamat, K. "A boundary crossing model of counterparty risk," *Journal of Economic Dynamics and Control*, vol. 27, no. 10, 2003, pp. 1771–99.

Hayt, G., "How to price a credit derivative," *Risk Magazine*, February 2000, p. 60.

Heath, D., R. Jarrow, and A. Morton, "Bond Pricing and the Term Structure of Interest Rates, A New Methodology," *Econometrica*, 60, no. 1, 1992, pp. 77–105.

Henn, M., "Valuation of Credit Risky Contingent Claims," Unpublished Dissertation 1997, University of St. Gallen.

Ho, T. and S. Lee, "Term Structure Movements and Pricing Interest Rate Contingent Claims," *Journal of Finance*, 41, 1986, pp. 1011–29.

Hull, J. and A. White, "Pricing Interest Rate Derivatives Securities," *Review of Financial Studies*, 3, no. 4, 1990, pp. 573–92.

Hull J. and A. White, "Forward Rate Volatilities, Swap Rate Volatilities, and Implementation of the LIBOR Market Model," *Journal of Fixed Income*, September 2000a, vol. 10, issue 2, pp. 46–63.

Hull, J. and A. White, "Valuing Credit Default Swaps I: No Counterparty Default Risk," *Journal of Derivatives*, vol. 8, issue 1, Fall 2000, pp. 29–41.

Hull, J. and A. White, "Valuing Credit Default Swaps II: Modeling Default Correlations," *Journal of Derivatives*, vol. 8, issue 3, Spring 2001, pp. 12–22.

Iben, T. and R. Litterman, "Corporate Bond Valuation and the Term Structure of Credit Spreads," *Review of Portfolio Management*, Spring 1991, pp. 52–64.

Jamshidian, F., "Libor and Swap Market Models," *Finance and Stochastics*, 1, 1997, pp. 293–330.

Jarrow, R., D. Lando and S. Turnbull, "A Markov Model for the Term Structure of Credit Risk Spreads," *The Review of Financial Studies 1997*, vol. 10, no. 2, pp. 1–42.

Jarrow, R. and S. Turnbull, "Pricing Derivatives on Financial Securities Subject to Credit Risk," *Journal of Finance*, vol. L, no. 1, March 1995, pp. 53–85.

Jarrow, R. and S. Turnbull, "The Intersection of market and credit risk," *Journal of Banking & Finance*, 24, 2000, pp. 271–99.

Jarrow, R. and Y. Yildirim, "Valuing Default Swaps under Market and Credit Risk Correlation," *The Journal of Fixed Income*, March 2002, pp. 7–19.

Jones, E., S. Mason and E. Rosenfeld, "Contingent Claim Analysis of Corporate Structures: An Empirical Investigation," *Journal of Finance*, 39(3), July 1984, pp. 611–37.

Kamakura, "Comparison of the Merton and Jarrow Credit Models for Pricing Risky Debt," Internal Kamakura paper to be received at http://www.kamakuraco.com.

Kettunen, J., D. Ksendzvosky, and G. Meissner, "Pricing Default Swaps including Reference Asset–Counterparty Default Correlation," *Hawaii Pacific University Working Paper*, 2003.

Kim, J., K. Ramaswamy, and S. Sundaresan, "Does Default Risk in Coupons Affect the Valuation of Corporate Bonds?: A Contingent Claim Model," *Financial Management*, 22(3), 1993, pp. 117–31.

Lando, D., "On Cox Processes and Credit-Risky Securities," *Review of Derivatives Research*, 2, 1998, pp. 99–120.

Longstaff, F. and E. Schwartz, "A Simple Approach to Valuing Risky Fixed and Floating Rate Debt," *Journal of Finance*, No. 3, July 1995, pp. 789–819.

Madan, B. and H. Unal, "Pricing the Risk of Default," *Review of Derivatives Research*, 2(2/3), 1998, pp. 121–60.

Martin, R., K. Thompson, and C. Brown, "Price and Probability." *Risk Magazine*, January 2001, pp. 115–17.

Mashal, R. and M. Naldi, "Pricing Multiname Credit Derivatives: Heavy Tailed Hybrid Approach," *Columbia University Working Paper*, www.columbia.edu.

Merton, R., "The Theory of Rational Option Pricing," *Bell Journal of Economics and Management Science*, vol. 4, no. 1, Spring 1973, pp. 141–83.

Merton, R., "On the Pricing of Corporate Debt: The Risk Structure of Interest Rates," *Journal of Finance* 29, 1974, pp. 449–70.

Miltersen, K., K. Sandmann, and D. Sondermann, "Closed Form Solutions for Term Structure Derivatives with LogNormal Interest Rates," *Journal of Finance*, 52, no. 1, March 1997, pp. 409–30.

O'Kane D., et al., *The Lehman Brothers Guide to Exotic Credit Derivatives*, Risk Waters Group, 2003.

Rebonato, R., Modern pricing of interest-rate derivatives: the LIBOR market model and beyond, Woodstock, NJ: Princeton University Press, 2002.

Rendleman, R. and B. Bartter, "Two State Option Pricing," *Journal of Finance*, 34, 1997, pp. 1092–110.

Schmidt, W. and I. Ward, "Pricing default baskets," *Risk Magazine*, January 2000, pp. 111–14.

Schoenbucher, J., "Term Structure Modelling of Defaultable Bonds," *Review of Derivatives Research*, 2(2/3), 1997, pp. 161–92.

Sharpe, W., "Bank Capital Adequacy, Deposit Insurance, and Security Values," *Journal of Financial and Quantitative Analysis*, November 1978, pp. 701–18.

Smithson, C., "Wonderful Life," *RISK Magazine*, December 1992, pp. 23–32.

Vasicek, O., "An Equilibrium Characterization of the Term Structure," *Journal of Economics*, 5, 1977, pp. 177–88.

Wei, J., "Rating- and Firm Value-Based Valuation of Credit Swaps," *The Journal Fixed Income*, 2, 2001, pp. 53–64.

Questions and Problems

Answers, available for instructors, are on the Internet. Please email gmeissne@aol.com for the site.

5.1 *Explain why the pricing of credit derivatives is more difficult than the pricing of derivatives in the equity, commodity, foreign exchange, or fixed income markets.*

5.2 *What are the three main approaches for pricing credit derivatives? Characterize and criticize them briefly.*

5.3 *Of the numerous input factors, which ones do you believe are the most important for pricing a credit derivative? Discuss.*

5.4 *Explain why in trading practice the default swap premium is often derived from the asset swap spread.*

5.5 *Derive the price range of a default swap using hedging arguments.*

5.6 *Derive the probability of default for period 1 in a simple 1-step binomial tree. Using this result, derive the probability of default for period 2 in a 2-step binomial model.*

5.7 *Explain the market price of risk equation:* $\chi_i = \dfrac{\mu_i - r}{\sigma_i}$. *Give a numerical example showing that the market price of risk decreases for an asset that has a higher market price of risk than the arbitrage-free market price of risk* χ_M.

5.8 *Explain why a zero-coupon bond is not a martingale. Do you think a stock price is a martingale?*

5.9 *Show that the Black-Scholes equation for a put* $P = -SN(-d_1) + Ke^{-rT}N(-d_2)$ *with*

$$d_1 = \frac{\ln\left(\frac{S}{Ke^{-rT}}\right) + \frac{1}{2}\sigma^2 T}{\sigma\sqrt{T}} \quad and \quad d_2 = d_1 - \sigma\sqrt{T}$$

satisfies the PDE:

$$D = \frac{\partial D}{\partial t}\frac{1}{r} + \frac{\partial D}{\partial S}S + \frac{1}{2}\frac{\partial^2 D}{\partial S^2}\frac{1}{r}\sigma^2 S^2.$$

5.10 *Do you think it is reasonable to value a credit-spread option on a modified Black-Scholes equation, where the spread is modeled as a single variable? What are the drawbacks?*

5.11 *Discuss the original Merton equation* $E_0 = V_0 N(d1) - De^{-rT}N(d_2)$ *where*

$$d_1 = \frac{\ln\left(\frac{V_0}{De^{-rT}}\right) + \frac{1}{2}\sigma_V^2 T}{\sigma_V\sqrt{T}} \quad and \quad d_2 = d_1 - \sigma_V\sqrt{T}.$$

What is the probability of default in the Merton model? Explain.

5.12 *The probability of default in the original Merton model can also be derived via a put option. Explain.*

5.13 *Discuss the derivation of the probability of default in first-time passage models. Why have first-time passage models not been too successful in trading practice?*

5.14 *Discuss the vulnerable option pricing approach in the Jarrow Turnbull 1995 model.*

5.15 *Why is it necessary to transform historical transition probabilities into risk-neutral (martingale) transition probabilities in the derivatives pricing process? When should historical probabilities, and when should risk-neutral probabilities be applied?*

5.16 *Why is the reference asset–counterparty default correlation important when pricing default swaps? Discuss how the reference asset–counterparty default correlation can be incorporated in a default swap pricing process.*

5.17 *Show how TRORs can easily be evaluated on the basis of default swap pricing.*

Notes

1 Altman, E., "Measuring Corporate Bond Mortality and Performance," *Journal of Finance*, 44, 1989, pp. 909–21.

2 Black, F. and M. Scholes, "The Pricing of Options and Corporate Liabilities," *Journal of Political Economy*, 81, May–June 1973, pp. 637–54.

3 Merton had outlined the basic principle of arbitrage-free derivatives pricing. See Merton, R. "Theory of Rational Option Pricing," *Bell Journal of Economics and Management Science*, vol. 4, no. 1, Spring 1973, pp. 141–83.

4 See Meissner, G., "Pricing Default Swaps – Which Default Probabilities, Which Default Correlations Should Be Included?" Hawaii University Working Paper, 2004.

5 For reasons of simplicity we have not included arrows for the bond sale from bank B to the bond buyer at time t_0 and no arrows for the cash returns at time t_1.

6 In many reduced form models such as Jarrow and Turnbull (1995), Lando (1998), and Duffie and Singleton (1999), a "hazard rate" (also called default intensity) is used to model default. The hazard rate h, multiplied by a certain time period results in the default probability. The λ_t

used in figure 5.5 and throughout this book already incorporates the time period. Hence λ_t is the risk-neutral default probability for period t to t + 1. Naturally, if the time period for the possible default is 1, the hazard rate and the default probability are identical.

7 For an explanation of forward rates see Hull, J., "Options, Futures and Other Derivatives," Prentice Hall, 2002, 4th edn, pp. 98ff and Meissner, G., *Trading Financial Derivatives*, Simon and Schuster, 1998, pp. 84ff.

8 Earlier in the book we used the notation e^x (e = Euler's number). For convenience we are now using $\exp(x) = e^x$.

9 W. Sharpe, "Evaluating Mutual Fund Performance," *Journal of Business*, (39) 1966, pp. 138–99.

10 See K. Ito, "On Stochastic Differential Equations," *Memoirs, American Mathematical Society*, 4, 1951, pp. 1–51.

11 For a proof see http://www.dersoft.com/bspdeproof.doc.

12 Margrave, W., "The value of an option to exchange one asset for another," *Journal of Finance* 33, 1978, pp. 177–86.

13 See Hull, J. and A. White, "Pricing Interest Rate Derivative Securities," *Review of Financial Studies*, 3, 4 1990, pp. 573–92, and Hull J. and A. White, "Numerical procedures for implementing term structure models I: single factor models," *The Journal of Derivatives*, 2, 1994, pp. 7–16.

14 Merton, R., "On the Pricing of Corporate Debt: The Risk Structure of Interest Rates," *Journal of Finance* 29, 1974, pp. 449–70.

15 The value of N(−1.7695) = 3.84% can be found in table A.1 in the appendix or with Excel function normsdist(−1.7695) = 3.84%.

16 See for example P. Crosbie, "Modeling Default Risk," in *Credit Derivatives: Trading & Management of Credit and Default Risk*, Risk Books; Jones E., S. Mason and E. Rosenfeld, "Contingent Claim Analysis of Corporate Structures: An Empirical Investigation," *Journal of Finance*, 1984, 39(3), pp. 611–28, and Kamakura, "Comparison of the Merton and Jarrow Credit Models for Pricing Risky Debt," *Internal Kamakura paper* to be received at www.Kamakuraco.com.

17 Black, F. and J. Cox, "Valuing Corporate Securities: Some Effects of Bond Indenture Provisions," *The Journal of Finance*, 31, 1976, pp. 351–67.

18 Kim, J., K. Ramaswamy, and S. Sundaresan, "Does Default Risk in Coupons Affect the Valuation of Corporate Bonds?: A Contingent Claim Model," *Financial Management*, 22(3), 1993, pp. 117–31.

19 Cox, J., J. Ingersoll and S. Ross, "A Theory of the Term Structure of Interest Rates," *Econometrica*, 53 (1985), pp. 385–407.

20 Longstaff, F. and E. Schwartz, "A Simple Approach to Valuing Risky Fixed and Floating Rate Debt," *The Journal of Finance*, no. 3, July 1995, pp. 789–819.

21 Vasicek, O., "An Equilibrium Characterization of the Term Structure," *Journal of Economics*, 5, 1977, pp. 177–88.

22 Briys, E. and F. de Varenne, "Valuing Risky Fixed Rate Debt: An Extension," *Journal of Financial and Quantitative Analysis*," vol. 32, no. 2, June 1997, pp. 239–48.

23 Hull, J. and A. White, "Pricing Interest Rate Derivative Securities," *The Review of Financial Studies*, 3(4), 1990, pp. 573–92.

24 Jarrow, R. and S. Turnbull, "Pricing Derivatives on Financial Securities Subject to Credit Risk," *Journal of Finance*, vol. L, no. 1, March 1995, pp. 53–85.

25 Jarrow and Turnbull use $\lambda\mu$, where μ represents a time period, and call $\lambda\mu$ pseudo- or martingale probability. We will drop the variable μ, hence our λ_t already incorporates the length of the time period t to t + 1, in which default occurs.

26 Jarrow and Turnbull derive the bond price as $B_{0,2} = P_{0,2}\ \{\lambda_0\ RR + (1 - \lambda_0)[\ \lambda_1 RR + (1 - \lambda_1)]\}$ (equation 28, p. 66 of Jarrow, R., and S. Turnbull, "Pricing Derivatives on Financial Securities Subject to Credit Risk," *Journal of Finance*, vol. L, no. 1, March 1995, pp. 53–85). This is slightly inconsistent since the weighted default value at time 1, λ_0 RR, is discounted with the risk-free bond price with maturity 2.

27 For the derivation of equation (5.36) see G. Meissner, *Trading Financial Derivatives – Futures, Swaps and Options in Theory and Application*, Simon and Schuster, 1997.

28 Jarrow, R., D. Lando, and S. Turnbull, "A Markov Model for the Term Structure of Credit Risk Spreads," *The Review of Financial Studies*, 1997, vol. 10, no. 2, pp. 1–42.

29 The derivation of equation (5.41) can be found at www.dersoft.com/541.doc.

30 A credit value at risk analysis addresses the question: What is the maximum amount we can lose due to a certain type of credit risk, within a certain time frame, with a certain probability? See chapter 6 for a detailed analysis of VAR.

31 Hull, J. and A. White, "Valuing Credit Default Swaps I: No Counterparty Default Risk," *Journal of Derivatives*, Fall 2000, vol. 8, issue 1, pp. 29–41.

32 The Libor Market Model is credited to three groups of authors: Brace, A., D. Gatarek, and M. Musiela, (BGM) "The Market Model of Interest Rate Dynamics," *Mathematical Finance*, 7, no. 2, 1997, pp. 127–55; Jamshidian, F., "Libor and Swap Market Models," *Finance and Stochastics*, 1 1997, pp. 293–330; and Miltersen, K., K. Sandmann, and D. Sondermann, "Closed Form Solutions for Term Structure Derivatives with LogNormal Interest Rates," *Journal of Finance*, 52, no. 1, March 1997, pp. 409–30. In the following, we will use the notation of Hull, J. and A. White, "Forward Rate Volatilities, Swap Rate Volatilities, and Implementation of the LIBOR Market Model," *Journal of Fixed Income*, September 2000a, vol. 10, issue 2, pp. 46–63 and Hull, J., *Options, Futures and Other Derivatives*, Prentice Hall, 2002.

33 Heath, D., R. Jarrow, and A. Morton, "Bond Pricing and the Term Structure of Interest Rates, A New Methodology," *Econometrica*, 60, no. 1, 1992, pp. 77–105.

34 Calculations for premium payments and payoffs are more complicated when the observed time step is different to the time interval of premium payments or the time interval of coupon payments of the reference asset. The reason is that it is necessary to keep track of the accrued interest and the accumulated premium payment.

35 See Duffie, D. and D. Lando, "Term Structures of Credit Spreads with Incomplete Accounting Information," *Econometrica*, 69(3), pp. 633–64; see also Kamakura's hybrid Jarrow-Merton model, KPD-JM, at www.kamakuraco.com. See also Mashal, R., M. Naldi, "Pricing Multiname Credit Derivatives: Heavy Tailed Hybrid Approach," *Columbia University Working Paper*, www.columbia.edu/rm586/.

Chapter Six
Risk Management with Credit Derivatives

Any virtue can become a vice if taken to an extreme, and models are only approximations of a complex real world. The practitioners should use the models only tentatively, assessing their limitations carefully in each application. (Robert Merton in 1998, just before the LTCM crash nearly caused a global financial meltdown)

In chapter 4 we have discussed how individual credit derivatives such as default swaps, TRORs, and credit-spread options hedge single asset exposure. We will now analyze how the credit risk of a *portfolio* of credit risky assets can be evaluated and managed. *Risk management* is the process of identifying risk, measuring the risk, and managing it. Managing risk means reducing the risk to levels that regulators require and that the management is comfortable with. Risk can be reduced by:

- simply eliminating risky positions (e.g. selling the risky asset);
- entering into a cash position that offsets the risk (e.g. a long position in a risky bond can be offset by shorting a bond with a high correlation to the risky bond);
- reducing the risk by entering into a derivate position (e.g. buying a default swap to hedge default risk).

The VAR Concept

The VAR (value at risk) concept is widely accepted and established in the risk management divisions of financial and non-financial institutions. VAR answers the crucial question: what is the maximum amount we can lose due to a certain type of risk[1], within a certain time frame, with a certain probability? VAR is expressed as a single number and is therefore easily understood by the senior management. Before we look how to derive a credit VAR number, let's first investigate VAR due to market risk, termed market VAR.

Market VAR for a single linear asset

A linear asset is an asset that moves by x units if the underlying instrument moves by x units. Stocks, currencies and commodities are linear assets. Derivatives are non-linear assets. Let's consider a credit-spread put option: If the credit-spread moves by x units, the credit-spread put price will move by more or less than x.

For a single linear asset S, the market VAR is the worst loss due to market price movements. Market VAR is the difference between the mean return μ of an asset S and a maximum loss return m:

$$VAR(S) = \mu - m. \tag{6.1}$$

If we assume that the return of S, $(S_i - S_{i-1})/S_{i-1}$, is normally distributed, we can express the maximum loss return m via a confidence interval expressed by α, the mean μ, and the standard deviation σ (the third and fourth moment of a normal distribution, skewness, and kurtosis are 0):

$$m = -\alpha\sigma + \mu \tag{6.2}$$

where

α: x-axis value of a cumulative distribution; e.g. for a cumulative normal distribution N, a 95% confidence interval gives $\alpha = 1.65$; for a 99% confidence interval $\alpha = 2.33$; formally: $N(1.65) = 95\%$, $N(2.33) = 99\%$, (see table A.1 in the appendix)

$\sigma(S)$: standard deviation, Std, of returns $((S_i - S_{i-1})/S_{i-1})$; $\sigma(S)$ can be more conveniently interpreted as the volatility of asset price S, calculated as $\sigma(S) = \sqrt{\frac{1}{n-1}\sum_{i=1}^{n}[\ln(S_i/S_{i-1}) - \mu]^2}$ where $\mu = \frac{1}{n}\sum_{i=1}^{n}\ln(S_i/S_{i-1})$. This is because the standard deviation of returns Std $((S_i - S_{i-1})/S_{i-1})$ is equal to the volatility of prices, $\sigma(S_i)$, hence Std $((S_i - S_{i-1})/S_{i-1}) = \sigma(S_i)$.

Combining equations (6.1) and (6.2), we derive for VAR:

$$VAR(S) = \alpha\sigma. \tag{6.3}$$

Equation (6.3) states that the maximum loss, VAR, is simply expressed as the volatility of an asset price σ, which is adjusted by the choice of a certain confidence level, expressed by α. In case of a normally distributed return, as seen in figure 6.1, the mean is zero and the standard deviation is unity.[2] Hence for the standardized normal distribution as in figure 6.1, we derive a VAR of α. More precisely, VAR is the distance from the mean of zero to $-\alpha$, which is α.

In figure 6.1 we chose an alpha of -1.65. Since $N(-1.65) = 5\%$, this means that there is a 5% chance that the loss will be higher than 1.65 standard deviations. It also means that there is a 95% probability that the loss will not exceed 1.65 standard deviations.

If we assume that the underlying asset return is not normally distributed, we can generate α from existing tables of other distributions. This concept will be applied to credit VAR, termed CAR.

Market VAR for a certain time frame

The volatility σ in equation (6.3) is expressed as a daily volatility, i.e. for the time horizon of one day. This is typically the case in reality since end-of-day prices are used. Volatility can

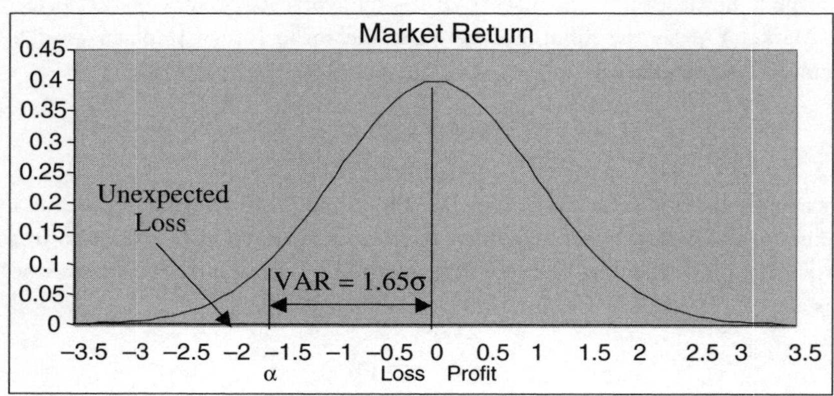

Figure 6.1: VAR, which represents the maximum expected loss due to market price changes, on a 95% confidence level and the unexpected loss

easily be transformed into any time frame by multiplying it with the square root of that time frame. For example a daily volatility, σ_{daily}, is transformed into a yearly volatility, σ_{yearly}, by multiplying by $\sqrt{252}$, assuming there are 252 trading days in a year: $\sigma_{daily} \times \sqrt{252} = \sigma_{yearly}$. A daily volatility is transformed into a 10-day volatility by multiplying by the square root of 10: $\sigma_{daily} \times \sqrt{10} = \sigma_{10day}$.

Using this transformation and adding the notional amount N to equation (6.3), we derive the VAR for an x-day time period as:

$$\mathrm{VAR}(S) = N\alpha\sigma\sqrt{x} \tag{6.4}$$

where σ is the daily volatility and x is expressed in days.

In equation (6.4) we are using the volatility concept, which calculates the standard deviation of relative price differences: $(S_i - S_{i-1})/S_{i-1} \approx \ln(S_i/S_{i-1})$. Since we are applying the normal standard distribution to calculate VAR, we are implicitly assuming that the relative change of the price of asset S, $(S_i - S_{i-1})/S_{i-1}$, termed market return, is normally distributed, see figure 6.1. Also, since the volatility is calculated around the mean (of relative price changes), the VAR that we are calculating is the VAR with respect to that mean.

Let's explain equation (6.4) in a numerical example.

Example 6.1: A company owns \$1,000,000 worth of asset S. The daily volatility of asset S is 1%. What is the 10-day market VAR for a confidence level of 99%?

We first find the value for α for the 99% confidence level from table A.1 in the appendix, or with Excel function normsinv(0.99) = 2.33. Following equation (6.4) the market VAR is: VAR (S) = \$1,000,000 × 0.01 × 2.33 × $\sqrt{10}$ = \$73,681. Hence, the company is 99% sure that it will not lose more than \$73,681 within the next 10 days due to market price changes of asset S.

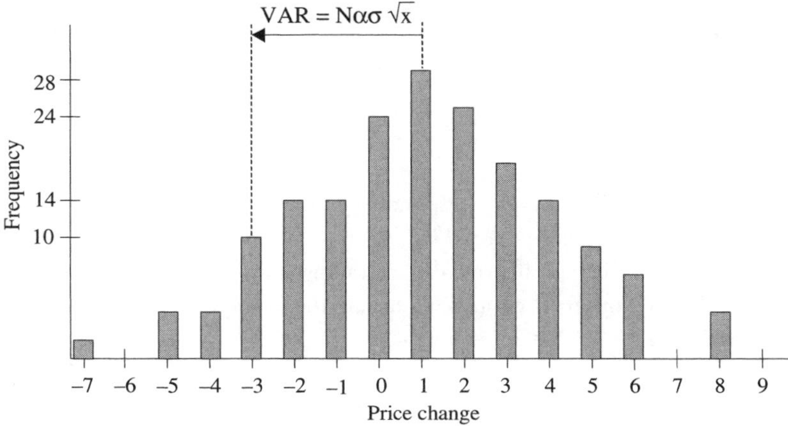

Figure 6.2: The VAR in a numerical example

The number \$73,681 is the 10-day VAR on a 99% confidence level. This means that on average once in a hundred 10-day periods (so once every 1,000 days), this VAR number of \$73,681 will be exceeded. If we have roughly 252 trading days in a year, a company will expect to exceed the VAR roughly once every 4 years. The Basel Committee of the BIS considers this as too often. Hence, they require that banks hold 3-times the 10-day VAR, which means that they will expect to exceed their VAR approximately once every 12 years. In example 6.1, a VAR capital charge of \$73,681 × 3 = \$221,043 is required by the BIS regulators.

Currently investment banks use a daily time horizon for their trading books to calculate the VAR. This is in line with the daily marking to market of the trading portfolio. For investment portfolios such as retirement funds, which are less volatile, typically a monthly time horizon for VAR is applied.

Accumulated expected loss

As derived from equation (6.4), VAR is the notional amount N times the absolute α-value, multiplied with the volatility σ of the asset for a time period of x days. Let's have a look at a numerical example in figure 6.2.

In figure 6.2, VAR is 4. This can be derived by the numerical values of N = \$100, $\alpha = 1.65$, $\sigma = 2.425\%$, for a one-day time horizon, so $x = 1$. Hence, from equation (6.4), VAR = \$100 × 1.65 × 0.02425 × $\sqrt{1}$ = \$4. Naturally, if the position in the asset would be N = \$1,000,000, the VAR would result in \$40,000.

From figure 6.2, we can also derive the accumulated expected loss, AEL, within VAR. It can be interpreted as the sum of all losses, which will not be exceeded for a certain time frame, for a certain probability. It is the surface from d to the mean, where d is the value on the x-axis corresponding to a certain α. In figure 6.2, $d = -3$. Since the mean is 1, AEL is the area from −3 to 1. So in figure 6.2 the accumulated expected loss AEL, is 4 × 10 +

$3 \times 14 + 2 \times 14 + 1 \times 24 = 134$. For continuous time and continuous price change, the accumulated expected loss is:

$$\mathrm{AEL} = \int_{d}^{mean} \phi(x)dx \tag{6.5}$$

where d is the value on the x-axis corresponding to a certain α.

We can also derive the *average expected loss*, AVEL, which is the accumulated loss per unit of observation. This unit is typically one day in trading practice. If so, in figure 6.2 we have $10 + 14 + 14 + 24 = 62$ observation days. Hence, in the example in figure 6.2, the expected loss per day, AVEL, is $134/62 = 2.16$. Formally,

$$\mathrm{AVEL} = \frac{1}{n}\sum_{i=1}^{n} d_i \Delta P_i \tag{6.6}$$

where n is the total number of days, d_i the number of days on which the i-th price change occurred, and ΔP_i the price change for d_i.

As mentioned above, VAR expresses the expected worst loss for a certain time frame for with a certain probability. Hence the *unexpected* accumulated loss, UAL, is the area from $-\infty$ to d. For continuous price change we derive:

$$\mathrm{UAL} = \int_{-\infty}^{d} \phi(x)dx. \tag{6.7}$$

VAR with respect to zero

In equations (6.3) and (6.4) we have calculated the VAR with respect to the return mean, which may not be zero as in figure 6.2. If we choose to disregard this positive mean and want to derive the VAR with respect to a relative price change of zero, which gives us the absolute loss, we have to adjust equation (6.4). We derive:

$$\mathrm{VAR(zero)} = N\sigma(S)\alpha\sqrt{x} - \mu x \tag{6.8}$$

where x is the time period of observation, expressed in days, and μ is the return mean of the underlying asset.

Using the same values as above, i.e. $N = \$100$, $\alpha = 1.65$, $\sigma = 2.425\%$, $x = 1$, and $\mu = 1$, from figure 6.2 we derive, following equation (6.8), $\mathrm{VAR(zero)} = \$100 \times 1.65 \times 0.02425 \times \sqrt{1} - 1 \times 1 = \$3$. This result can be directly observed from figure 6.2 as the distance between 0 and -3 on the x-axis.

Market VAR for a portfolio of linear assets

In order to derive the market VAR for a portfolio of linear assets, we have to take into account the correlation of the assets ρ of a portfolio P. We can slightly alter equation (6.4):

$$\text{VAR(P)} = \sigma(\text{P})\alpha\sqrt{\text{x}} \tag{6.9}$$

where the volatility $\sigma(P)$ is now defined as:

$$\sigma(\text{P}) = \sqrt{\sum_{i=1}^{n}\sum_{j=1}^{n}\rho_{i,j}\beta_i\beta_j\sigma_i\sigma_j}, \tag{6.10}$$

where β_i and β_j are the invested notional amounts (price S times quantity q) of asset i and j, respectively, and $\rho_{i,j}$ is the correlation coefficient of the returns of i and j. Hence, the term $\sigma(P)$ includes the notional amounts of assets i and j via β_i and β_j. Therefore the notional amount N does not appear in equation (6.9).

Example 6.2: Given is a portfolio of two assets i and j. \$1,000,000 is invested in asset i, which has a daily volatility of 1%. \$2,000,000 is invested in asset j, which has a daily volatility of 3%. The correlation coefficient of the assets is +0.5. What is the 10-day market VAR on a 95% confidence level?

From equation (6.10), we first derive $\sigma(P)$ as:

$$\begin{aligned}&1\times1{,}000{,}000\times1{,}000{,}000\times0.1\times0.01+0.5\times1{,}000{,}000\times2{,}000{,}000\times0.01\times0.03\\&\quad+0.5\times2{,}000{,}000\times1{,}000{,}000\times0.03\times0.01+1\times2{,}000{,}000\times2{,}000{,}000\times0.03\times0.03\\&\quad=4.300.000.000.\\&\sqrt{4{,}300{,}000{,}000}=65{,}574.\end{aligned}$$

We find the value of α for the 95% confidence level from table A.1 in the appendix or with Excel function normsinv(0.95) = 1.65.

Following equation (6.9), the VAR for the portfolio of the two linear assets is:

$$\$65{,}574\times1.65\times\sqrt{10}=\$342{,}149.$$

Hence, we are 95% sure that the portfolio will not result in a higher loss than \$342,149 in the next 10 days due to market price changes of assets i and j.

Market VAR for non-linear assets

In order to derive the VAR for non-linear assets, we have to include the non-linearity feature in the calculation. For bonds the non-linearity is measured by the first and second partial mathematical derivative, duration and convexity (ignoring higher orders). For options the non-linearity feature is measured by the first and second partial mathematical derivative, delta and gamma. Let's discuss how the VAR for options can be derived.

Market VAR for a portfolio of options

The non-linearity of options is measured by the delta and gamma (ignoring the third and higher orders). The delta δ is the first partial mathematical derivate of an option function with respect to the underlying asset. Expressing δ for a discrete change in the underlying price S, we have:

$$\delta = \frac{\Delta P}{\Delta S} \tag{6.11}$$

where P is the option portfolio value and S the price of an asset in the portfolio.

Equation (6.11) expresses how much the portfolio value changes, ΔP, for a discrete change of the price, ΔS, of an asset in the portfolio.

In order to capture the curvature of the option function (the change of the delta) we use the second mathematical derivative, the gamma Γ:

$$\Gamma = \frac{\Delta^2 P}{\Delta S^2}. \tag{6.12}$$

Equation (6.12) expresses how much the delta of portfolio changes, $\Delta\delta = \Delta^2 P$, for a discrete change of the price, ΔS, of an asset in the portfolio.

To derive the VAR value for a portfolio of options, we have to ideally include the delta and gamma in equation (6.10) (while ignoring higher orders) and we can then apply equation (6.9).

To find the impact of delta and gamma on the portfolio, typically a Taylor series approximation[3] is applied in practice. It results in:

$$\frac{\Delta P}{\Delta S} = \delta + 0.5\Gamma\Delta S \tag{6.13}$$

where ΔP is again a discrete change of the portfolio for ΔS, a discrete change in the price of an asset price in the portfolio, δ is the delta, $\delta = \Delta P/\Delta S$, and $\Gamma = \Delta^2 P/\Delta S^2$.

The Taylor approximation gives good results for small changes in S and small gamma values. However, for big changes in the underlying S and high gamma values, equation (6.13) overestimates portfolio changes. Since big changes of the underlying are crucial in risk management, the Taylor series approximation of equation (6.13) cannot be considered a good choice. This is why in trading practice, often just the delta, the delta + 0.5 times gamma, or delta + gamma are applied. For a test of these approximations see www.dersoft.com/Taylortest.xls.

In the following analysis we will use the approximation delta + gamma. In most cases this approximation does not significantly overestimate portfolio changes for big changes in the underlying S and mostly gives better results than just using the delta.

The delta and gamma will be included in equation (6.10) via the β terms. Hence, we apply equation (6.14):

$$\sigma(P) = \sqrt{\sum_{i=1}^{n}\sum_{j=1}^{n} \rho_{i,j}\beta_i^*\beta_j^*\sigma_i\sigma_j}, \tag{6.14}$$

where β^* is defined as the notional amount invested in an asset (price S × quantity q) times delta plus gamma: $\beta^* = (S \times q)\ (\delta + \Gamma)$.

Example 6.3: A portfolio consists of two options. Option 1 on stock i has a delta of 0.4 and a gamma of 0.04. Option 2 on stock j has a delta of 0.5 and a gamma of 0.05. Stock i has a price of $60 and stock j has a price of $70. The daily volatility of asset i is 1%, the daily volatility of asset j is 3%. The correlation coefficient of the daily changes between asset i and asset j is +0.5. The portfolio consists of 100 shares of stock i and 200 shares of stock j. What is the 10-day VAR of the portfolio on a 99% confidence interval?

First we derive $\beta_i^* = (60 \times 100) \times (0.4 + 0.04) = 2{,}640$ and $\beta_j^* = (70 \times 200) \times (0.5 + 0.05) = 7{,}700$.

The α-value, representing a 99% confidence level, can be again found in table A.1 in the appendix or with Excel function normsinv(0.99) = 2.33.

Using equation (6.14), the value of $\sigma(P)$ is:

$$1 \times 2{,}640 \times 2{,}640 \times 0.01 \times 0.01 + 0.5 \times 2{,}640 \times 7{,}700 \times 0.01 \times 0.03$$
$$+ 0.5 \times 7{,}700 \times 2{,}640 \times 0.03 \times 0.01 + 1 \times 7{,}700 \times 7{,}700 \times 0.03 \times 0.03 = 60{,}156.$$
$$\sqrt{60{,}156} = 245.$$

Using equation (6.9), the VAR value for the option portfolio is:

$$245 \times 2.33 \times \sqrt{10} = 1{,}805.$$

Hence we are 99% certain that the option portfolio will not result in a loss of more than $1,805 within a 10-day time horizon due to price fluctuation of the underlying assets in the portfolio.

See www.dersoft.com/ex63.xls for this example.

Credit at Risk (CAR)

In analogy to market VAR, credit at risk (CAR) can be defined as the maximum loss due to default or credit deterioration risk, within a certain time frame, with a certain probability. To calculate VAR we used two inputs: The volatility of daily prices σ, and a certain confidence level of the normal distribution, represented by α, see equation (6.3). Both inputs are problematic when calculating CAR. Daily changes in the credit quality of a debtor are currently not available. Hence, CAR is usually calculated for a larger time frame than VAR, usually for one year. Also, the normal distribution cannot be applied since credit returns are highly skewed, as seen in figure 6.3.

Figure 6.3 shows the probability of moving from one credit class to another within a certain time frame, typically a year. Hence figure 6.3 reflects the transition matrix for a single A rated asset as in table 5.5, including asset prices.

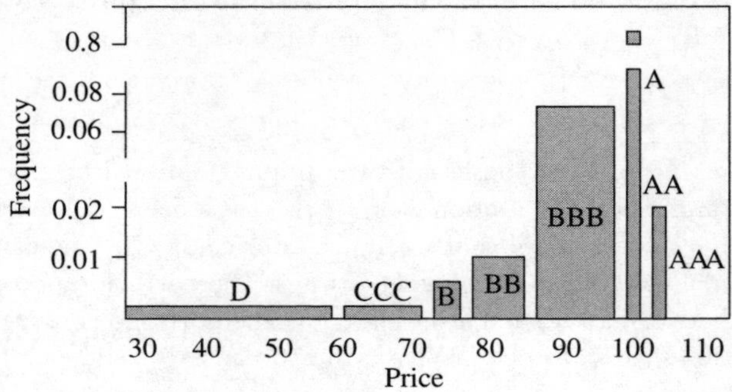

Figure 6.3: Probability credit distribution of a bond currently rate A

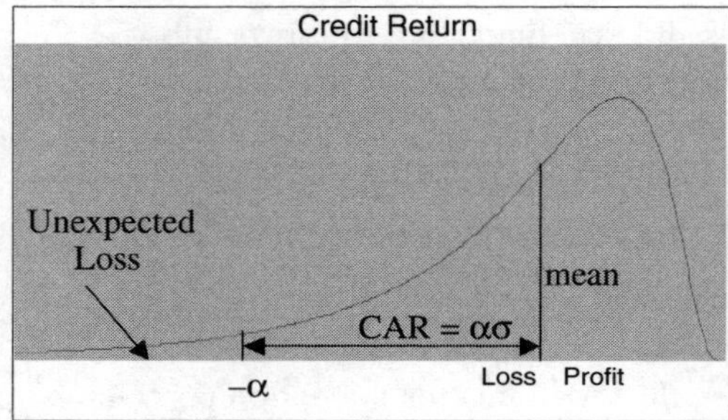

Figure 6.4: CAR, which represents the expected loss due to credit deterioration, and the unexpected loss

Naturally, staying in the same credit class, in figure 6.3 class A has the highest probability. Figure 6.3 shows that in case of an upgrade of the bond from single A to AA or AAA, the price increase of the bond is rather small. But in case of a downgrade, the price decrease is significant. The event of a strong price decrease, however, has a low probability, as seen in figure 6.3. For continuous credit classes, we derive from figure 6.3 in combination with the VAR concept of figure 6.1, figure 6.4.

Using the concept of equation (6.3), CAR can be approximately derived as the credit-volatility of the underlying asset σ multiplied with a certain confidence level, which is represented by α. This is an approximation, since the third and fourth moment of the underlying distribution are not implicitly included, but only comprised by α:

$$\text{CAR} = \alpha\sigma \tag{6.15}$$

where α is the value expressing a certain confidence level for a certain credit distribution and σ is annual credit volatility.

Adding the notional amount N and a time frame z, expressed in years, we derive:

$$\text{CAR} = \text{N}\alpha\sigma\sqrt{\text{z}}. \tag{6.16}$$

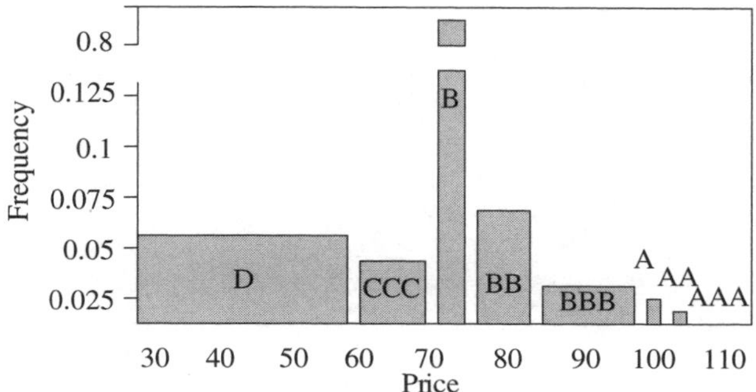

Figure 6.5: Credit and price distribution of a downgraded bond, currently rated B

Finding the annual credit volatility σ for the underlying credit is currently (year 2004) not easy, since the market for credit is still in its infancy. However, with a growing credit market, more data and data providers will be available to generate reliable and consistent credit volatility data.

A more critical question when evaluating CAR in equation (6.16) is to find a credit function that gives realistic values for α. This is not an easy task, since the credit distribution function of an asset differs with respect to the current rating. Investment grade bonds (rated AAA to BBB) principally have a credit function as shaped as in figure 6.3 and 6.4. However, bonds that have been downgraded to junk bond status (rated lower than BBB to CCC), can be assumed to have a more normally shaped credit distribution, typically with a fat left tail as seen in figure 6.5.

Since the bond in figure 6.5 has a current price of slightly above 70, we can assume that it was downgraded from a higher rating and its inception price of 100, assuming no interest rate effects. In figure 6.5 we can also observe that junk bonds typically have a higher probability to default (rating D) than to be downgraded (to CCC).

For a newly issued bond with a junk rating (with a par price of 100), the distribution would be a combination of figures 6.3 and 6.5. Hence, the question which distribution to use depends on the current rating, the past rating change, the recovery rate, and factors such as country, sector, seniority, maturity, coupon, yield, duration, convexity, and higher orders of the credit function.

Determining CAR of investment grade bonds

As derived above, for investment grade bonds we can generally assume a credit distribution as in figures 6.3 and 6.4. Figures 6.3 and 6.4 equate roughly to an inversely scaled lognormal distribution. The well-known lognormal distribution is:

$$\varphi(x) = \frac{1}{\sigma(x-\theta)\sqrt{2\pi}} e^{-\frac{(\ln(x-\theta)-\mu)^2}{2\sigma^2}} \tag{6.17}$$

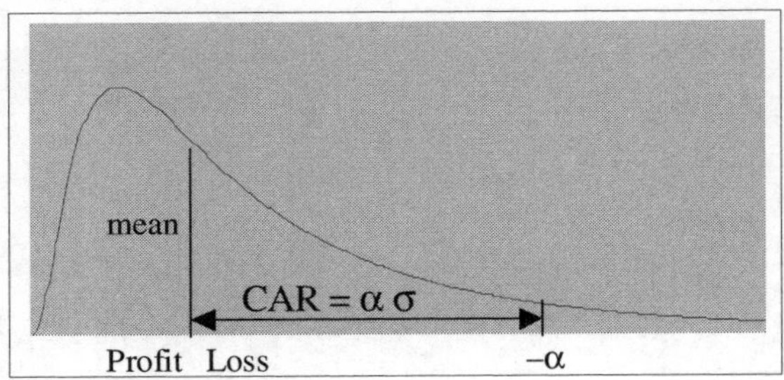

Figure 6.6: Lognormal distribution with $\mu = 0$, $\sigma = 0.6$ and $\theta =$ zero

where μ is a scale parameter, σ is a shape parameter, and θ is a location parameter, which allows a linear (horizontal) transformation of the distribution. Using $\ln e^x = e^{\ln x} = x$, we derive some important properties of the lognormal distribution. If a variable X is lognormally distributed, the logarithm of X, ln (X), is normally distributed. This property is used by Black-Scholes in the equation (5.9):

$$d_1 = \frac{\ln\left(\frac{S}{Ke^{-rT}}\right) + \frac{1}{2}\sigma^2 T}{\sigma\sqrt{T}}.$$

Since the stock price S in the term d_1 is assumed to be lognormally distributed, $\ln(S/Ke^{-rt})$ is normally distributed. Hence to derive $N(d_1)$, we can use tables of a normal distribution. Also, if x is normally distributed, then $X = e^x$ is lognormally distributed.

Assuming ln(X) is normally distributed, we derive from the properties of the normal distribution the mean $\mu = E(\ln(X))$ and the variance $\sigma^2 = \text{Var}(\ln(X))$.[4] From the properties of the lognormal distribution, we derive $E(X) = e^{\mu+\sigma^2/2}$ and $\text{Var}(X) = e^{\mu+\sigma^2/2}(e^{\sigma^2} - 1)$. For $\mu = 0$ and small σ^2 it follows that $E(X) \approx 1$ and $\sigma(X) \approx \sqrt{\text{Var}(X)}$. See spreadsheet www.dersoft.com/lnd.xls for a lognormal distribution. Graphically equation (6.16) with an inverse scaling of the x-axis compared to figure 6.4 is as shown in figure 6.6.

For the lognormal distribution, software such as Statistica or SAS exists, which gives α-values for certain confidence levels and certain values of μ and σ. Table A.2 in the appendix also gives α-values for a lognormal distribution. Let's derive CAR in a numerical example.

Example 6.4: The annual credit volatility (the standard deviation of credit quality changes) of asset i is 5%. Assuming the credit changes of asset i are roughly lognormally distributed with $\mu = 0$ as in figures 6.4 and 6.6, what is the 1-year CAR on a 95% confidence level for a notional amount of \$1,000,000?

From table A.2 in the appendix, or with statistical software we derive α for a 95% confidence level of 4.175. (This is derived from $N(d = 1) = 0.5$ and $N(d = 5.175) =$

0.95, see table A.2.) From equation (6.16) we derive a CAR of $1{,}000{,}000 \times 4.175 \times 0.05 \times \sqrt{1} = \$208{,}750$.

Hence we are 95% sure that asset i will not result in a loss of more than $208,750 due to credit deterioration within one year.[5]

Accumulated expected credit loss

As derived for market VAR in equation (6.5), we can easily derive the accumulated expected credit loss, AECL, within CAR. It can be interpreted as the sum of all losses, which will not be exceeded for a certain time frame, for a certain probability due to credit risk. It is the surface from the mean to d (see figure 6.5), where d is a value on the x-axis representing a certain α. Hence we derive:

$$AECL = \int_{mean}^{d} \varphi(x)dx. \tag{6.18}$$

To evaluate the integral of equation (6.18), we can use statistical software such as Statistica or SAS. Alternatively, table A.2 in the appendix gives values for equation (6.18).

Equation (6.18) expresses the expected accumulated credit loss. The unexpected accumulated credit loss, UACL, is the area from d to infinity, where d again corresponds to a certain α-value. Hence:

$$UACL = \int_{d}^{\infty} \varphi(x)dx. \tag{6.19}$$

CAR for a portfolio of assets

In order to evaluate the CAR for a portfolio of assets, we can apply the portfolio concept for market risk, VAR, equations (6.9) to (6.14). Let's incorporate the fact that credit risk is typically non-linear: If the credit quality of a highly rated asset changes by one unit (for example from AA to A) the resulting price change of the portfolio will typically not be one. Furthermore, the magnitude of the price change will typically be different for lower rate assets (for example from B to CCC). Hence, we have to apply equations (6.11) to (6.14). Slightly altering equations (6.11) to (6.14), we derive for the credit-delta δ_c:

$$\delta_c = \frac{\Delta P}{\Delta c} \tag{6.11a}$$

where P is the portfolio value and c the credit quality of an asset in the portfolio.

Equation (6.11a) expresses how much the portfolio value changes, ΔP, for a discrete change of the credit quality, Δc, of an asset in the portfolio. The credit ratings AAA to D are ordinal measures. In order to derive metric measures, we can assign asset prices to each credit rating on the basis of historical data.

In order to capture the curvature of the credit function (the change of the delta) we use the second mathematical derivative, the credit-gamma Γ_c:

$$\Gamma_c = \frac{\Delta^2 P}{\Delta c^2}. \tag{6.12a}$$

Equation (6.12a) expresses how much the portfolio delta changes, $\Delta\delta = \Delta^2 P$, for a discrete change in the credit quality, Δc, of an asset in the portfolio.

To derive the CAR value for a portfolio of credits, we have to again include the delta and gamma in equation (6.10a). The delta and gamma are included in equation (6.10a) via the β terms. Hence we derive:

$$\sigma_c(P) = \sqrt{\sum_{i=1}^{n}\sum_{j=1}^{n}\rho_{i,j}\beta_i^*\beta_j^*\sigma_i\sigma_j} \tag{6.10a}$$

where β^* is defined as the notional amount invested in an asset (price $S \times$ quantity q) times the credit-delta plus the credit-gamma: $\beta^* = (S \times q)\ (\delta_c + \Gamma_c)$. For a discussion on this approximation, see the above section "Market VAR for a portfolio of options" and www.dersoft.com/Taylortest.xls. σ_i and σ_j in equation (6.10a) and consequently $\sigma_c(P)$ are expressed as annual volatilities.

To evaluate CAR, we use the result of (6.10a) and input it into the following equation:

$$CAR = \alpha\sigma_c(P)\sqrt{z} \tag{6.15a}$$

where z is a time period, expressed in years.

The notional amount N is again not included in equation (6.15a), since it is included in the β^* terms of equation (6.10a). Let's now derive the portfolio CAR in a numerical example.

Example 6.5: A portfolio consists of two assets. Asset i has a credit-delta of 2 (meaning that if the credit quality of asset i changes by one unit, the portfolio value changes by 2) and a credit-gamma of 0.3. Asset j has a credit-delta of 3 and a credit-gamma of 0.4. Asset i has a price of \$90 and asset j has a price of \$95. The annual credit-volatility of asset i is 4%, the annual credit-volatility of asset j is 5%. The correlation coefficient of the annual credit-volatility changes of asset i and asset j is +0.3. The portfolio consists of 10,000 assets of i and 20,000 assets of j. What is the 1-year CAR of the portfolio on a 95% confidence level assuming the credit quality changes are roughly lognormally distributed?

First we derive $\beta_i^* = (90 \times 10{,}000) \times (2 + 0.3) = 2{,}070{,}000$ and $\beta_j^* = (95 \times 20{,}000) \times (3 + 0.4) = 6{,}460{,}000$.

Using equation (6.10a), the value of $\sigma_c(P)$ is:

$1 \times 2{,}070{,}000 \times 2{,}070{,}000 \times 0.04 \times 0.04 + 0.3 \times 2{,}070{,}000 \times 6{,}460{,}000 \times 0.04 \times 0.05$
$+ 0.3 \times 6{,}460{,}000 \times 2{,}070{,}000 \times 0.05 \times 0.04 + 1 \times 6{,}460{,}000 \times 6{,}460{,}000 \times 0.05 \times 0.05$
$= 127{,}231{,}480{,}000.$

$\sqrt{127{,}231{,}480{,}000} = 356{,}695.$

Using equation (6.15a), the CAR of the portfolio is:

$$356{,}695 \times 4.18 \times \sqrt{1} = 1{,}490{,}985.$$

Hence, we are 95% certain that the portfolio will not lose more than $1,490,985 within 1 year due to credit deterioration risk.
See www.dersoft.com/ex65 for this example.

Reducing portfolio CAR with credit derivatives

If the senior management is concerned with the CAR number, it may require the traders to reduce CAR. As explained in the beginning of the chapter, this can be done in principally three ways:

- simply eliminating risky positions (e.g. selling the risky asset);
- entering into a cash position that offsets the credit risk (e.g. a long position in a risky bond can be offset by shorting a bond with a high correlation to the risky bond);
- reducing the risk by entering into a derivate position.

In chapter 4, we have already explained how credit derivatives can reduce the risk of a single asset. We can use this concept to derive the impact of this single asset hedge on a portfolio of assets.

Reducing CAR with default swaps

Let's reconsider example 6.5 and let's hedge asset j with a default swap. As mentioned in chapter 4 (see example 4.25), the BIS grants an 80% risk offset for positions in the trading book that are hedged with a default swap.

Example 6.6: As in example 6.5, we assume that a portfolio consists of two assets. Asset i has a credit-delta of 2 and a credit-gamma of 0.3. Asset j has a credit-delta of 3 and a credit-gamma of 0.4. Asset i has a price of $90 and asset j has a price of $95. The annual credit-volatility of asset i is 4%, the annual credit-volatility of asset j is 5%. The correlation coefficient of the annual credit-volatility changes of asset i and asset j is +0.3. The portfolio consists of 10,000 assets of i and 20,000 assets of j.
In example 6.5, we derived a CAR of $1,490,985 on a 95% confidence level for a 1-year time horizon. Let's assume the combined risk-ratio of equation (4.6) is

smaller than 8% and traders have to reduce CAR. To reduce the CAR number, the traders buy a default swap on asset j with the same notional amount as asset j. The BIS grants an 80% risk offset for positions hedged with a default swap (see section "Regulatory Capital Relief" in chapter 4). Since β_j^* expresses the credit risk (i.e. how much the value of asset j changes for a change in credit quality), we can do the approximation of relating the 80% capital relief to β_j^*. Hence, we derive the reduced β_j^* as $0.2 \times (95 \times 20{,}000) \times (3 + 0.4) = 1{,}292{,}000$.

Using equation (6.10a), the value of $\sigma_c(P)$ is:

$$1 \times 2{,}070{,}000 \times 2{,}070{,}000 \times 0.04 \times 0.04 + 0.3 \times 2{,}070{,}000 \times 1{,}292{,}000 \times 0.04 \times 0.05$$

$$+ 0.3 \times 1{,}292{,}000 \times 2{,}070{,}000 \times 0.05 \times 0.04 + 1 \times 1{,}292{,}000 \times 1{,}292{,}000 \times 0.05 \times 0.05$$

$$= 14{,}238{,}218{,}000.$$

$$\sqrt{14{,}238{,}328{,}000} = 119{,}324.$$

Using equation (6.15a) the CAR of the portfolio is:

$$\$119{,}324 \times 4.18 \times \sqrt{1} = \$498{,}774.$$

Consequently, with a default swap that grants an 80% risk offset, the portfolio CAR reduces from $1,490,985 to $498,774. If the default swap had been on asset i, the CAR would reduce to $1,372,496, which the capable reader may verify herself.

See www.dersoft.com/ex66.xls for this example.

Reducing CAR with TRORs

As mentioned earlier in chapter 4, the BIS grants a 100% risk offset for positions hedged in the trading book with a TROR. Let's alter again example 6.5 and hedge asset j with a TROR.

Example 6.7: As in example 6.5, we assume that a portfolio consists of two assets. Asset i has a credit-delta of 2 and a credit-gamma of 0.3. Asset j has a credit-delta of 3 and a credit-gamma of 0.4. Asset i has a price of $90 and asset j has a price of $95. The annual credit-volatility of asset i is 4%, the annual credit-volatility of asset j is 5%. The correlation coefficient of the annual credit-volatility changes of asset i and asset j is +0.3. The portfolio consists of 10,000 assets of i and 20,000 assets of j.

In example 6.5 we derived a CAR of $1,490,985 on a 95% confidence level for a 1-year time horizon. Let's again assume the combined risk-ratio of equation (4.6) is smaller than 8% and traders have to reduce CAR. The traders enter into a TROR on asset j where they pay the TROR and receive 6ML. The TROR has the same notional amount as asset j. Since the BIS grants a 100% risk offset for hedged TROR positions in the trading book, the CAR of asset j is zero. Hence, the CAR of the portfolio is simply the CAR of asset i. From equation (6.15a), the CAR of asset i is $(90 \times 10{,}000) \times (2 + 0.3) \times 4.18 \times 0.04 = 346{,}104$. This result can also be derived with equations (6.15a) and (6.10a) with $\beta_j^* = 0$.

Hence, we find that the portfolio CAR when asset j is hedged with a TROR that has a 100% risk offset, reduces from \$1,490,985 to \$346,104. Had the TROR been done on asset i, the portfolio CAR would reduce to \$1,350,140, which the reader may verify again her/himself.

Reducing CAR with credit-spread options

In chapter 2, section "Hedging with credit-spread options," we concluded that a credit-spread put hedges a long position in an asset with respect to credit deterioration risk and default risk. Hence a credit-spread put provides a hedge with respect to the same risks as a default swap. The BIS has not specifically granted a certain risk offset for credit-spread options. However, from our conclusion in chapter 2, the BIS should grant a similar offset as for default swaps, which is – as mentioned above – 80%. In this case, hedging the portfolio in example 6.6 with a credit-spread put would result in the same reduction of the CAR as hedging with a default swap.

The correlation of credit risk management with market risk management and operational risk management

As discussed in chapter 4, market risk and credit risk are clearly related: A decrease in the market price of an asset due to interest rate increases, can increase the probability of default, and hence reduce the credit quality of a firm. Conversely, a decrease in the credit quality can increase the sensitivity of the firm to market price changes, and hence increase market risk. Empirical studies confirm this correlation – see Duffee (1998), as well as Das and Tufano (1996) and Longstaff and Schwartz (1995).

We can assume that the impact of credit risk on operational risk is rather small. For example, a credit quality deterioration should not significantly increase the exposure to legal or criminal risks. However, operational risk can impact credit risk. If a company suffers from operational damage, the default risk may increase. Consequently, the correlation between market risk, credit risk, and operational risk should ideally be incorporated when calculating portfolio risk.

As mentioned in chapter 4, equation (4.6), in October 2002 the BIS defined a combined minimum capital requirement ratio for market, credit, and operational risk. However, equation (4.6) does not incorporate any correlation between the three types of risk. In addition, the five credit risk management models discussed below do not include a correlation between the risks. They assume that credit risk, market risk, and operational risk are independent and add the risk numbers. This leads to an overstating of the total risk number.

So far we have discussed theoretical aspects of market and credit risk management. In the following, we will analyze and compare five established credit risk management models.

Recent Advances in Credit Risk Management – A Comparison of Five Models[6]

In the following, we will discuss five of the most widely used credit risk models in today's risk-management practice. Three of the five models have their roots in the Black-Scholes-Merton contingent claim methodology: KMV's *Portfolio Manager*, JP Morgan's *CreditMetrics* and Kamakura's *Risk Manager*. Furthermore, CSFP's actuarial-based *Credit+* and McKinsey's econometric-based *Portfolio View* will be analyzed.

Credit risk models – structural versus reduced form

A key debate among academics and credit risk managers is whether *structural models* or *reduced form models* are more appropriate to model the default process of a company.[7] Both models have their roots in the Merton contingent claim methodology, though the structural models have closer ties to Merton. Structural models endogenize the bankruptcy process by modeling assets and liabilities of a company as in the Merton model. The total loss distribution is often derived with the help of empirical databases.[8]

Reduced form models exogenously derive the risk-neutral probability of default by modeling the credit-spread of the company's risky bond.[9] They abstract from the company's specific data, therefore being called "reduced" form.

Reduced form models derive the risk-neutral default probability[10] from the price of a credit-risky zero-coupon bond B:

$$B = e^{-rT}N[(1-\lambda)+\lambda RR] \tag{6.20}$$

where e^{-rT} is the discount factor, N is the notional amount of the bond, $0 \leq \lambda \leq 1$ is the risk-neutral probability of default, and $0 \leq RR \leq 1$ is the recovery rate. It is easy to see that if the default probability λ is zero, the bond price will be the (now risk-free) discounted notional amount $e^{-rT}N$. In case the default is certain (i.e. $\lambda = 1$), the bond price B will be the discounted notional amount $e^{-rT}N$ multiplied by the recovery rate. If the recovery rate RR is zero, it has no effect on the bond price. If the recovery rate is 1, the default probability λ is irrelevant for deriving the bond price.

The elegant equation (6.20) has a drawback though. It has 2 unknowns, λ and RR. Solving for λ gives the probability of default as:

$$\lambda = \left(\frac{1}{1-RR}\right)\left(1-\frac{Be^{rT}}{N}\right). \tag{6.21}$$

To derive λ, RR has to be determined exogenously. This is typically the case in reduced form models.[11]

Developed reduced form models add realism to equations (6.20) and (6.21). In an often-cited article, Jarrow, Lando, and Turnbull (1997) include credit ratings of the company and model the transition of the credit rating via a Markov process through eight discrete credit states, from AAA to default. (See chapter 5.) Jarrow (1997) addresses the drawback of focusing on illiquid debt prices by including equity prices in the model. The equity price process contains a "bubble" component, relating to jumps in high-tech stocks. Debt prices include a liquidity premium due to the large spread in risky debt bonds. Further contributions of reduced form modeling are Brennan-Schwartz (1980); Iben-Litterman (1991); Longstaff-Schwartz (1995); Das-Tufano (1996); Duffee (1998); Schoenbucher (1997); Henn (1997); Duffie-Singleton (1997); Brooks-Yan (1998); Madan-Unal (1998); Duffie-Singleton (1999); Duffie (1999); Duffie-Lando (2001); Das-Sundaram (2000); Hull-White (2000); Wei (2001); Martin-Thompson-Brown (2001); and Jarrow-Yildirim (2002). For a survey article comparing the default swap evaluation equations of the Jarrow-Turnbull (1995), Brooks-Yan (1998), Duffee (1998), Das-Sundaram (2000), and Hull-White (2000) models, see Cheng (2001).

Key features of credit risk models

Credit risk models have to answer several critical questions. For a single credit they are:

- *Default risk:* What is the probability of default of a single debtor?
- *Credit deterioration or migration risk:* What is the probability of change in asset value due to changes in credit rating of the debtor?
- *Loss amount:* Given default or downgrade, what is the extent of the loss?

For a portfolio of assets the same questions arise on an aggregate level. Therefore, *default correlations*, the extent to which the default and migration risk of debtors are related, have to be considered.

Addressing all issues in a single model is not a trivial matter. Arguably, the most critical feature is the probability of default. Nonetheless, with the exception of CSFP's actuarial model, all models discussed below also include migration risk.

Credit risk models can be classified due to various criteria. The most crucial criteria are as follows.

A first broad categorization can be the *model type*, which reflects the principal conceptual framework. Structural models and reduced form models, as well as actuarial and econometric frameworks can be differentiated. The modeled *input variables* differ strongly among the credit risk models. Merton-based structural models postulate a stochastic process for the assets and liabilities of a company. In most reduced form models the term structure of credit risky spreads is Markovian, i.e. the stochastic process for the credit spread only depends on credit spread at the beginning of the process, not its past process. Actuarial models input a univariate "risk-factor" and econometric models use macroeconomic variables such as the unemployment rate, inflation rate, GDP growth rate, long-term interest rates, etc., as inputs.

On first sight *distributional assumptions* of the underlying variables and the aggregate default probability vary strongly in today's credit risk models. In Merton's model the underlying asset follows a lognormal distribution, which implies a normal distribution of asset returns. However, today's credit risk management models often derived the default distribution with the help of empirical databases.[12] Reduced form models typically use a discrete binomial, multinomial, or continuous term structure framework to model short-term interest rates. The bankruptcy process can be approximated as a Cox process (a double Poisson process). The processes are usually assumed to be independent of each other although new approaches dispense with the independence assumption.[13] Actuarial models use a gamma distribution to model the "risk-factor" and aggregate default probabilities with the actuarial-standard Poisson distribution. In econometric models the macroeconomic variables are assumed normally distributed and are transformed into default probabilities, often scaled with the help of a logit function.

As mentioned in the beginning of this chapter, in reality the density distribution of credit risk is highly skewed and can be approximated by the density of a lognormal distribution, see figures 6.3 to 6.6.

The default distribution assumptions of certain credit models can be harmonized and expressed for a portfolio with identical first two moments (mean μ and standard deviation σ). CSFP's actuarial model applies a specific form of the gamma distribution:

$$f(x) = \frac{1}{\beta^{\alpha}\Gamma(\alpha)} e^{-\frac{x}{\beta}} x^{\alpha-1},$$

where

$$\Gamma(\alpha) = \int_{x=0}^{\infty} e^{-x} x^{\alpha-1} dx \quad \text{and} \quad \alpha = \mu^2/\sigma^2 \quad \text{and} \quad \beta = \sigma^2/\mu.^{14}$$

Koyluoglu and Hickman show that a special case of the Merton approach results in:

$$f(x) = \frac{\sqrt{(1-x)}\varphi\left(\frac{c - \sqrt{1-\rho}\Phi^{-1}(x)}{\sqrt{\rho}}\right)}{\sqrt{\rho}\varphi(\Phi^{-1}(x))}$$

where c is a critical value for the normally distributed underlying variable, ρ is the asset correlation, $\varphi(x)$ is the standard normal density, and $\Phi^{-1}(x)$ is the inverse cumulative standard normal density. For McKinsey's econometric model, the probability function can be shown to be:

$$f(x) = \frac{1}{Vx(1-x)}\varphi\left\{\frac{\ln((1-x)/x) - U}{V}\right\}$$

where U and V represent a constant and a random term of the macroeconomic regression, respectively.[15] Applying these equations, we derive the default distribution probability functions for the different models. They are shown in figure 6.7.

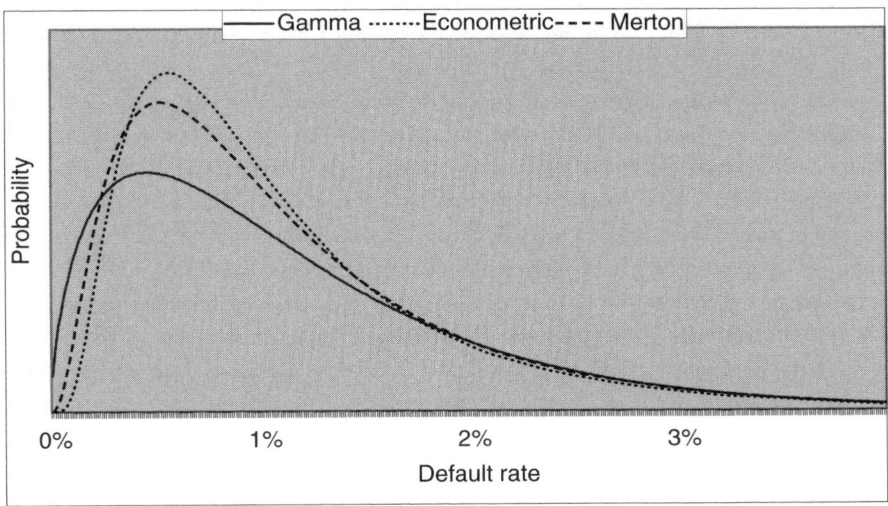

Figure 6.7: Default rate distribution for different models

Table 6.1: Skewness and kurtosis of the default rate distribution for different models with harmonized input parameters

	Skewness	Kurtosis
Gamma	0.8326	−0.7917
Econometric	1.2441	0.1606
Merton	1.0997	−0.2064

From figure 6.7 we can see that the distributions of the different models are quite similar, as seen in table 6.1 which lists the similar third and fourth moments, skewness and kurtosis.[16]

Figure 6.7 also shows that the models are virtually identical for crucial higher default rates, resulting in even closer third and fourth moments for these default rates than in table 6.1.

Correlations assumptions: In chapter 5, we had derived an equation (5.61) to evaluate the joint probability of default for two entities whose default probability is correlated:

$$\lambda(r \cap c) = \rho(\lambda^r, \lambda^c)\sqrt{\left[\lambda^r - (\lambda^r)^2\right]\left[\lambda^c - (\lambda^c)^2\right]} + \left[\lambda^r \lambda^c\right].$$

Following the *CAPM* school of thought, a portfolio is exposed to *systematic risk* (also called market risk or common risk) and *unsystematic risk* (also called company specific or idiosyncratic risk). The diversifiable unsystematic risk is not correlated and therefore does not contribute to the asset return correlation. However, the systematic risk influences the asset return correlation (e.g. the joint default probability of the two companies in the same industry should be higher than the joint default probability of two companies in different industries) and should be included in the process of deriving joint probabilities of default.

Ideally, all systematic based correlations of assets in a portfolio should be analyzed to derive joint probabilities of default. However, the number of covariance terms C in a covariance matrix increases exponentially with the number of assets n: $C = n(n - 1)/2$. Therefore the need for aggregating correlations is evident. KMV's structural model uses a three level factor structure with k common factors to aggregate correlations. This reduces the covariance terms to $kn + k(k - 1)/2$. JP Morgan's CreditMetrics assumes that companies with the same credit rating have homogeneous default rate probabilities. CSFP's actuarial model assumes a pair-wise correlation of systematic factors in each sector and aggregates default rate probabilities among sectors. In McKinsey's econometric model the regression coefficients include correlations of the systematic factors. Reduced form models include company correlations in the stochastic Markov process of modeling credit-spreads.

Bottom-up versus top-down: The term bottom-up refers to an inductive procedure, i.e. analyzing sub-units to assess characteristics of a whole population. Thus, for credit models it means analyzing credit risk for a single asset and aggregating risks via correlation and distributional assumptions. This procedure is appropriate if the single assets are relatively heterogeneous and the number of assets is low. The top-down approach is a deductive procedure, i.e. analyzing characteristics of a population to generate results for individual units. In today's credit risk models the inductive bottom-up process is dominating. Only CSFP's actuarial model, which analyzes homogeneously assumed credits on a sector level, can be considered top-down.

Economic data: Default rates of companies are higher in a recession than they are in an economic expansion. Therefore, including macroeconomic data, such as the GDP growth rate, inflation rate, interest rates, the unemployment rate, etc., in a credit risk model is beneficial for the process of generating realistic default rate probabilities. Naturally, the cost of modeling economic data is an increase in the complexity of the model. Of the credit models that are discussed here, naturally McKinsey's econometric model incorporates economic data. Furthermore, KMV's Portfolio Manager and JP Morgan's CreditMetrics as well as new developments in reduced form models can include economic variables.

The Models in Detail

KMV's Portfolio Manager[17]

One of the most widely employed credit risk management models in today's practice is Moody's-KMV's Portfolio Manager. Moody's acquired KMV in April 2002 to create Moody's KMV (M-KMV). In the following, we will refer to the Moody's-KMV model as the KMV model or KMV's Portfolio Manager.

Of all the three Merton-based models discussed here, KMV's model has the closest ties to the original Merton model. The underlying variable is the firm's assets, which grow with

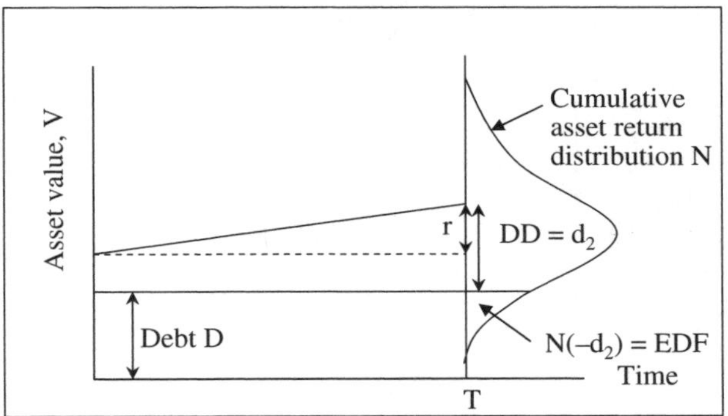

Figure 6.8: Deriving the default probability EDF in the KMV model

the expected return of the asset including servicing debt and dividends. The change in the firm's assets V is monitored against the change of the firm's debt. Bankruptcy principally occurs when the asset value drops below a default point Dp, which KMV defines as between short and long term debt. A *distance to default*, DD is defined $DD = \frac{V - Dp}{V\sigma_V}$. DD is mathematically identical with risk-neutral d_2 from the Merton model:

$$DD = d_2 = \frac{\ln\left(\frac{V}{De^{-rT}}\right) - \frac{1}{2}\sigma_V^2 T}{\sigma_V \sqrt{T}}.$$

The probability of default, termed *expected default frequency*, EDF, is a representation of the risk-neutral $N(-d_2)$ from the Merton model; N is again the cumulative distribution of asset returns. N is not necessarily normally or lognormally distributed, but derived with the help of empirical asset return data. Graphically, a simplified version of KMV's model can be seen in figure 6.8, where r is the expected asset growth rate of the asset value and the time horizon is T.

Figure 6.8 outlines the basic relationship between the default probability EDF and the distance to default DD. The higher the debt and the lower the asset growth, the lower the distance to default, thus the higher the default probability EDF. Therefore, the default probability EDF has an inverse relationship to the distance to default, as shown in figure 6.9.

The individual firm-specific functional relationship EDF (DD) can either be derived by this theoretical approach, which includes default correlations, or with economic data. In the latest version of Portfolio Manager, clients can also choose to derive EDFs on the basis of KMV's large historical internal database. KMV claims that their EDFs have high predictive power, i.e. increase sharply before the actual default occurs.[18] In 2001, KMV launched an Internet version called CreditEdge, which provides daily upgrades of EDFs for more than 25,000 publicly traded companies.[19]

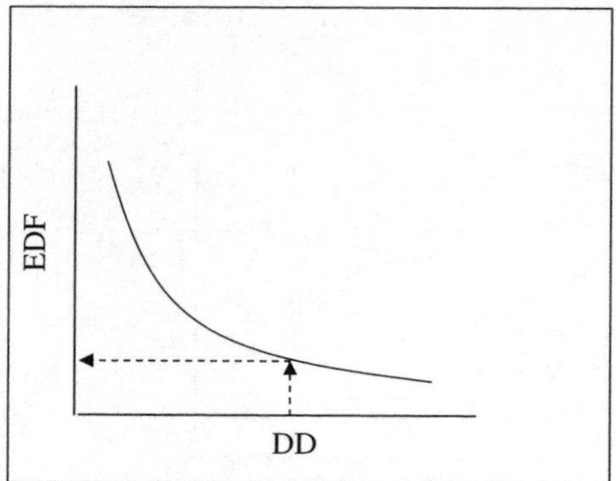

Figure 6.9: The default probability EDF as a function of the distance to default DD

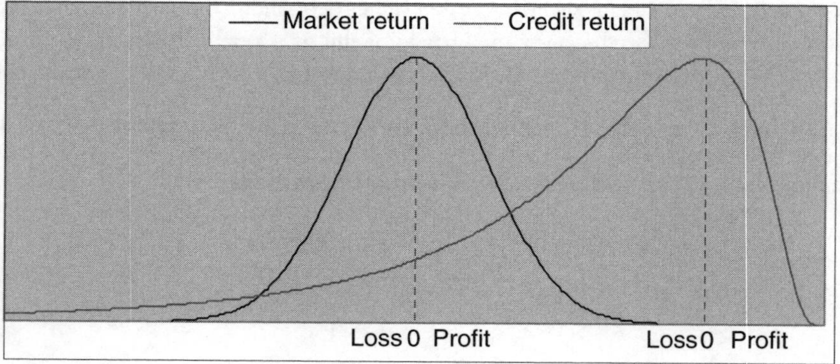

Figure 6.10: Credit return and market return for investment grade bonds

JP Morgan's CreditMetrics[20]

In 1998 JP Morgan spun off its credit risk management software development division into RiskMetrics Group (RMG). In the following, we will refer to JP Morgan's/RMG's model as JP Morgan's model or CreditMetrics.

The Merton-based CreditMetrics model estimates the value change of a portfolio by modeling the change in credit quality on the basis of historical transition matrices. As discussed in the beginning of the chapter (see figures 6.3 to 6.6), in practice, credit quality changes cannot be assumed to be normally distributed, but are highly skewed as seen in figure 6.10.

As mentioned, the credit return distribution in figure 6.10 is typical for investment grade bonds (AAA to BBB). For junk bonds, which have been downgraded, the distribution function will be more normally distributed as shown in figure 6.5.

The basis for modeling credit quality changes in JP Morgan's approach is the transition matrix, which provides historical probabilities of transition from one credit state to another. A transition matrix was displayed in chapter 5, table 5.5 (reproduced below).

One-year historical transition matrix of year 2002 (numbers in %)

		Rating at Year-end								
		Aaa	**Aa**	**A**	**Baa**	**Ba**	**B**	**Caa**	**Default**	**WR**
Initial	Aaa	86.82	7.75	0	0	0	0	0	0	5.43
Rating	Aa	1.38	82.23	12.12	0.14	0	0	0	0	4.13
	A	0	2.18	82.83	8.86	1.01	0.47	0.08	0.16	4.43
	Baa	0.17	0.17	2.46	79.47	7.55	2.04	1.87	1.19	5.09
	Ba	0	0.18	0.18	2.39	72.38	13.26	2.03	1.47	8.10
	B	0	0	0.14	0.41	2.71	72.9	9.76	4.88	9.21
	Caa	0	0	0	0	0.34	3.42	56.85	27.74	11.64

Source: Moody's Investor Service, April 2003. WR represents companies that had been rated initially but are not rated at year-end

Historical transition matrices often contain anomalies. In table 5.5 for example, the probability of an A rated company to move to Aaa is lower (0%) than the probability of a Baa rated company to move to Aaa (0.17%). CreditMetrics uses Markov processes to smooth these anomalies.

In order to derive the cumulative default distribution for a portfolio, Monte Carlo simulation generates a path and terminal value for the credit rating changes of each asset. The terminal value is stored and added to derive the cumulative default distribution.

The credit rating changes of the assets can be assumed to be correlated. CreditMetrics incorporates these correlations derived from equity price correlations via a *copula* approach. This approach derives the distribution of random variables from their marginal distributions. The non-normal univariate variables are joined to multivariate normal variables. The derivation of joint transition correlations of various companies can then be achieved using properties of the multivariate normal distribution.[21]

CreditGrades is the latest version of CreditMetrics. It is an equity-based model, which also includes balance sheet information to derive the credit-spread of publicly traded companies. CreditGrades addresses a major problem of CreditMetrics, which applied credit rating as a primary resource to evaluate the potential credit migration and default probability. As a consequence, in the CreditMetrics model, two corporate bonds within the same rating class could not be differentiated with respect to transition- and default probability. CreditGrades estimates the issuer-specific risk that allows default probability differentiation across issuers even within a certain rating/sector/maturity bucket. Further new developments of RMG are CreditManager, which allows portfolio credit risk management as well as CDOManager for synthetic structures and a platform for valuing hedge fund exposure.

Kamakura's Risk Manager[22]

Kamakura's original Risk Manager is a reduced form model, based on the findings of Kamakura's research director Robert Jarrow. As discussed, reduced form models exogenously generate an arbitrage-free process for the spread between risk-free and risky bonds to derive the default probability. Reduced form models use the arbitrage-free martingale framework, which underlies the Merton model.

As mentioned above, key equations in the reduced form models are equations (6.20) and (6.21). Thus implementing reduced form models requires a liquid bond market. This is often not the case in reality, especially compared with rather liquid equity prices. Also, reduced form models assume that the risky bond prices incorporate the correct default information, and thus assume that the risky bond market is "default-efficient." This is not the case in reality. Credit risky bond prices often overstate the probability of default compared to historical default rates.[23]

The reliance on bond data must be seen as a drawback of reduced form models. Consequently new reduced form approaches incorporate equity prices. Jarrow (1997, 2001) treats equity as "last seniority" debt and models the equity value ξ as the sum of the present value of liquidating dividends paid in case of default S, a bubble component θ, and the present value of regular dividends D:

$$\xi(t) = S(t) + \theta(t) + \sum_{t}^{T} D_t e^{-rt} \qquad (6.22)$$

where r is defined as the zero-coupon bond yield of a bond issued by the risky firm, reflecting the risk of the dividends. The bubble component θ in equation (6.22) is introduced to reflect inflated stock prices, especially high-tech stock prices. However, since most high-tech stocks do not pay a dividend, equation (6.22) cannot be used to model them. Nevertheless, the introduction of bond illiquidity premiums, macroeconomic data, and company correlations in the default process is adding realism to reduced form models.

In the recent past, Kamakura has integrated features from structural models in its software. A "Merton Structural" model that derives default probabilities as well as a hybrid "Jarrow-Merton" are available. Since November 2002 Kamakura also provides daily default probabilities for listed companies.

CSFP's Credit Risk+[24]

In November 1998, CSFP (Credit Suisse Financial Products) was merged into CSFB (Credit Suisse First Boston). However, we will still refer to CSFP's approach as CSFP's model or CSFP's Credit Risk+. This model utilizes concepts applied in the actuarial industry. Similar to reduced form models, Credit Risk+ is non-causal, i.e. it does not analyze the reasons of the default. Furthermore, Credit Risk+ models only default risk, not migration risk. The relative simplicity of the models allows a specification of the loss distribution as a convenient closed form solution.

The probability of n defaults, f(n), is assumed to follow the well-known one parameter Poisson distribution:

$$f(n) = \frac{e^{-\mu}\mu^{n}}{n!} \qquad (6.23)$$

where μ is the expected number of defaults, derived as the sum of probabilities of default for each counterpart i, p_i, so $\mu = \sum_{i=1}^{n} p_i$. The Poisson distribution has a mean μ and a standard deviation $\sqrt{\mu}$, and the default events of counterparties i are independent. CSFP acknowledges that in reality default rate standard deviations are much larger than $\sqrt{\mu}$ and that defaults are correlated. These issues are addressed by modeling the mean default rate μ itself as a Gamma distributed variable with mean μ and volatility σ_μ.

Correlations are not modeled explicitly but are incorporated by the default rate volatility σ_μ and sector aggregate analysis. Each sector is assumed to share the same systematic risk factors. CSFP justifies not explicitly modeling correlations with the instability of default rate correlations and the lack of empirical data. CSFP also questions the approach of other models of deriving default correlations from equity correlations, claiming the instability of this dependence. CSFP's computationally and mathematically straightforward top-down model is suited for portfolios of homogeneous credits.

McKinsey's Credit Portfolio View[25]

McKinsey's Credit Portfolio View derives migration probabilities and the default distribution with a macroeconomic-based, multi-factor, lagged, linear regression analysis. Company-specific data are not analyzed. The core model can be specified with three equations.

The probability of default for a single creditor in a country or sector j and time t, $p_{j,t}$ is scaled between 0 and 1 by the logit function:

$$p_{j,t} = \frac{1}{1+e^{-Y_{j,t}}},$$

where Y is a macroeconomic index, derived by the linear regression:

$$Y_{j,t} = \beta_{j,0} + \beta_{j,1}x_{j,1,t} + \beta_{j,2}x_{j,2,t} + \ldots + \beta_{j,t}x_{j,m,t} + v_{j,t}.$$

The m macroeconomic variables x_i, e.g. GDP growth rate, inflation, unemployment rate, etc., of country or sector j, are each derived by a linear, autoregressive, two-period lagged function:

$$x_{i,j,t} = \alpha_{i,j,t} + \alpha_{i,j,1}x_{i,j,t-1} + \alpha_{i,j,2}x_{i,j,t-2} + \upsilon_{i,j,t}$$

where $v_{j,t}$ and $\upsilon_{i,j,t}$ are normally distributed innovations.

Simplified, McKinsey's model can be expressed as shown in figure 6.11.

The probability density distribution $f(p_i)$ can be derived from the individual p_is by Monte Carlo simulation.

McKinsey conducts empirical tests to verify their claim that systematic portfolio risk is largely driven by macroeconomic data. McKinsey finds that much of the variation of default

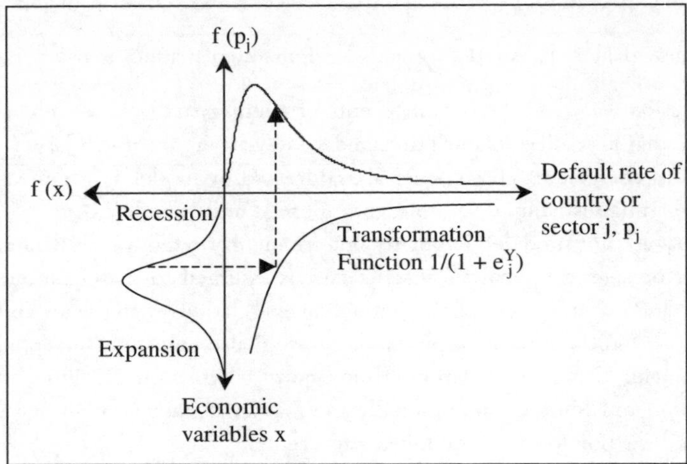

Figure 6.11: Probability density generation in the McKinsey model

rate risk can be explained by their model, shown in an R^2 of 0.9 for most of 10 industrial countries. McKinsey also justifies their multi-factor model by a principal component analysis, finding that second and third factors contribute with 10.2% and 6.2%, respectively, to the explanation of correlated systematic default risk.

Results

A summary of the models is given in table 6.2.

So what's the best model?

Which model a credit risk manager should use depends on the nature of the credit-risky portfolio, scope of the risk-management, and availability of data. For heterogeneous portfolios depending highly on specific company data, structural models are relevant. For portfolios with underlying liquid bond markets, reduced form models can be appropriate. Their arbitrage-free pricing framework can also be a good fit for trading desks. For managers of homogeneous portfolios, not concerned with migration risk, computationally less demanding actuarial models may be sufficient. For homogeneous portfolios with high dependence on economic conditions, econometric models can be the right choice.

Furthermore the models are becoming more and more similar, since the architects of the models are implementing the advantageous features of their competitors (e.g. reduced form approaches modeling equity prices rather than illiquid bond prices). It can be expected that the conceptual differences of the models will further decrease over time.

It should also be noted that the mathematical framework of today's models produce quite similar results, if input parameters are harmonized. Nevertheless, input parameter harmo-

Table 6.2: Summary of key features of the credit models

	KMV's Portfolio Manager	**JP Morgan's CreditMetrics**	**Kamakura's Risk Manager**	**CSFP's Credit Risk+**	**McKinsey's Credit Portfolio View**
Model type	Merton-based. Structural	Merton-based. Structural/ Reduced Form	Merton-based. Reduced From	Actuarial	Econometric
Underlying variables	Firm's assets	Credit changes	Bond spread	Risk factor	Macroeconomic variables
Distribution assumptions	Lognormal/ empirical for firm's assets	Empirical for credit changes	Binomial for bond spread; Poisson to aggregate	Gamma for risk factor; Poisson to aggregate	Normal for macro-variables; Logit to aggregate
Correlation assumptions	Asset correlation approximated by equity correlation	Asset correlation approximated by equity correlation within rating classes	Default rates and recovery rates correlated within rating classes	Default rates correlated within sectors	Macroeconomic variables correlated on country or sector level
Includes migration risk	Yes	Yes	Yes	No	Yes
Includes economic factors	Can	Can	Can	No	Yes
Bottom-up/ Top-down	Bottom-up	Bottom-up	Bottom-up	Top-down	Bottom-up

nization, though theoretically possible, might not be reasonable. Input variables of the models do vary and it might not be sensible to align company specific data of structural models with bond spread data of reduced form models or macroeconomic data of econometric models.

Further research will focus on models that integrate market, credit, and operational risk in a coherent way, as well as combining structural and reduced form models. The implementation of credit-risky derivatives also awaits further research.

Summary of Chapter 6

Credit at Risk, CAR, answers the crucial question: What is the maximum loss due to default or credit deterioration risk, within a certain time frame, with a certain probability?

To calculate CAR, we can apply the concept of the established market VAR. However, the two inputs: volatility of credit quality σ and a certain confidence level, expressed by α, are problematic when calculating CAR. Daily changes in the credit quality of a debtor are not available. Hence, CAR is usually calculated for a longer time frame than VAR, typically for one year. Also, the distribution of credit quality is highly skewed, which prohibits the use of the convenient normal distribution. An inversely scaled lognormal distribution gives a reasonable approximation of the skewed credit quality.

An analysis of five of the most widely used credit risk management software tools finds that the models produce quite similar results, if the input variables are harmonized. Nevertheless, the input variables are quite different in nature and an alignment, while possible, might not be reasonable. Differences in the models can be expected to decrease in the future, since the architects of the models are integrating positive components of their competitors.

The question which model a credit risk manager should implement depends on the nature of the credit-risky portfolio, scope of the risk-management, and availability of data. For heterogeneous portfolios depending highly on specific company data, structural models are relevant. For portfolios with underlying liquid bond markets, reduced form models can be appropriate. Their arbitrage-free pricing framework can also be a good fit for trading desks. For managers of homogeneous portfolios, not concerned with migration risk, computationally less demanding actuarial models may be sufficient. For homogeneous portfolios with high dependence on economic conditions, econometric models can be appropriate.

References and Suggestions for Further Reading

Altman, E., "Measuring Corporate Bond Mortality and Performance," *Journal of Finance*, 44, 1989, pp. 902–22.

Black, F., and M. Scholes, "The Pricing of Options and Corporate Liabilities," *The Journal of Political Economy*, May–June 1973, pp. 637–59.

Brooks, R., and D. Y. Yan, "Pricing Credit Default Swaps and the Implied Default Probability," *Derivatives Quarterly*, Winter 1998, pp. 34–41.

Cass, D., "KMV gives itself a CreditEdge," *Risk Magazine*, July 2001, p. 10.

Cheng, W., "Recent Advances in Default Swap Valuation," *The Journal of Fixed Income*, 1, 2001, pp. 18–27.

Crouhy, M., D. Galai, and R. Mark, "A Comparative Analysis of Current Credit Risk Models," *Journal of Banking and Finance*, 24, 2000, pp. 59–117.

CSFP, "Credit Risk+, A Credit Risk Management Framework," Internal Publication, 1997.

Das, S., and K. Sundaram, "A Direct Approach to Arbitrage-Free Pricing of Credit Derivatives," *Management Science*, January 2000, vol. 46, issue 1, pp. 46–63.

Das, S. R., and P. Tufano, "Pricing credit sensitive debt when interest rates, credit ratings and credit spreads are stochastic," *Journal of Financial Engineering*, 5(2), 1996, pp. 161–98.

Duffee, G., "On measuring credit risks of derivative instruments," *Journal of Banking and Finance*, 20, 1996, pp. 805–33.

Duffee, G. R., "The relationship between treasury yields and corporate bond yield spreads," *Journal of Finance*, 53(6), 1998, pp. 2225–41.

Duffie, D., and D. Lando, "Term Structures of Credit Spreads with Incomplete Accounting Information," *Econometrica*, 69(3), 2001, pp. 633–64.

Duffie, D., and K. Singleton, "An Econometric Model of the Term Structure of Interest-Rate Swap Yields," *Journal of Finance*, 52(4), 1997, pp. 1287–321.

Duffie, D., and K. Singleton, "Modeling the term structure of defaultable bonds," *Review of Financial Studies*, 12, 1999, pp. 687–720.

Gordy, M., "A Comparative Anatomy of Credit Risk Models," *Journal of Banking and Finance*, 24, 2000, pp. 119–49.

Henn, M., "Valuation of Credit Risky Contingent Claims," Unpublished Dissertation 1997, University of St. Gallen.

Hull J., and A. White, "Forward Rate Volatilities, Swap Rate Volatilities, and Implementation of the LIBOR Market Model," *Journal of Fixed Income*, September 2000, vol. 10, issue 2, pp. 46–63.

Iben, T., and R. Litterman, "Corporate Bond Valuation and the Term Structure of Credit Spreads," *Review of Portfolio Management*, Spring 1991, pp. 52–64.

Jarrow R., "Default Parameter Estimation using Market Prices," *Financial Analyst Journal*, 57(5), September/October 1997, pp. 75–91.

Jarrow, R., "An Introduction to Kamakura Credit Risk Modeling," Kamakura Corporation, 2001.

Jarrow, R., D. Lando, and S. Turnbull, "A Markov Model for the Term Structure of Credit Risk Spreads," *The Review of Financial Studies*, no. 2, 1997, pp. 481–523.

Jarrow, R., and S. Turnbull, "Pricing Derivatives on Financial Securities Subject to Credit Risk," *Journal of Finance*, March 1995, pp. 53–85.

Jarrow, R., and R. van Deventer, *Integrating Interest Rate Risk and Credit Risk in Asset and Liability Management*, Risk Publications, Fall 1998.

Jarrow, R., and D. van Deventer, *Practical Use of Credit Risk Models in Loan Portfolio and Counterparty Exposure Management*, Risk Publications, 1999.

Jarrow, R., and Y. Yildirim, "Pricing Default Swaps under Market and Credit Correlation," *The Journal of Fixed Income*, March 2002, pp. 7–20.

Jorion, P., *Value at Risk*, McGraw-Hill, 2000.

KMV, "Portfolio Management of Default Risk," KMV internal publication, 1998.

KMV, "Uses and Abuses of Bond Default Rates," KMV internal publication, 1998.

KMV, "Modeling Default Risk," KMV internal publication, 1999.

Koyluoglu, U., and A. Hickman, "Reconcilable Differences," *Risk Magazine*, October 1998, pp. 56–62.

Lando, D., "On Cox Processes and Credit Risky Securities," *Review of Derivatives Research*, 2, 1998, pp. 99–120.

Longstaff, F., and E. Schwartz, "A Simple Approach to Valuing Risky Fixed and Floating Rate Debt," *The Journal of Finance*, no. 3, July 1995, pp. 789–819.

Madan, B., and H. Unal, "Pricing the Risk of Default," *Review of Derivatives Research*, 2(2/3), 1998, pp. 121–60.

Martin, R., K. Thompson, and C. Brown, "Price and Probability." *Risk Magazine*, January 2001, pp. 115–17.

Meissner, G., and K. Nielsen, "Recent Advances in Credit Risk Management – A Comparison of 5 models," *Derivatives Use, Trading and Regulation*, vol. 7, no. 2, 2001, pp. 76–93.

Merton, R., "Theory of Rational Option Pricing," *Bell Journal of Economics and Management Science*, 4(1), Spring 1973, pp. 141–83.

Morgan J. P., Risk Metrics Group. "CreditMetrics™-Technical Document," Internal JP Morgan Publication, 1997.

Naftci, S., *An Introduction to the Mathematics of Financial Derivatives*, San Diego: Harcourt Inc., 1996.

O'Kane D., et al., "The Lehman Brothers Guide to Exotic Credit Derivatives," Risk Waters Group, 2003.

Platen, E., "An introduction to numerical methods for stochastic differential equations," *Acta Numerica*, 1999, pp. 195–244.

Romano, C., "Applying Copula Function to Risk Management," Working Paper, www.icer.it/workshop/Romano.pdf.

Roncalli, T., "Copulas: A Tool for Modeling Dependence in Finance," Working Paper, www.gloriamundi.org/picsresources/jr.pdf.

Schoenbucher, J., "Term Structure Modelling of Defaultable Bonds," *Review of Derivatives Research*, 2(2/3), 1997, pp. 161–92.

Wei, J., "Rating- and Firm Value-Based Valuation of Credit Swaps," *The Journal Fixed Income*, 2, 2001, pp. 53–64.

Wilson, T., "Portfolio Credit Risk," *Economic Policy Review*, 14(3), October 1998, pp. 51–96.

Wilson, T., "Portfolio Credit Risk (I)," *Risk Magazine*, September 1997, pp. 111–19.

Wilson, T., "Portfolio Credit Risk (II)," *Risk Magazine*, October 1997, pp. 56–61.

Questions and Problems

Answers, available for instructors, are on the Internet. Please email gmeissne@aol.com for the site.

6.1 *How can risk generally be reduced in the financial markets? Name three transactions.*

6.2 *Define market VAR. What are the assumptions of market VAR?*

6.3 *How is credit at risk, CAR, related to market value at risk, VAR? Why is it more difficult to calculate CAR, compared with VAR?*

6.4 *Can we assume that the probability distribution for CAR is constant? Derive the probability distribution for a bond that was issued with CCC rating and has since been upgraded to BB.*

6.5 *Discuss how CAR can be reduced with a default swap. Compare this reduction with the reduction of CAR using a TROR and a credit-spread option.*

6.6 *How is credit risk management related to market risk management and operational risk management? Should this correlation be taken into account when calculating a combined market, credit, and operational risk number?*

6.7 *What are key questions that a credit risk management model has to answer? Categorize current credit risk management models. What are key features of credit risk management models?*

6.8 *Discuss the reduced form equation* $B = e^{-rT}N[(1 - \lambda) + \lambda\, RR]$. *What are the shortcomings of this equation?*

6.9 *How is the distance to default DD in the KMV model related to* d_2 *in the original Merton model? How is the expected default frequency, EDF, related to* $N(-d_2)$ *in the original Merton model?*

6.10 *Discuss which credit risk management model is best suited in which environment. Do you believe any model is superior?*

Notes

1 For the different types of risk, see figure 4.1.

2 This means that the standard deviation of the standard normal distribution is 1. It also means that the (absolute) units on the x-axis represent standard deviations from the zero mean. One standard deviation from the mean represents 34.13% (0.8413 − 0.5 in table A.1 in the appendix), two standard deviations from the mean is 47.72% (0.9772 − 0.5 in table A.1 in the appendix).

3 See Naftci, S., "An Introduction to the Mathematics of Financial Derivatives," San Diego: Harcourt Inc., 1996, pp. 58ff for an introduction on Taylor series expansion. See Platen, E., "An introduction to numerical methods for stochastic differential equations," *Acta Numerica*, 1999, pp. 195–244, for a detailed analysis on Taylor series expansion.

4 From basic statistics

$$E(X) = \sum_{i}^{n} x_i P(x_i)$$

for discrete distributions (P = Probability) and

$$E(X) = \int_{-\infty}^{\infty} x f(x) dx$$

for continuous distributions. Also

$$Var(X) = \sum_{i}^{n} (x_i - \mu) P(x_i)$$

for discrete distributions and

$$Var(X) = \int_{-\infty}^{\infty} (x - \mu)^2 f(x) dx$$

for continuous distributions.

5 In this example we have made the simplifying assumption that credit risk is linear, i.e. that the credit delta is 1. See example 6.6 for a credit delta unequal to 1.

6 The following analysis is based on the article: Meissner, G., and K. Nielsen, "Recent Advances in Credit Risk Management – A Comparison of 5 models," *Derivatives Use, Trading and Regulation*, vol. 7, no. 2, 2001, pp. 76–93. A survey on software companies that sell derivatives software can be found each year in the January issue of *Risk Magazine*.

7 See chapter 5 for a detailed discussion of structural models versus reduced form models for pricing credit derivatives.

8 See, for example, KMV, "Modeling Default Risk," KMV internal publication, 1999.

9 See Jarrow and Turnbull (1995); Jarrow, Lando, and Turnbull (1997); and Duffie and Singleton (1999).

10 For the difference between the hazard rate also called default intensity, and default probability, see chapter 5.

11 Jarrow, R., "Default Parameter Estimation using Market Prices," *Financial Analyst Journal*, September/October 1997, 57(5), pp. 75–91.

12 See, for example, KMV, "Modeling Default Risk," KMV internal publication, 1999.

13 See Jarrow and Turnbull (1995) and Lando (1998).

14 Credit Risk+, "A Credit Risk Management Framework," 1997.

15 Koyluoglu, U., and A. Hickman, "Reconcilable Differences," *Risk Magazine*, October 1998.

16 For more on skewness and kurtosis see http://mathworld.wolfram.com/Skewness.html and http://mathworld.wolfram.com/Kurtosis.html.

17 See www.moodyskmv.com; KMV, "Modeling default risk," 1999; KMV, "Uses and Abuses of Bond Default Rates," 1998; KMV, "A Comment on Market vs. Accounting-Based Measures of Default Risk," 1993; KMV, "Portfolio Management of Default Risk," 1998.

18 KMV, "A Comment on Market vs. Accounting-Based Measures of Default Risk," KMV internal publication, 1993.

19 Cass, D., "KMV gives itself a CreditEdge," *Risk Magazine*, July 2001, p. 10.

20 See www.riskmetrics.com; see also "Introduction to CreditMetrics", JP Morgan internal publication, 1997.

21 For a good introduction to copulas see Romano, C., "Applying copula function to Risk Management," www.icer.it/workshop/Romano.pdf; and Rank, J., "Copulas in Financial Risk Management," Oxford University, www.gloriamundi.org/picsresources/jr.pdf.

22 See www.kamakuraco.com; Jarrow, R., "An Introduction to Kamakura Credit Risk Modeling," Kamakura Corporation, 2001; Jarrow, R., and R. van Deventer, *Integrating Interest Rate Risk and Credit Risk in Asset and Liability Management*, Risk Publications, 1998; Jarrow, R., "Default Parameter Estimation Using Market Prices," *Financial Analyst Journal*, September/October 1997, 57(5), pp. 75–91.

23 One of the first studies to point this out was Altman, E., "Measuring Corporate Bond Mortality and Performance," *Journal of Finance*, 44, 1989, pp. 902–22.

24 See http://www.csfb.com/creditrisk/ and CSFP, "Credit Risk+, A Credit Risk Management Framework," 1997, CSFP internal publication.

25 Wilson, G., "Portfolio Credit Risk," *Economic Policy Review*, October 1998, 14(3) pp. 51–96; Wilson, T., "Portfolio Credit Risk (I)," *Risk Magazine*, September 1997, pp. 111–19; Wilson, T., "Portfolio Credit Risk (II)," *Risk Magazine*, October 1997, pp. 56–61.

Appendix

Table A.1: Cumulative standard normal distribution table (with $\mu = 0$ and $\sigma = 1$). The numbers in the table show N(d), see equations (5.9) and (5.9a)

d	0.00	0.01	0.02	0.03	0.04	0.05	0.06	0.07	0.08	0.09
−0.0	0.5000	0.4960	0.4920	0.4880	0.4840	0.4801	0.4761	0.4721	0.4681	0.4641
−0.1	0.4602	0.4562	0.4522	0.4483	0.4443	0.4404	0.4364	0.4325	0.4286	0.4247
−0.2	0.4207	0.4168	0.4129	0.4090	0.4052	0.4013	0.3974	0.3936	0.3897	0.3859
−0.3	0.3821	0.3783	0.3745	0.3707	0.3669	0.3632	0.3594	0.3557	0.3520	0.3483
−0.4	0.3446	0.3409	0.3372	0.3336	0.3300	0.3264	0.3228	0.3192	0.3156	0.3121
−0.5	0.3085	0.3050	0.3015	0.2981	0.2946	0.2912	0.2877	0.2843	0.2810	0.2776
−0.6	0.2743	0.2709	0.2676	0.2643	0.2611	0.2578	0.2546	0.2514	0.2483	0.2451
−0.7	0.2420	0.2389	0.2358	0.2327	0.2296	0.2266	0.2236	0.2206	0.2177	0.2148
−0.8	0.2119	0.2090	0.2061	0.2033	0.2005	0.1977	0.1949	0.1922	0.1894	0.1867
−0.9	0.1841	0.1814	0.1788	0.1762	0.1736	0.1711	0.1685	0.1660	0.1635	0.1611
−1.0	0.1587	0.1562	0.1539	0.1515	0.1492	0.1469	0.1446	0.1423	0.1401	0.1379
−1.1	0.1357	0.1335	0.1314	0.1292	0.1271	0.1251	0.1230	0.1210	0.1190	0.1170
−1.2	0.1151	0.1131	0.1112	0.1093	0.1075	0.1056	0.1038	0.1020	0.1003	0.0985
−1.3	0.0968	0.0951	0.0934	0.0918	0.0901	0.0885	0.0869	0.0853	0.0838	0.0823
−1.4	0.0808	0.0793	0.0778	0.0764	0.0749	0.0735	0.0721	0.0708	0.0694	0.0681
−1.5	0.0668	0.0655	0.0643	0.0630	0.0618	0.0606	0.0594	0.0582	0.0571	0.0559
−1.6	0.0548	0.0537	0.0526	0.0516	0.0505	**0.0495**	0.0485	0.0475	0.0465	0.0455
−1.7	0.0466	0.0436	0.0427	0.0418	0.0409	0.0401	0.0392	0.0384	0.0375	0.0367
−1.8	0.0359	0.0351	0.0344	0.0336	0.0329	0.0322	0.0314	0.0307	0.0301	0.0294
−1.9	0.0287	0.0281	0.0274	0.0268	0.0262	0.0256	0.0250	0.0244	0.0239	0.0233
−2.0	0.0228	0.0222	0.0217	0.0212	0.0207	0.0202	0.0197	0.0192	0.0188	0.0183
−2.1	0.0179	0.0174	0.0170	0.0166	0.0162	0.0158	0.0154	0.0150	0.0146	0.0143
−2.2	0.0139	0.0136	0.0132	0.0129	0.0125	0.0122	0.0119	0.0116	0.0113	0.0110
−2.3	0.0107	0.0104	0.0102	**0.0099**	0.0096	0.0094	0.0091	0.0089	0.0087	0.0084
−2.4	0.0082	0.0080	0.0078	0.0075	0.0073	0.0071	0.0069	0.0068	0.0066	0.0064
−2.5	0.0062	0.0060	0.0059	0.0057	0.0055	0.0054	0.0052	0.0051	0.0049	0.0048
−2.6	0.0047	0.0045	0.0044	0.0043	0.0041	0.0040	0.0039	0.0038	0.0037	0.0036
−2.7	0.0035	0.0034	0.0033	0.0032	0.0031	0.0030	0.0029	0.0028	0.0027	0.0026
−2.8	0.0026	0.0025	0.0024	0.0023	0.0023	0.0022	0.0021	0.0021	0.0020	0.0019
−2.9	0.0019	0.0018	0.0018	0.0017	0.0016	0.0016	0.0015	0.0015	0.0014	0.0014
−3.0	0.0014	0.0013	0.0013	0.0012	0.0012	0.0011	0.0011	0.0011	0.0010	0.0010
−3.1	0.0010	0.0009	0.0009	0.0009	0.0008	0.0008	0.0008	0.0008	0.0007	0.0007
−3.2	0.0007	0.0007	0.0006	0.0006	0.0006	0.0006	0.0006	0.0005	0.0005	0.0005
−3.3	0.0005	0.0005	0.0005	0.0004	0.0004	0.0004	0.0004	0.0004	0.0004	0.0003
−3.4	0.0003	0.0003	0.0003	0.0003	0.0003	0.0003	0.0003	0.0003	0.0003	0.0002
−3.5	0.0002	0.0002	0.0002	0.0002	0.0002	0.0002	0.0002	0.0002	0.0002	0.0002
−3.6	0.0002	0.0002	0.0001	0.0001	0.0001	0.0001	0.0001	0.0001	0.0001	0.0001
−3.7	0.0001	0.0001	0.0001	0.0001	0.0001	0.0001	0.0001	0.0001	0.0001	0.0001
−3.8	0.0001	0.0001	0.0001	0.0001	0.0001	0.0001	0.0001	0.0001	0.0001	0.0001
−3.9	0.0000	0.0000	0.0000	0.0000	0.0000	0.0000	0.0000	0.0000	0.0000	0.0000
−4.0	0.0000	0.0000	0.0000	0.0000	0.0000	0.0000	0.0000	0.0000	0.0000	0.0000

Table A.1: *Continued*

d	0.00	0.01	0.02	0.03	0.04	0.05	0.06	0.07	0.08	0.09
0.0	**0.5000**	0.5040	0.5080	0.5120	0.5160	0.5199	0.5239	0.5279	0.5319	0.5359
0.1	0.5398	0.5438	0.5478	0.5517	0.5557	0.5596	0.5636	0.5675	0.5714	0.5753
0.2	0.5793	0.5832	0.5871	0.5910	0.5948	0.5987	0.6026	0.6064	0.6103	0.6141
0.3	0.6179	0.6217	0.6255	0.6293	0.6331	0.6368	0.6406	0.6443	0.6480	0.6517
0.4	0.6651	0.6591	0.6628	0.6664	0.6700	0.6736	0.6772	0.6808	0.6844	0.6879
0.5	0.6915	0.6950	0.6985	0.7019	0.7054	0.7088	0.7123	0.7157	0.7190	0.7224
0.6	0.7257	0.7291	0.7324	0.7357	0.7389	0.7422	0.7454	0.7486	0.7517	0.7549
0.7	0.7580	0.7611	0.7642	0.7673	0.7704	0.7734	0.7764	0.7794	0.7823	0.7852
0.8	0.7881	0.7910	0.7939	0.7967	0.7995	0.8023	0.8051	0.8078	0.8106	0.8133
0.9	0.8159	0.8186	0.8212	0.8238	0.8264	0.8289	0.8315	0.8340	0.8365	0.8389
1.0	**0.8413**	0.8348	0.8461	0.8485	0.8508	0.8531	0.8554	0.8577	0.8599	0.8621
1.1	0.8643	0.8665	0.8686	0.8708	0.8729	0.8749	0.8770	0.8790	0.8810	0.8830
1.2	0.8849	0.8869	0.8888	0.8907	0.8925	0.8944	0.8962	0.8980	0.8997	0.9015
1.3	0.9032	0.9049	0.9066	0.9082	0.9099	0.9115	0.9131	0.9147	0.9162	0.9177
1.4	0.9192	0.9207	0.9222	0.9236	0.9251	0.9265	0.9279	0.9292	0.9306	0.9319
1.5	0.9332	0.9345	0.9357	0.9370	0.9382	0.9394	0.9406	0.9418	0.9429	0.9441
1.6	0.9452	0.9463	0.9474	0.9484	0.9495	**0.9505**	0.9515	0.9525	0.9535	0.9545
1.7	0.9554	0.9564	0.9573	0.9582	0.9591	0.9599	0.9608	0.9616	0.9625	0.9633
1.8	0.9641	0.9649	0.9656	0.9664	0.9671	0.9678	0.9686	0.9693	0.9699	0.9706
1.9	0.9713	0.9719	0.9726	0.9732	0.9738	0.9744	0.9750	0.9756	0.9761	0.9767
2.0	**0.9772**	0.9778	0.9783	0.9788	0.9793	0.9798	0.9803	0.9808	0.9812	0.9817
2.1	0.9821	0.9826	0.9830	0.9834	0.9838	0.9842	0.9846	0.9850	0.9854	0.9857
2.2	0.9861	0.9864	0.9868	0.9871	0.9875	0.9878	0.9881	0.9884	0.9887	0.9890
2.3	0.9893	0.9896	0.9898	0.9901	0.9904	0.9906	0.9909	0.9911	0.9913	0.9916
2.4	0.9918	0.9920	0.9922	0.9925	0.9927	0.9929	0.9931	0.9932	0.9934	0.9936
2.5	0.9938	0.9940	0.9941	0.9943	0.9945	0.9946	0.9948	0.9949	0.9951	0.9952
2.6	0.9953	0.9955	0.9956	0.9957	0.9959	0.9960	0.9961	0.9962	0.9963	0.9964
2.7	0.9965	0.9966	0.9967	0.9968	0.9969	0.9970	0.9971	0.9972	0.9973	0.9974
2.8	0.9974	0.9975	0.9976	0.9977	0.9977	0.9978	0.9979	0.9979	0.9980	0.9981
2.9	0.9981	0.9982	0.9982	0.9983	0.9984	0.9984	0.9985	0.9985	0.9986	0.9986
3.0	0.9986	0.9987	0.9987	0.9988	0.9988	0.9989	0.9989	0.9989	0.9990	0.9990
3.1	0.9990	0.9991	0.9991	0.9991	0.9992	0.9992	0.9992	0.9992	0.9993	0.9993
3.2	0.9993	0.9993	0.9994	0.9994	0.9994	0.9994	0.9994	0.9995	0.9995	0.9995
3.3	0.9995	0.9995	0.9995	0.9996	0.9996	0.9996	0.9996	0.9996	0.9996	0.9997
3.4	0.9997	0.9997	0.9997	0.9997	0.9997	0.9997	0.9997	0.9997	0.9997	0.9998
3.5	0.9998	0.9998	0.9998	0.9998	0.9998	0.9998	0.9998	0.9998	0.9998	0.9998
3.6	0.9999	0.9999	0.9999	0.9999	0.9999	0.9999	0.9999	0.9999	0.9999	0.9999
3.7	0.9999	0.9999	0.9999	0.9999	0.9999	0.9999	0.9999	0.9999	0.9999	0.9999
3.8	0.9999	0.9999	0.9999	0.9999	0.9999	0.9999	0.9999	0.9999	0.9999	0.9999
3.9	1.0000	1.0000	1.0000	1.0000	1.0000	1.0000	1.0000	1.0000	1.0000	1.0000
4.0	1.0000	1.0000	1.0000	1.0000	1.0000	1.0000	1.0000	1.0000	1.0000	1.0000

Table A.2: Cumulative standard lognormal distribution (with $\theta = 0$, $\mu = 0$, and $\sigma = 1$)

d	**0.000**	**0.025**	**0.05**	**0.075**	**0.1**	**0.125**	**0.15**	**0.175**	**0.2**	**0.225**
0.00	0.0000	0.0001	0.0014	0.0048	0.0107	0.0188	0.0289	0.0407	0.0538	0.0679
0.25	0.0828	0.0984	0.1143	0.1305	0.1469	0.1633	0.1798	0.1961	0.2123	0.2283
0.50	0.2441	0.2597	0.2750	0.2900	0.3047	0.3192	0.3333	0.3471	0.3607	0.3739
0.75	0.3868	0.3994	0.4117	0.4237	0.4354	0.4469	0.4580	0.4689	0.4795	0.4899
1.00	**0.5000**	0.5098	0.5195	0.5288	0.5380	0.5469	0.5556	0.5641	0.5723	0.5804
1.25	0.5883	0.5960	0.6035	0.6108	0.6180	0.6249	0.6317	0.6384	0.6449	0.6512
1.50	0.6574	0.6635	0.6694	0.6752	0.6808	0.6863	0.6917	0.6970	0.7022	0.7072
1.75	0.7121	0.7169	0.7217	0.7263	0.7308	0.7352	0.7395	0.7437	0.7479	0.7519
2.00	0.7559	0.7598	0.7636	0.7673	0.7709	0.7745	0.7780	0.7814	0.7848	0.7881
2.25	0.7913	0.7945	0.7976	0.8006	0.8036	0.8065	0.8093	0.8121	0.8149	0.8176
2.50	0.8202	0.8228	0.8254	0.8279	0.8303	0.8327	0.8351	0.8374	0.8397	0.8419
2.75	0.8441	0.8463	0.8484	0.8505	0.8525	0.8545	0.8565	0.8584	0.8603	0.8622
3.00	0.8640	0.8658	0.8676	0.8693	0.8711	0.8727	0.8744	0.8760	0.8776	0.8792
3.25	0.8807	0.8823	0.8837	0.8852	0.8867	0.8881	0.8895	0.8909	0.8922	0.8935
3.50	0.8949	0.8961	0.8974	0.8987	0.8999	0.9011	0.9023	0.9035	0.9046	0.9058
3.75	0.9069	0.9080	0.9091	0.9101	0.9112	0.9122	0.9132	0.9142	0.9152	0.9162
4.00	0.9172	0.9181	0.9191	0.9200	0.9209	0.9218	0.9226	0.9235	0.9244	0.9252
4.25	0.9260	0.9269	0.9277	0.9285	0.9292	0.9300	0.9308	0.9315	0.9323	0.9330
4.50	0.9337	0.9344	0.9351	0.9358	0.9365	0.9372	0.9378	0.9385	0.9391	0.9398
4.75	0.9404	0.9410	0.9416	0.9422	0.9428	0.9434	0.9440	0.9446	0.9451	0.9457
5.00	0.9462	0.9468	0.9473	0.9478	0.9484	0.9489	0.9494	**0.9499**	0.9504	0.9509
5.25	0.9514	0.9518	0.9523	0.9528	0.9532	0.9537	0.9541	0.9546	0.9550	0.9555
5.50	0.9559	0.9563	0.9567	0.9571	0.9575	0.9579	0.9583	0.9587	0.9591	0.9595
5.75	0.9599	0.9602	0.9606	0.9610	0.9613	0.9617	0.9620	0.9624	0.9627	0.9631
6.00	0.9634	0.9637	0.9641	0.9644	0.9647	0.9650	0.9653	0.9657	0.9660	0.9663
6.25	0.9666	0.9669	0.9672	0.9674	0.9677	0.9680	0.9683	0.9686	0.9688	0.9691
6.50	0.9694	0.9696	0.9699	0.9702	0.9704	0.9707	0.9709	0.9712	0.9714	0.9717
6.75	0.9719	0.9721	0.9724	0.9726	0.9728	0.9731	0.9733	0.9735	0.9737	0.9740
7.00	0.9742	0.9744	0.9746	0.9748	0.9750	0.9752	0.9754	0.9756	0.9758	0.9760
7.25	0.9762	0.9764	0.9766	0.9768	0.9770	0.9771	0.9773	0.9775	0.9777	0.9779
7.50	0.9780	0.9782	0.9784	0.9786	0.9787	0.9789	0.9791	0.9792	0.9794	0.9795
7.75	0.9797	0.9799	0.9800	0.9802	0.9803	0.9805	0.9806	0.9808	0.9809	0.9811
8.00	0.9812	0.9814	0.9815	0.9816	0.9818	0.9819	0.9820	0.9822	0.9823	0.9824
8.25	0.9826	0.9827	0.9828	0.9830	0.9831	0.9832	0.9833	0.9835	0.9836	0.9837
8.50	0.9838	0.9839	0.9841	0.9842	0.9843	0.9844	0.9845	0.9846	0.9847	0.9849
8.75	0.9850	0.9851	0.9852	0.9853	0.9854	0.9855	0.9856	0.9857	0.9858	0.9859
9.00	0.9860	0.9861	0.9862	0.9863	0.9864	0.9865	0.9866	0.9867	0.9868	0.9869
9.25	0.9869	0.9870	0.9871	0.9872	0.9873	0.9874	0.9875	0.9876	0.9876	0.9877
9.50	0.9878	0.9879	0.9880	0.9881	0.9881	0.9882	0.9883	0.9884	0.9885	0.9885
9.75	0.9886	0.9887	0.9888	0.9888	0.9889	0.9890	0.9891	0.9891	0.9892	0.9893
10.00	0.9893	0.9894	0.9895	0.9896	0.9896	0.9897	0.9898	0.9898	0.9899	0.9900

Glossary of Notation

a: Mean reversion: The degree with which a variable is drawn to its long-term mean b.

b: Long-term mean of a variable; in term structure models, the long-term mean of interest rate r.

B: Price of a risky bond.

c_t: Coupon of a bond, paid at time t.

C: Price of a call, European style.

Cr: Credit quality.

d_1, d_2: Intermediate results in the Black-Scholes model; d_1 and d_2 represent x-axis values of the standard normal distribution.

d: The default swap premium compared to the asset swap spread x. When d is used in conjunction with a variable, it represents an infinitesimal small change in that variable.

dz: Wiener process, which involves the multiplication of a random drawing from a standardized normal distribution with the square root of the time interval between two samples.

D: Duration of a bond. In chapter 5: A company's debt; also a derivative in chapter 5.

$D_{t,T,V}$: A derivative viewed at time t with maturity T, where the counterpart has, on a netted basis, a future obligation.

$e = 2.7182\ldots$

E: Expectation value. In chapter 5, shareholders' equity.

E_0: Present value of equity.

$'E$: Present value of an exchange option.

F: Face value of a risky bond.

g: Risk weight of the protection seller.

h: Hazard rate, also called default intensity. The hazard rate multiplied by a certain time frame, results in the risk-neutral default probability λ for that time frame.

i: Horizontal parameter of node (i,j) in a Hull-White model.

I: The return of the firm's equity or asset index.

j: Vertical parameter of node (i,j) in a Hull-White model.

k: Exogenous constant in the Black and Cox exponential default boundary.

K: Strike price.

n_m: Number of nodes on each side of the central node at time $m\Delta t$ in a Hull-White trinomial model.

N: The notional amount of a security. In chapter 5, the cumulative standard normal distribution.

O: Operational status.

P: In chapter 3, price of a European style put. In chapter 5, probability. Also the price of a risk-free bond price in the Jarrow-Turnbull 1995 and the Briys-de Varenne 1997 model. In chapter 6, an option portfolio.

P_{m+1}: Zero-coupon bond maturing at time m + 1 in a Hull-White trinomial model.

q (k,j): Probability of moving from node (m,k) to node (m + 1,j);

Q_m: Used in the Hull-White trinomial model to derive the present value of a security at time m that pays $1 if node (i,j) is reached and zero otherwise.

r: In chapter 2, the return on a risk-free asset. In chapter 4, risk weight of the underlying obligor. In chapter 5, short-term interest rate. Also risk-free return.

r*: The risk weight for the buyer of credit derivatives as defined by the New Basel Capital Accord.

R: Discrete interest rate for time Δt in a term structure model.

R*: Discrete interest rate for time Δt on a tree that is evenly spaced and has a zero slope.

R_{oc}: Measures the impact of operational damage on credit quality.

RR_c: Recovery rate of the counterparty.

RR_r: Recovery rate of the reference entity.

s: Default swap premium.

S: Stock price. In chapter 5, it denotes the credit-spread in the modified Black-Scholes equation.

t: A certain point in time. If specific points in time are necessary, an index is attached to t. For example, t_n is the point in time in n years.

T: Maturity date of the option or bond.

V: Value of a company's assets.

V_0: Current value of assets.

w: Weight applied to the underlying exposure; set to 0.15 by the BIS for all credit derivatives recognized as giving protection. Also a parameter in term structure models.

W: Wealth.

x: Asset swap spread; the spread above Libor, which represents the credit quality difference to a risk-free asset.

y_1, y_2: Yield of risk-free and risky assets, respectively.

y: Yield of a bond; represents the profit of a bond, if the bond is purchased at the current market price and held to maturity, assuming the bond does not default.

z: Underlying variable in a Wiener process.

α: Drift rate for the short interest rate in the Das-Sundaram model. In the Hull-White model, a variable that transforms an evenly spaced zero-slope tree into a tree that matches the upward (or downward) slope of the term structure. In chapter 6, x-axis value of a cumulative distribution.

β: Drift rate of the swap rate in the Das-Sundaram Model. In chapter 6, invested notional amounts (price S times quantity q).

Γ: Second partial derivative of an option function; measure of the curvature of an option function; change in the delta.

γ: Exogenous constant in the Black and Cox exponential default boundary.

∂: Partial derivative operator.

Δ: Discrete change in a variable.

Λ: Transition Matrix in Jarrow-Lando-Turnbull 1997 model.

π_t: risk-neutral probability of no default by counterparty or reference asset during the life of the swap.

η: Risk premium or risk adjustment, which transforms historical transition probabilities into martingale probabilities; also exogenous constant in the Longstaff-Schwartz 1995 model.

θ: In a term structure model, it is the function chosen so that the model fits the current term structure. In chapter 5, also used for trading strategy.

λ^r_t: Exogenous, risk-neutral probability of default of reference entity r, during time t to t + 1, which is expressed in years as $\Delta\tau_t$, viewed at time 0, given no earlier default of the reference entity r (λ^r is used instead of λ if counterparty default risk λ^c is part of the analysis).

λ^c_t: Exogenous, risk-neutral probability of default of counterparty c, during time t to t + 1, which is expressed in years as $\Delta\tau_t$, viewed at time 0, given no earlier default of the counterparty c.

μ: Drift rate or the average expected growth rate of the relative change of a stock price. In chapter 5, it is the expected return of a risky asset.

κ: Probability of default of the counterparty.

ρ: Correlation coefficient.

σ: Volatility of the underlying asset.

ν: Volatility of the swap rate in the Das-Sundaram model.

ϕ_t: Risk-neutral probability of default of a counterparty at time t and no earlier default of the reference entity.

Glossary of Terms

Accrued Interest The accumulated interest of an investment from the last payment date.

Actuarial Risk The risk that an insurer made substantially incorrect assumptions on determining the expected net present value of the contract.

Add-up credit default swap or **linear credit default swap** A default swap in which the investor is exposed to all reference entities of a basket.

American-Style Options Options that can be exercised at any time before or at the option maturity date.

Antithetic Variable Technique A method to reduce computations when simulating trials (as in the Monte Carlo method) by changing the sign of the random sample.

Arbitrage A risk-free profit, achieved by simultaneously buying and selling equivalent securities on different markets. In trading practice often more widely defined as a strategy trying to exploit price differences.

Asset Swap A swap based on the fixed rate of an asset. Typically that fixed rate is swapped into Libor plus a spread.

Asset Swap Spread Spread over Libor that is paid in an asset swap. Reflects the credit quality of the issuer.

Attachment point The number or the amount of defaults necessary to trigger a payoff in a basket default swap or a tranche of a CDO.

Back testing Testing how well current VAR or CAR numbers or other methods would have performed in the past.

Backwardation Backwardation is the situation in the commodity market where the futures price is lower than the spot price. See also contango.

Bank for International Settlements (BIS) The BIS is an international organization which fosters cooperation among central banks and other agencies in pursuit of monetary and financial stability.

Banking book constitutes the account where a bank's conventional transactions such as loans, bonds, deposits, and revolving credit facilities are recorded. (compare Trading book.)

Bankruptcy A party not honoring its obligations to its creditors and whose assets are therefore administered by a trustee.

Barrier option An option, which can be knocked-in or knocked-out. A barrier option is cheaper than a standard option.

Basel Committee Committee of the BIS, established in 1975. It functions as a supervisory authority, establishing the regulatory framework for financial institutions.

Basis The difference between the spot price and the futures price of a security.

Basis Point One hundredth of one percentage point, i.e. 0.01%.

Basis Risk The risk that the basis changes.

Basket Credit Default Swap A default swap with several reference entities.

Bid The highest price a buyer is willing to pay for a security.

Binary Default Swap also called Digital Default Swap. The payoff in the event of default is a fixed amount, which is specified at the commencement of the swap.

Binomial Model A model in which the price of a security can only move two (bi) ways, typically up or down.

BIS See Bank for International Settlements.

BISTRO Broad Index Securitized Trust Obligation; First synthetic structure issued by JP Morgan in 1997 in the form of a CLO (collateralized loan obligation).

Black-Scholes Model A mathematical model suggested by Fisher Black and Myron Scholes in 1973 to find a theoretical price for European options on an underlying security that pays no dividends.

Brady Bonds Bonds issued by emerging countries in the early 1990s, which were guaranteed by US Treasury bonds.

Calibration The process of finding values for the input parameters of a model, so that the model's output matches market values.

Call option The right but not the obligation to buy an underlying asset at the strike price at a certain date (European style) or during a certain period (American style).

Cancelable Default Swap A swap, in which one or both parties have the right to terminate the swap.

Cap A contract, which gives the cap owner the right to pay a fixed interest rate (strike) and receive a Libor rate. If the cap owner has a floating rate loan, the cap acts as an insurance against rising interest rates.

Capital Adequacy Capital requirements set by the Basel Committee of the BIS for different types of risk.

Capital Asset Pricing Model (CAPM) A model that demonstrates the relationship between risk and return.

Caplet A single interest rate option of a cap.

CAR Credit at Risk, the maximum loss in a certain time frame, with a certain probability, due to credit risk.

Cash Settlement Type of settlement of derivatives where a cash amount is paid to the profiteer. See also physical settlement.

CDO See collateralized bond obligation.

CME Chicago Mercantile Exchange.

Collar The purchase of a call and simultaneous sell of a put, where the call strike is higher than the put strike. In the interest rate market, the purchase of a cap and simultaneous sell of a floor, where the cap strike is higher than the floor strike.

Collateral An asset pledged by a debtor as a guarantee for repayment.

Collateralized Bond Obligation (CBO) A tranched debt structure in with each tranche reflects a different credit risk profile. Bonds serve as collateral.

Collateralized Debt Obligation (CDO) A term that refers to a collateralized bond obligation (CBO), collateralized loan obligation (CLO), or collateralized mortgage obligation (CMO).

Collateralized Loan Obligation (CLO) A tranched debt structure in which each tranche reflects a different credit risk profile. Loans serve as collateral.

Collateralized Mortgage Obligation (CMO) A tranched debt structure in which each tranche reflects a different prepayment option. Mortgages serve as collateral.

Contango The situation in the commodity market where the futures price is higher than the spot price. See also backwardation.

Contingent Default Swap Swap in which the payoff is triggered if both the standard credit event and an additional event occur.

Continuously Compounded Interest Rate An interest rate, where interest is compounded in infinitesimally short time units. (See also instantaneous interest rate.)

Control Variate Technique A method to reduce computations when simulating trials (as in the Monte Carlo method) applicable for two similar derivatives.

Convertible A bond issued by a company that can be converted into shares of that company during the life of the bond.

Convertible Arbitrage A long position in convertible security and a short position in the underlying stock.

Convexity The second partial derivative of a bond with respect to the yield. Convexity measures the curvature of the bond function or the change in the duration for an infinitesimally small change of the yield.

Copula A function, applied in risk management, that joins univariate distribution functions to form multivariate distribution functions.

Correlation Demonstrates the extent to which two variables move together over time.

Correlation Coefficient A standardized statistical measure that takes values between −1 and +1; defined as the covariance divided by the standard deviations of the two variables.

Counterparty A partner in a financial transaction.

Counterparty Risk The risk that the counterparty does not honor its obligation.

Covariance A statistical measure that shows the extent to which two variables are related to each other.

Coverage Ratios Ratios that are analyzed to help determine the credit rating of synthetic structures.

Covered Call A short call option position and a long position in the underlying security.

Covered Call Writing See covered call.

Credit at Risk (CAR) The maximum loss in a certain time frame, with a certain probability, due to credit risk.

Credit Default Swap See default swap.

Credit Derivative A Future, Swap, or Option that transfers credit risk from one counterparty to another.

Credit Deterioration Risk The risk that the credit quality of the debtor decreases. In this case, the value of the assets of the debtor will decrease, resulting in a financial loss for the creditor. (See also migration risk.)

Credit Event The ISDA 1999 documentation defines six credit events: Bankruptcy, Failure to pay, Obligation Acceleration, Obligation Default, Repudiation/Moratorium, and Restructuring.

Credit Linked Note A security in which the interest payment and/or repayment of the notional is linked to a credit event.

CreditMetrics A transition-matrix based model developed by JP Morgan to value portfolio credit risk.

Credit Rating An assessment of the credit quality of a debtor, expressed in categories from AAA to D.

Credit Risk The risk of a financial loss due to a reduction in the credit quality of a debtor. Consists of credit deterioration risk and default risk.

Credit Risk+ An actuarial based model developed by Credit [??Swiss] Suisse Financial Products to value portfolio credit risk.

Credit Risk Premium See credit-spread.

Credit-spread (also referred to as **credit risk premium**) The excess in yield of a security with credit risk over a comparable security without credit risk.

Credit-spread Option A credit-spread put option generates a payoff if the creditworthiness of a security falls below a strike level. A credit-spread call option generates a payoff if the creditworthiness of a security is above a strike level.

Credit-spread Range Note In a credit-spread range note, the investor receives an above market coupon if the credit spread stays within a predetermined range, and may additionally incur a penalty if the credit-spread is outside a predetermined range.

Credit-spread Swap A swap that exchanges a fixed credit-spread for Libor.

Credit Triangle An approximate relationship between the swap premium s, the hazard rate λ, and the recovery rate RR; see equation (5.45).

Credit Value at Risk See credit at risk.

Currency Swap An exchange of interest rate payments in different currencies on a pre-determined notional amount and in reference to pre-determined interest rate indices.

Default A party not honoring its obligations to its creditors.

Default Correlation A measure of joint default probability of two or more firms.

Default Exposure (also called **loss given default**) The amount of loss that will be incurred if the reference asset or counterparty defaults.

Default Intensity See hazard rate.

Default Probability The likelihood that a debt instrument or counterparty will default within a certain time. See also hazard rate.

Default Risk The risk that a debtor may be unable to make interest and notional payments.

Default Swap (also **credit default swap**) An insurance against default if the underlying asset is owned. The default swap buyer makes an upfront or annual payments. The default swap seller promises to make a payment in case of default of a reference asset.

Default Swap Option The right to enter into a default swap (see also cancelable default swap)

Default Swap Premium (also termed default swap spread, fee, or fixed rate) Price of a default swap.

Default Swap Spread See default swap premium.

Delta The change in the value of a derivative for an infinitesimally small change in the price (or rate) of the underlying security.

Derivatives A security whose value is at least in part derived from the price of an underlying asset.

Digital Default Swap See binary default swap.

Discount Factor The number that a cash flow occurring at a future date is multiplied with, to bring it to its present value.

Discount Rate The interest rate that is used in the discount factor.

Distance to Default A term derived by KMV displaying the difference between the value of assets and the value of liabilities at a certain future point in time. Mathematically identical with the risk-neutral d_2 in the Merton model.

Drift Rate The average change of a variable in a stochastic process.

Duration A measure of the relative change in the value of a bond with respect to a change in its yield to maturity. Also measures the average time that an investor has to wait to get his investment back.

Economic Capital Capital that is required to protect against unexpected loss.

Efficient Market Hypothesis A hypothesis that asset prices include all relevant information. Past asset price patterns are irrelevant.

Equity Swap A swap in which the price or return of an equity or equity index is exchanged against Libor.

European Style Option An option that can only be exercised on the maturity date.

Excess Yield The difference between the yield of a risky bond and the yield of a risk-free bond.

Exchange Option An option to exchange one asset for another.

Exotic Option Options, whose payoff, evaluation and hedging is different, typically more complex than that of standard options.

Expected Default Frequency (EDF) A term from KMV's model for the probability of default. Real world representation of the risk-netural $N(-d_2)$ in the Merton model.

Fair Value Value of a futures contract that does not offer any arbitrage opportunities with respect to the cash market.

Finite Difference Method A method to solve differential equations by transferring the differential equations into difference equations and solving these iteratively.

Firm Value Model A type of structural model. In firm value models, bankruptcy occurs when the asset value of a company is below the debt value at the maturity of the debt.

First Time Passage Model A type of structural model. In first time passage models, bankruptcy occurs when the asset value drops below a pre-defined, usually exogenous barrier, allowing for bankruptcy before the maturity of the debt.

First-to-default Basket Credit Swap See N-to-default basket swap.

Floating Rate An interest rate that periodically changes according to a certain reference rate i.e. Libor.

Floor Opposite of a cap. A contract which gives the floor owner the right to receive a fixed interest rate (strike) and pay a Libor rate.

Forward A transaction in which the price is fixed today, but settlement takes place at a future date.

Funded Transaction A transaction in which the buyer pays an upfront premium as in a purchase of a bond, an option or CDO (see unfunded transaction).

Future A standardized forward that trades on an exchange. The notional, price, maturity, quality, deliverability, type of settlement, trading hours, etc., are standardized.

Gamma Second partial derivative of the option function with respect to the underlying price. A measure for the curvature of the option function. Gamma is the change in the delta of an option for an infinitesimally small change in the price of the underlying.

Generalized Wiener Process A process in which a variable grows with an average drift rate. Superimposed on this growth rate is a stochastic term, which adds volatility to the process.

Geometric Brownian Motion A process in which the relative change of a variable follows a generalized Wiener process.

Haircut A factor, input into an equation that changes the exposure in a collateralized transaction. Supervisors may allow banks to calculate their own haircuts if certain standards are met.

Hazard Rate (also termed **default intensity**) The risk-neutral probability of default. Multiplied with a certain time frame, results in the probability of default.

Hedging Reducing risk, i.e. entering into a second trade to reduce the risk of an original trade.

Iboxx An index based on default swap prices. Launched as a rival index to the Trac-x.

Implied Volatility Volatility that is implied by observed option prices when inverting the option pricing (typically Black-Scholes) formula.

In Arrears Refers to a later date, at which a payment is made.

Instantaneous Interest Rate An interest rate that is applied to an infinitesimal short period of time (see also continuously compounded interest rate).

Interest Rate Coverage Ratio Determines the credit quality of a synthetic structure. It is derived by dividing the total interest rates to be received in a structure by the interest rate liability of each tranche.

Interest Rate Swap An exchange of interest rate payments on a pre-determined notional amount and in reference to pre-determined interest rate indices.

Intrinsic Value The payoff when the option is exercised. For a call, the intrinsic value is the maximum of the spot price minus the strike price and zero; For a put the intrinsic value is the maximum of the strike price minus the spot price and zero.

Investment Grade Bond A bond with a rating of BBB and higher.

Junk Bond (also **High Yield Bond**) A bond with a rating lower than BBB.

KMV Market-leading software company for managing credit portfolio risk. Main product is Portfolio Manager.

Knock-In Option Type of barrier option. It gets knocked-in (starts existing) if the underlying price reaches or breaks a certain level.

Knock-out Option Type of barrier option. It gets knocked-out (stops existing) when the underlying price reaches or breaks a certain level.

Kurtosis Fourth moment of a distribution; measure of the fatness of the tails of the distribution.

Libor London Interbank Offered Rate; an interest rate paid by highly rated borrowers; fixed daily in London.

Libor Market Model A term structure model, in which interest rates are conveniently expressed as discrete forward rates.

Liquidity Premium Premium, which lowers an asset price due to asset illiquitity.

Lognormal Distribution A distribution with a fat right tail. A variable follows a lognormal distribution if the logarithm of the variable is normal. Often applied for stock price behavior, as in the Black-Scholes model.

Long Position A trading position, which generates a profit if the underlying instrument increases in price (opposite of short position).

Loss Given Default (LGD) See default exposure.

Market Price of Risk See Sharpe ratio.

Market Risk The risk of loss due to an unfavorable movement in market factors.

Markov Process A stochastic process assuming that all information about a variable is already incorporated in the current price. Hence past price patterns are irrelevant.

Mark-to-Market The daily adjustment of an account to reflect profits and losses.

Martingale Process A stochastic process with a zero drift rate. Hence the expected future value of a variable is the current value.

Maturity The date a transaction or a financial instrument is due to end.

Mean Reversion The tendency for a price or a rate to revert back towards its long-term mean.

Migration Probability The probability of a firm's credit rating to move to another rating.

Migration Risk The risk of a debtor being downgraded to a lower rating category; equivalent to credit deterioration risk of rated companies.

Monte Carlo Simulation A technique for approximating the price of a derivative by randomly sampling the evolution of the underlying security.

Moratorium/Repudiation (a) A standstill or deferral of the reference entity with respect to the underlying reference obligation; or, (b) if the reference entity disaffirms, disclaims, repudiates, or rejects the validity of the reference obligation.

Netting Offsetting assets with liabilities in the event of default.

Newton-Raphson Method (also called **Newton method**) An iterative search procedure for finding the solution of complex, but differentiable equations.

Normal Distribution (also **Gaussian Distribution** or **Bell Curve**) A probability distribution forming a symmetrical curve. Often assumed for the return of securities.

Notching Automatically downgrading a single debt in a CDO that had not been rated. This leads to a downgrading of the entire CDO structure.

Notional Amount (also called **Principal Amount**) Dollar amount of a security or transaction. In swaps used as the basis for payment calculations.

N-to-default basket swap A swap in which a payoff is triggered when the N-th reference entity defaults. If $N = 1$, this swap is a first-to-default basket credit swap.

Numeraire The price of a security in which other securities are measured.

Obligation Acceleration An obligation that has become payable before it otherwise would have been due to a credit event.

Off-Balance-Sheet A transaction that does not have to be included in the figures on the balance sheet of the party concerned.

Offset The process whereby purchases and sales of identical contracts are netted out, leaving only the net profit (or loss).

Operational Risk The risk of direct or indirect loss resulting from inadequate or failed internal processes, people, and systems or from external events (BIS definition).

Overcollateralization ratio Measures how many times the collateral (assets) in a synthetic structure can cover the liabilities that an SPV owes its investors.

Over the Counter (OTC) A transaction dealt directly between counterparties, hence not on an exchange.

Physical Settlement Type of settlement of derivatives where physical delivery and payment of the underlying asset takes place (see cash settlement).

Pit The area of the floor of an exchange where a certain contract is traded.

Poisson Distribution A distribution with a mean μ and a standard deviation $\sqrt{\mu}$, often applied in the actuarial industry.

Portfolio View McKinsey's econometric-based model to manage portfolio credit risk.

Premium The price of a financial transaction (see also credit risk premium and credit spread).

Present Value Current value of discounted future cash flows.

Principal Component Analysis A method of deriving risk values by defining historically based components that explain the risk.

Put option The right but not the obligation to sell an underlying asset at the strike price at a certain date (European style) or during a certain period (American style).

Put–Call Parity An equation stating that a put price + the underlying price is equal to the call price + the discounted strike. This holds for European style calls and puts with identical strike and maturity. If put–call parity is violated, arbitrage opportunities exist.

QBI Quarterly Bankruptcy Index, an index based on personal bankruptcy filings in a certain quarter.

QBI Futures Contract A futures contract based on the QBI, traded on the CME.

QBI Options Contract An option contract on the Future QBI Contract, traded on the CME.

Random Walk A term expressing the random, not predictable process of a variable. The randomness is typically generated by a drawing from a standard normal distribution.

Range note (also called fairways) In a range note, the owner receives an above market coupon, if a certain variable, e.g. the 6ML (6 Month Libor), stays inside a predetermined range, and may additionally incur a penalty if the variable is outside a predetermined range (see also Credit-spread range note).

Recovery Rate The percentage of the notional amount that a creditor receives in case of default.

Reduced Form Model A type of model that does not include the asset–liability structure of the firm to generate default probabilities. Rather, reduced form models use debt prices as a main input to model the bankruptcy process.

Reference Obligation The obligation that, if in default, triggers the default swap payment.

Repo Repurchase agreement. A securitized loan: In a Repo, a security is sold with a guarantee that it will be repurchased at a later date at a fixed price.

Repudiation See moratorium.

Risk-Adjusted Return on Capital (RAROC) The expected return divided by the economic capital that is required to support the transaction.

Risk Averse An attitude toward risk that causes an investor to prefer an investment with a certain return to an investment with the same expected return but higher uncertainty.

Risk-free Rate An interest rate that can be achieved without risk. Typically the interest rate for securities issued by an AAA-rated government.

Risk-neutral An attitude toward risk that leads an investor to be indifferent between investment A with a certain expected return and investment B with the same expected return but higher uncertainty.

Sharpe Ratio (also termed **Market Price of Risk**) Return of a risky asset minus the return of the risk-free asset, divided by the standard deviation of the risky asset.

Short Position A trading position, which generates a profit if the underlying instrument decreases in price (opposite to long position).

Short Selling Selling a security that is borrowed.

Short Squeeze A term for traders buying a security to increase the price since they know the security has to be bought back by (short) sellers.

Short Straddle An option strategy where both a call and a put with the same strike price, same underlying, and same maturity are sold.

Skewness Third moment of a distribution function. Measure of the asymmetry of a distribution.

Smile Effect A term referring to the higher implied volatilities of out-of-the-money options and in-the-money options compared to at-the-money options.

Solvency The ability of a corporation to meet its long-term obligations.

Special-Purpose Corporation (SPC) See special-purpose vehicle.

Special-Purpose Entity (SPE) See special-purpose vehicle.

Special-Purpose Vehicle (SPV) Legal entity, separate from the parent bank, typically highly rated.

Spot Price The price of a security for immediate (in practice often two days) delivery.

Stochastic Process A process tracking the movement of a random variable.

Straddle An options strategy where you buy both a call and a put with the same strike price on the same underlying asset.

Strangle An option strategy consisting of a call and a put with different strike prices on the same underlying asset and same maturity.

Stress Testing Testing how well CAR or VAR would have performed assuming extreme market moves.

Strike Price For a call option, the price at which the underlying security may be bought; for a put option, the price at which the underlying security may be sold.

Structural Model A type of model that derives the probability of default by analyzing the capital structure of a firm, especially the value of the firm's assets compared to the value of the firm's debt.

Swap The agreement between two parties to exchange a series of cash flows.

Swaption (also **swap option**) An option on a swap. A payer swaption allows the owner to pay a fixed swap rate and to receive a floating rate. A receiver swaption allows the owner to receive a swap rate and to pay a floating rate.

Synthetic Structure A financial structure in which credit risk is assumed by a credit derivative.

Systematic Risk (also called **market risk** or **common risk**) Risk associated with the movement of a market or market segment as opposed to distinct elements of risk associated with a specific security. Systematic risk cannot be diversified away.

Term Structure Model A stochastic, binomial, or multinomial discrete or continuous model for the process of short-term interest rates.

Theta The change in price of a derivative for an infinitesimal change in time.

Time Value The portion of an option's premium that is attributed to uncertainty. Time value equals the option price minus the intrinsic value.

Total Rate of Return Swap (TROR) An unfunded long or short position in bond or loan. One party pays Libor + a spread, the other party pays the return (price change + coupon).

Trac-x (also termed Dow Jones Trac-x) A family of credit derivatives indexes based on a certain basket of default swaps.

Trading book Comprises instruments that are explicitly held with trading intent or in order to hedge other positions in the trading book. (Compare Banking book.)

Tranches Segments of deals or structures, typically with different risk levels.

Transition Matrix A matrix showing the probability of a firm to move to other rating categories within a certain time frame.

Uncovered (Naked) Option An option without a position in the underlying that could be used to fulfill the obligation of the option.

Unexpected Loss Loss amount exceeding VAR or CAR.

Underlying The security that a derivative is based on and which at least in part determines the price of the derivative.

Unfunded Transaction A transaction in which the buyer does not pay an upfront premium as in a swap, a futures contract or a TROR (see **funded transaction**)

Unsystematic Risk (also called **idiosyncratic risk** or **specific risk**) Risk that can be largely eliminated by diversification within an asset class.

VAR Value at Risk; the maximum loss in a certain time frame, with a certain probability, due to a certain type of risk.

Vega First partial derivative of the option function with respect to implied volatility. A measurement of the sensitivity of the value of an option to changes in implied volatility.

Volatility A measure of the degree of movements in the relative price of a security. The standard deviation of relative price movements.

Vulnerable Option An option, whose price includes the possibility of default of the option seller.

Wiener Process A process in which the movement of a variable for a certain time interval is determined by a random drawing from a distribution, multiplied by the square root of the time interval.

Yield Curve Shows the relationship between yields and their maturities.

Zero-Coupon Bond A bond that does not pay any coupons.

Index

Note: "n." after a page reference indicates the number of a note on that page.